PERSPECTIVES
IN
NEURAL COMPUTING

J. G. Taylor and C. L. T. Mannion (Eds.)

THEORY AND APPLICATIONS OF NEURAL NETWORKS

Proceedings of the First British Neural
Network Society Meeting, London

Springer-Verlag
London Berlin Heidelberg New York
Paris Tokyo Hong Kong
Barcelona Budapest

J. G. Taylor, BA, BSc, MA, PhD, FInstP
Department of Mathematics, King's College, Strand, London WC2R 2LS, UK

C. L. T. Mannion, BSc, PhD, MInstP
Department of Electrical Engineering, University of Surrey, Guildford, Surrey, GU2 5XH, UK

Series Editors
J. G. Taylor, BA, BSc, MA, PhD, FInstP
Department of Mathematics, King's College, Strand, London WC2R 2LS, UK

C. L. T. Mannion, BSc, PhD, MInstP
Department of Electrical Engineering, University of Surrey, Guildford, Surrey, GU2 5XH, UK

ISBN-13: 978-3-540-19650-1   e-ISBN-13: 978-1-4471-1833-6
DOI: 10.1007/978-1-4471-1833-6

British Library Cataloguing in Publication Data
British Neural Network Society Meeting (1st : 1990 : King's College, London)
Theory and applications of neural networks. – (Perspectives in neural computing)
I. Title II. Taylor, John, *1931–* III. Mannion, C. L. T. IV. Series
006.3

Library of Congress Data available

34/3830–543210 Printed on acid-free paper

PREFACE

This volume contains the papers from the first British Neural Network Society meeting held at Queen Elizabeth Hall, King's College, London on 18–20 April 1990. The meeting was sponsored by the London Mathematical Society.

The papers include introductory tutorial lectures, invited, and contributed papers. The invited contributions were given by experts from the United States, Finland, Denmark, Germany and the United Kingdom. The majority of the contributed papers came from workers in the United Kingdom.

The first day was devoted to tutorials. Professor Stephen Grossberg was a guest speaker on the first day giving a thorough introduction to his Adaptive Resonance Theory of neural networks. Subsequent tutorials on the first day covered dynamical systems and neural networks, realistic neural modelling, pattern recognition using neural networks, and a review of hardware for neural network simulations.

The contributed papers, given on the second day, demonstrated the breadth of interests of workers in the field. They covered topics in pattern recognition, multi-layer feedforward neural networks, network dynamics, memory and learning. The ordering of the papers in this volume is as they were given at the meeting.

On the final day talks were given by Professor Kohonen (on self organising maps), Professor Kürten (on the dynamics of random and structured nets) and Professor Cotterill (on modelling the visual cortex). Dr A. Mayes presented a paper on various models for amnesia. The editors have taken the opportunity to include a paper of their own which was not presented at the meeting.

November 1990

J.G. Taylor
C.L.T. Mannion

ACKNOWLEDGEMENTS

We would like to thank all those people and organisations involved in the meeting. In particular the London Mathematical Society for their financial support, Mrs Marion Harris for her invaluable secretarial and administrative help, and Linda Schofield for assistance with the production of this volume.

CONTENTS

Invited Papers

Additional Paper (not given at conference)

CONTRIBUTORS

Allinson, N.M.
Dr, Department of Electronics, University of York, Heslington, York YO1 5DD, UK

Bishop, C.M.
Dr, Culham Laboratory, Abingdon, Oxon, UK

Boullart, L.
Dr, Ghent State University, Kon Albertlaan 29, 9000 Ghent, Belgium

Bressloff, P.C.
Dr, Long Range Research, GEC-Hirst Research, East Lane, Wembley, Middlesex, UK

Calliauw, L.
Dr, Ghent State University, Kon Albertlaan 29, 9000 Ghent, Belgium

Carpenter, G.A.
Dr, Center for Adaptive Systems, University of Boston, 111 Cummington Street, Boston, MA 02215, USA

Child, T.M.
Dr, Information Technology Institute, University of Salford, The Crescent, Salford M5 4WT, UK

Christensen, S.S.
Dr, Department of Molecular Biophysics, The Technical University of Denmark, Building 307, DK-2800 Lyngby, Denmark

Cooper, G.S.
Dr, Information Technology Institute, University of Salford, The Crescent, Salford M5 4WT, UK

Cotterill, R.M.J.
Professor, Department of Molecular Biophysics, The Technical University of Denmark, Building 307, DK-2800 Lyngby, Denmark

Fletcher, P.
Dr, Department of Computer Science, University of Keele, Keele, Staffordshire ST5 5BG, UK

Gardner-Medwin, A.R.
Dr, Department of Physiology, University College London, Gower Street, London WC1E 6BT, UK, and The Physiological Laboratory, Cambridge CB2 3EG, UK

Gorse, D.
Dr, Department of Computer Science, University College London, Gower Street, London WC1E 6BT, UK

Grossberg, S.
Professor, Center for Adaptive Systems, University of Boston, 111 Cummington Street, Boston, MA 02215, USA

Hill, D.
Dr, Department of Mathematics and Statistics, University of Birmingham, Birmingham B15 2TT, UK

Kohonen, T.
Professor, Computer and Information Science Laboratory, University of Helsinki, Rakentajapaukio 2C, SF 02150 Espoo, Finland

Kürten, K.E.
Professor, Department of Theoretical Physics, University of Koln, Zulpichen Strasse 77, D-5000 Koln, Germany

Mannion, C.L.T.
Dr, Department of Electronic and Electrical Engineering, University of Surrey, Guildford, Surrey GU2 5XH, UK

Mayes, A.
Dr, Department of Psychology, University of Manchester, 10 Adria Road, Didsbury, Manchester M20 0SE, UK

Nielsen, C.
Dr, Department of Molecular Biophysics, The Technical University of Denmark, Building 307, DK-2800 Lyngby, Denmark

Otte, G.
Dr, Department of Neurology, Ghent State University, Bylokehof 24, 9000 Ghent, Belgium

Praet, M.
Dr, Ghent State University, Kon Albertlaan 29, 9000 Ghent, Belgium

Roels, L.
Dr, Ghent State University, Kon Albertlaan 29, 9000 Ghent, Belgium

Sieben, G.
Dr, Department of Pathology, Ghent State University, Kon Albertlaan 29, 9000 Ghent, Belgium

Taylor, J.G.
Professor, Department of Mathematics, King's College London, Strand, London WC2R 2LS, UK

Taylor, R.W.
Dr, Department of Electronics, University of York, Heslington, York YO1 5DD, UK

Vercauteren, L.
Dr, Automatic Control Laboratory, Ghent State University, Grote Steenweg Noord, 9710 Ghent-ZWijnaarde, Belgium

Whittle, P.
Professor, Statistical Laboratory, University of Cambridge, 16 Mill Lane, Cambridge CB2 2SB, UK

INVITED
LECTURE

SELF-ORGANIZING CORTICAL NETWORKS

FOR DISTRIBUTED HYPOTHESIS TESTING

AND RECOGNITION LEARNING

Gail A. Carpenter† and Stephen Grossberg‡
Center for Adaptive Systems. Boston University, 111 Cummington Street, Boston, MA 02215 USA

1. AUTONOMOUS LEARNING AND RECOGNITION IN A CHANGING WORLD.

Adaptive Resonance Theory, or ART, was introduced in 1976 [1.2] in order to analyse how brain networks can learn sensory and cognitive recognition codes in a stable fashion in response to arbitrary sequences of input patterns presented under real-time conditions. ART networks are at present the only computationally realized biological theory that analyses how fast, yet stable, real-time learning of recognition codes can be accomplished in response to an arbitrary stream of input patterns. Such a general-purpose learning ability is needed by any autonomous learning agent that hopes to learn successfully about unexpected events in an unpredictable environment. One cannot *restrict* the agent's processing capability if one cannot *predict* the environment in which it must function. Other learning theories do not have one or more essential properties that are needed for autonomous learning under real-time conditions (Table 1).

The ability of ART networks to carry out fast stable real-time learning is derived from their incorporation of architectural elements that have been derived from a behavioral and neural analysis of human and mammalian learning data [3-5] and a mathematical and computational analysis of how to design networks that rigorously implement these biological heuristics [6-9]. Such an interdisciplinary analysis has

† Supported in part by British Petroleum (89-A-1204). DARPA (AFOSR 90-0083), and the National Science Foundation (NSF IRI-90-00530).

‡ Supported in part by the Air Force Office of Scientific Research (AFOSR 90-0128 and AFOSR 90-0175), the Army Research Office (ARO DAAL-03-88-K-0088), and the National Science Foundation (NSF IRI-87-16960).

Acknowledgements: The authors wish to thank Diana Meyers. Cynthia E. Bradford and Carol Yanakakis Jefferson for their valuable assistance in the preparation of the manuscript.

TABLE 1

ART Architecture	Alternative Learning Properties
Real-time (on-line) learning	Lab-time (off-line) learning
Nonstationary world	Stationary world
Self-organizing (unsupervised)	Teacher supplies correct answer (supervised)
Memory self-stabilizes in response to arbitrarily many inputs	Capacity catastrophe in response to arbitrarily many inputs
Effective use of full memory capacity	Can only use partial memory capacity
Maintain plasticity in an unexpected world	Externally shut off plasticity to prevent capacity catastrophe
Learn internal top-down expectations	Externally impose costs
Active attentional focus regulates learning	Passive learning
Slow or fast learning	Slow learning or oscillation catastrophe
Learn in approximate-match phase	Learn in mismatch phase
Use self-regulating hypothesis testing to globally reorganize the energy landscape	Use noise to perturb system out of local minima in a fixed energy landscape
Fast adaptive search for best match	Search tree
Rapid direct access to codes of familiar events	Recognition time increases with code complexity
Variable error criterion (vigilance parameter) sets coarseness of recognition code in response to environmental feedback	Fixed error criterion in response to environmental feedback
All properties scale to arbitrarily large system capacities	Key properties deteriorate as system capacity is increased

required that ART architectures be simultaneously developed to realize both macroscopic design principles and microscopic mechanistic constraints. Correspondingly, the data explanations and predictions of the theory have ranged from microscopic neurobiological assertions about membrane and neurotransmitter dynamics to more macroscopic network assertions about resonance, attention, and learning, to still more macroscopic assertions about uncertainty principles and complementarity principles that bind together network subsystems into a total architectural design.

2.   INTERDISCIPLINARY PREDICTIONS CONCERNING NEURAL MECHANISMS OF ATTENTION, RESONANCE, AND LEARNING.

For example, concerning membrane and neurotransmitter dynamics, it was predicted in 1972 that norepinephrine and acetylcholine jointly control cortical plasticity [10]. In 1976, this prediction was refined to hypothesize that norepinephrine and acetylcholine control cortical plasticity during the critical period in visual cortex [2]. Several studies have described relevant data [11-13]. These theoretical results built upon earlier predictions from the 1960's that synaptic plasticity is controlled by processes in which an inward Na^+ current and an outward K^+ current interact synergetically with an inward Ca^{++} current that competes with an Mg^{++} current [14-16]. Recent data about the role of NMDA receptors have refined contemporary understanding of such synergetic interactions [17]. These currents were predicted to control an associative learning law in which synaptic efficacy is gated by postsynaptic activity such that, with the learning gate open, synaptic strength can either increase or decrease [1,3,18,19]. Such a gated learning law has recently been discovered in visual cortex and hippocampus [20-24]. It is the basic learning law used in the ART models.

Concerning more global network-level constraints on information processing and learning, a role for attention in the regulation of cortical plasticity was predicted in 1976 [2] and subsequently reported [25]. Standing waves of resonant cortical activity were predicted to subserve these cortical dynamics [2,19]. Several labs have recently reported such resonant standing waves [26,27]. A top-down template matching event that regulates selective attention was predicted at the same time [2,28(reprinted in 3)]. It has the properties of the subsequently reported Processing Negativity (PN) event-related potential [29,30]. Different properties of match/mismatch in visual thalamocortical interactions were also predicted [2,31], and have recently received experimental support [32]. Sequences of internal processing events were predicted to occur during conditions of top-down mismatch and memory search. These events were interpreted in terms of the event-related potentials P120, N200, and P300 [28(reprinted in 3), 33(reprinted in 4)]. Supportive data have subsequently been reported [34,35].

Although ART is surely an incomplete theory some of whose hypotheses are bound to be incorrect, it is at present the only neural learning theory in which such a wide range of interdisciplinary phenomena have been successfully predicted. It is to be hoped that more systematic cooperation between experimental and theoretical neuroscientists will facilitate further testing of such interdisciplinary predictions, especially of key predictions which have not yet received either support or disconfirmation from neurobiological experiments. For example, we predict that cortical matching obeys a 2/3 Matching Rule [4,6-8].

3. CONTROL OF DISTRIBUTED HYPOTHESIS TESTING BY INTERACTIONS BETWEEN STM, MTM, AND LTM: THE ROLE OF HABITUATING CHEMICAL TRANSMITTERS.

The present chapter summarizes results that are also concerned with the neural control of cellular properties such as transmitter dynamics and network properties such as resonance, attention, and learning. In particular, we summarize model mechanisms capable of implementing parallel search of compressed or distributed recognition codes in a neural network hierarchy. The search process is a form of hypothesis testing capable of discovering appropriate representations of a nonstationary input environment. The search process functions well with either fast learning or slow learning, and can robustly cope with sequences of asynchronous input patterns in real-time. Such a search process emerges when computational properties of Short Term Memory (STM), Medium Term Memory (MTM), and Long Term Memory (LTM) are suitably organized. STM and LTM are familiar ingredients: STM concerns cell activations, whereas LTM concerns changes due to learning in adaptive weights. MTM concerns the dynamics of chemical transmitters at the synapse, including the processes of release, inactivation, and modulation.

When these processes are embedded within an Adaptive Resonance Theory architecture, called ART 3, useful search properties emerge. A key part of the search process utilizes formal analogs of synergetic interactions between ions such as Na^+ and Ca^{2+}, regulated by specific and nonspecific signal pathways. These interactions control a nonlinear feedback process that enables the spatial pattern of presynaptic MTM transmitter to model the spatial pattern of postsynaptic STM activation that constitutes the recognition code. If activation of the recognition code leads to a predictive failure that causes a reset event, the postsynaptic STM activation pattern is restored to its equilibrium values, but the presynaptic MTM transmitter pattern remains unchanged. The hypothesis or recognition code that is next selected is hereby biased against those features that were most responsible for the predictive failure. When no reset event follows such a hypothesis, the network's STM patterns become resonant and generate a focus of attention that selectively drives learned changes in the LTM traces which support the resonance. The remainder of this chapter describes how the MTM transmitter dynamics interact with STM and LTM to control the hypothesis testing process.

4. CONTROL OF RECOGNITION AND SEARCH BY COMPLEMENTARY ATTENTIONAL AND ORIENTING SUBSYSTEMS.

Adaptive Resonance Theory was derived from an analysis of the instabilities inherent in feedforward adaptive coding structures [1,2]. More recent work has led to the development of three classes of ART neural network architectures, specified as systems of differential equations.

The first class, ART 1, self-organizes recognition categories for arbitrary sequences of binary input patterns [6]. A second class, ART 2, does the same for either binary or analog inputs [7].

Both ART 1 and ART 2 use a maximally compressed, or choice, pattern recognition code. Such a code is a limiting case of the partially compressed recognition codes that are typically used in explanations by ART of biological data [3-5], and which are the subject of ART 3. Partially compressed recognition codes have been mathematically analysed in models for competitive learning, also called self-organizing feature maps, which are incorporated into ART models as part of their bottom-up dynamics [1,3,36]. Indeed, the coding instabilities of self-organizing feature maps, whether compressed or distributed, led to the introduction of ART in 1976. The basic equations and main computational properties of these models had by then been described by Grossberg [37,1,28] and Malsburg [38,39] and were followed by applications and expositions of Kohonen [36]. The name "GKM model" may thus be used to summarize this historical development.

Maximally compressed, or winner-take-all, codes were used in ART 1 and ART 2 to enable a rigorous analysis to be made of how the bottom-up and top-down dynamics of ART systems can be joined together in a real-time self-organizing system capable of learning a stable pattern recognition code in response to an arbitrary sequence of input patterns. These results provide a computational foundation for designing ART systems capable of stably learning partially compressed recognition codes. The present results about ART 3 contribute to such a design.

The main elements of a typical ART 1 module are illustrated in Figure 1. F_1 and F_2 are fields of network nodes. An input is initially represented as a pattern of activity across the nodes, or feature detectors, of field F_1. The pattern of activity across F_2 corresponds to the category representation. Because patterns of activity in both fields may persist after input offset yet may also be quickly inhibited, these patterns are called short term memory, or STM, representations. The two fields, linked both bottom-up and top-down by adaptive filters, constitute the Attentional Subsystem. Because the connection weights defining the adaptive filters may be modified by inputs and may persist for very long times after input offset, these connection weights are called long term memory, or LTM, variables.

An auxiliary Orienting Subsystem becomes active during search. This search process is the subject of the present chapter.

5. AN ART SEARCH CYCLE.

Figure 2 illustrates a typical ART search cycle. An input pattern **I** registers itself as a pattern **X** of activity across F_1 (Figure 2a). The F_1 output signal vector **S** is then transmitted through the multiple converging and diverging weighted adaptive filter pathways emanating from F_1, sending a net input signal vector **T** to F_2. The internal

ART 1 MODULE

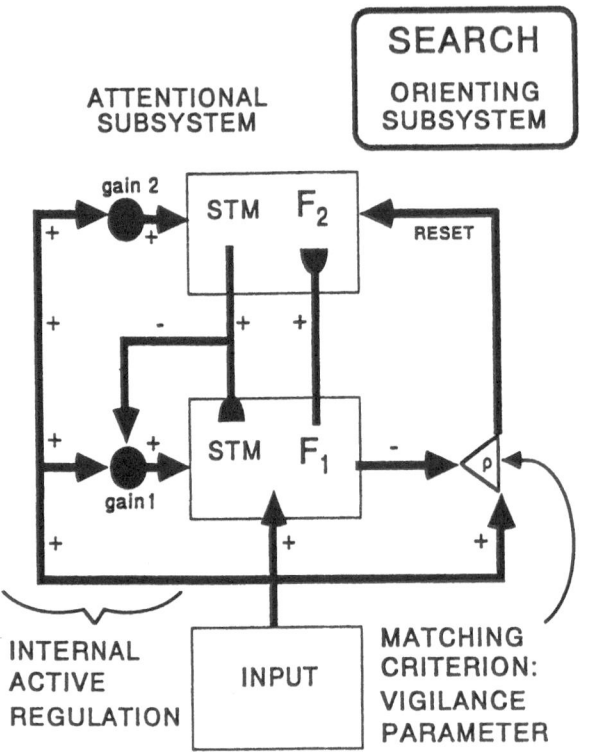

Figure 1. Typical ART 1 neural network module [6].

competitive dynamics of F_2 contrast-enhance $\mathbf{T}$. The F_2 activity vector $\mathbf{Y}$ therefore registers a compressed representation of the filtered $F_1 \rightarrow F_2$ input and corresponds, in the winner-take-all case, to a category representation for the input active at F_1. These are the standard operations of self-organizing feature maps. In ART, vector $\mathbf{Y}$ generates a signal vector $\mathbf{U}$ that is sent top-down through the second adaptive filter, giving rise to a net top-down signal vector $\mathbf{V}$ to F_1 (Figure 2b). F_1 now receives two input vectors, $\mathbf{I}$ and $\mathbf{V}$. An ART system is designed to carry out a matching process whereby the original activity pattern $\mathbf{X}$ due to input pattern $\mathbf{I}$ may be modified by the *template pattern* $\mathbf{V}$ that is associated with the current active category. If $\mathbf{I}$ and $\mathbf{V}$ are not sufficiently similar according to a matching criterion established by a dimensionless *vigilance parameter* ρ, a reset signal quickly and enduringly shuts off the active category representation (Figure 2c), allowing a new category to become active. Search ensues (Figure 2d) until either an adequate match is made or a new category is established. The search process is not, however, exhaustive. Only those representations that are similar enough to the input

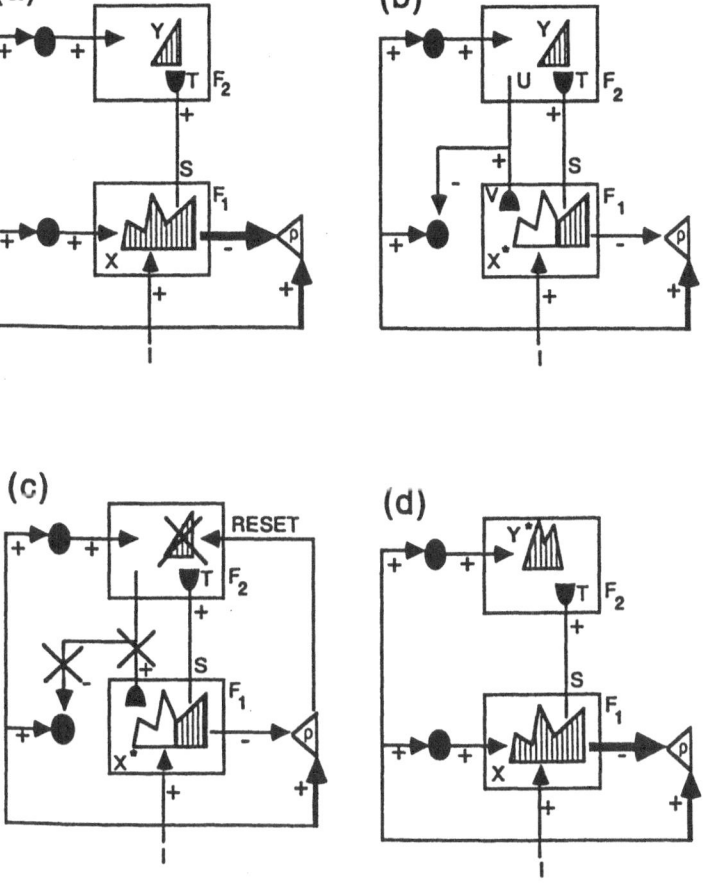

Figure 2. ART search cycle [6].

pattern are searched before a new representation is selected.

In earlier treatments (e.g. [6]), we proposed that the enduring shut-off of erroneous category representations by a nonspecific reset signal could occur at F_2 if F_2 were organized as a gated dipole field, whose dynamics depend on habituative transmitter gates. Though the new search process does not use a gated dipole field, it does retain and extend the core idea that habituative transmitter dynamics, operating as a MTM, can enable a robust search process when appropriately embedded in an ART system.

6. ART 2: THREE-LAYER COMPETITIVE FIELDS.

Figure 3 shows the principal elements of a typical ART 2 module. It shares many characteristics of the ART 1 module, having both an input representation field F_1 and a category representation field F_2, as well as Attentional and Orienting Subsystems. Figure 3 also illustrates one of the main differences between the examples of ART 1

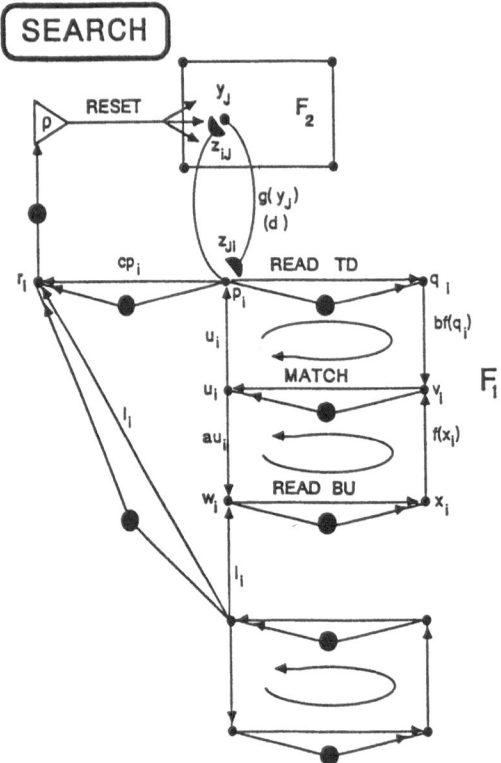

Figure 3. Typical ART 2 neural network module, with three-layer F_1 field [7]. Large filled circles are gain control nuclei that nonspecifically inhibit target nodes in proportion to the Euclidean norm of activity in their source fields.

and ART 2 modules so far explicitly developed; namely, the ART 2 examples all have three processing layers within the F_1 field. These three processing layers allow the ART 2 system to stably categorize sequences of analog input patterns that can, in general, be arbitrarily close to one another. Unlike in models such as back propagation, this category learning process is stable even in the fast learning situation, in which the LTM variables are allowed to go to equilibrium on each learning trial. In Figure 3, one F_1 layer reads in the bottom-up input, one layer reads in the top-down filtered input from F_2, and a middle layer matches patterns from the top and bottom layers before sending a composite pattern back through the F_1 feedback loop. Both F_1 and F_2 are shunting competitive networks that contrast-enhance and normalize their activation patterns [16].

In many applications, ART modules are often embedded in larger architectures that are hierarchically organized. When an ART module is embedded in a network hierarchy, it is no longer possible to make a sharp distinction between the characteristics of the input representation field F_1 and the category representation field F_2. In order for them to serve both functions, the basic structures of all the network fields in a hierarchical ART system should be homologous, in so far as possible. This constraint is satisfied if all fields of the hierarchy are endowed with the F_1 structure of an ART 2 module (Figure 3). Such a design is sufficient for the F_2 field as well as the F_1 field because the principal property required of a category representation field, namely that input patterns be contrast-enhanced and normalized, is a property of the three-layer F_1 structure.

7. HYPOTHESIS TESTING AND MEMORY SEARCH IN AN ART HIERARCHY.

We now consider the problem of implementing hypothesis testing and parallel memory search among the distributed codes of a hierarchical ART system. Assume that a top-down/bottom-up mismatch has occurred somewhere in the system. How can a reset signal search the hierarchy in such a way that an appropriate new category is selected? The search scheme for ART 1 and ART 2 modules incorporates an asymmetry in the design of levels F_1 and F_2 that is inappropriate for ART hierarchies whose fields are homologous. The ART 3 search mechanism described below eliminates that asymmetry.

A key observation is that a reset signal can act upon an ART hierarchy *between* its fields $F_a, F_b, F_c \ldots$ (Figure 4). Locating the site of action of the reset signal between the fields allows each individual field to carry out its pattern processing function without introducing processing biases directly into a field's internal feedback loops.

8. THE ROLE OF HABITUATIVE CHEMICAL TRANSMITTERS IN ART SEARCH.

The computational requirements of the ART search process can be fulfilled by formal properties of neurotransmitters (Figure 5), if these properties are appropriately embedded in the total architecture model. The main properties used are illustrated in Figure 6, which is taken from Ito [40]. In particular, the ART 3 search equations incorporate the dynamics of production and release of a chemical transmitter substance; the inactivation of transmitter at postsynaptic binding sites; and the modulation of these processes via a nonspecific control signal. The net effect of these transmitter processes is to alter the ionic permeability at the postsynaptic membrane site, thus effecting excitation or inhibition of the postsynaptic cell.

The notation to describe these transmitter properties is summarized in Figure 7, for a synapse between the ith presynaptic node and the jth postsynaptic node. The presynaptic signal, or action potential, S_i arrives at a synapse whose adaptive weight, or long term

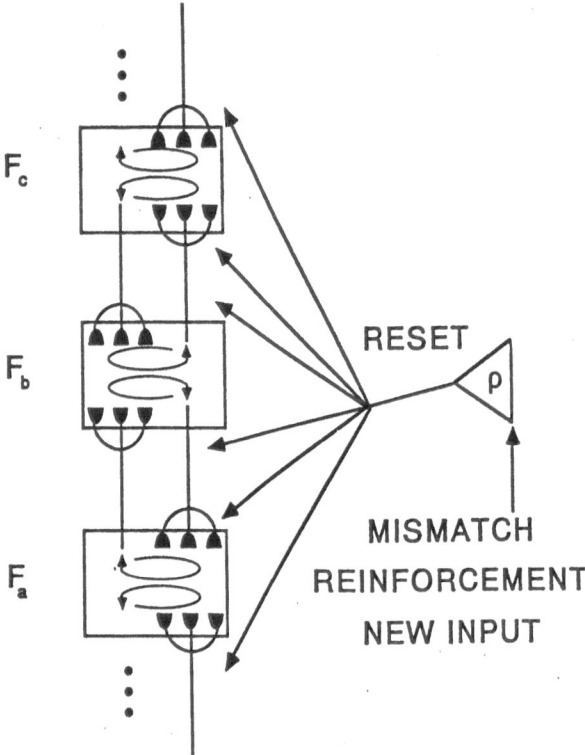

INTERFIELD RESET

F_c

F_b

F_a

RESET

ρ

MISMATCH
REINFORCEMENT
NEW INPUT

Figure 4. Interfield reset in an ART bidirectional hierarchy.

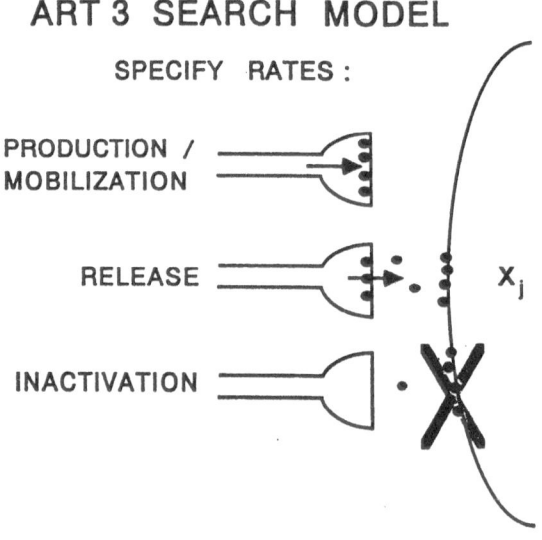

ART 3 SEARCH MODEL

SPECIFY RATES :

PRODUCTION /
MOBILIZATION

RELEASE

x_j

INACTIVATION

Figure 5. The ART search model specifies rate equations for transmitter production, release, and inactivation.

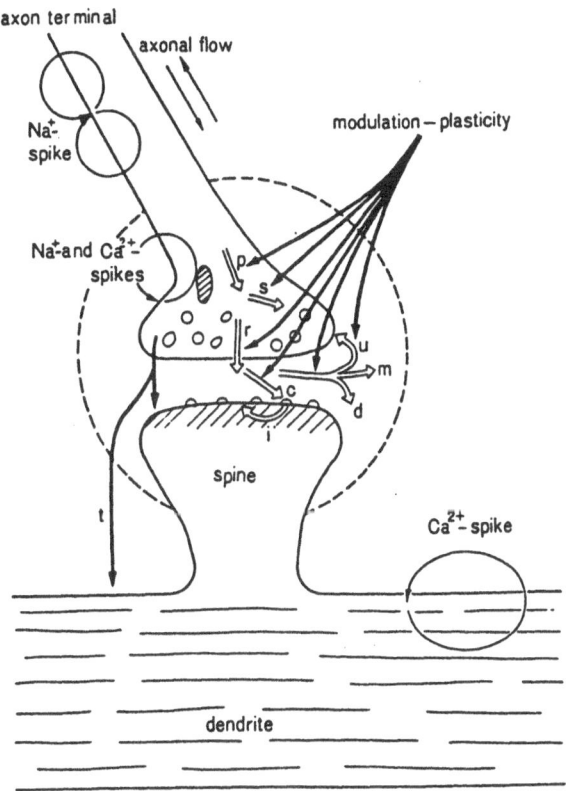

Figure 6. Schematic diagram showing electrical, ionic, and chemical events in a dendritic spine synapse. Open arrows indicate steps from production of neurotransmitter substance (p) to storage (s) or release (r) to reaction with subsynaptic receptors (c), leading to change of ionic permeability of subsynaptic membrane (i) or to removal to extracellular space (m), enzymatic destruction (d), or uptake by presynaptic terminal (u).t, action of trophic substance [40, p.52]. (Reprinted with permission.)

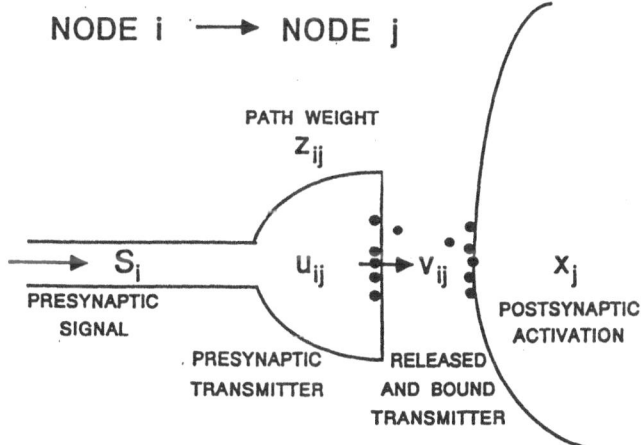

Figure 7. Notation for the ART chemical synapse.

memory trace, is denoted z_{ij}. The variable z_{ij} is identified with the maximum amount of available transmitter. When the transmitter at this synapse is fully accumulated, the amount of transmitter u_{ij} available for release is equal to z_{ij}. When a signal S_i arrives, transmitter is typically released. Variables v_{ij} and w_{ij} denote the amount of transmitter released into the extracellular space from the bottom-up filter and intrafield feedback, respectively. A fraction of this total transmitter pool is assumed to be bound at the postsynaptic cell surface and the remainder rendered ineffective in the extracellular space. Finally, x_j denotes the activity, or membrane potential, of the postsynaptic cell.

9.   EQUATIONS FOR TRANSMITTER PRODUCTION, RELEASE, AND INACTIVATION.

The search mechanism works well if it possesses a few basic properties. These properties can be realized using one of several closely related sets of equations, with corresponding differences in biophysical interpretation. An illustrative systems of equations is described below.

Equations (1)–(3) govern the dynamics of the variables z_{ij}, u_{ij}, v_{ij}, w_{ij}, and x_j at the ij^{th} pathway and j^{th} node of an ART 3 system.

Presynaptic Transmitter

$$\frac{du_{ij}}{dt} = (z_{ij} - u_{ij}) - u_{ij}[\text{release rate}] \tag{1}$$

Bound Transmitter in Bottom-Up Filter

$$\frac{dv_{ij}}{dt} = -v_{ij} + u_{ij}[\text{release rate}] - v_{ij}[\text{inactivation rate}]$$
$$= -v_{ij} + u_{ij}[\text{release rate}] - v_{ij}[\text{reset signal}] \tag{2}$$

Bound Transmitter in Intrafield Feedback Pathways

$$\frac{d}{dt}w_j = -w_j + [\text{intrafield feedback}] - w_j[\text{inactivation rate}]$$
$$= -w_j + [\text{intrafield feedback}] - w_j[\text{reset signal}] \tag{3}$$

14

Postsynaptic Activation

$$\epsilon\frac{dx_j}{dt} = -x_j + (A - x_j)[\text{excitatory inputs}]$$
$$- (B + x_j)[\text{inhibitory inputs}]$$
$$= -x_j + (A - x_j)\left[\sum_i v_{ij} + w_j\right] \tag{4}$$
$$- (B + x_j)[\text{internode competition}]$$

Equation (1) says that presynaptic transmitter is produced and/or mobilized until the amount u_{ij} of transmitter available for release reaches the maximum level z_{ij}. The adaptive weight z_{ij} itself changes on the slower time scale of learning, but remains essentially constant on the time scale of a single reset event. Available presynaptic transmitter u_{ij} is released at a rate that is specified below.

A fraction of presynaptic transmitter becomes postsynaptic bound transmitter after being released. For simplicity, we ignore the fraction of released transmitter that is inactivated in the extracellular space. Equation (2) says that the bound transmitter is inactivated by the reset signal. Equation (3) posits a similar process for the transmitter released from intrafield feedback pathways.

Equation (4) for the postsynaptic activity x_j is a shunting membrane equation such that excitatory inputs drive x_j up toward a maximum depolarized level equal to A; inhibitory inputs drive x_j down toward a minimum hyperpolarized level equal to $-B$; and activity passively decays to a resting level equal to 0 in the absence of inputs. The net effect of bound transmitter at all synapses converging on the jth node is assumed to be excitatory, via the term

$$\sum_i v_{ij} + w_j. \tag{5}$$

Bottom-up signals and internal feedback from within the target field are excitatory (Figure 3), whereas the competitive interactions from other intrafield nodes are inhibitory. Parameter ϵ is small, corresponding to the assumption that activation dynamics are fast relative to the transmitter accumulation rate, equal to 1 in equation (1).

The ART 3 system can be simplified for purposes of simulation. Suppose that $\varepsilon << 1$ in (4); the reset signals in (2) and (3) are either 0 or $>> 1$; and net intrafield feedback is excitatory. Then equations (1), (6), (7), and (8) below approximate the main properties of ART 3 system dynamics.

Simplified ART 3 Equations

$$\frac{du_{ij}}{dt} = (z_{ij} - u_{ij}) - u_{ij}[\text{release rate}] \tag{1}$$

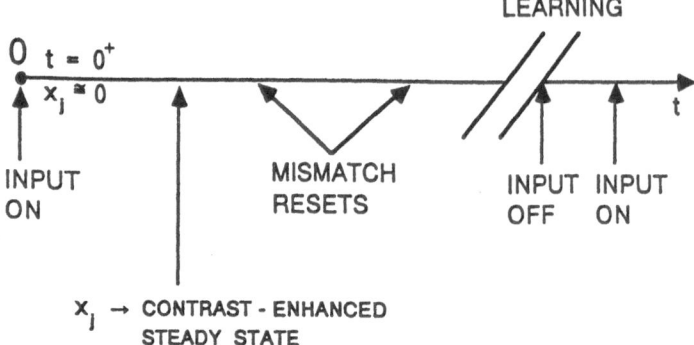

Figure 8. The system is designed to carry out necessary computations at critical junctures of the search process.

$$\begin{cases} \frac{dv_{ij}}{dt} = -v_{ij} + u_{ij} \ [\text{release rate}] & \text{if reset} = 0 \\[2mm] v_{ij}(t) = 0 & \text{if reset} \gg 1 \end{cases} \tag{6}$$

$$\begin{cases} \frac{d}{dt} w_j = -w_j + [\text{intrafield feedback}] & \text{if reset} = 0 \\[2mm] w_{ij}(t) = 0 & \text{if reset} \gg 1 \end{cases} \tag{7}$$

$$x_j(t) = \begin{cases} \sum_i v_{ij} + w_j & \text{if reset} = 0 \\[2mm] 0 & \text{if reset} \gg 1. \end{cases} \tag{8}$$

10. TRANSMITTER RELEASE RATE.

The transmitter release and inactivation rates in equations (1)-(3) will now be specified. Then we trace the dynamics of the system (Figure 8) during a brief time interval after the input turns on ($t = 0^+$), when the signal S_i first arrives at the synapse; when subsequent internal feedback signals act from within the target field, following contrast-enhancement of the inputs; and when a reset signal implements a rapid and enduring inhibition of erroneously selected pattern features. We begin with the

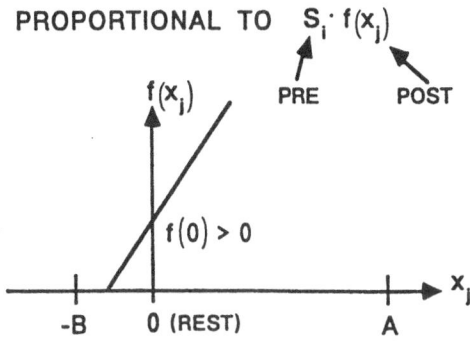

Figure 9. The ART Search Hypothesis 1 specifies the transmitter release rate.

ART Search Hypothesis 1:

Presynaptic transmitter u_{ij} is released at a rate jointly proportional to the presynaptic signal S_i and a function $f(x_j)$ of the postsynaptic activity. That is, in equations (1), (2), and (6),

$$\text{release rate} = S_i f(x_j). \tag{9}$$

The function $f(x_j)$ in equation (9) has the qualitative properties illustrated in Figure 11, where $f(x_j)$ has a positive value when x_j is at its 0 resting level, so that transmitter u_{ij} can be released when the signal S_i arrives at the synapse. In addition, $f(x_j)$ equals 0 when x_j is significantly hyperpolarized, but rises steeply when x_j is near 0. In our computer simulations, $f(x_j)$ is linear above a small negative threshold.

The form factor $S_i f(x_j)$ is a familiar one in the neuroscience and neural network literatures. In particular, such a product is often used to model associative learning, where it links the rate of learning in the ijth pathway to the presynaptic signal S_i and the postsynaptic activity x_j. Associative learning occurs, however, on a time scale that is much slower than the time scale of transmitter release. On the fast time scale of transmitter release, the form factor $S_i f(x_j)$ may be compared to interactions between voltages and ions, such as those in Figure 8, where the presynaptic signal depends on the Na^+ ion, the postsynaptic signal on the Ca^{2+} ion, and transmitter release on the *joint* fluxes of these two ions. The ART Search Hypothesis 1 formalizes this type of synergetic relationship between presynaptic and postsynaptic processes in effecting transmitter release. Moreover, the rate of transmitter release is typically a function of the concentration of Ca^{2+} in the extracellular space, and this function has qualitative properties similar to the function $f(x_j)$ shown in Figure 9 [41, p.84; 42, p.244].

11. SYSTEM DYNAMICS AT INPUT ONSET: AN APPROXI-MATELY LINEAR FILTER.

Some implications of the ART Search Hypothesis 1 will now be summarized. Assume that at time $t = 0$ transmitter u_{ij} has accumulated to its maximal level z_{ij} and that activity x_j and bound transmitter v_{ij} equal 0. Consider a time interval $t = 0^+$ immediately after a signal S_i arrives at the synapse. During this brief initial interval, the ART equations approximate the linear filter dynamics typical of many neural network models. In particular, equations (2) and (9) imply that the amount of bound transmitter is determined by equation

$$\frac{dv_{ij}}{dt} = -v_{ij} + u_{ij}S_i f(x_j) - v_{ij}[\text{inactivation rate}]. \qquad (10)$$

Thus at times $t = 0^+$,

$$\frac{dv_{ij}}{dt} \approx z_{ij}S_i f(0) \qquad (11)$$

and so

$$v_{ij}(t) \approx K(t)S_i z_{ij} \quad \text{for times } t = 0^+. \qquad (12)$$

Because equation (12) holds at all the synapses adjacent to cell j, equation (6) implies that

$$x_j(t) \approx \sum_i K(t)S_i z_{ij} = K(t)\mathbf{S} \cdot \mathbf{z}_j \quad \text{for times } t = 0^+. \qquad (13)$$

Here $\mathbf{S}$ denotes the vector $(S_1 \ldots S_n)$, $\mathbf{z}_j$ denotes the vector $(z_{1j} \ldots z_{nj})$, and $i = 1 \ldots n$. Thus in the initial moments after a signal arrives at the synapse, the small amplitude activity x_j at the postsynaptic cell grows in proportion to the dot product of the incoming signal vector $\mathbf{S}$ times the adaptive weight vector $\mathbf{z}_j$.

18

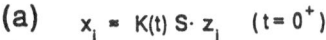
(a) $\quad x_j = K(t) \, S \cdot z_j \quad (t = 0^+)$

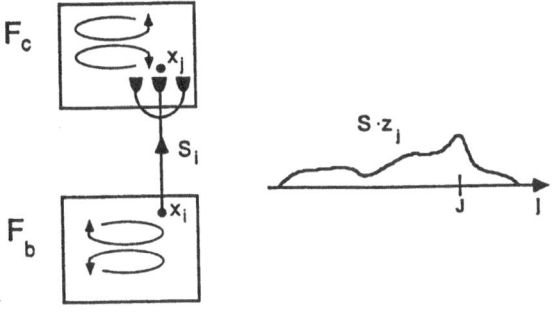

(b) FEEDBACK CONTRAST ENHANCES x_j

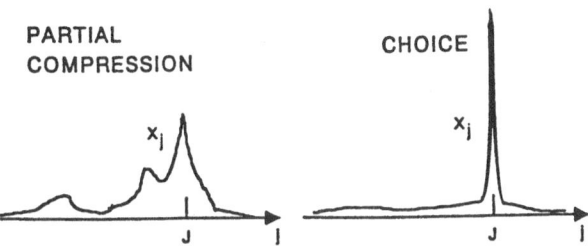

PARTIAL
COMPRESSION

CHOICE

Figure 10. (a) If transmitter is fully accumulated at $t = 0$, low-amplitude postsynaptic STM activity x_j is initially proportional to the dot product of the signal vector $\mathbf{S}$ and the weight vector $\mathbf{z}_j$. (b) Intrafield feedback rapidly contrast-enhances the initial STM activity pattern. Large-amplitude activity is then concentrated at one or more nodes.

12. SYSTEM DYNAMICS AFTER INTRAFIELD FEEDBACK: AMPLIFICATION OF TRANSMITTER RELEASE BY POSTSYNAPTIC CONTRAST ENHANCEMENT AND ATTENTION.

In the next time interval, the intrafield feedback signal contrast-enhances the initial signal pattern (13) via equation (6) and amplifies the total activity across field F_c in Figure 10a, thereby starting to generate an attentive focus. Figure 10b shows typical contrast-enhanced activity profiles: partial compression of the initial signal pattern; or maximal compression, or choice, where only one postsynaptic node remains active due to the strong competition within the field F_c.

In summary, the model behaves initially like a linear filter. The resulting pattern of activity across postsynaptic cells is contrast-enhanced, as required in the ART 2 model as well as in the many other neural network models that incorporate competitive learning [20]. These models implicitly assume that intracellular transmitter u_{ij} is always accumulated up to its target level z_{ij} and that postsynaptic activity x_j does not alter the rate of transmitter release:

$$u_{ij} \approx z_{ij} \quad \text{and} \quad v_{ij} \approx z_{ij}S_i. \qquad (14)$$

We now suggest how nonlinearities of synaptic transmission and neuromodulation can, when embedded in an ART circuit, help to correct coding errors by triggering a parallel search. allow the system to respond adaptively to reinforcement, and rapidly reset itself to changing input patterns. In equation (10), term

$$u_{ij}S_i f(x_j) \qquad (15)$$

for the amount of transmitter released per unit time implies that the original incoming weighted signal $z_{ij}S_i$ is distorted both by depletion of the presynaptic transmitter u_{ij} and by the activity level x_j of the postsynaptic cell. If these two nonlinearities are significant, the net signal in the ijth pathway depends jointly on the maximal weighted signal $z_{ij}S_i$; the prior activity in the pathway, as reflected in the amount of depletion of the transmitter u_{ij}; and the immediate context in which the signal is sent, as reflected in the target cell activity x_j. In particular, once activity in a postsynaptic cell becomes large, this activity dominates the transmitter release rate, via the term $f(x_j)$ in (15). In other words, although linear filtering properties initially determine the small-amplitude activity pattern of the target field F_c, once intrafield feedback amplifies and contrast-enhances the postsynaptic activity x_j (Figure 10b), it plays a major role in determining the amount of released transmitter v_{ij} (Figure 11). In particular, the postsynaptic activity pattern across the field F_c that represents the recognition code (Figure 10b) is imparted to the pattern of released transmitter (Figure 11), which then also represents the recognition code, rather than the initial filtered pattern $\mathbf{S} \cdot \mathbf{z}_j$.

13. SYSTEM DYNAMICS DURING RESET: INACTIVATION OF BOUND TRANSMITTER CHANNELS.

The dynamics of transmitter release implied by the ART Search Hypothesis 1 can be used to implement the reset process, by postulating the

ART Search Hypothesis 2:

The nonspecific reset signal quickly inactivates postsynaptic membrane channels at which transmitter is bound (Figure 12).

The reset signal in equations (5) and (6) may be interpreted as assignment of a large value to the inactivation rate in a manner analogous to the action of a neuromodulator (Figure 8). Inhibition of

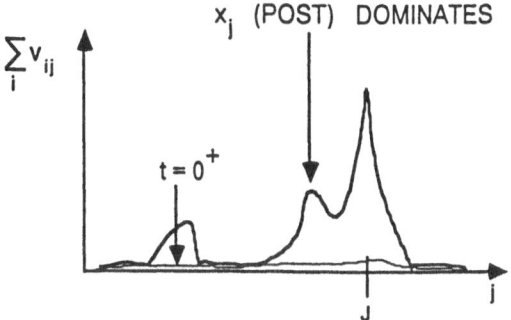

Figure 11. The ART Search Hypothesis 1 implies that large amounts of transmitter (v_{ij}) are released only adjacent to postsynaptic nodes with large-amplitude activity (x_j). Competition within the postsynaptic field therefore transforms the initial low-amplitude distributed pattern of released and bound transmitter into a large-amplitude contrast-enhanced pattern.

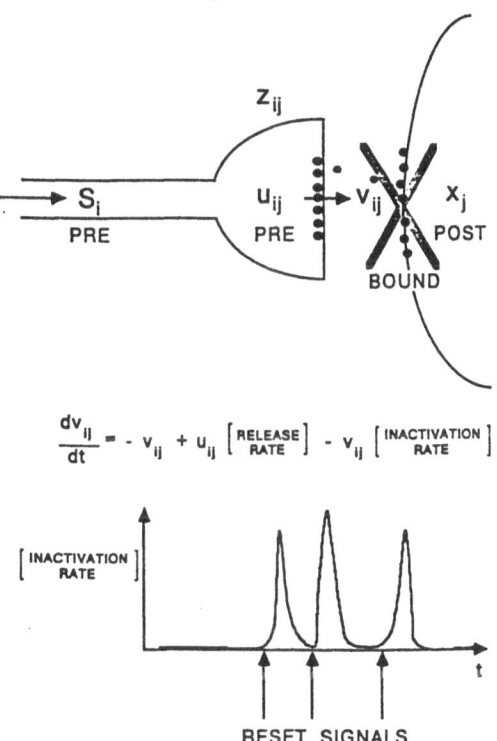

Figure 12. The ART Search Hypothesis 2 specifies a high rate of inactivation of bound transmitter following a reset signal. Postsynaptic action of the nonspecific reset signal is similar to that of a neuromodulator.

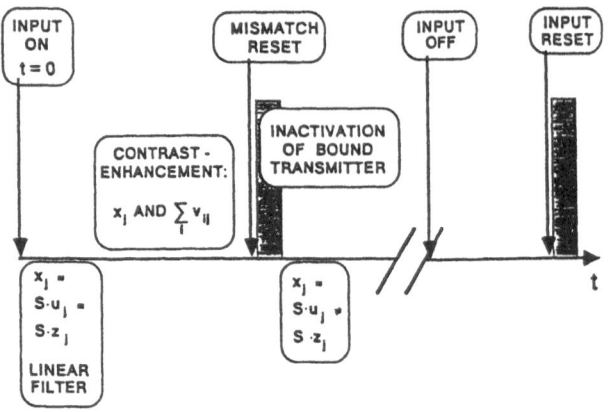

Figure 13. An ART 3 search cycle: Initial read-out of bottom-up signals behaves like a linear filter. Read-out leads to contrast-enhancement and amplification both of the postsynaptic activity pattern and the presynaptic transmitter pattern. A mismatch causes a reset event that inactivates the channels at which transmitter is postsynaptically bound. The reset event biases the network's short term memory representation against the previously most active feature detectors. After such a reset event, the adaptive filter delivers a smaller signal to the previously most active feature detectors, thereby testing a different hypothesis.

postsynaptic nodes breaks the strong intrafield feedback loops that implement ART 2 and ART 3 matching and contrast-enhancement (equation (3) or (6)).

The pattern of released transmitter provides a representation of the postsynaptic recognition code. The arrival of a reset signal implies that some part of the system has judged this code to be erroneous, according to some criterion. The ART Search Hypothesis 1 implies that the largest concentrations of bound extracellular transmitter are adjacent to the nodes which the system, based on its past experiences, deems the most likely representation of the data. Correspondingly, the presynaptic transmitter stores of the most active postsynaptic cells are selectively inactivated. If the hypothesis corresponding to this representation is supported, then the selective presynaptic transmitter inactivation does not compromise the postsynaptic representation. On the other hand, the ART Search Hypothesis 2 implies that a reset event restores postsynaptic activation to an unbiased baseline of inactivation, and leaves the selective presynaptic transmitter inactivation intact. This is the basis for calling the postsynaptic activation pattern Short-Term Memory, or STM, and the presynaptic transmitter pattern Medium-Term Memory, or MTM.

In summary, after a reset event occurs, the system maintains a presynaptic MTM bias against postsynaptic activation of those nodes which were most responsible for the predictive failure that led to the reset event. Although the transmitter signal pattern $\mathbf{S} \cdot \mathbf{u}_j$ originally sent to target nodes at times $t = 0^+$ was proportional to $\mathbf{S} \cdot \mathbf{z}_j$, as in equation (12), the transmitter signal pattern $\mathbf{S} \cdot \mathbf{u}_j$ after the reset event is no longer proportional to $\mathbf{S} \cdot \mathbf{z}_j$. Instead, it is selectively biased against those features that were previously most active (Figure 15). The new signal pattern $\mathbf{S} \cdot \mathbf{u}_j$ will lead to selection of another contrast-enhanced representation, with more activation given to previously unattended features. This representation may or may not then be reset. This search process continues until an acceptable match is found, whence an attentive resonance is established and learning triggered in those adaptive weights, or LTM traces, which abut resonant activations.

14. SUMMARY OF SYSTEM DYNAMICS DURING A SEARCH, RESONANT ATTENTION, AND LEARNING CYCLE.

Figure 14 summarizes system dynamics of the ART search model during a single input presentation. Initially the transmitted signal pattern $\mathbf{S} \cdot \mathbf{u}_j$, as well as the postsynaptic activity x_j, are proportional to the weighted signal pattern $\mathbf{S} \cdot \mathbf{z}_j$ of the linear filter. The postsynaptic activity pattern is then contrast-enhanced, due to the internal competitive dynamics of the target field. The ART Search Hypothesis 1 implies that the transmitter release rate is greatly amplified in proportion to the level of postsynaptic activity. A subsequent reset signal selectively inactivates transmitter in those pathways that caused an error. Following the reset wave, the new signal $\mathbf{S} \cdot \mathbf{u}_j$ is no longer proportional to $\mathbf{S} \cdot \mathbf{z}_j$ but is, rather, biased against the previously active representation, thereby causing a shift in the attentive focus to a potentially more predictive pattern of features in short term memory. A series of such reset events may ensue, until an adequate match or a new category is found, thereby allowing the network to go into resonance and to maintain its attentional focus. New code learning can then occur on a time scale that is long relative to that of the search process.

Mathematical details and computer simulations of these ART 3 interactions are described in Carpenter and Grossberg [9]. Taken together, they illustrate how functional analyses of cellular and network neurobiological processes and of behavioral processes of attention and learning can be joined in a multi-level interdisciplinary theory for enhancing our understanding of behavioral adaptation to a changing world.

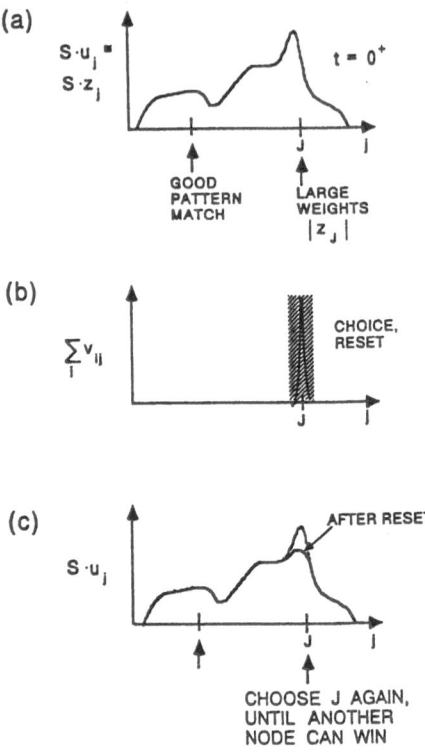

Figure 14. Change of transmitter and short term memory patterns due to search: (a) Initially the signal pattern $S \cdot u_j$ may deliver a bigger input to nodes whose adaptive weights z_J are larger than to nodes whose adaptive weights better match the input pattern; (b) contrast enhancement and amplification select the preferred nodes in short term memory; (c) a reset event biases the transmitted signal pattern $S \cdot u_j$ against these preferred nodes. More than one reset event may be needed to accumulate sufficient bias to select a new representation capable of supporting resonant attention and learning.

REFERENCES

[1] Grossberg, S., Adaptive pattern classification and universal recoding, I: Parallel development and coding of neural feature detectors. *Biological Cybernetics*, 1976a; **23**: 121–134.

[2] Grossberg, S., Adaptive pattern classification and universal recoding, II: Feedback, expectation, olfaction, and illusions. *Biological Cybernetics*, 1976b; **23**: 187–202.

[3] Grossberg, S., **Studies of mind and brain: Neural principles of learning, perception, development, cognition, and motor**

control. Boston: Reidel Press, 1982.

[4] Grossberg, S. (Ed.), **The adaptive brain, I: cognition, learning, reinforcement, and rhythm**, Amsterdam: Elsevier/North-Holland, 1987.

[5] Grossberg, S. (Ed.), **Neural networks and natural intelligence**. Cambridge, MA: MIT Press, 1988.

[6] Carpenter, G.A. and Grossberg, S., A massively parallel architecture for a self-organizing neural pattern recognition machine. *Computer Vision, Graphics, and Image Processing*, 1987a; **37**: 54–115.

[7] Carpenter, G.A. and Grossberg, S., ART 2: Self-organization of stable category recognition codes for analog input patterns. *Applied Optics*, 1987b; **26**: 4919–4930.

[8] Carpenter, G.A. and Grossberg, S., The ART of adaptive pattern recognition by a self-organizing neural network. *Computer:* Special issue on Artificial Neural Systems, 1988; **21**: 77–88.

[9] Carpenter, G.A. and Grossberg, S., ART 3: Hierarchical search using chemical transmitters in self-organizing pattern recognition architectures. *Neural Networks*, 1990; **3**: 129-152.

[10] Grossberg, S., A neural theory of punishment and avoidance, II. Quantitative theory. *Mathematical Biosciences*, 1972; **15**: 253-285.

[11] Bear, M.F. and Singer, W., Modulation of visual cortical plasticity by acetylcholine and noradrenaline. *Nature*, 1986; **320**: 172–176.

[12] Kasamatsu, T. and Pettigrew, J.D., Depletion of brain catecholamines: Failure of ocular dominance shift after monocular occlusion in kittens. *Science*, 1976; **194**: 206–208.

[13] Pettigrew, J.D. and Kasamatsu, T., Local perfusion of noradrenaline maintains visual cortical plasticity. *Nature*, 1978; **271**: 761–763.

[14] Grossberg, S., Some physiological and biochemical consequences of psychological postulates. *Proceedings of the National Academy of Sciences*, 1968; **60**: 758–765.

[15] Grossberg, S., On the production and release of chemical transmitters and related topics in cellular control. *Journal of Theoretical Biology*, 1969; **22**: 325–364.

[16] Grossberg, S., Classical and instrumental learning by neural networks. **Progress in theoretical biology**, Rosen, R. and Snell, F. (Eds.), New York: Academic Press, **3**, 1974.

[17] Kleinschmidt, A., Bear, M.F., and Singer, W., Blockade of "NMDA" receptors disrupts experience-dependent plasticity of kitten striate cortex. *Science*, 1987; **238**: 355–358.

[18] Grossberg, S., On learning and energy-entropy dependence in recurrent and nonrecurrent signed networks. *Journal of Statistical Physics*, 1969b; **1**: 319–350.

[19] Grossberg, S., A theory of visual coding, memory, and development. **Formal theories of visual perception**, Leeuwenberg, E. and Buffart, H. (Eds.), New York: Wiley and Sons, 1978.

[20] Levy, W.B., Associative changes at the synapse: LTP in the hippocampus. **Synaptic modification, neuron selectivity, and nervous system organization**.

Levy, W.B., Anderson, J., and Lehmkuhle, S. (Eds.), Hillsdale, NJ: Erlbaum, 1985; 5–33.

[21] Levy, W.B., Brassel, S.E., and Moore, S.D., Partial quantification of the associative synaptic learning rule of the dentate gyrus. *Neuroscience*, 1983; **8**: 799–808.

[22] Levy, W.B. and Desmond, N.L., The rules of elemental synaptic plasticity. **Synaptic modification, neuron selectivity, and nervous system organization**. Levy, W.B., Anderson, J., and Lehmkuhle, S. (Eds.), Hillsdale, NJ: Erlbaum, 1985; 105–121.

[23] Rauschecker, J.P. and Singer, W., Changes in the circuitry of the kitten's visual cortex are gated by postsynaptic activity. *Nature*, 1979; **280**: 58–60.

[24] Singer, W., Neuronal activity as a shaping factor in the self-organization of neuron assemblies. **Synergetics of the brain**. Basar, E., Flohr, H. Haken, H., and Mandell, A.J. (Eds.), New York: Springer-Verlag, 1983.

[25] Singer, W., The role of attention in developmental plasticity. *Human Neurobiology*, 1982; **1**: 41–43.

[26] Eckhorn, R., Bauer, R., Jordan, W., Brosch, M., Kruse, W., Munk, M., and Reitboeck, H.J., Coherent oscillations: A mechanism of future linking in the visual cortex? *Biological Cybernetics*, 1988; **60**: 121–130.

[27] Gray, C.M., Konig, P., Engel, A.K., and Singer, W., Oscillatory responses in cat visual cortex exhibit inter-columnar synchronization which reflects global stimulus properties. *Nature*, 1989; **338**: 334–337.

[28] Grossberg, S., A theory of human memory: Self-organization and performance of sensory-motor codes, maps, and plans, **Progress in theoretical biology**, 5, Rosen, R. and Snell, F. (Eds.), New York, Academic Press, 1978, 233-374.

[29] Näätänen, R., Gaillard, A., and Mäntysalo, S., The N1 effect of

selective attention reinterpreted, *Acta Psyologica*, 1978; **42**: 313-329.

[30] Näätänen, R., Processing negativity: An evoked potential reflection of selective attention, *Psychological Bulletin*, 1982; **92**: 605-540.

[31] Grossberg, S., How does a brain build a cognitive code? *Psychological Review*, 1980; **87**: 1-51.

[32] Varela, F.J. and Singer, W., Neuronal dynamics in the visual corticothalamic pathway revealed through binocular rivalry. *Experimental Brain Research*, 1987; **66**: 10-20.

[33] Grossberg, S., Some psychophysiological and pharmacological correlates of a developmental, cognitive, and motivational theory. **Brain and information: Event related potentials**. Karrer, R., Cohen, J., and Tueting, P. (Eds.), New York: New York Academy of Sciences, 1984, 58-151.

[34] Banquet, J.-P., Massioui, F. El, and Godet, J.L., ERP-RT chronometry and learning in normal and depressed subjects. **Cerebral psychophysiology: Studies in event-related potentials**, McCallum, W.C., Zappoli, R., and Denoth, F. (Eds.) Amsterdam: Elsevier, 1986.

[35] Banquet, J.-P. and Grossberg, S., Probing cognitive processes through the structure of event-related potentials during learning: An experimental and theoretical analysis. *Applied Optics*, 1987; **26**: 4931-4946

[36] Kohonen, T., **Self-organization and associative memory**. New York: Springer-Verlag, 1984.

[37] Grossberg, S., Neural expectation: Cerebellar and retinal analogs of cells fired by learnable or unlearned pattern classes. *Kybernetik*, 1972; **10**: 49-57.

[38] Malsburg, C. von der, Self-organization of orientation sensitive cells in the striate cortex. *Kybernetik*, 1973; **14**: 85-100.

[39] Willshaw, D.J. and Malsburg, C. von der, How patterned neural connections can be set up by self-organization. *Proceedings of the Royal Society of London (b)*, 1976; **194**: 431-445.

[40] Ito, M., **The cerebellum and neural control**. New York: Raven Press, 1984.

[41] Kandel, E.R. and Schwartz, J.H., **Principles of neural science**, New York: Elsevier/North-Holland, 1981.

[42] Kuffler, S.W., Nicholls, J.G., and Martin, A.R., **From neuron to brain, 2nd edition.** Sunderland, MA: Sinauer Associates, 1984.

TUTORIALS

DYNAMICAL SYSTEMS AND ARTIFICIAL NEURAL NETWORKS

J.G.Taylor

Department of Mathematics,
King's College, Strand,
London,WC2R 2LS,UK.

ABSTRACT

After a brief account of the range of complexities of model neurons, a dynamical systems primer is given which outlines the main features of asymptotia, stability and bifurcation analysis. This is then applied to gain insights into the possible dynamical behaviour of model nets, including oscillatory assemblies.

INTRODUCTION

After the great flurry of activity in artificial neural nets of the last few years it is becoming clear that it is necessary to gain a deeper understanding of the dynamics of such nets both for their ongoing and their longer-term learning abilities. The ideal approach would be in terms of a framework which would allow the rapid appreciation of the powers of a net constructed of whatever architechture and sorts of neurons. Such a powerful framework does not seem to be available, yet the approach through the theory of dynamical systems grants a limited sort of understanding along those lines. That is why it was thought appropriate to include a tutorial on the subject here. The use of the concepts from dynamical systems begins to give a general impresion of what the features of a net are, with some hint at the dependence of these properties on those of the neurons and topology of the net.

In particular it will be seen that we can begin to describe the following features about net activity:

1. the dynamical evolution of the net,

2. the nature of the attractors of the net (fixed points, cycles and strange attractors),

3. how to train the net to accomplish certain tasks (learning algorithms, memory capacity),

4. stability of the net under either training or testing regimes,

5. dependence of the net activity on the initial states in which it has been set up.

Such features are at the heart of study in neural nets; although we will not be able to give very detailed answers, the general feature give valuable insights into net activity.

It should be noted immediately that the study of any dynamical system depends on having a reasonably clear picture of the mathematical structure under investigation. Neural nets may be said to present somewhat of a moving target in that respect, since there is a very large range of models that are presently being studied. These range all the way from the most simple formal neurons of McCulloch and Pitts [1] and Caianiello [2] to models of almost real neurons [3]. There are also a variety of learning rules. Whilst it is better to try to aim for simplicity in such modelling it is worth while noting Einstein's dictum "you can make a model simple but not too simple". That is why an analysis of the varieties of properties which neurons may possess is given in the next section (temporal summation, noise, non-linearity, etc). This allows us to begin to approach the level of complexity of the living neuron, and to appreciate the nature of the mathematical structure needed in that modelling. In so doing we are thus able to give the study of neural nets room for future manouevres.

It is appropriate to point out here that there is also the important approach to the study of nets that considers the information transfer as the crucial aspect of study. Such items as maximising the information-theoretic capacity by the coding of inputs by a net, the process of redundancy reduction by lateral inhibition, of maximisation of information throughput are all needed to be analysed of part of the study of neural nets We agree that such an approach is of great value, and should be married to the one we are developing here. Again the details of the net may be of importance in determining the information-theoretic powers it possesses, so that the present study would seem to be needed as much as the information one.

The tutorial covers the following topics:
1. Models of Neural nets.
2. Dynamical Systems Primer.
3. Applications to Neural Nets.
4. Conclusions.

One of the crucial lessons that has been gained in the development of dynamical systems theory is of the importance of reducing a system ,if of high dimension, to one of much lower dimension. The presence of order parameters are very important in such an approach, and the development of mean activity analyses(mean field theories in statistical mechanical language) is an indication of how such an approach might proceed. In the context of turbulence it is usual to have a system which moves always to lower dimensions due to the presence of dissipation. Such ideas are of value to have in the backs of our minds when we consider neural nets as dynamical systems.

1. MODELS OF NEURAL NETS

1.1 Single Neurons.

There are two extreme ways of approaching the problem of modelling neural nets. The first of these starts at the most complex, and attempts to model the system with no appeal to simplicity. This is the approach of, say [3]. While admirable , and very likely necessary if one wishes to get the best from the system it may be that one may not see very clearly what different features of the model are actually achieving. The other approach is to start from the simplest model and gradually add to it . That is the method to be used here. By it we hope to be able to get a clearer picture of what makes a neuron "tick".

We start, then, with the simplest case of discrete time, taken to run in unit steps. The activity of the i'th neuron is described by the function $u_i(t)$, which satisfies the dynamical equation

$$u_i(t+1)= \theta(\Sigma a_{ij}u_j(t)-s_i)\qquad\qquad(1)$$

In this equation the connection or weight matrix is the set of a_{ij} and the quantities s_i are the thresholds of the neurons. The summation in (1) is over the labels j of the N neurons of the net. The θ-function is the unit step function: $\theta(x) = 1$ $(x>0)$, $\theta(x) = 0(x<0)$. This equation was first written down in [2]. It is simply interpreted as that the i'th neuron is active if the total activity arriving on it one unit of time earlier, obtained as a suitably weighted sum of inputs from the other neurons, is larger than a given threshold; otherwise it is inactive.

The first extension of this model is to take account of temporal summation on the membranes of the cells. That may be done by extending the summation in the activity in the θ-function in (1) to be over activities from a set of earlier times, as

$$u_i(t+1) = \theta(\Sigma a_{ij} e^{-r/\tau} u_j(t-r) - s_i) \tag{2}$$

The summation in (2) is now over the label j on the neuron and over the time-step r back in the past. The parameter τ denotes the membrane time-constant, and determines the range of r over which that summation is expected to be of importance. We note that as τ tends to zero then the right hand side of (2) becomes that of (1), since only the term r=0 can contribute in the sum over r in (2).

It is possible to consider the summation over r in the variable in the θ -function in (2) as a discrete approximation to an integral. The equation (2) then becomes

$$u_i(t+1) = \theta(\ \Sigma \int_0^t a_{ij} e^{-(t-t')/\tau} u_j(t')dt' - s_i) \tag{3}$$

where the symbols in (3) have the same meaning as before. It is convenient to introduce the function $V_i(t)$ to represent the variable in the θ-function in (2), and then it can easily be seen that $V_i(t)$ satisfies the equations

$$\dot{V}_i(t) = -(1/\tau)V_i(t) + \Sigma a_{ij} u_j(t) \tag{4a}$$

$$u_i(t+1) = \theta(\ V_i(t) - s_i) \tag{4b}$$

where u_i denotes the binary activity as in (1) but V_i is now a continuous variable.

There has been much interest in the results of time averaging the activity in (4a) so as to lead to the nonlinear system

$$\dot{V}_i = -(1/\tau)V_i + \Sigma \ a_{ij}F(V_j(t-1)) \qquad\qquad (5)$$

in which the function F denotes the degree of nonlinearity that arises in the output function (4b) averaged over the few time steps. This is achieved in detail by replacing u_j (t) in (4a) by its time average $U_i(t)$ =<u_i(t)>, where < > denotes the time averaging process. The quantity $U_i(t)$ is then considered to be the nonlinear function $F(V_j(t-1))$ in the right hand side of (5).

The equations (4) have not yet taken proper account of the manner in which activity arrives on a cell. This is in terms of a change Δg of the conductance on the cell surface, since the part (4a) is meant to describe the current conservation on the cell surface. Thus the modified equations are now

$$\dot{V}_i = -(1/\tau)V_i + \underset{j}{\Sigma} \ \Delta g_{ij}(t) \ (S_{ij} - V_i) \qquad\qquad (6a)$$

$$\Delta g_{ij}(t) = w_{ij}u_j(t) \qquad\qquad (6b)$$

$$u_j(t+1) = \theta(\ V_i(t) - s_i) \qquad\qquad (6c)$$

The quantity S_{ij} is termed the reversal potential of the particular synapse j on the i'th cell; in (6b) the conductance change is taken to be simply proportional to the binary activity of the j'th neuron which synapses onto the i'th neuron being considered. Time averaging of (6) has also been analysed extensively, especially by Grossberg [4], leading to the shunting-inhibition equations

$$\dot{V}_{i} = -(1/\tau)V_i + \Sigma(S_{ij} - V_{ij}(t))F_j(V_j(t)) \qquad\qquad (7)$$

This system of equations has nice stability properties which will be discussed later.

It is now possble to include the effect of cell geometry in (6) by considering that a cell is built up of a set of cylinders, each of which is an equipotential [5]. The resulting system of equations for the current flow through the compartments has been studied by many authors [6], and has the same form as the set of equations (6) ,with the label i now denoting the different compartments, with an added term $\Sigma(V_i - V_j)/R_{ij}$ on the right of (6a) ,where R_{ij} is the membrane resistance between the compartments i and j. The form of these equations are thus

$$C_i \dot{V}_i = -V_i/R_i + \Sigma(V_j - V_i)/R_{ij} + \Sigma \Delta g_{ik}(S_{ik} - V_i) \qquad (8)$$

Much use has been made of this model in the hippocampal simulations in [3], to which we refer the interested reader. This approach is also considered further by Dr. Mannion in his tutorial.

It is possible to add synaptic noise directly to the simple model (1) by interpreting the weights a_{ij} as a product of a post-synaptic efficiency factor ϵ_{ij} a random variable q_{ij} which denotes the amount of chemical transmitter substance in the synaptic cleft. This is released into the cleft in a discrete set of packets or quanta, as discovered by Katz [7]. This release was modelled as having a Poisson distribution in 1971 [8] but there are many possible distributions. One favored now amongst the neurophysiologists is the single vesicle distribution, this being the Bernoulli distribution with a probability p for emission of a vesicle on arrival of a nerve impulse (and 1-p for the emission when there is no impulse) and the resulting distribution function p( ) for the amount of chemical transmitter q_{ij} being

$$p(q_{ij}) = p\ \delta(q_{ij} - q_0) + (1-p)\ \delta(q_{ij}) \qquad (9)$$

where q_0 is the content of a single vesicle of transmitter substance. It also possible to use a binomial distribution. One may extend such a randomisation of variables to the threshold parameters s_i, thereby obtaining the spin-glass approach to neural nets. This has been worked out in the framework of random iteration networks in [9], and is described in Dr Bressloff's contribution to this Conference. There is also an extension of the noisy neuron which considers fully nonlinear (sigma-pi) units, in which there are nonlinear terms in the activity on the right hand side of (1) of form

36

$$\Sigma(\ a_{ijk}\ u_i u_j u_k + a_{ijkl} u_i u_j u_k u_l + \ldots) \tag{10}$$

where the summation in (10) is over all the doubly repeated indices i,j,k,l, etc. The further variables a_{ijk}, etc can also be given a stochastic character. This maximally nonlinear and stochastic approach has been developed at the theoretical, software and hardware level elsewhere in terms of probabilistic RAMs, or pRAMs[10], and certain developments, especially associated with reinforcement training considered in Dr Gorse's talk at this conference.

The next property which can be included in the neuron model is that of the production of the nerve impulse. That may be described in terms of the membrane potential V without use of any thresholding, such as was used in equations (6c). The equations satisfied by V are such as to make it change in a very fast fashion when a suitably large input arrives, so obviating the need to put in the thresholding θ-function as if by hand.

The most complete approach to the nonlinear active membrane properties of membrane is through the Hodgkin-Huxley equations [11]. These are a somewhat complicated four variable non-linear system of equations. However it is possible to get a feeling for the system by considering a simplified system which only requires the use of two independent variables instead of the four of the H-H system. That is the FitzHugh-Nagumo model [12],[13] which uses an extra recovery variable W in addition to the potential V. For a single neuron, without any extra compartments (which may easily be added if so desired) the model equations are

$$\dot{V} = c(V + W - (1/3)V^3 + W + I) \tag{11a}$$

$$\dot{W} = -(1/c)(V + a - bW) \tag{11b}$$

where a,b and c are suitable parameters, and I denotes any external current (which may arise from other neurons). We will discuss the dynamics of equations (11) in a later section; it will be considered in more detail in the accompanying paper in these Proceedings with Conal Mannion in the context of oscillatory neuronal assemblies.

The Hodgkin-Huxley equations are concerned with a more detailed description of the ionic currents involved in the nerve impulse. The basic equation of current conservation is, as always,

$$C\dot{V} = \Sigma g_i (V_i - V) \tag{12}$$

The summation in (12) is over the various ions: sodium, potassium, calcium, etc. Each of the associated conductances has its time-dependence modelled by presumed molecular concentration variables n,h,m, etc. The conductances depend nonlinearly on these concentrations, as

$$g_K = g_{K0} n^4 \tag{13a}$$

$$g_{Na} = g_{Na0} m^3 h \tag{13b}$$

where the parameters with the suffix zero are constants, and the concentration variables m,n,h satisfy rate equations of the form

$$\dot{n} = \alpha_n (1-n) - \beta_n n$$

$$\dot{m} = \alpha_m (1-m) - \beta_m m$$

$$\dot{h} = \alpha_h (1-h) - \beta_h h \tag{14}$$

$$\alpha_n = .01(V+1)/(e^{(V+10/10)} - 1)$$

$$\beta_n = .125 e^{V/80}$$

where there are similar expressions for the remaining variables [11]. It is the high nonlinearity of these variables in V that leads to the catastrophic type of activity of the nerve impulse.

There are numerous further effects that could be included in the formal neuron. A partial list is:

a) dendritic spikes, which would lead to the inclusion of further nonlinearities inside the θ-function in (1) or later equations, or of similar nonlinear equations to (11),(12),(13),(14) for dendritic compartment potential variables.

b) synaptic channels opening and closing, so causing the conductance change Δg used above to be smeared out in time by the alpha-function of Jack et al [14], as

$$\Delta g(t) \rightarrow \int dt' e^{-\alpha(t-t')} \alpha^2 (t-t') \Delta g(t') \tag{15}$$

where the parameter α is the inverse of the channel gate opening time.

c) second messengers, which can lead to modifications of the synaptic parameters, possibly related to learning,

d) slow ionic channels, which can lead to long-lasting ionic currents on the cell surface,

e) more exotic synapses than the usual dendro-axonal one, such as axo-axonal, serial, reciprocal dendro-dendritic, etc.(all of which will change the nonlinearity in the models by increasing the number of inter-related variables).

In general the model we end up with for a neuron is that of a stochastic, time delayed nonlinear system of equations in the vector variable we denote $\underline{X}$, with dynamical equations

$$\dot{\underline{X}} = G(\{X(t' \leq t)\}, \epsilon, p) \tag{16}$$

where the parameters ϵ and p are the synaptic efficiences and the transmitter probability distribution functions described earlier. The structure of equation (16) is therefore that for which we have been searching.

1.2 Learning Rules.

In the previous sub-section we only considered time dependence of the activity variables of the neurons. It is now necessary to discuss the various learning rules in which there is modification of the parameters. These latter are solely the connection weights a_{ij} in the original simple equations (1) (possibly together with the thresholds s_i), but in the more complex models there are both the synaptic efficiences $\bar{a}_{ij}$ and the probability distribution functions p_{ij} for the chemical transmitters (or the associated moments of these transmitters). Extensions mentioned at the end of the previous sub-section included the α-parameters, which may also be adaptive. Our discussion must therefore encompass a range of parameters, which we denote generically by $\underline{a}$.

There are three distinct classes of learning rules. These are

(a) Supervised

There exists an error function, which we denote $E(\underline{a})$, depending on the parameters, which is to be minimised. Then it is usual to modify $\underline{a}$ by gradient descent, so that the dynamics for $\underline{a}$ is

$$\underline{a} = -\lambda \underline{d}E \qquad (15)$$

where $\underline{d}$ denotes the partial derivative with respect to $\underline{a}$, and λ to a learning rate. This learning rule may lead to trapping in false minima; stochastic methods to avoid such are under active discussion, but are not part of our present analysis.

(b) Reward

In this case it is assumed that there exists a reward function of the output so that parameters are increased to values that produce an output obtaining a reward from the environment and decreased away from values that do not lead to a reward. A typical rule for this is (see Dr. Gorse's talk for more details).

$$\Delta\underline{a} = \lambda[r(\underline{x}-\underline{a})+\mu(1-r)(1-\underline{x}-\underline{a})] \qquad (16)$$

where the output of the machine under consideration is a binary stream $\underline{x}$ with mean $\underline{a}$ and r is a binary reward. Thus the first term on the right-hand side of (16) will increase the probability of obtaining rewarded outputs (r=1), the second term decrease the probability of unrewarded or penalised outputs (r=0). The rates of these changes are λ and $\lambda\mu$ respectively. The dynamics of (16) is an interesting one involving stochastic iterated function systems, and some of its features in the context of stochastic associative learning automata are analysed elsewhere (15).

(c) Unsupervised

There are a variety of modification rules here, starting with the Hebbian type.

$$w_{ij} = f(in_j, out_i) \qquad (17)$$

where f is some function of the input in_j from the j'th neuron onto the i'th neuron and out_i is the output of the latter. Rules similar to (17) can also be considered for the synaptic efficiencies and moments of the transmitter distributions, and some features of these are discussed in (9). There are other learning rules which also have some neurophysiological support, such as the co-operative learning rule.

$$w_{ij} = [\epsilon \; \theta(V_i-V_+)-\epsilon_- \; \theta(V_--V_i)]u_j(\underset{j}{\Sigma}u_j') \qquad (18)$$

where the first (second) term in the right hand side of (18) leads to long-term potentiation (depression) (LTP or LTD), with thresholds $V_+(V_-)$ which may be different from the cell firing threshold. The summation over j' in (18) is over synapses close to the j'th so that effects of activity near the jth may lead to long-term structural changes on concomitant activity at the jth synapse (16).

In general we may append learning rules of form

$$\Delta\underline{a} = \underline{H}(\underline{a},\underline{X}) \qquad (19)$$

to the dynamical equations (14).

1.3 Neural Net Taxonomy
Careful analysis of living nervous systems has lead to the recognition of broad areas of specialisation of parts of nerve nets. We only attempt a very broad survey here, and propose the subdivision of net function into

I. Preprocessors
This is performed by the retina for vision, cochlea for audition, nasal epithelium for olfaction.

II. Processors

These are input-output devices, with feedback, in which learning may occur, but usually only over a critical period (as in the development of orientation detectors in visual cortex of kittens). Thus the lateral geniculate nucleus (LGN) and visual cortex (areas 17, 18 and 19) are to be regarded as such direct information processing areas.

III. Semantic and Procedural

These nets set up storage of causal relations between inputs, such as in the relations between phonemes in a word or words in a sentence, and also include procedural skills involving such phenomena as reading mirror writing. They are located in associative cortex, cerebellum and cerebellar nuclei.

IV. Episodic

Particular events are stored in such nets, being related to specific experiences (encoded by nets of type III). It is likely that storage of typical sequences is occurring, as indicated by results of operations on conscious patients (17). The areas of cortex associated with such storage are in the temporal lobe; the hippocampus is clearly implicated in such storage since its loss causes almost complete inability to store new information (18).

V. Drive Centres

These function as generators of global reward centres to the cortex, and apparently are themselves coded by assessment of various chemical levels (hormones, etc) in the body. The hypothalamus is well-known as being a central nucleus of this sort.

VI. Attentional

These function to increase the excitability of areas of cortex, brought about by particularly important inputs (which may be internally generated). Various centres, such as the locus coeruleus (involved in the sleep/waking cycle) and the reticular formation of the brain stem and thalamus are also of this character.

The above division is not necessarily mutually exclusive, nor is it complete. Nets involved in forward planning, such as the frontal lobes, should also be considered in a fuller discussion.

The purpose of presenting such a taxonomy is to indicate the range of functions of living nerve nets, and the problems they pose in understanding how these functions are achieved. This requires appreciation of coding and learning rules, as well as architecture and the important single neuron properties which are needed to support such activities. Some of these aspects will be considered briefly later in the tutorial.

2. DYNAMICAL SYSTEMS PRIMER

2.1 Introduction

We will avoid giving a sequence of very precise definitions, with all the epsilantics, since although that is necessary to have ultimately if detailed results are to be proved, the purpose of this tutorial is to give a general impression of the basic ideas and how they are used.

In general a dynamical system is one for which there exist state variables for the system whose temporal development is the main object of study. If $\underline{x}(t)$ denotes the vector of state variables at time t, it is assumed that there is some general specification of the time variation of $\underline{x}(t)$ in terms of its value for earlier times. This is the manner in which causality is brought into the dynamics. The dynamical equation is therefore of form

$$\underline{x}(t) = \underline{F}(\{\underline{x}(t')\})_{t' < t} \tag{20}$$

where $\underline{F}$ is a functional of the values of the state variables for earlier times.

The description of a dynamical system (20) is more general than we need, however, since the conclusion of the last section was that the most general form of dynamics we need to consider is

$$\dot{\underline{x}}(t) = \underline{F}((\underline{x}(t'))_{t' < t}, t) \tag{21}$$

where the non-linearities $\underline{F}$ in (20) and (21) are generic. The first-order differential character of (21) also fits in with much of the thrust of the modern development of dynamical systems theory in its emergence from Hamiltonian dynamics (19), since the dynamical equations for variables q, p arising from a Hamiltonian H(q,p) are the first order ones

$$\dot{q} = \partial H/\partial p, \quad \dot{p} = -\partial H/\partial q$$

Moreover, provided the state variable is suitably interpreted in (21) it can encompass the differential learning laws of section 1.3. The discrete version of (21):

$$\underline{x}(t+1) = \underline{F}((\underline{x}(t'))_{t' < t}, t) \tag{22}$$

also encompasses the discrete time neuronal models discussed at the beginning of section 1.

We note that if t is absent in the function $\underline{F}$, then the system is called autonomous. A non-autonomous system can always be reduced to an autonomous one by introducing an extra state variable y, with $\dot{y}=1$.

Most investigation of dynamical systems does not involve time delays, so is of form

$$\dot{\underline{x}}(t) = \underline{F}(\underline{x}(t)) \tag{23}$$

or in the discrete case

$$\underline{x}(t+1) = \underline{F}(\underline{x}(t)) \tag{24}$$

However time delays are important to consider [20], arising either from synaptic or axonal sources. They lead to less stability than for the non-delay equations; we will consider these questions later.

We add here, for completeness, that formally a dynamical system is a flow on a differentiable manifold M arising from the vector field $\underline{F}$ of (23), this being a map from M to the tangent space TM. However such a definition is not so natural for the more general time-delayed equation (22); for this one needs to consider the end points of whole solution curves, where the whole curve determines the value of F, on the right hand side of (22).

There are two aspects of the above equation (21) to (24) which we wish to investigate:

a. the evolution for fixed parameters, and its stability under changes of initial conditions.

b. changes of the dynamics as parameters change (or there are more general perturbations).

We discuss (a) in the next sub-section and (b) in the following one.

2.2 Dynamical Evolution

The state space will be assumed here to be n-dimensional real space, $\underline{R}^n$, and the system will be (23). Then the following features are of interest.

i. Existence of solutions

There exist local solutions to (23), starting from a given point $\underline{x}_o$ in $\underline{R}^n$ [21]. Thus there exists a function $\Phi(t)$ of the time axis $\underline{R}$ into $\underline{R}^n$ with

$$\dot{\Phi}(t) = \underline{F}(\Phi(t)), \quad \Phi(o) = x_0 \tag{25}$$

The function $\Phi(t)$ is called a solution curve, based at x_0. The range of t over which this solution exists and lies in a given bounded set is not generally known (that is why the solution is called local), although if the solution is defined to lie in a compact space, such as a torus, then the solution will exist globally.

If the solution curve Φ based at x_0 is regarded as a function of x_0 then as x_0 itself varies the motion defines a flow in R^n. This and the solution curve itself are shown in Figure 1.

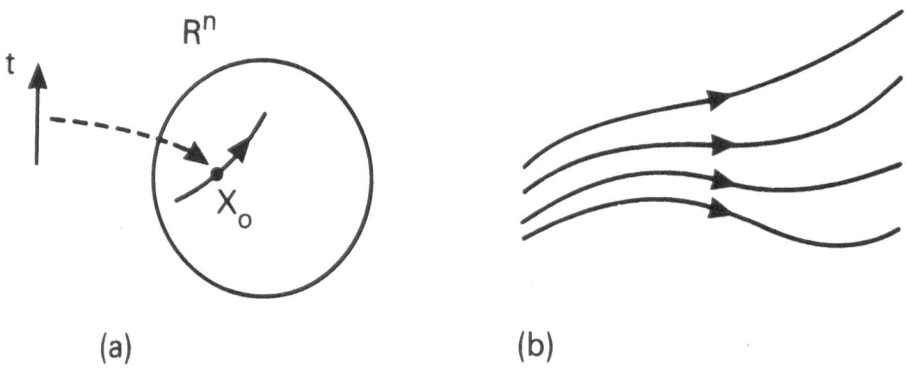

(a)   (b)

Figure 1: (a) The solution curve $\Phi(t)$ based at x_0
           (b) The flow $\Phi(t,x_0)$ generated by Φ as x_0
               varies.

ii. Special Solutions
(a) A fixed point $\bar{x}$ is a zero of the mapping F of (23), so that

$$F(\bar{x}) = 0 \tag{26}$$

Then from (23), x is a constant solution of the system. This is also termed an equilibrium point.

(b) A periodic solution $x(t)$ is one which satisfies (23) and for which

$$\underline{x}(t) = \underline{x}(t+T) \tag{23}$$

for some value T. The least such T for which (27) is valid is called the period of the solution.

(c) A quasi-periodic solution satisfies (23) and has solution curve of form

$$\Phi(t) = \Psi(f_1(t), \ldots, f_n(t)) \tag{28}$$

where Ψ is a general function of its variables, the i'th one, $f_i(t)$ being periodic of period T_i. If all the T_i are equal (or more generally commensurate) then the solution will be periodic, but that will not be so if they are incommensurate (so that their ratios are not all rational numbers).

iii. Stability

A fixed point $\bar{x}$ is said to be neutrally stable if a solution curve based at $\underline{x}_0$ near $\bar{x}$ remains near $\bar{x}$, as shown in Fig.2(a). The fixed point is termed asymptotically stable if it is neutrally stable and also $\Phi(t)$ tends to $\bar{x}$ as t tends to infinity for any x_0 near $\bar{x}$; this is shown in Fig.2(b). Finally, it is unstable otherwise.

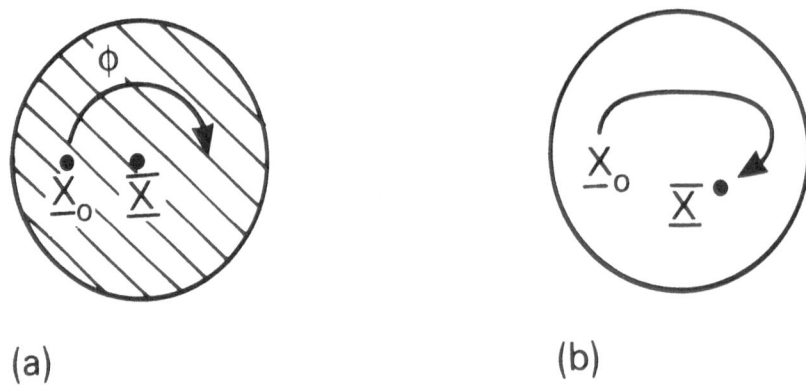

(a)   (b)

Figure 2:   (a) A neutrally stable fixed point;   U is a
               neighbourhood of $\bar{x}$.
             (b) An asymptotically stable fixed point $\bar{x}$.

      The variety of fixed points include sources, sinks and saddles, as
shown in the two-dimensional case in Fig.3.   Sources and saddles are
unstable, sinks asymptotically stable.

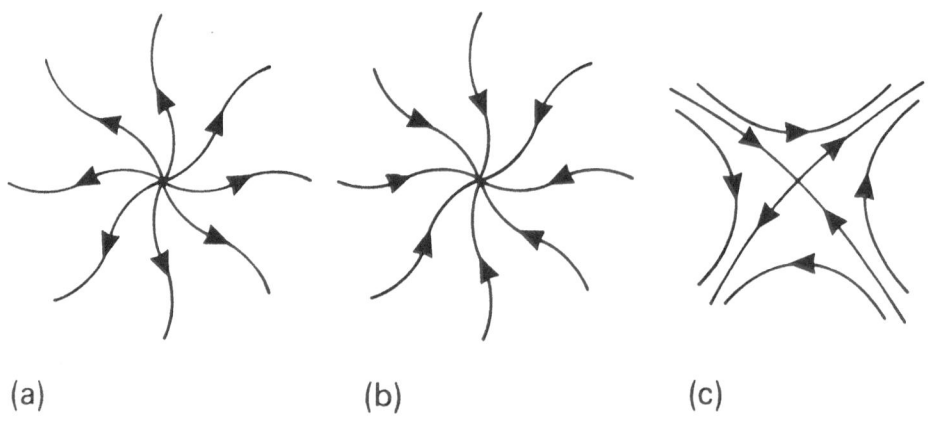

(a)   (b)   (c)

Figure 3:   (a) A source fixed point.
             (b) A sink fixed point.
             (c) A saddle fixed point.

It is also possible to define orbital stability for a periodic orbit: if the solution is given a small pertubation, the resulting motion lies in a neighbourhood of the periodic orbit. This is shown in Fig.4.

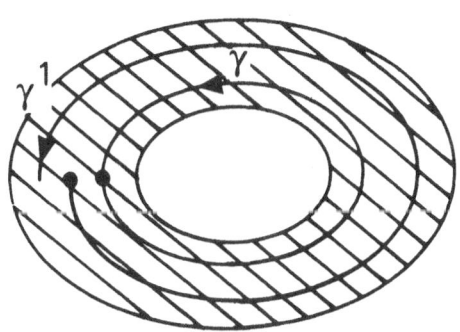

Figure 4: Orbital stability of the periodic orbit γ occurs if there is a neighbourhood U of γ in which a perturbed solution curve γ^1 of γ moves subsequently.

iv. Local Stability Analysis

This may be achieved easily if there exists a Liapunov function $V(\underline{x})$ with the properties that

$$V(\overline{\underline{x}}) = 0$$

$$V(\underline{x}) > 0 \quad (\underline{x} \neq \overline{\underline{x}}) \tag{29}$$

$$\dot{V}(\underline{x}) < 0 \quad \text{(on solution curves)}$$

The conditions (29) then ensure that solution curves can only enter and not leave a level surface of V (one defined by the set of $\underline{x}$

with $V(\underline{x})$ = positive constant with $\overline{\underline{x}}$ inside the surface) and move towards the fixed point $\overline{\underline{x}}$ in the interior. This shows asymptotic stability of $\overline{\underline{x}}$, as can be seen in Fig.5, where starting from a point in

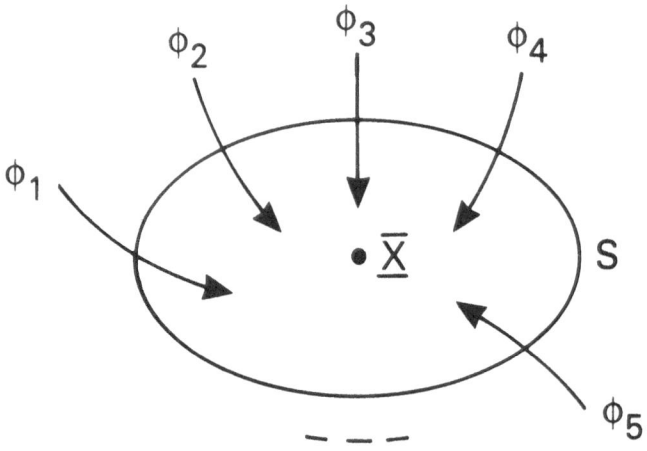

Figure 5: S is a level surface of V, and the solution curves Φ_1, Φ_2, Φ_3, Φ_4, ... all cross S into the interior.

S near to $\overline{\underline{x}}$ always leads asymptotically to $\overline{\underline{x}}$. This is a powerful result, but there is no general method for construction of a Liapunov function for an arbitrary system (23).

Linearisation about the fixed point is important to get a general picture of local stability. In terms of the small state vector

$$\underline{Y} = \underline{x} - \overline{\underline{x}} \tag{30a}$$

the dynamical system becomes

$$\dot{\underline{Y}} = D\underline{Y} + O\,(\underline{Y}^2) \tag{30b}$$

where the matrix D is the Jacobian matrix of $\underline{F}$ at $\underline{\bar{x}}$:

$$D_{ij} = \delta F_i / \delta Y_j \,\Big|_{\underline{x}=\underline{\bar{x}}} \tag{30c}$$

For small t, the solution of (30b) will be

$$\underline{Y} = \exp[Dt]\underline{Y}(o) \tag{31}$$

The nature of the ensuing motion is therefore determined by the eigenvalues λ of D, since in a basis for $\underline{Y}$ composed of the corresponding eigenvectors the motion will correspond to multiplication by the factor $\exp(\lambda t)$. Thus the division of the eigenvalues into three sets is clearly appropriate:

$$E^s = \{\lambda : Re\lambda < 0\}$$
$$E^u = \{\lambda : Re\lambda > 0\} \tag{32}$$
$$E^c = \{\lambda : Re\ \lambda = 0\}$$

The sets of associated eigenvectors are called the stable, unstable and centre manifolds respectively. It is clear from (31) and (32) that the motion along each of these manifolds have exponential decay for E^s, exponential growth in E^u and neither of these in E^c. In the absence of degenerate eigenvalues the latter case will correspond to oscillation of constant amplitude.

If there are no eigenvalues with Re λ = 0, so that E^c is empty, then $\underline{\bar{x}}$ is called a hyperbolic fixed point. At such a point local stability of the solutions is determined by the linearised analysis (30), and in particular there are manifolds W^s and W^u tangent to E^s and E^u (the stable manifold theorem for a fixed point [21]), so that the stability description of the motion can be extended smoothly away from $\underline{\bar{x}}$; the situation in this case is shown in Figure 6.

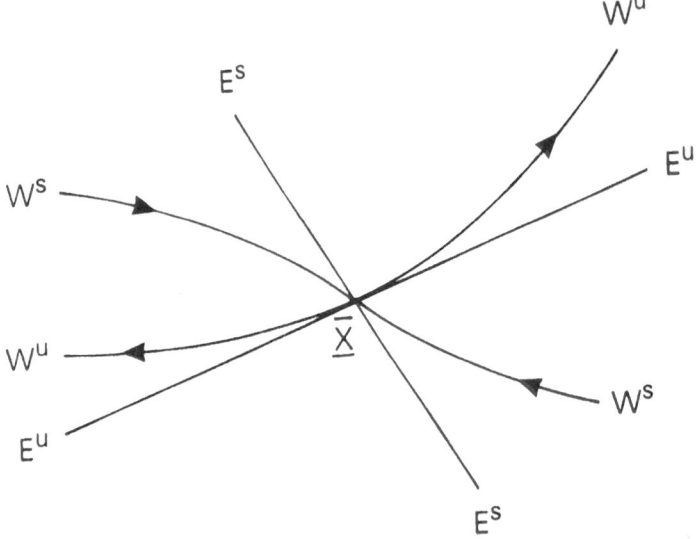

Figure 6: The stable and unstable manifolds of the motion
W^s, W^u are tangent to the corresponding manifolds
of the linearised motion (30) at the fixed point $\bar{x}$.

v. Asymptopia

An attracting set is one defined so that all orbits based near it
converge to it asymptotically. The domain or basin attraction of the
attracting set. A is the set of points whose orbits ultimately end at
A. A typical attracting set is shown in Fig. 7. An attractor is defined
as an attracting set with a dense orbit. This definition is so designed
as to cover the notion of a strange attractor, although it is often very
difficult to show that dense orbits exist. There are numerous detailed
definitions of attractors (see, for example, this discussion in [21],
although these do not help to clarity these objects further from our
point of view.

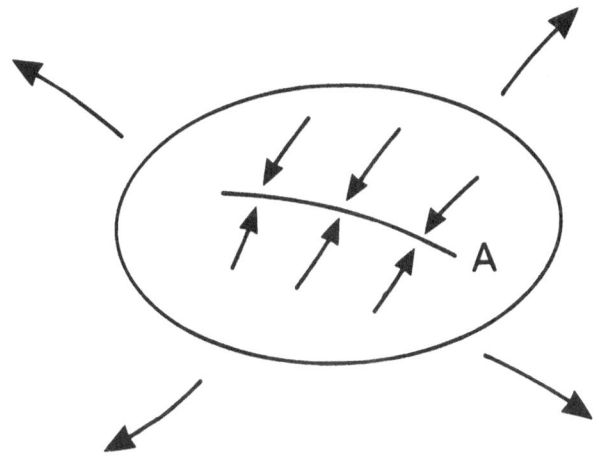

Figure 7: The attracting set A, with its basin of attraction B.

vi. Stability of Closed Orbits

This can be investigated by considering the Poincare map of the orbit and nearby ones. This is done by cutting the orbit by a plane Π and determining where a (not necessarily periodic) orbit sends a point q_1 on its return to Π, as in Fig.8; q_1 is sent to q_2 on completing the orbit. The Poincare map clearly has the point p (the intersection of the periodic

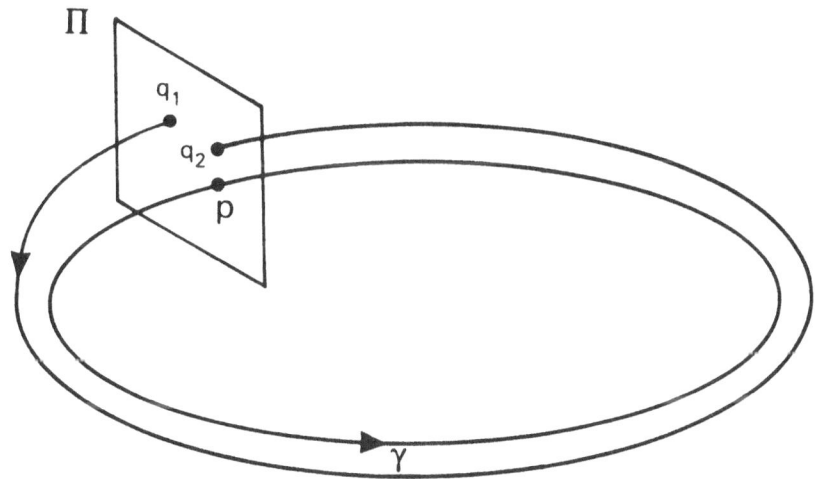

Figure 8: The Poincare map P is obtained by determining the point $q_2 = P(q_1)$ into which a point q_1 on Π returns to q_2

53

orbit γ with Π) as fixed point. The stability of γ may be shown to be given by that of the map P in Π; this latter has already been discussed earlier for continuous flows and this consideration easily extends to iterated maps such as P.

2.3 Bifurcations

At a bifurcation there occurs a change in the qualitative structure of the solutions. This modification arises for special values of the parameters. Thus for the case

$$\dot{x} = F(x,a) \tag{33}$$

with dependence being made explicit on the parameters a, the set of fixed points $\bar{x}$ satisfying

$$F(\bar{x},a) = 0 \tag{34}$$

will form, in general a smooth curve $\bar{x} = \bar{x}(a)$, being a branch of equilibria. However this branch will not be smooth at values of a for which the matrix $(\partial F/\partial x)|_{\bar{x}}$ is singular. As an example, consider

$$F(x,a) = ax-x^3$$
$$F' = a-3x^2 \tag{35}$$

The curves $\bar{x}=\bar{x}(a)$ or

$$\bar{x} = 0 \quad (a<0 \text{ or } a>0)$$
$$\bar{x} = \pm \sqrt{a} \quad (a>0) \tag{36}$$

which have the form shown in Fig. 9; the sign of F′ has already been noted as determining the stability of the fixed point, and is marked on the branches. F′ is zero on the equilibrium branches at the origin, where the single stable fixed point $\bar{x} = 0$ splits into three branches as a is increased. The bifurcation at a=0 is called a pitchfork bifurcation.

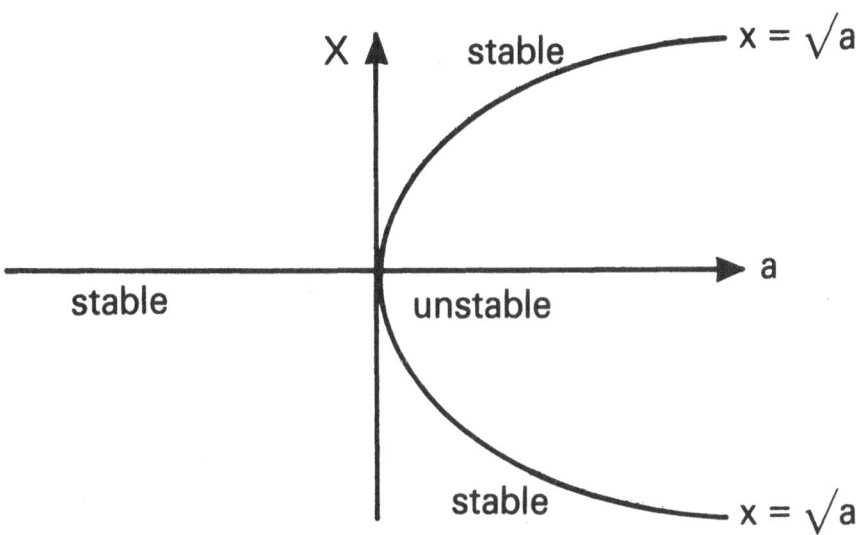

Figure 9: The pitchfork bifurcation diagram, showing how the single solution branch for a<0 bifurcates into two stable and are unstable branches for a>0.

From the earlier discussion it is clear that a bifurcation arises from eigenvalues in the centre manifold W^c defined earlier.

Other one parameter bifurcaions are the transcritical, the saddle-node and the Hopf ones, shown in Fig. 10. The first of

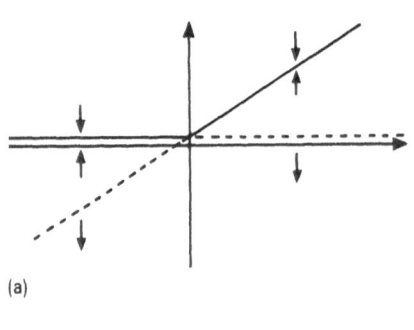

(a)

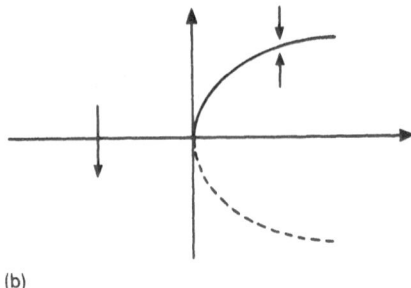

(b)

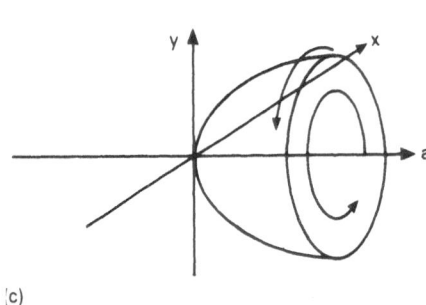

(c)

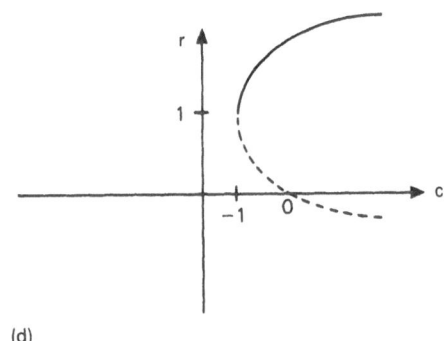

(d)

Figure 10: (a) Transcritical bifurcation
(b) Saddle-node bifurcation
(c) Hopf supercritical bifurcation
(d) Sub-critical Hopf bifurcation;
These are described in the text. The continuous
(dashed) lines are stable (unstable) equilibria;
the arrows indicate the directions of flow near
the bifurcations.

these arises in the example

$$\dot{x} = ax - x^2$$

where there is exchange of stability between the two branches. The
saddle node can be seen in the example

$$\dot{x} = a - x^2$$

Finally the Hopf bifurcation occurs in the system

$$\dot{x} = -y + x(a - (x^2 + y^2))$$

56

$$\dot{y} = x + y(a-(x^2+y^2))$$

where the stable node at x=y=0 for a negative becomes unstable for a positive and motion then converges to the stable periodic orbit x^2+y^2=a. This bifurcation is called a soft excitation [22] since the periodic orbit begins with zero amplitude. It is called more specifically a supercritical Hopf bifurcation to distinguish it from the subcritical case which can arise, say in

$$r = r(c+2r^2-r^4)$$
$$\dot{\theta} = 2\pi$$

whose bifurcation diagram is also shown in Fig. 10. This is a hard excitation [22] since the amplitude is non-zero when the fixed point at r=0 loses its stability and the stable periodic orbit with r=0 suddenly appears. This system has the interesting property of hysterisis, as well as that of having a black hole, arising when the periodic orbit can be perturbed to the fixed point at r=0 by a suitable disturbance.

Similar bifurcations occur in maps, together with the extra flip bifurcation (period doubling), as seen for the map $x \rightarrow -(1+a)x+x^3$, where there is an orbit of period 2 between the upper and lower curves in Figure 11.

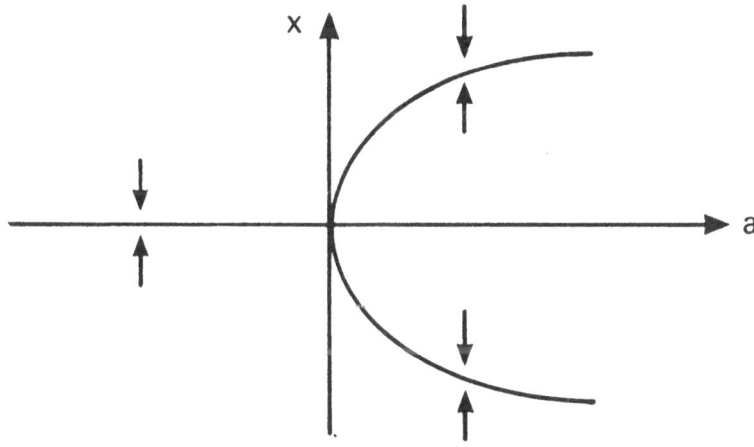

Figure 11: The flip bifurcation at a=0 in the map
$x \rightarrow -(1+a)x+x^3$.

Finally, there are the well-known strange attractors which can arise if parameters in dissipative maps are chosen suitably. Thus in the Henon map

$$x \rightarrow y$$
$$y \rightarrow 1+bx-ay^2 \tag{37}$$

the curves of 10^4 iterates is shown in Fig.12 at various magnifications for a = 1.4, b = 0.3

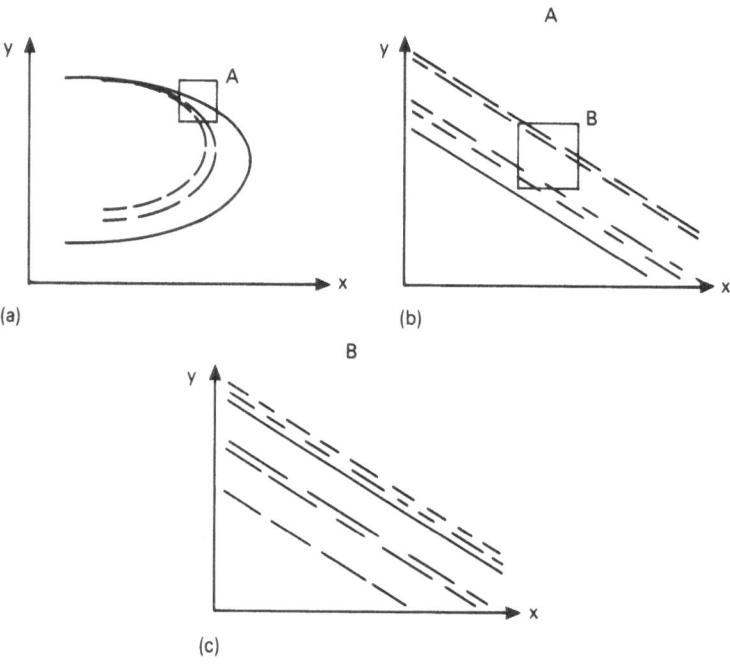

Figure 12: The Henon map of equation (37) at different levels of magnification.

Chaos is presently under very active analysis [23]. It can be characterised by a set of numbers. For example one can define the Liapunov exponents by

$$\lim_{n \to \infty}(1/n) \log \|DF^n(\underline{x}) \; \underline{v} \| \tag{38}$$

for normalised vectors $\underline{v}$. The exponents give the eigenvalues of DF^n for large n when $\underline{v}$ are chosen accordingly, and in general correspond to ratios of principal axes of the evolutionary states of a small ball in the state space. If an exponent is negative then motion along that direction will be periodic. A chaotic system is defined by some mathematicians as one for which typical orbits in the attractor have positive Liapunov exponent. Another parameter characterising the activity is

$$\rho = \lim_{\epsilon \to 0}(1/n) \sum_{t=0}^{n-1} \|\underline{x}(t)\| \tag{40}$$

and is used, for example, in analysis of the possible chaotic dynamics of periodically forced neurons [24].

Attractor dimensions may be defined, say, by coverings of the attractor by small hypercubes. If $n(\epsilon)$ is the minimum number of N-dimensional cubes of size ϵ needed to cover a set of points in N dimensions, then the capacity dimension of the set is defined by

$$d = \lim_{\Sigma \to 0}[\log n(\epsilon)/\log(1/\epsilon)] \tag{40}$$

The triadic Cantor set, obtained by continually removing the middle third of intervals on the unit line, has d=log2/log3; it is a fractal set. It is not easy to obtain the capacity (or other) dimension of attractors from simulation or data [25].

3. DYNAMICAL SYSTEMS AND ARTIFICIAL NEURAL NETWORKS

3.1 Introduction

There is still a long way to go before it can be claimed that we understand how the cortex works and what are effective algorithms we can extract from it for artificial neural networks. In particular it is unclear for such algorithms what is

(a) Efficient from a purely information-theoretic point of view: we are presented with a wide range of problems and modalities (segmentation, fusion, storage at semantic and episodic levels, etc)

(b) Used by the brain; for example is chaos used in olfractory cortex, as suggested by Freeman [38], or used in single neurons, since even these latter are very subtle?

Dynamical systems theory can only indicate what is the general nature of the dynamics of such systems. As mentioned earlier, information theory will have to be brought in to allow a proper assessment of the value of one or other of the dynamical properties of a system in information processing.

3.2 Model of Nerve Impulse

The Hodgkin-Huxley equations [11] were described in sub-section one. The manner in which these equations generate a nerve impulse has been elegantly described by Fitzhugh [12], but it is simpler to explain such features in terms of the similar but computationally cheaper Fitzhugh-Nagumo model [12, 13]. The equations for this were given earlier, and are

$$\frac{dV}{dt} = c\left[V - \frac{1}{3}V^3 + W+I\right]$$

$$\frac{dW}{dt} = -\frac{1}{c}(V-a+bW) \tag{40}$$

The null-clines of V and W, that is the curves on which V and W vanish, are sketched in Fig.13. The point of intersection of these two will be an equilibrium point.

60

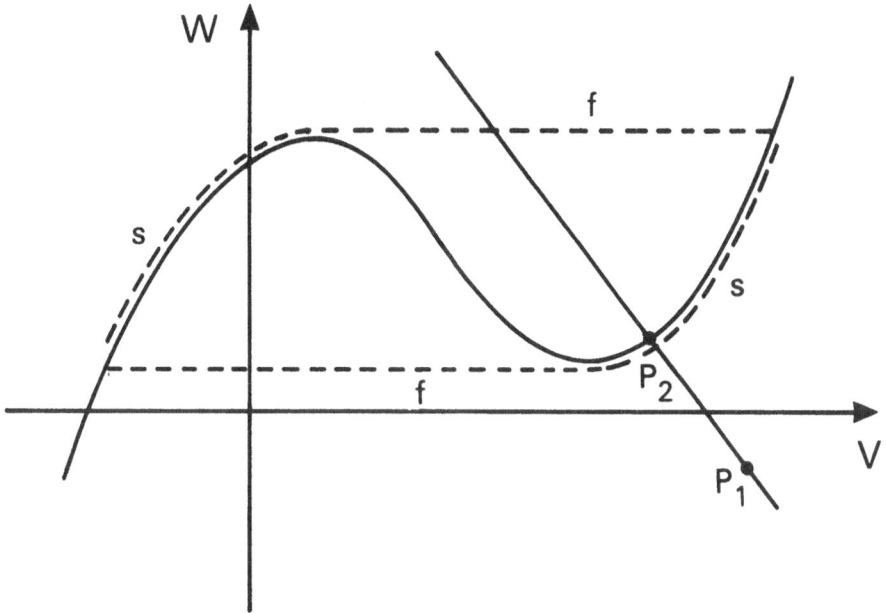

Figure 13: Null-clines of the FH-N model, equations (40).
P_1 is the asymptotically stable fixed point when
I=0. Motion around the curve tfsf, in the
direction of the arrows, occurs when I is chosen
so that P_2 is unstable; s denotes slow, f fast
motion along the curve.

When I=0, this point is P_1, and may be chosen stable. When a, b, c are
chosen so that the equilibrium is unstable when the W null-cline
intersects the V null-cline between the humps then a limit cycle is set
up, and denoted sfsf (s = slow, f = fast), as shown in Fig.13. This
motion is a simplified model of the nerve impulse.

This model may be extended to include, for example, further
recovery variables to give complex spiking or take account of slow ionic
currents. Thus one may take the system

$$\dot{V} = c\left[V - \frac{1}{3}V^3 - W - U + I\right]$$

$$\dot{W} = -\frac{1}{c}\left[V + a - bW\right]$$

$$\dot{U} - \frac{1}{c}\left[V + d - eV\right] \tag{41}$$

with U much slower than W: e<<b. More complicated models, such as in [27] model a switch from silent to bursting activity, as in Fig.14. The range and possible uses of such variety of cell responses is analysed in [28].

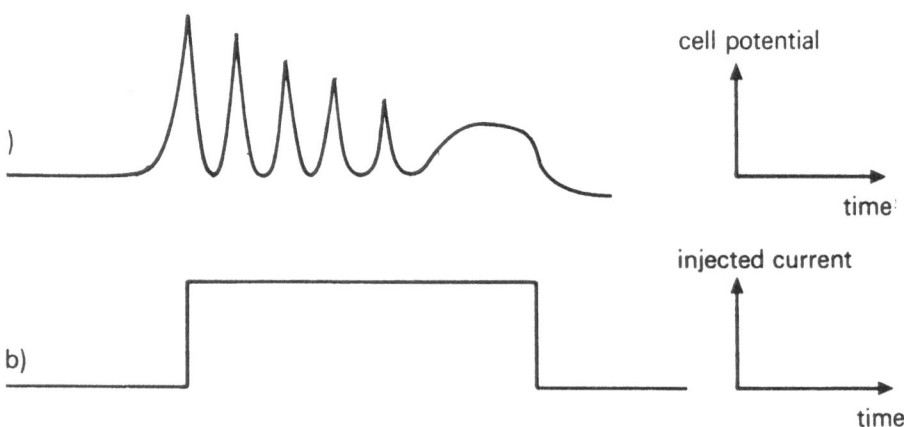

Figure 14: Bursting activity of a hippocampal cell.

3.3 Convergent Dynamics of Nets

For given inputs I and initial states $\underline{x}$(o) the final states $\underline{x}$(∞) will be functionals of these two sets of variables.

$$\underline{x}(\infty) = \underline{x}_\infty(\underline{x}(o), I) \qquad (42)$$

The dependence on one or other of these two types of variables may be emphasized, when initial state dependence is to be singled out leading to auto-associative nets [29], [30], and for inputs being singled out giving the 'continuous mapper' nets of feedforward character. One of the immediate questions of interest for the first class of nets is as to the construction of a given set of basins of attraction. But more generally it is of value to know if the dynamics is asymptotically convergent.   That can be answered by the construction of Liapunov functions, as considered in the previous section.

Convergence theorems for the shunting-inhibition equations (7) of Cohen-Grossberg [4], of form

$$\dot{x}_i = F_i(\underline{x}) = a_i(x)[b_i(x_i) - \sum_k c_{ik} d_k(x_k)]$$

$$= -c_i x_i + \Sigma T_{ij} g(x_j) \qquad (43)$$

can be proven by use of the Liapunov function

$$V(x) = -\frac{1}{2} \sum_i c_i x_i^2 + \frac{1}{2} \sum_{j,k} T_{jk}\, g(x_k)\, g(x_j) \qquad (44)$$

In fact, this energy function was already used by Hopfield in his well-known paper [29].

Convergence theorems can also be proven when there is no obvious Liapunov function, as in the case [32].

$$\dot{\underline{x}} = \underline{F}(\underline{x}, I)$$

$$\underline{D}\,\underline{F} = \underline{A} : \quad \underline{A} < -\mu, \text{ in } L_2 \qquad (44)$$

63

In fact this system can be proven to have globally asymptotic convergence and a strict Liapunov function obtained for it. The particular 'additive' model

$$x_i = -c_i x_i + W_{ij} \ \sigma_j(x_j - s_j) + I_i \qquad (45)$$

which is a leaky integration model with mean firing rate approximation is globally asymptotically stable if

$$0 \leq \sigma_j' \leq \gamma$$

$$\gamma\left[W_{ii} + \frac{1}{2} \sum_{j \neq i} \left\{ |W_{ij}| + |W_{ji}| \right\}\right] < c_i$$

where these conditions correspond to the need for sufficiently small gains relative to the self-inhibition term.

Cascades of convergent nets can also be proven convergent [31]. For example global asymptotic convergence is preserved under cascading. This is an important property if modellers wish to use a modular approach to net design.

3.4 Time Delayed Neural Nets (TDNNs)

Typically a time-delayed equation has the form

$$\dot{x} = F(\dot{x}_t, t) \qquad (46)$$

where X_t is a functional of x on the interval (-r+t,t).

Then boundary values involve the set of values of the state variable $x(\sigma)$, for σ belonging to the whole of (-r,o) [20]. As an example, consider

$$\underline{x}(t) = A\underline{x}(t-r)+B\underline{x}(t-s) \qquad (47)$$

$$r/s \text{ irrational, } s > r > 0$$

Then this requires the boundary values of x(t) for t in the interval (-s,o). Time averaged neural net equations, with time delay, are of form [32]

$$\dot{u}_i(t) = -u_i(t)+\Sigma w_{ij}f(u_j(t-\tau)) \qquad (48)$$

If one considers the linearised solution near $\underline{u}=\underline{o}$, one obtains, in a basis of u_i's in which the connection matrix is diagonal,

$$\dot{x}_i(t) = -x_i(t)+\beta \lambda_i x_i(t-T) \qquad (49)$$

where the gain is f'(o) equal to β, and λ_i are the eigenvalues of the connection matrix W_{ij}. Then if one tries the solution, for complex s_i,

$$x_i(t) = x_i(o)e^{s_it} \qquad (50)$$

in (49), one obtains the conditions

$$(s_i+1)e^{s_it} = \beta\lambda_i \qquad (51)$$

For stability of (50) one needs $Res_i<0$, for any i.

For zero time delay the stability region is shown in Figure 15(a); the loss of stability when W is symmetric corresponds to a pitchfork bifurcation as λ increases through its critical value $1/\beta$. For $\tau\neq0$ the corresponding situation is depicted in Figure 15(b) for different values of τ. It can be seen that the stability decreases as τ increases, and one way of generating oscillations is to

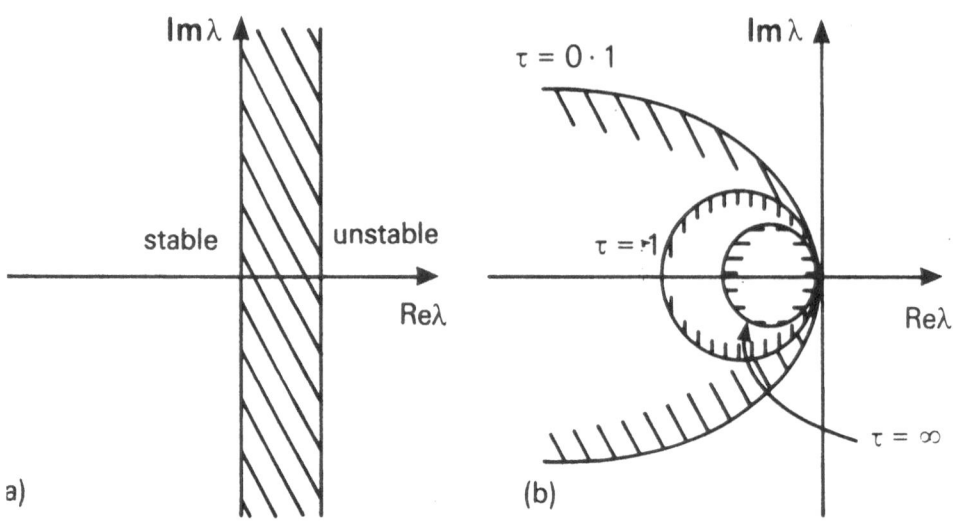

Figure 15: (a) Regions of (un)stability in the λ-plane for
the equations (49), for τ=0,
(b) Decreasing regions of stability for
increasing values of τ.

increase τ sufficiently.

It is possible to develop dynamics and bifurcation theory for TDDNs, but one has to work with states of the net given by activities over an interval of time (in other words, with function spaces), as was indicated earlier. Since the state space is infinite dimensional there is expected to be a much wider variety of dynamics of such systems. But there is only a fragmentary theory yet.

3.5 Cortical Oscillations

There is now well-known data on the existence of stimulus-evoked (but not stimulus-linked) oscillations of feature-detector cells in the cat visual cortex, in particular in areas 17 and 19 [33], [34]. Various interesting attempts have been made made to model these oscillations, both using phase variables θ belonging to an S^1 [35], incorporating coupled inhibitory-excitatory pairs of mean-firing rate neurons [36] and most recently utilising the non-linear properties of active membrane [37]. The inhibitory-excitatory system has also been used in modelling observed [38] cortical oscillations associated with olfaction in the olfactory bulb and cortex [39].

The olfactory data is clear as to the presence of both excitatory (mitral) and inhibitory (granule) cells, there being a 90° phase difference between the oscillations of a pair of such cells, which are coupled by known reciprocal dendro-dendrite synapses. However the nature of the coding of information in that system is not resolved, especially in learning, since the hippocampus is known to be necessary in olfactory learning.

In visual cortex the cross-correlation data [33] indicates the possibility of cortical assemblies being set up which comprise cells with the sensitivity to the same features, such as orientation of an illuminated edge. These assemblies may therefore produce binding or fusion of responses to different parts of an object, so as to give recognition of the total object. It is not clear yet exactly how this binding may be achieved, since, as noted above, there are various levels at which modelling is being pursued. A very simple version of binding would be by means of later neurons which respond to a set of precursor neurons acting in phase but not active if the precursor activity is out of phase. In this sub-section we well briefly consider the olfactory cortical oscillations, describe a system, the accessory olfactory bulb (AOB), where there is no hippocampal involvement, and conclude with comments on the visual oscillations.

The basic form of coupled feedback inhibition has dynamical equations for the mean firing rate vectors X and Y of the excitatory and inhibiting neurons which are of form (see equations ())

$$\dot{X} = -\alpha X - HF(Y) + I \qquad (52a)$$

$$\dot{Y} = -\alpha Y + WG(X) \qquad (52b)$$

In (52), I is the input vector (assumed only to input on the excitatory neurons), α^{-1} are the common time constants of all neurons, F and G are the non-linear response functions of the Y and X neurons respectively, and H and W are their connection matrices, assumed positive (so with only non-negative eigenvalues.

For reasonably steady inputs, (52) may be linearised about the steady values X_o, Y_o, to give the linear equations

$$\dot{x} = -hy - \alpha x \qquad (53a)$$

$$\dot{y} = wx - \alpha y \qquad (53b)$$

where h and w are matrices derived from H and W with the non-linear matrix functions $F'(Y_o)$, $G^1(X_o)$ being absorbed into their definition:

$$h = HF'(Y_o), \quad w = WG'(X_o)$$

The system (53) has oscillatory solutions, especially as it can be put into the obviously oscillatory form

$$\ddot{x} + 2\alpha\dot{x} + (hw + \alpha^2)x = 0 \qquad (54)$$

We refer the reader to [39] where the spatial dependence of the oscillations is analysed by simulation, and also to [40] for a valuable discussion of the manner in which oscillations bifurcate on odour stimulation.

In the AOB it appears possible to consider a learning paradigm in which a change of the AOB transfer function can be studied. This may be seen directly from (53), for which the transfer function is

$$T = [(i\nu + \alpha) + hw/(i\nu + \alpha) \qquad (55)$$

where ν is the Fourier frequency. If learning is assumed to proceed by increasing w, the form of T shifts from one which is a low pass filter to one which is peaked at higher frequency, as shown in Figure 16. The response of the AOB

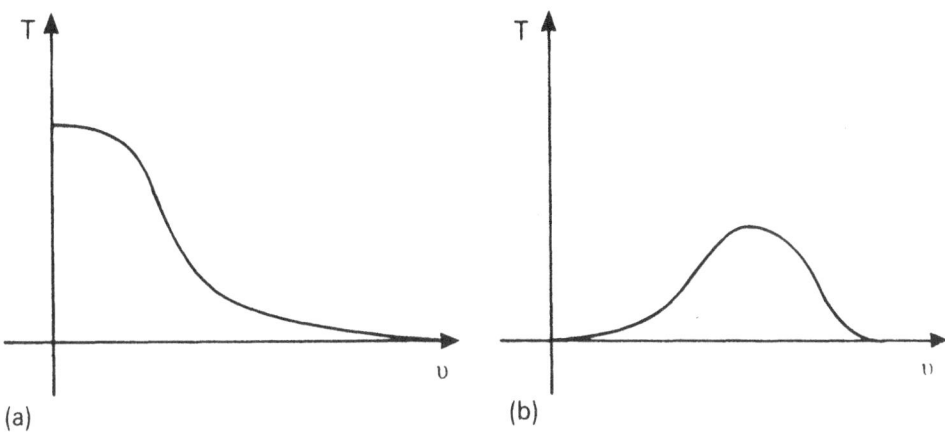

Figure 16: (a) Transfer function of AOB for small
excitatory synaptic weights w
(b) The same but when w has increased by
learning.

has therefore been shifted to a higher frequency. This can be tested
directly in the case of pregnancy block in pregnant mice [41], and the
experiments are presently being considered to see if T does change, for
certain parts of the AOB, in the manner of Figure 16.

Finally we turn to visual cortical oscillations. We do not
discuss the S^1-type of models since there is no good evidence for the
existence of bursters (central pattern generators) especially in layers
2/3. In addition it seems necessary to allow for bifurcations, and in
general greater temporal accuracy in neuronal models, in order to
understand the more detailed results reported in [42]. The same comment
applies to the mean firing models of [36], and that is one of the main
reasons we turned to the use of the Fitz-Hugh-Nagumo model [37]. This
model can also include feedback-inhibition oscillators, in particular to
determine how crucial the presence of inhibitory interneurons are in
explaining the data of [42].

The basic model is a set of time-delayed coupled van der Pol
oscillators, in which there is both external input and that from other
oscillators. The set of equations describing the system is therefore

$$x_i = c[y_i + x_i - \frac{1}{3} x_i{}^3 + \Sigma a_{ij} x_j (t-t_j) + I_i(t)] \tag{56a}$$

$$\dot{y}_i = - \frac{1}{c} [x_i - a + by_i] \tag{56b}$$

The constants a, b, c are so chosen that when the y_i null-clines cross the x_i null-clines between the humps of the cubic-curves of the latter, with non-zero external input, the equilibrium point is unstable and a limit cycle oscillation results. In particular when the time delays are zero and the a_{ij}'s are small, first order perturbation in them leads to the possibility of doing a careful analytic determination of parameter ranges leading to synchronised oscillations.
This can be seen most simply in the case N=2.
For $a_{11}=a_{22}=0$, $a_{12}=a_{21}=d$ the equilibrium points satisfy the equations

$$^1/_3 \bar{x}_1 3 + \bar{x}_1 ((1/b)-1) - d\bar{x}_2 = (a/b) \tag{57a}$$
$$^1/_3 \bar{x}_2 3 + \bar{x}_2 ((1/b)-1) - d\bar{x}_1 = (a/b) \tag{57b}$$

The equations (57) may be shown to have only one solution if

$$1/b > 1+d \tag{58}$$

The stability of this solution is determined by the Jacobian matrix (30c), following the discussion in subsection 2.2, part (iii). The eigenvalues λ can be shown to arise from the equations

$$(\lambda - \lambda_1)^2 (\lambda - \lambda_2)^2 = (\lambda + (b/c)^2) c^2 d^2 \tag{59}$$

where λ_1, λ_2 are the eigenvalues of the N=1 problem, so satisfy the conditions, for i=1,2,

$$\lambda^2_i + [b/c - (1-\bar{x})c]\lambda_i + [1 - (1-\bar{x}^2)b] = 0 \qquad (60)$$

with $\bar{x}$ the x_1 co-ordinate of the point of intersection of either of the x-null-clines (56a) in the absence of external current or input from the other cell. As in the case of the non-interacting neurons, the single fixed point will be unstable if

$$\bar{x}_2 < (1 - b/c^2 - d) \qquad (61)$$

This extends the condition of instability of p450 of [12]; for the condition (61) to be effective requires

$$d < 1 - (b/c^2) \qquad (62)$$

Thus the conditions enlarging those of (3) of (12) are

$$\sqrt{1+d} \; [1 - (2b/3) - (d/3) + d^2/3] < a < \sqrt{1+d}$$
$$\qquad (6.3)$$
$$0 < b < 1, \quad b < c^2$$

and (58), (61). A choice of values are, for example, a=0.7, b=0.8, d=0.05, c=3.

With these values a suitable level of external input will perturb the cells into a stable limit cycle, since the corresponding x value will satisfy (61). Simulation of the coupled system was performed using a Runge-Kutta variable step programme. The result for a fourth-order run with external currents in (56a) of values

$$-\exp[-(t-100)^2/90] \; -\exp[-(t-50)^2/900] \qquad (65)$$

lead to the results of Fig.18 where the coupling is shown in Figure 17. It is clear that synchronisation of the nerve impulses has occurred due

71

to the below-threshold inputs from the other active cells. Such a feature, together with various other properties of this system, are considered in the adjoining paper with CLT Mannion in this volume and in [37].

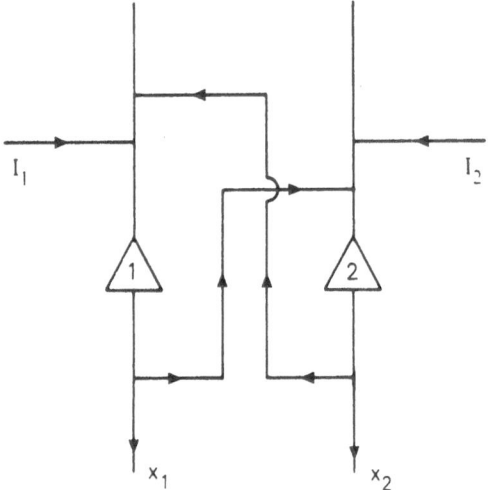

Figure 17: Two interacting vander Pol oscillators (56) with parameter values (64) and external currents (65).

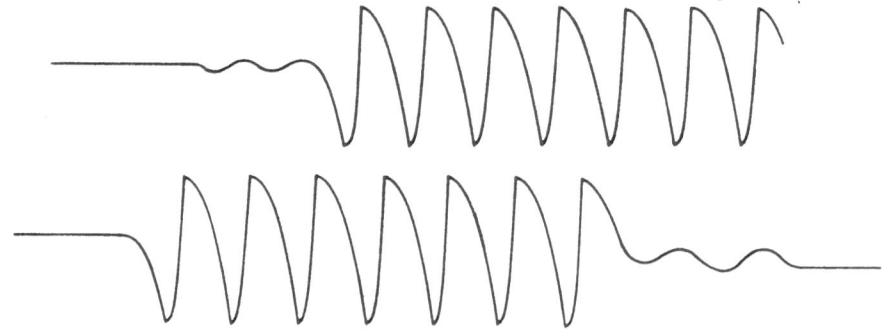

Figure 18: The time-development of the activities x_1 (top curve) and x_2 (bottom curve) for a pair of neurons coupled according to Figure 17 with parameters and currents as in (64), (65).

4. CONCLUSIONS

Some of the paradigms possible for neural networks have been briefly investigated in the previous section, aided by the dynamical systems approach presented in survey form in the previous section. New paradigms have also been shortly considered, based on some of the further properties of living neurons beyond those normally used in artificial neural net modelling. In particular coupled oscillator models were discussed briefly, although the major part of the discussion is given in the adjoining paper. Various further paradigms, in particular that using leaky integrator neurons for storing temporal sequences, was not discussed here, but is being studied elsewhere [43]. Since cortical pyramidal cells may have time constants of the order of 50msec or more [44] it is clearly necessary to take account of membrane time constants with similar care to synaptic, compartmental and active membrane effects.

What can we conclude about the value of the new paradigms mentioned above for artificial neural networks, as compared to the simpler ones of mean firing rate or binary decision neurons mentioned at the very beginning? I think the best answer I can give at this stage is that it is too early to say how to achieve real progress in reverse engineering. Perhaps there are already available, in the standard algorithms, system which will be powerful enough for a range of task domains once good hardware implementations become available. That is a view that is gaining strong support in the neural net community. On the other hand such artificial net algorithms as are presently available are clearly not going to produce intelligent robots. To have a robot with planning and problem-solving capabilities seems in principle to be beyond present nets. Since there is an existing model inside our own heads worth understanding it would seem necessary to continue modelling subtleties of neurons, and their circuits, till the main principles used by the brain are understood. Not till then will we be able to dispense with this or that subtlety.

REFERENCES

[1] W. S. McCulloch and W. Pitts, "A logical calculus of ideas immanent in nervous activity", Bull Math.Biophys. 5, 1943.

[2] E. Caianiello, "Outline of a theory of thought processes and thinking machines", J.Theor.Biol. 1, 209-235, 1961.

[3] R. D. Traub, R. Miles and R. K. Wong, "Models of Synchronised Hippocampal Bursts in the Presence of Inhibition", J.Neurophysiol., 58, 739-764, 1987.

[4] M. Cohen and S. Grossberg, "Absolute stability of global pattern formation and parallel memory storage by competitive neural networks", IEEE Trans SMC, 13, 815-826, 1983.

[5] W. Rall, "Theoretical significance of dendritic trees for neuronal input-output relations", in Neural Theory and Modelling, (ed. R. Reiss), Stanford Univ.Press, 1964.

[6] D. H. Perkel, B. Mulloney and R. Budelli, "Quantitative Methods for Predicting Neuronal Behaviour", Neuroscience, 6, 823-937, 1981.

[7] B. Katz, The Release of Neural Transmitter Substances, Thomas, Springfield,

[8] J. G. Taylor, "Spontaneous Behaviour in Neural Networks", J.Theor.Biol., 36, 513-528, 1972.

[9] P. C. Bressloff and J. G. Taylor, "Random Iterative Networks", Phys.Rev., A41, 1126-1137, 1990.

[10] D. Gorse and J. G. Taylor, "On the Equivalence and Properties of Noisy Neural and Probability RAMNets", Phys.lett. A131, 326-332, 1988; ibid, "An analysis of noisy RAM and neural nets", Physica, D34, 90-114, 1989.

[11] A. L. Hodgkin and A. F. Huxley, "A quantitative description of membrane current and its applications to conductors and encitation in nerve", J.Physiol., 117, 500-44, 1952.

[12] R. FitzHugh, "Impulses and Physiological States in Theoretical Models of Nerve Membrane", Biophys.J., 1, 445-466, 1961.

[13] J. S. Nagumo, S. Arimoto and S. Yoshizawa, "An active pulse transmission line simulating nerve anon", Proc.IRE, 50, 2061-2070, 1962.

[14] J. Jack, D. Noble and R. Tsien, Electric Current Flow in Excitable Cells, Clarendon Press, Oxford, 1975.

[15] D. Gorse and J. G. Taylor, "A General Model of Stochastic Neural Processing", Biol. Cybern. (to appear).

[16] G. M. Edelman, "Population Rules for Synapses in Networks", pp.711-758 in Synaptic Function, ed. Edelman, Gall and Cowan, Wiley, 1987.

[17] W. Penfold and Perot, Brain, 86, 595-696, 1963.

[18] L. R. Squire, <u>Memory and Brain</u>, Oxford Univ.Press, 1987.

[19] M. Tabor, <u>Chaos and Integrability in Non-Linear Dynamics</u>, Wiley, 1989.

[20] J. Hale, <u>Theory of Functional Differential Equations</u>, Springer, 1977.

[21] J. Guckenheimer and P. Holmes, <u>Non-Linear Oscillations, Dynamical Systems and Bifurcation of Vector Fields</u>, Springer, 1983.

[22] L. Glass and M. C. Mackay, <u>The Rythms of Life</u>, Princeton Univ.Press, 1988.

[23] S. N. Rasban, <u>The Chaotic Dynamics of Non-Linear Systems</u>, Wiley, 1990.

[24] K. Aihara, T. Takabe and M. Toyoda, "Chaotic Neural Networks", Phys.Lett., A<u>144</u>, 333-340, 1990.

[25] A. Babloyantz and A. Destenke, "Low-Dimensional chaos in an instance of epilepsy", Proc.Nat.Acad.Sci., <u>83</u>, 3513-17, 1986.

[26] Y. Yao and W. Freeman, Model of Biological Pattern Recognition with Spatially Chaotic Dynamics, Neural Networks, <u>3</u>, 153-170, 1990.

[27] R. Rose and J. Hindmarsh, "A model of a thalamic neuron", Proc.Roy.Soc., B<u>225</u>, 161-193, 1985.

[28] R. R. Llinas, "The Intrinsic Electrophysiological Properties of Mammalian Neurons", Science, <u>242</u>, 1654-1664, 1988.

[29] J. J. Hopfield, "Neural networks and physical systems with emergent collective computational abilities", Proc.Nat.Acad.Sci.USA., <u>79</u>, 2554-2558, 1982.

[30] T. Kohonen, <u>Self-Organisation and Associative Memories</u>, Springer, 1984.

[31] M. Hirsch, "Convergent Activation Dynamics in Continuous Time Networks", Neural Networks, <u>2</u>, 331-350, 1989.

[32] C. M. Marcus and R. Westervelt, Phys.Rev., A<u>39</u>, 347-359, 1989.

[33] C. M. Gray and W. Singer, "Stimulus-specific neuronal oscillations in the cat visual cortex: a cortical functional unit", Soc.Neurosci.Abstr. 404.3, 1987; ibid, "Stimulus-dependent neuronal oscillations in the cat visual cortex area 17", Neuroscience Suppl., <u>22</u>, 1301, 1987; C. M. Gray, P. Konig, A. K. Engel and W. Singer, "Oscillatory responses in cat visual cortex exhibit inter-columnar synchronization which reflects global stimulus properties", Nature, <u>338</u>, 334-7, 1989.

[34] R. Eckhorn, R. Bauer, W. Jordan, M. Brosch, W. Kruse, M. Munk and H. J. Roitboeck, "Coherent Oscillations: A Mechanism of Feature Linking in the Visual Cortex?", Biol. Cybern., <u>60</u>, 121-130, 1988.

[35] D. M. Kammen, P. J. Holmes and C. Koch, "Cortical architecture and oscillation in neuronal networks", pp.273-284 in Models of Brain Function, ed. R. J. M. Cotterill, Camb.Univ.Press, 1989; P. Baldi, J. Buchmann and J. Meir, "Computing with Arrays of Coupled Oscillators", 908-911, Proc.INNC '90, publ. Kluwer Academic, London, 1990.

[36] P. Konig and T. B. Schillen, "Simulation of Delayed Oscillations with the MENS General Purpose Modelling Environment for Network Systems", in Parallel Processing in Neural Systems and Computers, ed. R. Echmiller, N. Holland, 1990.

[37] C. L. T. Mannion and J. G. Taylor, "Coupled Excitable Cells", Kings College pre-print, Aug 1990.

[38] W. Freeman, Mass Action in the Nervous System, Academic Press, 1975.

[39] Z. Li and J. J. Hopfield, "Modelling the Olfactory Bulb and its Neural Oscillatory Processings", Biol.Cybernet., 61, 379-392, 1989.

[40] B. Baird, "Non-Linear Dynamics of Pattern Formation and Pattern Recognition in the Rabbit Olfactory Bulb", Physica, 22, 150-175, 1986.

[41] E. B. Keverne and J. G. Taylor, "Accessory Olfactory Learning", Biol.Cybernet. (to appear).

[42] A. K. Engel, P. Konig, C. M. Grey and W. Singer, "Stimulus-Dependent Neuronal Oscillation in Cat Visual Cortex 1", Eur.J.Neurosci 2 588-606, (1990); ibid, 2, Eur.J. Neurosci 2, 607-619. Neurosci (to appear).

[43] M. Reiss and J. G. Taylor, "Storing Temporal Sequences", Kings College pre-print, Aug 1990.

[44] G. Major, A. Larkman and J. Jack, "Constraining non-uniqueness in passive electrical models of cortical pyramidal neurones", Proc.Physiol.Soc., Oxford Meeting 27-28 July 1990, p.23P, (1990).

Neural Modelling

Abstract. *Most current work in neural network modelling is concerned with simple binary units. The deficiencies of these units are widely recognised. This tutorial reviews some of the models that have been used to include more biological detail.*

C.L.T. Mannion
Electronic and Electrical Engineering,University of Surrey,
Guildford, Surrey GU2 5XH.

1.Introduction.

Recent progress in neural computing has largely been concerned with models using highly simplified units as representations of real neurons.The purpose of this review is to examine models that have been developed that go beyond these initial approximations. There are a number of motivations for this step. It may be desired to demonstrate that real understanding of the function of a particular region of the brain has been obtained, to investigate the extent to which biophysical detail is important for information processing or to provide a benchmark for testing standard connectionist models.

The realistic description of networks of neurons has many aspects. Factors that might be of interest include

a.detailed circuitry and the spatial distribution of morphologically distinct kinds of neurons.

b.the various ionic channels, their spatial distribution and the time history of the currents they allow

c.The connectivity and spatial extent of dendritic trees,the effects of propagation delay, active membrane, spines etc.

d.The detailed shape, firing frequency and adaptation of action potentials

e.Synaptic noise

For neural computing what is of interest is the effect (if any) of these details on the information processing capabilities of assemblies of neurons.

An immediate problem is that a lot of the precise anatomical and biophysical information required to build realistic models is not available. It is quite clear that a multidisciplinary effort involving physiologists, computer scientists and modellers is required to develop interesting and useful biologically detailed approximations.

Also it is necessary to consider what to do with the mass of output data that can be produced by such models(potentially information on all of a. to e. above). How can these results be used to understand the information processing capabilities of real neural networks?

In this tutorial it is intended to introduce some of the ways in which greater realism has been included in neural network models. In the next section some of the biophysical details that might be relevant for information processing are briefly mentioned. This is followed by an outline of a mean firing rate model. Subsequent sections contain an introduction to the modelling of neurons as electrical cables, compartmental models and their applications.

2. What to model

A variety of mechanisms for information processing based on loose analogies with networks of real neurons have been suggested.[1] Some of the most popular are

       a. Multi-layer perceptrons
       b. Spin glass models
       c. Self organising maps

In all of these an interconnected network of simple units is used, individual nodes sum their inputs and output a signal if a threshold is exceeded. These models have various learning rules and in general are expected to demonstrate those properties that are considered to distinguish biological systems from standard computers such as graceful degradation, generalisation etc.

These models have been criticised for a variety of reasons[2]. Some of the most common observations are
a. Real neurons are extremely complex. They have time and voltage dependent conductances spatially distributed over their surfaces, they exhibit complicated temporal behaviour. They come in many morphologically distinct types.

b. The patterns of connectivity are complicated including recurrent paths and can be modulated in time.

c. Real neural networks are not homogeneous.

d. The learning rules, often based on some variant of the Hebb rule, are unrealistic.

Detailed modelling is required to assess the importance of the above remarks with regard to the information processing capabilities of current connectionist architectures.

Reported results on stimulus induced oscillations and phase locking[3] in spatially separated regions of the visual cortex of the cat and the monkey have been interpreted as evidence for the use of correlated activity of assemblies of neurons for feature linking in visual scenes. It has been conjectured that the basic neural oscillators are coupled by modulation of postsynaptic activities.

Koch and Poggio[4] give an extensive discussion of the possible information processing function of detailed biophysical mechanisms. For instance they discuss the possibility that active membrane can function as a resonant filter the frequency response of which can be modulated by cellular calcium or active channel density. Bearing in mind the spatially extended nature of the dendritic tree this suggests that individual neurons might be powerful computational devices.

Llinas[5] reviews the electrical properties of neurons again emphasising the complexity of single neurons.He lists approximately sixty different voltage dependent ionic conductances for various neurons, in different locations, in the mammalian central nervous system. Ionic conductances are distributed non uniformly over the cell surface. The arrangement of some of these is such that individual neurons can exhibit oscillation and resonance. There is evidence that individual neurons can cause a cascade through various circuits so as to cause network oscillations that are used for motor control. Neuronal oscillations and bursting in the thalamus can gate the sleep wakefulness cycle and may be important for attentional mechanisms.

The above references discuss other examples where biophysical phenomena might be relevant to the understanding of the computational properties of a network and provide additional motivation for the development of detailed models.

3.Mean firing rate models.

Possibly the simplest elaboration beyond binary units is to consider nodes described by a continuous variable giving the frequency of firing of the action potential. Chen, Clark and Kurten[6,7] have discussed a mean firing rate model that addresses some of the criticisms levelled against the more common connectionist models. In addition to considering the neuron as a threshold unit that sums its inputs the existence of a refractory period(during which the node will not respond) , propagation delay on the dendritic tree, adaptation of a neuron to continued input,spontaneous activity and warm up at the axon hillock are all considered.

This leads to the following set of coupled first order ordinary differential equations for each node of a model network

$$a_{i1}^{-1}(dx_{i1}/dt) = -x_{i1}+r_i^{-1}(1/(1+exp[-(u_i-f_{i0})])) \qquad 3.1$$

$$a_{i2}^{-1}\ (du_i/dt) = -u_i+f_i+\Sigma_j c_{ij}x_{j1}+b_i x_{i2} \qquad 3.2$$

$$dx_{i2}/dt = x_{i1}-p_i x_{i2} \qquad 3.3$$

in the simplest case where response is immediate. Adding extra equations of the form 3.3 allows adaptation with a gradual response.

The details of the derivation of these equations can be found in Chen's thesis.The parameters in the above can be interpreted as follows

x_{i1} the firing rate

u_i the membrane potential

x_{i2} adaptation variable

r_i absolute refractory period

a_{i1} rise time at axon hillock where the action potential is generated

a_{i2} warmup time on the input tree associated with time course of potential

f_{i0} spontaneous firing in the absence of any input

b_i,p_i accomadation of neural firing rate to sustained input

f_i represents the input. Large excitatory and inhibitory inputs are controlled by the sigmoid function in 3.1. Chen's thesis gives an extensive analysis of the behaviour of single neurons of this type.

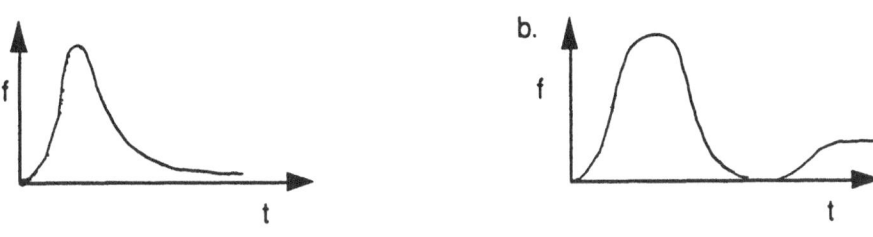

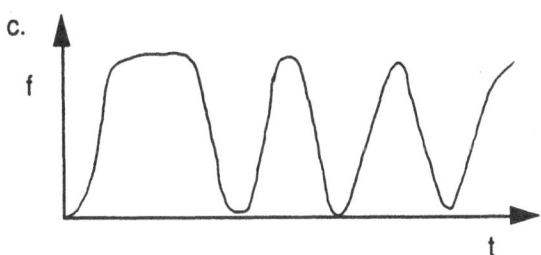

Fig.1 Results for a single neuron.
a.Response with immediate adaptation; b.Response with gradual adaptation
c.Oscillations for sufficently strong input.

Linear analysis about the equilibrium points determines conditions on the parameters for stable solutions.

Chen[6] determines analytically the conditions necessary for stable oscillations in a two neuron network. His results suggest that without adaptation it is difficult to observe oscillations even with strong interneuronal coupling.It is straightforward to connect a pair of these neurons together and exhibit antiphase oscillations in the firing rate. A fourth order Runge-Kutta algorithm with adaptive step size for the solution of coupled ordinary differential equations appears to give good results.

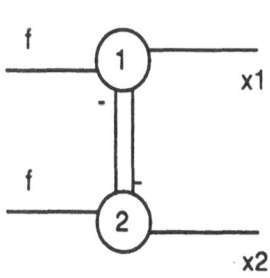

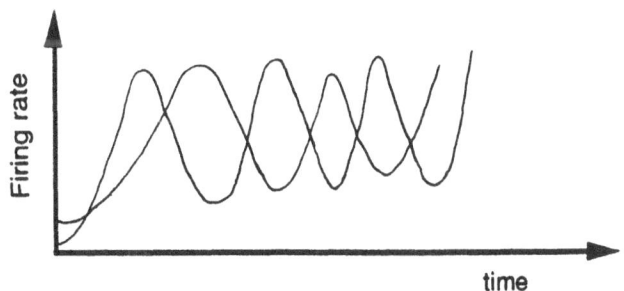

Fig.2. Two Neuron Circuit

3.1 Olfactory Bulb Model

Chen applies the above model to the olfactory bulb. In the basic circuit three kinds of cells are considered, mitral cells and two types of interneurons. The olfactory bulb is considered to be a three layered structure. Axons from receptor cells(R) in the olfactory mucosa ramify in spherical structures called glomeruli in the first layer of the bulb. Each mitral cell,with the cell body in the middle layer, has an unbranched dendrite which terminates in a glomerulus. Further connections, in the input layer, between mitral cells are mediated by one of the types of interneurons(Periglomular cells).

Each mitral cell also has dendritic branches in the middle layer and communication between these cells is mediated by the other type of interneurons(Granule Cells). A natural interpretation is that the PG cells are used for input processing and the granule cells for output control.

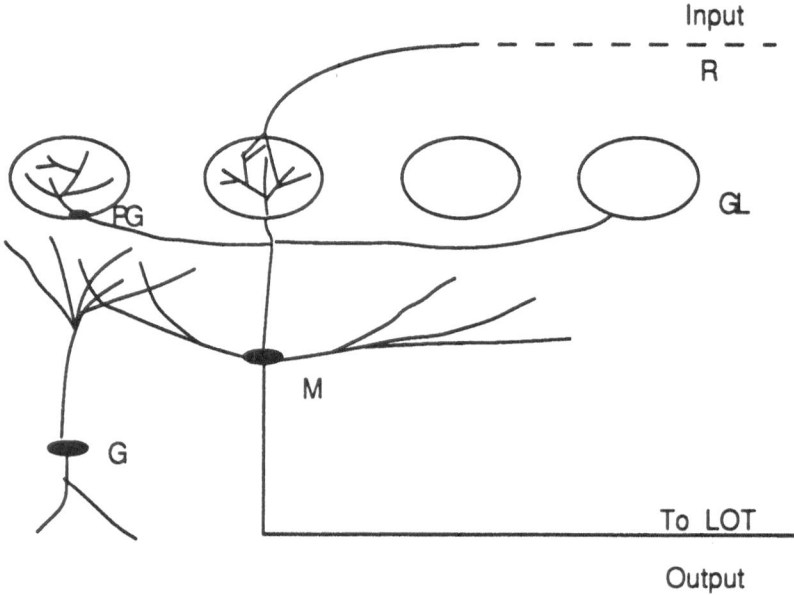

Fig. 3. Olfactory Bulb details; R: Receptor Cells, Gl:Glomeruli, M:Mitral Cells, PG:PeriGlomular Cells, G:Granule Cells

Cell Population Data

$R \approx 5 \times 10^7$
$R:M \approx 1000:1$
#olfactory axons:M:GL $\approx 2.5 \times 10^4:25:1$
$G:PG:M \approx 200:20:1$

The above tends to support the view that a considerable amount of processing is occurring within the olfactory bulb. Following the basic

82

circuit due to Shepherd[8] Chen suggests the following six neuron basic model circuit in the olfactory bulb.

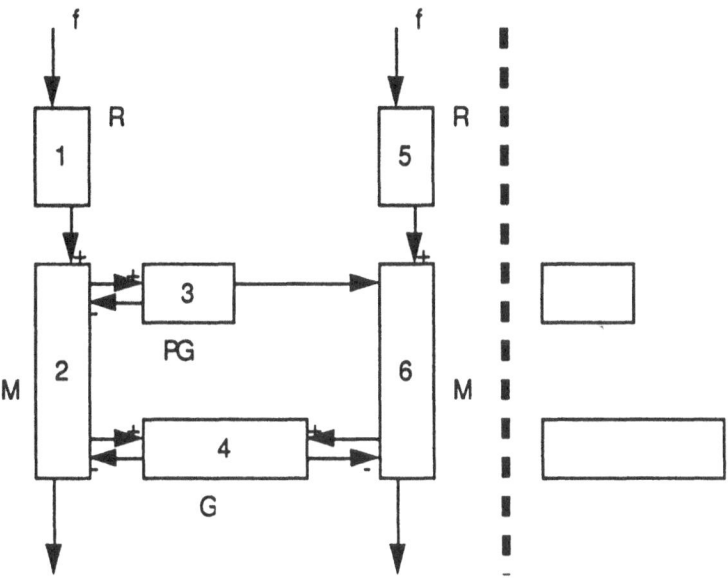

Fig.4. Olfactory bulb simulation circuit

It should be noted that the above circuit is not consistent with the population data given above.
The equations 3.1-3.3 can be applied and the result is eighteen coupled differential equations. For example the equation for the membrane potential for neuron 4 is given by

$$du_4/dt = a_2[-u_4+bx_{42}+c_{42}x_{21}+c_{46}x_{61}]$$

where c_{42},c_{46} are positive.

An extensive discussion of the results can be found in Chen's thesis and reference 7. The main results are
a.For a certain parameter range firing rates of mitral cells display sustained oscillations.
b.The period of these oscillations is strongly dependent on the adaptivity parameters(b,p).
c.Sustained oscillations can be seen in the subsystems of the basic circuit.
d.When oscillations do occur they occur at the same frequency.
e.Without adaptation it is not possible to produce oscillations in a small network.
f.The membrane potential term oscillates at the same frequency as the firing rate of the neuron.

Extending the basic circuit as indicated in Fig 4. Chen presents results for rings and chains of the basic circuit. A full description of the results can be found in the references. For rings of the basic circuit it is easy to find oscillations. For chains of the same circuit oscillations tend to interfere destructively. When oscillations do occur there are strong open boundary effects for chains of neurons.

It should be noted that even within the mean firing rate approximation a fairly complicated system of equations resulted from the inclusion of more realism at the level of individual nodes and this detail strongly influenced the development of oscillations in the network.

4. Cable Theory

In the next two sections models that include more detail, are based on simple mathematics, and have been used to give results in good agreement with experiment, are introduced.

A considerable body of theory has been developed for the interpretation of experimental results on cellular recordings on current conduction in nerve cells. The dendrites and axons of nerve cells can be idealised as cylindrical tubes of cell membrane. The membrane resistance is much higher than that of the core of the tube.Hence for short distances current can be imagined as tending to flow along the axis of the tube rather than through the cell membrane. This picture leads to the development of a one dimensional partial differential equation for current flow in parts of a neuron.

In order to derive the cable equation[9,10] uniform electrical and geometrical properties are assumed. In particular it is assumed that the internal potential in the section of cell being modelled is a function of distance along the section and time only giving

$$V_i = V_i(x,t) \qquad\qquad 4.1$$

and that

$$(\partial V / \partial x)_x = r_i(-i_a)_x . \qquad\qquad 4.2$$

The membrane current is obtained from the equation of continuity

$$\partial i_a / \partial x = -i_m \qquad\qquad 4.3$$

where i_a is the axial current along the tube.

Equations 4.1 and 4.2 can be combined to give

$$\partial^2 V/\partial x^2 = r_i i_m.$$
                                                        4.4

Assuming constant external extracellular potential, and that resting membrane battery is time and space independent and writing

$$V = V_i - V_e - E_r$$
                                                        4.5

gives

$$(r_m/r_i)(\partial^2 V/\partial x^2) = i_m r_m$$
                                                        4.6

The membrane current is due ionic channels in the cell membrane and a capacitative effect due to the polarisability of the molecules making up the membrane giving

$$i_m = c_m \partial V/\partial t + (V_i - V_m - E_r)/r_m .$$
                                                        4.7

So that

$$(r_m/r_i)(\partial^2 V/\partial t^2) = r_m c_m \partial V/\partial t + V$$
                                                        4.8

Puting $r_m c_m = \tau$ and $(r_i/r_m)^{1/2} = \lambda$ gives the telegraph equation

$$\lambda^2 \partial^2 V/\partial t^2 = \tau \partial V/\partial t + V$$
                                                        4.9

In order to solve this partial differential equation some initial conditions

$$V(x,0) = v_c(x)$$

and boundary conditions

a.Voltage clamp

$$V(0,t) = v \quad ; t>0$$

b.Sealed end

$$\partial V(0,t)/\partial x = 0 \quad ; t>0$$

c.Killed end
$$V(0,t) = 0 \quad ; t>0$$

will be required.

Typical solutions include

$$V(x,t) = \Sigma\ b_n Cos(\alpha_n x)exp-(1+\alpha_n^2)t \qquad\qquad 4.10$$

for a finite length cylinder with sealed end boundary conditions.$(\alpha_n = n\pi/L)$

The Greens function[11] solution giving the response at x=0 to an impulse given at time t = 0 at position y

$$G(0,y,t)\ =\ exp(-t)/(4\pi t)^{1/2}\Sigma\ [exp(-(2nL+y)^2/4t$$
$$+exp(-(2nL-y)^2/4t)] \qquad 4.11$$

gives some useful information about the effectiveness of synaptic input.

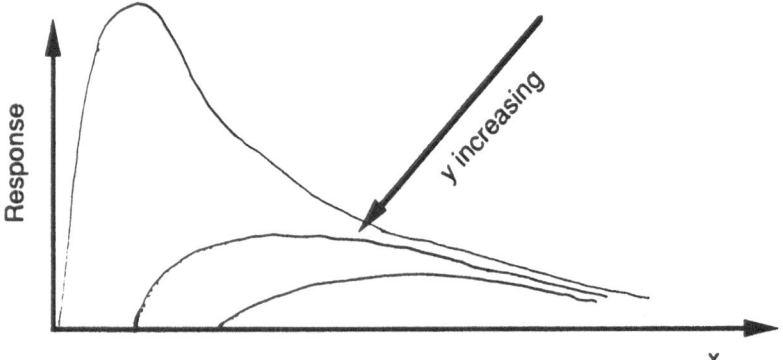

Fig.5. Plot of Greens function 4.11

Real neurons are not cylinders. Their dendritic trees have extensive structure. A dendritic tree can be represented as an equivalent cylinder provided some rather restrictive conditions concerning the geometry of the tree and in the transient case the distribution of inputs are satisfied. This allows the analysis of idealised model neurons with complicated geometry. Details can be found in references (10,11).

5. Compartmental Modelling

The assumptions in the derivation of the cable equation concerning spatial and electrical uniformity are fairly restrictive when one wishes to include more detail in neuron models. In order to get approximate solutions to more realistic models it is convenient to break neurons into compartments. The compartments are considered small enough to have uniform properties and inhomogeneities are concentrated between the cells. An individual compartment can represent a whole cell, a portion of a dendritic tree or axon or a cell body. In principle any geometry can be modelled, non-linearities can be dealt with and synaptic distribution taken into account. Essentially a lumped component model of the telegraph equation is being taken.

Consider the simplest case of three sections of a passive dendrite in series[10]. The membrane in each of these compartments can be modelled as an equivalent circuit consisting of a resistance and capacitance in parallel.

Applying the equation of continuity to compartment j gives

$$i_{mj} = i_{j-1,j} - i_{j,j+1} \qquad\qquad 5.1$$

where $i_{j-1,j}$ denotes the current between the j-1 and j compartments,etc. The membrane current for compartment j is the sum of the various ionic currents through the membrane and the capacitative current giving

$$i_{mj} = c_{mj} (dV_j/dt) + I \qquad\qquad 5.2$$

where I denotes the conductive membrane current.

The axial current in the jth compartment can be expressed in terms of the voltages between the compartments and the the lumped axial conductances to give

$$c_{mj}(dV_j/dt) + I + I_e = (V_{j-1} - V_j)g_{j-1,j} - (V_j - V_{j+1})g_{j,j+1} \qquad 5.3$$

where I_e denotes any external injected current.

The interesting term is the ionic current which can be considered to be the sum of three components in parallel corresponding to the leakage current, the synaptic channels and the active channels. Each of these currents can be modelled as a possibly time and voltage dependent conductance in series with a reversal potential.

The simplest of these, the leakage current, can be modelled as a constant conductance in series with a fixed voltage source.

The synaptic channels are thought to arise when neurotransmitters bind to receptors and open pores in the post synaptic membrane. These channels can be modelled as a time varying conductance in series with the appropriate reversal potential. The time varying conductance is usually taken to be given in the alpha function form due to Jack et al.

$$g_s(t) = \alpha^2 t e^{-\alpha t} \qquad\qquad 5.4$$

where $\alpha = 1/t_{peak}$, and t_{peak} is the time to peak.

Voltage and time dependent conductances may be included to model action potentials, rectification and shunting.

The final form of the compartmental equations can be written as

$$c_{mj} \; (dV_j/dt) \;\; = g_{j-1,j} V_j +$$

$$(g_{lj} + g_{sj} + g_{aj} + g_{j-1,j} + g_{j,j+1}) V_j +$$

$$g_{j,j+1} V_{j+1} +$$

$$g_{lj} E_{lj} + g_{sj} E_{sj} + g_{aj} E_{aj}. \qquad\qquad 5.5$$

Note that each of the separate membrane currents could have subcomponents with varying parameters.

Early results from compartmental models allowed the investigation of complicated branched model neurons. The effects of spatial and temporal distribution of inputs on the time course of the soma transient can be easily modelled using this approach.

A particular compartmental model consists of a set of coupled ordinary differential equations for the potential of a particular compartment. In the above only the simplest case has been considered. Similar arguments apply for branched structures but the calculation of the axial conductances at branches becomes slightly more complicated.

In matrix form the equations to be solved are

$$V = DV + b. \qquad\qquad 5.6$$

where the matrix D is, in general, sparse.

Perkel[12] discusses a number of approximate methods of solution for these equations. For instance the generation of an action potential and a refractory period can be approximated by regarding the neuron as a threshold unit and allowing the threshold θ to be governed by the following differential equation.

$$d\theta/dt = -(\theta-\theta_s)/\tau.$$

When physiological detail is the objective full numerical solution of the differential equations is required. Runge-Kutta adaptive step size methods can give good results but often quite different time scales for the various synaptic currents are involved in which case methods for stiff equations would be more appropriate.However the simple case shown below suggests another convenient method of solution .

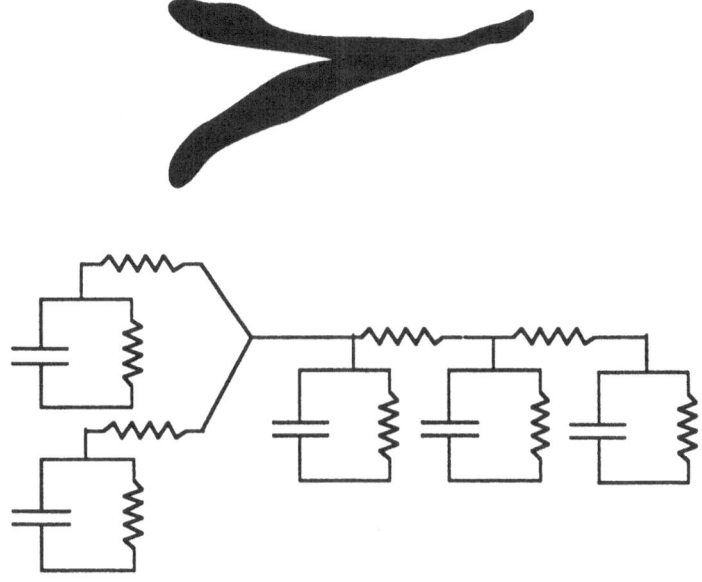

Fig.6. Section of neuron and equivalent circuit
(membrane potentials ommitted in this and subsequent diagrams)

It is clear that solving the above neuron for a given input is approximately equivalent to an electrical circuit problem. There are numerous packages available for solving such problems.One of the best known and most widely available is a batch mode fortran program known as SPICE[13].

SPICE takes as input a description of the circuit. Each circuit element is given a name(starting with R,C,L for resistors, capacitors and inductors respectively). A node is a point of connection between two circuit components. Each node must connect two circuit components. A number of voltage and current sources are provided with parametrised voltage and time dependencies. Nonlinear current and voltage controlled sources are also available. To use these it is necessary to supply the nodes between which the source is connected and current/voltage nodes that control the source.

Input consists of data lines and control lines. Data lines give the name of a component,the nodes it connects and the value of the component.Control lines give the type of analysis to be performed and the form of the output. Sources can be distributed around the circuit and output collected anywhere.

Applying SPICE to model a neuron involves constructing an appropriate compartmental representation (i.e dividing it into small enough regions for the assumption of isopotentiality to apply) and calculating appropriate axial resistance and membrane resistances and capacitances. A simple equivalent circuit for a section of neuron such as that shown below

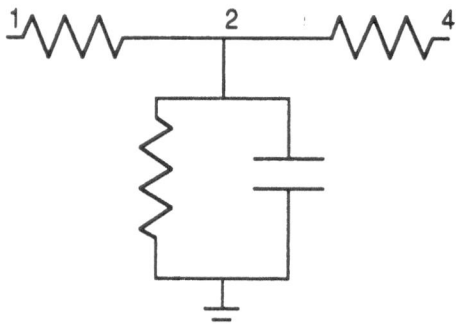

Fig.7. Compartmental model equivalent circuit

would be represented in SPICE by

R1 1 2 70M
R2 2 4 50M
RM 2 0 25M
CM 2 0 1PF

Terminating sections of neuron can be represented with a single axial resistance and branches taken care of with appropriate connectivity.

Synaptic inputs can be modelled in an analogue way[14a]. For a synaptic current from the above there are two things to be taken into account. The alpha function shape for the time varying conductance and the difference between the synaptic resting potential and that of the post synaptic cell. The first can be dealt with by deriving a circuit having the alpha function as a solution.The second aspect can be dealt with by using a polynomial, voltage-dependent source of the kind mentioned above.

Taking the alpha function in the form

$$g(t) = Atexp(t/t_{peak}) \qquad\qquad 5.7$$

the differential equation

$$dV/dt = (-1/t_{peak})V + Aexp(-t/t_{peak}) \qquad 5.8$$

has a solution of the form 5.7. This can be represented in SPICE in the following form

$$cdV/dt = -V/R + Iexp(-t/t_{peak}) \qquad 5.9$$

Adjusting cR and I/c gives the constants in the alpha function. To obtain the second part of the synaptic current a voltage dependent current source is used. Half a dozen lines of spice input suffice to describe the synaptic conductance.

Conduction in passive dendritic trees has been the main subject that has been discussed so far. The SPICE circuit analysis program can also be used to model active membrane phenomena[14b] such as the generation of an action potential using similar analogue ideas. The Hodgkin-Huxley equations are given by

$$cdV/dt = -g_{Na}m^4h(V-E_{Na}) -g_kn^4(V-E_k) -g_l(V-E_l) \qquad 5.10$$

$$dm/dt = \alpha_m(1-m) -\beta_m\, m \qquad 5.11$$

$$dh/dt = \alpha_h(1-h)-\beta_hh \qquad 5.12$$

$$dn/dt= \alpha_n(1-n) - \beta_nn \qquad 5.13$$

where the α_m, β_m are given by exponentials in V.

Each term of the equation can be represented by a SPICE circuit element using, where necessary, the polynomial sources mentioned earlier. The α and β functions in the equations for m,n,h are given by exponentials in the membrane potential. For efficiency reasons it is better to compute these using fitted polynomials. A single Hodgkin Huxley compartment needs about 60 lines of input. The full details of the SPICE input for all the Hodgkin Huxley equations can be found in the references.

The results of using SPICE are compared with the solutions of the Hodgkin -Huxley equations by Segev et al and are found to be in good agreement for the three following cases.
a. Space clamped
b. Action potential propagation
c. Action potential propagation through an axonal bifurcation.

For spiny neurons the majority of the synapses are on the spine heads.Analytical work suggests that passive spine heads might be important for integration. Active spine heads would imply synaptic amplification. The density and proximity suggest the possibility of electrical interactions between the spines. Segev et al give an example of the kind detailed modelling that can be carried out using SPICE. They consider the case shown below.

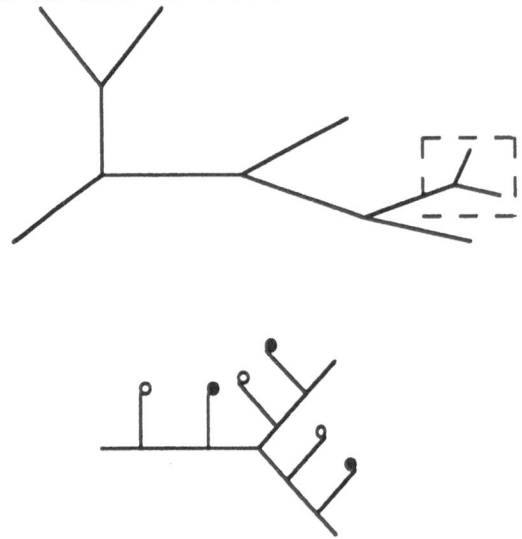

Fig.8. Schematic of complex model neuron and expanded diagram of inset

They find that exitatory input applied to the exciteable spines (filled in Fig. 8) are suffient to cause intra-spine action potentials and produce spikes in the bifurcating branch

Segev and his colleagues comment on the accuracy and computational cost of their model. With regard to accuracy there are two aspects to be considered: the anatomical and the electrical. The essential assumption of compartmental model is that the segments are sufficiently small to be assumed isopotential. If detailed investigations concerning the interaction of synaptic inputs is considered then it may be necessary to consider models with thousands of compartments. Segev et al report in 1985 that a model involving 300 compartments would typically be solved in minutes whereas the transient analysis of cat α motoneurons required 30 hrs of CPU time. Note that a three element representation of a patch of membrane can reduce that number of equations by a third. For transient analysis the choice of a three element representation can result in substantial inaccuracies.

6.Applications of Compartmental Modelling

a. Pyramidal Neurons in Rat Visual Cortex

In Stratford et al[15] the application of compartmental models to pyramidal neurons in layer 5 of the rat visual cortex is discussed. The compartmental model parameters(membrane resistivity, axial resistivity , somatic shunt conductance and membrane capacitance) were derived by fitting the output of the compartmental model to the results of experimental measurements.

These kinds of cell are reasonably complex. A schematic diagram is shown below.

Fig.9.Schematic of cortical pyramidal cell. (Dendritic spines not shown)

For the cell considered in the above reference approximately 8000 spines covered the membrane surface. Most of the excitatory inputs to the cell were made onto these dendritic spines. These neurons did not satisfy the criteria for modelling by cable theory and were modelled by a compartmental model.
Dendritic spines can make a considerable contribution to the membrane area which is required to calculate the membrane capacitance for the compartmental model. In this model the spines were included using a transformation of the length and diameter of the initial dendritic shafts. By not including all the spines in this way the effects of synaptic inputs on spines,active sites on spine heads etc can be included.

In a further approximation to collapse the number of compartments while retaining the essential features of the description the lengths of all dendrites were normalised and all the sections at the same normalised distance from the cell body represented by one compartment. This "cartoon " representation is reported as taking 15 CPU seconds as against 6000 for the full compartmental model for the simulation of a thirty msec transient. The responses of the simplified model were very accurate. Synaptic conductances were modelled using the alpha function mentioned earlier.

The main conclusions of this investigation were the following;
a.Membrane time constants could be much longer than previously thought.
b.These neurons were electrically very compact with regard to synaptic input on basal and proximal apical dendrites.
c.Synaptic input on the distal part of the apical dendrite suffered substantially greater attenuation and had a slower time course than similar inputs on the dendrites mentioned above.

It should be noted that the above mentioned work was carried out in order to assist with the interpretation of experimental results. A number of sets of parameter values were able to produce good agreement with measured values.

b. Olfactory Cortex

So far models involving detailed neural circuits (Section 2) and models involving biophysical detail at the level of individual neurons have been considered. In a realistic model both of these would need to be included.

Wilson and Bower[16] discuss a detailed compartmental model of the olfactory cortex in the context of a general purpose system they have developed for neural network simulation. At the gross anatomical level the olfactory cortex is a three layered structure. The cellular population of their model is composed of excitatory pyramidal neurons and two kinds of inhibitory interneurons. The initial layer of this part of the cortex takes inputs from mitral cells in the olfactory bulb(Section 2) and association fibres from other pyramidal cells. Layer two contains the cell bodies of pyramidal cells and and interneurons. Layer three contains basal dendrites of layer two pyramidal cells and the cell bodies of deep pyramidal cells. In the Wilson and Bower model only layer two pyramidal cell are simulated. The layering structure is important, however, as different compartments in the pyramidal cell model correspond to different layers and hence receive different inputs.

The network connections in the model are of three kinds:- input from the olfactory bulb, association fibres from other pyramidal neurons and inhibitory interconnections.

In the model sensory input from the olfactory bulb makes sparse excitatory contact with the pyramidal cells and feedforward interneurons. Variation of axonal velocity with axonal type is also taken into account. There is an exponential decrease in the influence of a particular synapse with increased distance from the site of stimulation.

Associative connections between pyramidal neurons are made in the model. These connections are made onto the basal dendrites of local pyramidal neurons and onto the apical dendrites outside a fixed radius.These connections are purely exitatory and decrease with distance.The spatial attenuation constants are different in different directions(fig12a). A schematic diagram of the connectivity implementing current shunting inhibition (fig 12c) and long duration inhibitory(Fig.12b) potential from the two kinds of interneurons used in the model is shown below. Note that these act on different spatial locations of the model pyramidal cells.

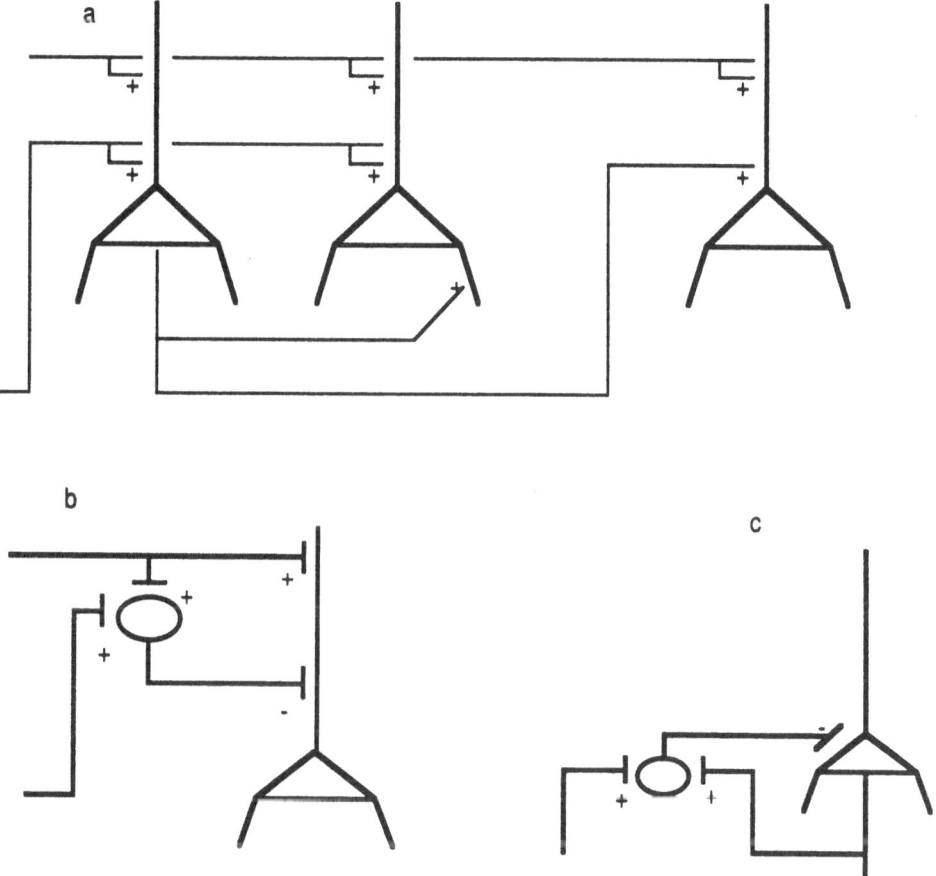

Fig.10. Connectivity for olfactory cortex model
a.Association fibres and inputs for pyramidal cells
b,c: connectivity for inhibitory interneurons

The various kinds of synaptic inputs (association, feedforward and feedback inhibitory, input) are all described by ionic channels with different time courses corresponding to observational results.

The two types of inhibitory interneurons are each modelled by a single compartmental model. The pyramidal neurons are represented by two different models in the course of simulation. A single compartmental model is used to establish the gross cortical behaviour. A five compartmental model is then used to take into account the detailed behaviour of the current flows within a neuron. The generation of an action potential is simulated by "pasting" in a unit amplitude pulse if a threshold is exceeded and the model neuron has not fired for a specified time.

The time delay from the generation of an action potential in a source cell to the target cell is the sum of the path length between the cells divided by the axon propagation velocity and the synaptic delay time. The total conductance in channel k of cell j due to input from cell i along a fibre q is given by

$$g_{ijkq}(t) = \int G_{jk}(\lambda) S_i(t-\lambda-t_{t(ijq)}) w_{ijq}(t-\lambda-t_{t(ijq)}) d\lambda$$

$$6.1$$

The total conductance change in channel k of cell j is obtained by summing expressions like 6.1 over all synaptic inputs to that channel.

The equation for the potential of a compartment is then given by

$$dV_j/dt = (1/c_m)\Sigma^{nchan} (E_k-V_j(t))g_{jk}(t) + I_a \ . \qquad 6.2$$

The output from the model consists of the membrane potential calculated by pasting in the waveform at the appropriate time and the gross field potential. This latter output can be directly related to the extensive experimental information available concerning field potentials in the olfactory cortex[17].

c. Other Models.

In the previous model a stereotyped pulse was pasted in when a threshold was exceeded. It would be useful to have a compartmental model in which the action potential was generated. This can be done in SPICE as was discussed earlier. There is some evidence that some pyramidal cells are electrically rather compact[15]. A two compartment model with one compartment representing the dendrites and cell body and another compartment representing the axon hillock might be appropriate. Using the FitzHugh-Nagumo equations to represent the action potential generation leads to the following equations.

$$_j\dot{V}_s = -(1/\tau)V_s + \Sigma_i \Delta g_{i(j)}(V^0_{ij} - {}_jV_s) + (R_s/R_{sh})(V^0_{i(j)} - {}_jV_s(t))$$

$$6.3$$

$$_j\dot{V}_h = V_h - (1/3)(V_h)^3 - W_h + (R_h/R_{hs})(V_s - V_h) \qquad 6.4$$

$$_j\dot{W}_h = (V_h + a - bW_h) \qquad 6.5$$

Where the $\Delta g_{i(j)}$ takes account of the history of the neurons connected to neuron j.

The full Hodgkin-Huxley equation could be used instead. These model neurons are being used[18] to investigate phase locking in systems of coupled neurons as in the simple example shown below.

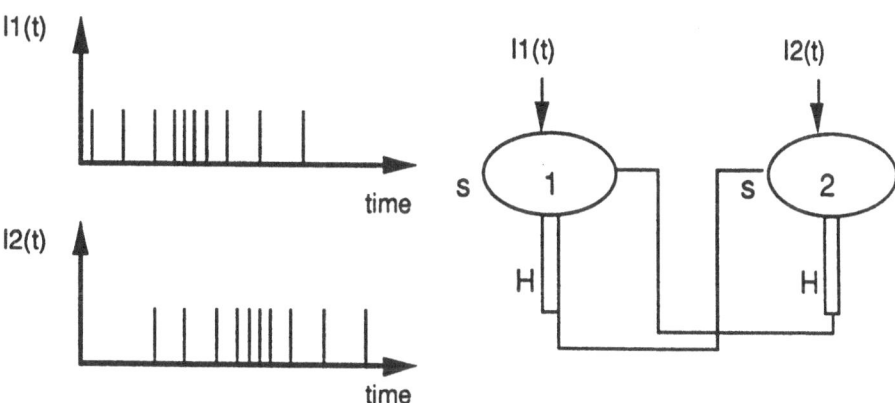

Fig.11. Inputs and coupled oscillator model

7.Conclusions.

Individual neurons are complicated objects. The information processing importance of this complexity needs careful examination.
Modelling large assemblies of neurons in reasonable biological detail is computationally tractable. SPICE provides a relatively easy way of dealing

with individual neurons and small circuits. It is necessary to develop custom codes for larger collections. Compartmental modelling looks likely to remain the method of choice for the future.

Realistic modelling is often constrained by the lack of experimental data. However where that information is available these detailed models can be used to provides constraints for functional models.

The results on cortical oscillations indicate how the the dynamical properties of individual neurons might be relevant to information processing. Hopefully the development of large scale,realistic simulations will provide further insights.

References

1. New Developments in Neural Computing
Edited by J.G. Taylor, C. L. T. Mannion; Adam Hilger 1989
2. The diversity of Neuronal Properties, C.Miall in
The Computing Neuron. Edited by R. Durbin, C. Miall, G. Mitchison.
Addison-Wesley 1989.
3. A Neural Network for feature linking via Synchronous Activity
R.Eckhorn, H.J. Reitboek, M. Arndt, P. Dicke in
Models of Brain Function. Edited by R.M.J. Cotterill. C.U.P. 1989
4. Biophysics of Computation: Neurons,Synapses and Membranes.
C. Koch, T. Poggio in
Synaptic Function edited by G.M. Edelman,W. Einar-Gall, W. Maxwell Cowan
5 The intrinsic electrophysiological properties of Mammalian Neurons.
R.R. Llinas. Science Vol242 1054 (1988)
6. The Dynamics of Neural Systems.J.W. Chen,
Ph.D. Dissertation, Physics Dept.,Washington University.,1986.
7. Analog simulation of circuits in the Olfactory Bulb, Chen,Clark,Kurten in
reference 3.
8. Perspectives in Memory Research.
M.S. Gazzaniga. MIT press 1988.
9. Electric current flow in excitable cells.
J.Jack,D. Noble, R. Tsien.
Oxford University Press 1975.
10. Methods in Neuronal Modelling. Edited by C.Koch,I. Segev
11. Introduction to theoretical neurobiology Vols 1,2.
H.C. Tuckwell . C.U.P 1988.
12. Quantitative methods for predicting neuronal behaviour.
D.H. Perkel, B. Mulloney, R.W. Budelli. Neuroscience 6,5,1981.
13. Computer aided circuit analysis using spice.
W. Banzhaf. Prentice Hall 1985.
14. a.Modelling the Electrical Behaviour of Anatomically Complex neurons
Using a Network Analysis Program:Passive Membrane.
b. Modelling the Electrical Behaviour of Anatomically Complex neurons
Using a Network Analysis Program: Active Membrane.
I.Segev,J.W.Fleshman,J.P.Miller andB.Bunow
Biol.Cyber. 53,27-40,1985.
15. The modelling of pyramidal neurons in the visual cortex.
K. Stratford,A. Larkman, A. Mason,G. Major and J.Jack
16. Wilson and Bower in ref 10
17. Mass Action in the Nervous System.

W.J. Freeman. Academic Press(1975)

18. Coupled excitable cells,C.L.T.Mannion,J.G. Taylor (these proceedings)

Self-Organising Neural Maps and their Applications

N. M. Allinson

ABSTRACT

This tutorial paper is an introduction to Kohonen's self-organising neural maps. It discusses their operating principles, relationship to classical pattern recognition and outlines various applications.

PATTERN RECOGNITION

The goal of pattern recognition is to classify objects into one of a number of categories or *classes*. The objects of interest are generically called *patterns* and may be images, speech signals or entries in a database. It is these patterns, which we can loosely define as *natural structure*, that give meaning to the events in the external world. Patterns are manifestations of rules, and through observing patterns we are able to propose rules and to form an understanding of the underlying processes. A sequence of spoken utterances only has meaning if we have heard it before, that it follows certain phonological rules and we can assign a meaning to this "word." That is we can give it a higher level of representation.

Objects are represented by taking a number of measurements. It is these measurements that form the *pattern vector*. Objects from the same class, since they will possess similar pattern vectors, will form clusters of points in the pattern space. It is this clustering which can be equated to the concept of natural structure. Figure 1 shows a simple example. If the clustered classes have a perceptual significance then we can give the clusters *labels* or names, such as triangles, squares or circles. We may take many measurements to produce this pattern vector. For example, a simple optical character reading system could consist of a sensor array of 7 x 5 photo-diodes, and hence results in a pattern vector of 35-dimensions. The pattern vector is transformed into another vector, whose components are termed *features*. The resulting *feature space* will contain less dimensions than the original pattern space but should collectively contain sufficient information for the accurate classification of patterns. For example, in our character reading example, it may be that only the area and perimeter of each character is sufficient for it to be identified. Hence the feature space will be two-dimensional.

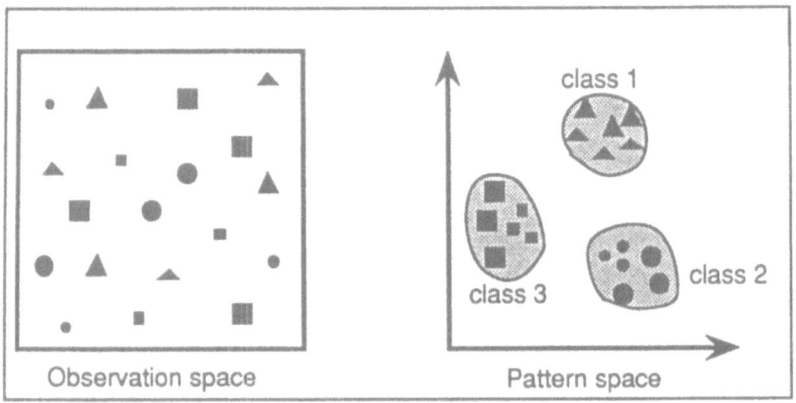

Figure 1   *Clustering of classes in pattern space.*

In reducing the number of dimensions from pattern space to feature space, there must be a loss of information. However, this process is essential since it permits the classification of clusters based on the simple partitioning of feature space, and in a complex many-layered neural system, such as the mammalian brain, the reduction in the number of dimensions is essential if the combinational explosion is to be avoided. Figure 2 shows two basic forms of clustering in pattern space. The transformation from pattern space to feature space for the meshed cluster example can be achieved by some form of smooth mapping function. However, the disjoint clusters belonging to the same class in famous the exclusive-OR problem can only be achieved by the employment some logical function - since there is no perceptual similar between the class clusters. Such patterns are said to contain *hidden structure*.

Supervised and Unsupervised Learning

Pattern classification can be divided into two distinct forms. *Supervised learning* is where each training input pattern is accompanied by its correct

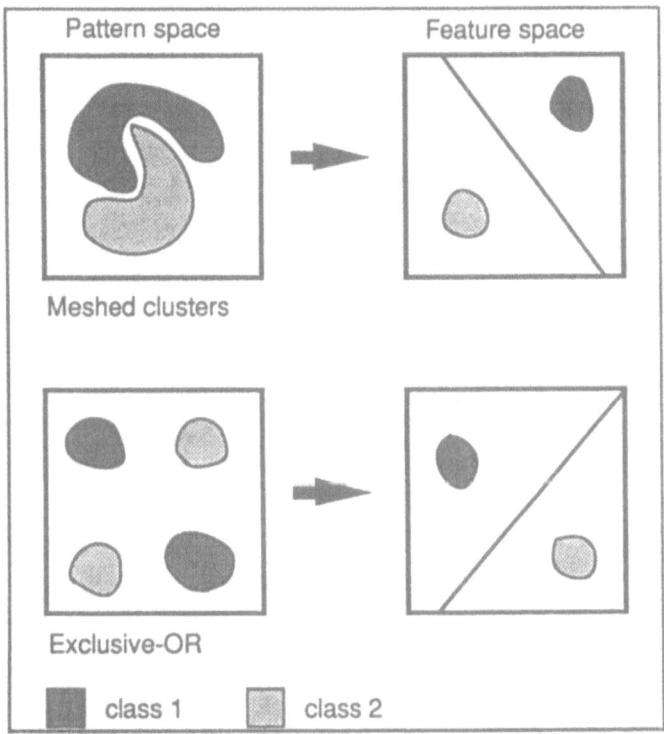

Pattern space   Feature space

Meshed clusters

Exclusive-OR

class 1   class 2

Figure 2   *Types of clustering in pattern space and the desired*
transformations in feature space.

class. Multi-layer perceptrons, the most common type of neural network architecture currently used, employ this form of learning. The difference between the network's current response and the desired one is used to change the synaptic weights of each neuron. Of course, such an approach must do more than just learn the class exemplars since all that the fully trained network would be able to do would be to *template match* on these exemplars. It must be able to *generalise*, that is to correctly assign similar patterns to the exemplars into their correct class.

For neural maps, *unsupervised learning* is employed. Representative training data is, again, applied but no indication of class membership provided. By applying some optimisation mechanism, the pattern data is segregated into clusters in the feature space in some meaningful manner. An alternate term for this type of learning is *self-organisation*. Unsupervised learning algorithms attempt to identify several prototypes in the data set that can serve as cluster centres. Unsupervised learning schemes can identify the natural structure in patterns but they can not, in general, discover the hidden structure. This means that unsupervised learning can not solve the exclusive-OR problem, unless the architecture of the network forces such an association.

Unsupervised learning may appear, therefore, to be a poor relation to supervised learning. This is not the case, especially, where we are concerned with perceptual data (such as speech or vision) since supervised paradigms assume that we already possess an accurate model of the underlying processes for assigning class membership - or at least, a knowledge of the number of classes and examples of each. Supervised learning schemes become difficult to implement where there is a hierarchy of networks, each reducing its input pattern space into a much lower dimensional output space. How should errors in the final output network be reflected back down the hierarchy? There are no easy answers. Only systems that are unsupervised in their training and possess an overall architecture that forces dimensionality reduction can hope to succeed.

Elements of Self-Organisation

The formation of distinct clusters in feature space implies the existence of two opposing effects. These are illustrated diagrammatically in Figure 3.

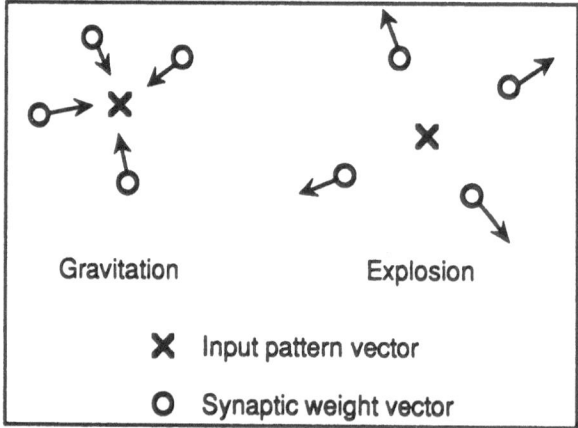

Figure 3   *The two opposing processes necessary in self-organising systems.*

A gravitational force of attraction that moves the synaptic weight vectors of the neurons towards the input pattern vector, and explosive force that repels the weight vectors so as to form distinct isolated clusters. Inherent in the operation of these forces is the requirement to measure the distance or *similarity* between the weight and pattern vectors. All neural implementations of self-organising structures employ some form of lateral communication between the neurons in a layer and some way of measuring the similarity of the weight and pattern vectors.

The next section summaries the work of Kohonen [1] in developing self-organising neural networks, which possess the additional property that the arrangement of features in the output space is topological.

SUMMARY OF KOHONEN'S SELF-ORGANISING FEATURE MAPS

Biological Background

An important property apparent in those parts of the mammalian brain, associated with sensory processing (eg, the visual and auditory cortex), is the existence of low, usually two, dimensional neural maps that reflect the topological ordering of the external stimuli. A schematic of a one dimensional map is illustrated in Figure 4 The overall input connectivity matrix, M, is composed of the modifiable synaptic weight vectors of each neuron. The output vector, y, is not only fed forward to another part of the cortex but also, via another set of synapses - the feedback connectivity matrix, N, back to the neurons in the array. The general set of differential equations that describe this system are,

$$\frac{dy}{dt} = f(x,y,M,N) \tag{1}$$

$$\frac{dM}{dt} = f'(x,y,M) \tag{2}$$

$$\frac{dN}{dt} = f''(y,N) \tag{3}$$

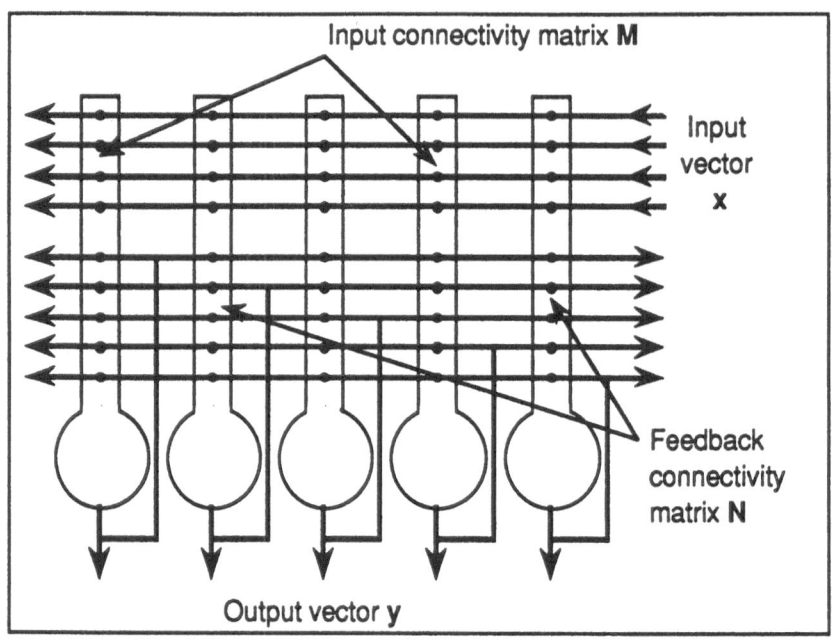

Figure 4   *One-dimensional neural array.*
The small black circles represent the individual synapses and
the larger empty circles represent the neuron's soma - each
with a single axon output.

Eq. (1) can be termed the *relaxation equation* since it relates the current
output of the system as a function of the current input vector, x, and the
state of the synaptic matrices. Eqs. (2) and (3) are related to how these
synaptic matrices are modified. That is how the system learns. There are,
of course, many different forms for the functions f, f' and f", and here we
will concentrate on a simple form that permits the formation of topological
maps. Due to the widely differing time scales of relaxation and adaptation,
these equations can be decoupled in the analysis. A widely observed form
of the lateral inhibition function in many biological systems - both
vertebrate and invertebrate - is the *Mexican hat* function (Figure 5). There
is a short-range area of lateral excitation around a point of excitation (with a
radius of 50-100 μm, in primates), then a wider annulus of inhibitory action
over a radius of 200-500 μm and finally a very weak excitatory connection
extending over several centimetres. We shall assume that N is of this
general form and that it is non-adaptive. The relaxation equation can be
specified as,

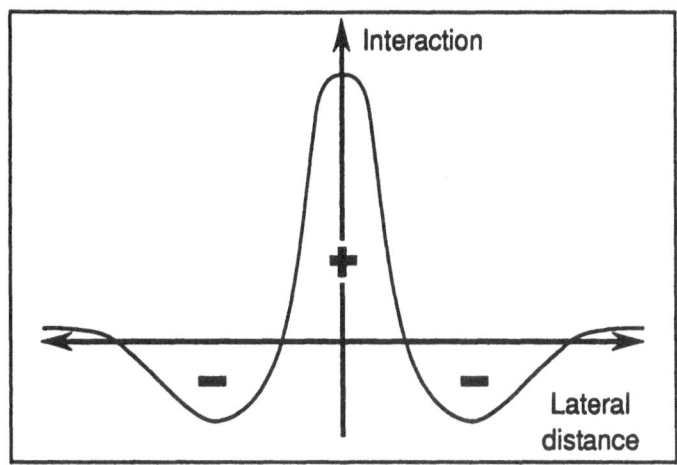

Figure 5   *General form of the Mexican hat lateral inhibition function.*

$$\frac{dy_i}{dt} = \sum_{j=1}^{n} m_{ij}x_{ij} - \sum_{k \in S_i} n_{ki}y_k - \gamma(y_i) \qquad (4)$$

The first term on the right-hand side represents the coupling of the input vector elements, x_{ij}, to the individual i^{th} neuron via its synaptic weight elements, m_{ij}. The second term incorporates the lateral interaction effects over the local neighbourhood, S_i. The final term is a non-linear leakage term which models the dynamic nature of neural responses. The adaptation equation is expressed as,

$$\frac{dm_{ij}}{dt} = \alpha y_i x_j - \beta(y_i)m_{ij} \qquad (5)$$

The first term is simply an expression of Hebb's law, namely that the synaptic connection is strengthened in proportion to the current input excitation and output response of the neuron. The second term is a non-linear forgetting term. Kohonen's work demonstrated that the detailed forms of the lateral interaction term and the non-linear terms were unimportant in forming *activity bubbles*. The formation of these isolated distinct regions of high neural excitation is illustrated in Figure 6. If the input vector is a smooth function, then a stationary bubble of constant radius is formed at the neuron where $m_i^T x$ is a maximum. Furthermore, if the forgetting term, β, in eq. (5) is assumed to possess a Taylor series

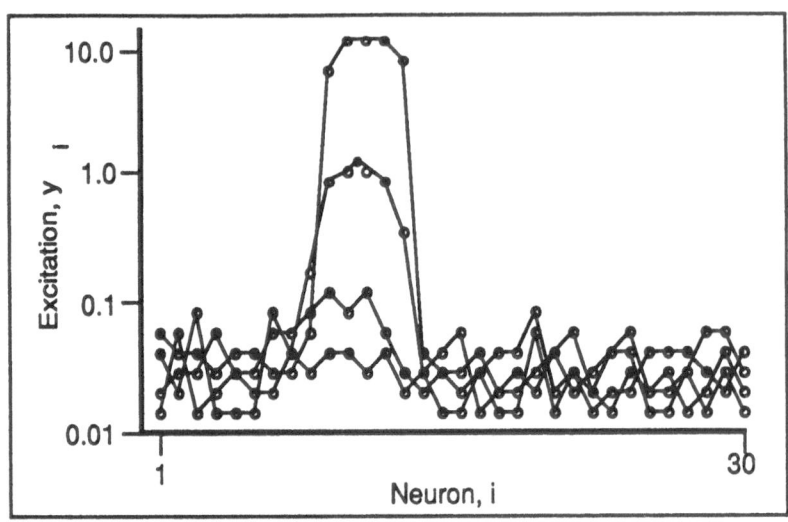

Figure 6   *Formation of an activity bubble over a number of iterations,*
            for a single line of neurons possessing a Mexican hat lateral
            inhibition profile. A random input vector is applied which
            causes the noisy low-level background responses of the
            neurons outside the bubble.

expansion with a zero constant term (that is the forgetting is active, being proportional to y_i), then this equation may be simplified to,

$$\frac{dm_{ij}}{dt} = \alpha(x_j - \beta m_{ij}) \qquad \text{inside the bubble} \qquad (6a)$$

$$\frac{dm_{ij}}{dt} = 0 \qquad \text{outside the bubble} \qquad (6b)$$

The condition for the location of the activity bubble now becomes the location where $\| x - m_i \|$.

Practical Realisation of Neural Maps

A computationally less intensive method for producing topological neural maps, that also overcomes the potential instability problems if the *Mexican hat* inhibition profile is employed, has also been developed by Kohonen. This method is applicable to one, two or even higher dimensional arrays of identical neurons. It will be described here for the

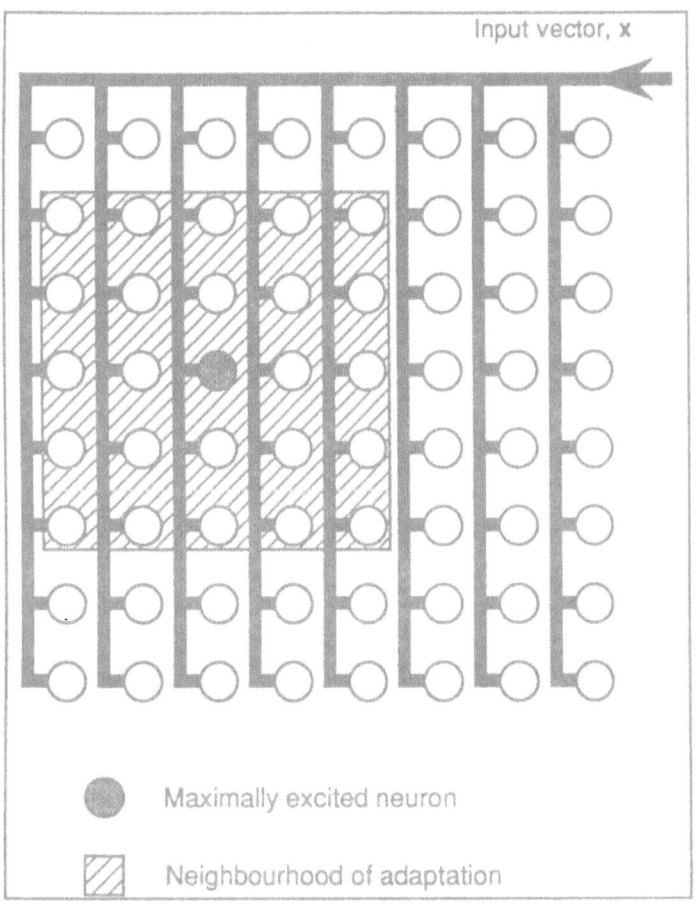

Figure 7   *Two dimensional self-organising neural map.*

case of a two-dimensional array (Figure 7). Initially, the weight vectors
areset to small random values. The input vector, x, is broadcast to all
neurons. Each neuron effectively performs a similarity analysis between x
and its weight vector, w_{ij}, where i,j = 1, 2, ..., K for a K x K array. Kohonen's
original work concentrated on using the Euclidean distance as the similarity
measure, that is,

$$d(x,w) = \| x - w \| = \sqrt{\sum_{i=1}^{N}(x_i - w_i)^2} \qquad (7)$$

Where N is the number of dimensions in the input vector. A number of
distance measures are possible and this aspect will be discussed later.

The neuron with its weight vector closest to the current input vector is identified, that is $\|x - w\|$ is a minimum. This is, of course, the neuron with the largest output response. A neighbourhood of $N_c \times N_c$ neurons, centred on this this neuron, is defined. All neurons within this neighbourhood are subject to adaptation so that their weight vectors become more like the current input vector. The weight vectors of neurons outside the neighbourhood are not changed. The process can be described by the following equations,

$$\frac{dw_{ij}}{dt} = \alpha^t(x - w_{ij}) \qquad \text{for } ij \in N_c \qquad (8)$$

$$w_{ij}^{t+1} = w_{ij}^t + \alpha^t(x^t - w_{ij}^t)$$

$$\frac{dw_{ij}}{dt} = 0 \qquad \text{for } ij \notin N_c$$

$$w_{ij}^{t+1} = w_{ij}^t$$

where $0 < \alpha^t < 1$.

This algorithm is repeated many thousands of times for different input vectors. Initially, both the neighbourhood, N_c, and the adaptation coefficient, α^t, are large. The learning phase proceeds by applying input vectors and allowing adaptation to occur. The values of N_c and α are reduced monotonically as learning progresses. There is a wide choice in the way these parameters can be modified. Typically, α^t varies as,

$$\alpha^t = k_1\left[1 - \frac{t}{10000}\right] \qquad \text{where } k_1 = 0.1$$

Though sometimes, it is an better to use a two-stage process in order to reduce the learning time. For example,

$$\alpha^t = k_1\left[1 - \frac{t}{2000}\right] \qquad \text{for the first 2000 learning cycles}$$

and $\qquad \alpha^t = k_2\left[1 - \frac{t}{10000}\right] \qquad$ for the remaining 8000 learning cycles, where $k_2 = 0.005$.

The neighbourhood size is reduced linearly over the first part of the learning phase. The topological optimisation of the fully trained network is strongly dependent on the values of these two parameters and on the manner in which they are reduced as training progresses. Though there are some pointers as to suitable values, and their dependences on, say, the size of the array, their exact values must be found by experimentation. Convergence of the algorithm is guarantied by $\alpha^t \rightarrow 0$ as $t \rightarrow \infty$. It can be seen that the *Mexican hat* profile has been replaced by a shrinking *top-hat* function. The optimum nature of the topological organisation of this approach has been proved for the one-dimensional case (see, for example refs [2,3]).

The order in which data is applied during training can be critical. As the global ordering is achieved during the early stages, then the initial training data must be truely representative of the complete training set. Even if this requirement is met, then the adapted map may organise to any one of a number of the possible reflections. Priming the synaptic weights prior to training may overcome these difficulties.

The optimum size of the output map depends on the expected number of features present in the data. Hence, a certain amount of experimentation may be necessary in order to achieve the correct size of the array.

After training, input signals are applied and though all neurons will be excited to some extent, there will be one neuron with its weight vector most closely matching that of the current input vector and this will possess the largest output response. Hence, there will be a clear excitation peak in the output map.

Simple Example

Figure 8(a) shows a training image of concentric black and white circles. The input signals to the map consists of 16 x 16 pixel patches taken at random from this image. The two-dimensional network possesses 16 x 16 neurons. The synaptic weights of these neurons in the fully trained network are shown in Figure 8(b). Notice that the network has 'discovered' that the natural structure of this image, at the scale of 16 x 16 pixel patches, is that of isolated line fragments of differing orientations. Lines with

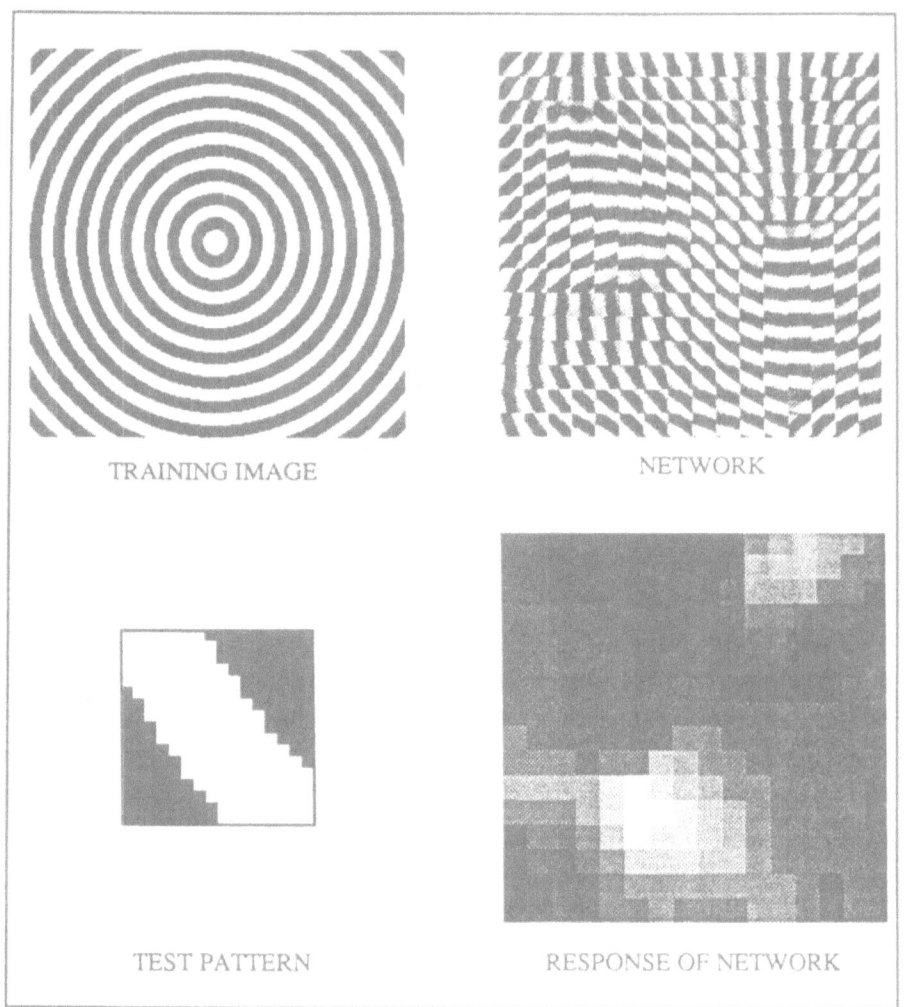

TRAINING IMAGE

NETWORK

TEST PATTERN

RESPONSE OF NETWORK

Figure 8   *Example of a two dimensional Kohonen network.*

(a)   *Training image of concentric circles.*

(b)   *Fully adapted 16 x 16 network, showing the final values of each neuron's synaptic weights.   Each neuron possesses a 256 element weight vector.*

(c)   *Test pattern - on an enlarged scale.*

(d)   *Resultant output map, showing the single excitation peak.*

similar orientations are physically close together in the output map and vice versa. If the test pattern of Figure 8(c) is applied to this trained network then the output response shown in Figure 8(d) is obtained. A single high peak is obtained that corresponds to the neuron with the best match of its weight vector and the test pattern vector.

Global and local ordering

The self-organising process means that the probability density function of the input vectors is mirrored in the density of the neurons in the output feature space. If the input data is strongly clustered then a large proportion of the neurons will be sensitised to input vectors near these clusters and relatively few far away from them. The topological organisation of the adapted neurons means that physically adjacent neurons in the output space will possess similar excitation signals. This is a very important property since it allows the network to generalise for novel data. Such topological organisation needs to impose both global and local ordering of the neural excitation pattern within the output map.

As explained above, the self-organising algorithm searches for the excitation peak in the neuron array, then a neighbourhood is defined around this peak. If the neighbourhood is large, it will tend to globally average the input vectors and the weight vectors will graviate towards their mean. The probability density mapping will become distorted, with the extremes suppressed and the central area exagerated. If the neighbourhood is small then the inverse occurs. Now, the weight vectors will provide a good probability density function mapping of the input vectors but at the expense of the global topology. The solution proposed by Kohonen is to employ shrinking neighbourhoods. Once the global ordering has been achieved in the initial stages of learning, then only more local ordering is necessary.

DATA DIMENSIONALITY

Though the input vector may be of high dimensionality, the inherent dimensionality of the data may be much lower. The self-organising process attempts to map the N-dimensional input vector onto the limited number of dimensions of the array. Only if the *inherent dimensionality* of the data matches that of the array will global ordering be achieved. If the inherent dimensionality of the data is greater than that of the array, the formation of the sensitised neurons in the output feature space can not map the probability density function in a direct way. For example, if the data is two-dimensional and the array possesses only one-dimension, then the result of training is shown in Figure 9. Here, the input vector samples had a uniform probability density. The network successfully manages to provide probability density function mapping by repeatedly contorting itself into recursive convolutions. The map is correctly topologically organised at a local level since the neurons are connected to their nearest neighbours in the feature space. The feature space is covered by a space-filling Peano curve.

Figure 9   *Two-dimensional Peano curve, resulting from the application of two-dimensional data to a one-dimensional array.*

Another example, that demonstrates the self-organising mechanism and dimensionality reduction is given in Figure 10. It is intended to map the points on the surface of a sphere (represented by the dotted circle) onto a one-dimensional map. The input vectors are randomly chosen points on the sphere's surface. At an early stage of the learning the neuron array is approximately aligned as a circle around the sphere. Points on the sphere near this circle are well represented, but points well away from it are not. The learning algorithm attempts to minimise the differences between the input and weight vectors. Hence, the one-dimensional array adapts to the

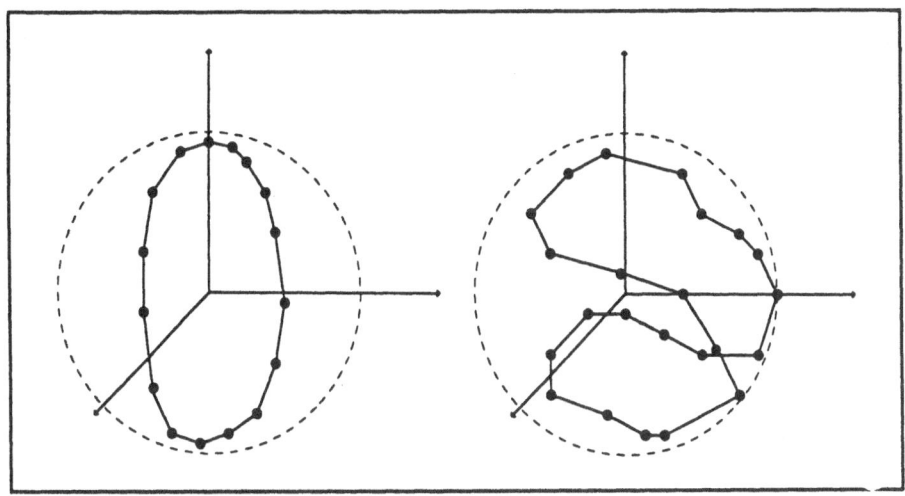

Figure 10   *Mapping of a one-dimensional array onto the surface of a sphere.*

shape shown in the right-hand figure. This shape is the optimum one, in the sense that the distance from any point on the sphere is a minimum distance away from the line. (Compare the shape of this line with the join between the two parts of a tennis ball) However, the projection of this line onto any of the indicated planes would result in a fairly meaningless shape. A further discussion of inherent dimensionality and methods for map projection are given in Tattersall, Linford and Linggard[4].

MEASURES OF SIMILARITY

Previously only the Euclidean metric was introduced as a similarity measure of the input and weight vectors, however a large number of such measures exist (see, for example, ref [5]). One that is of particular note is the normalised scalar product or *direction cosine*. A difficulty with the Euclidean metric is that different neurons in the array will become sensitized to different amplitudes of the same signal. In a number of application areas, for example image recognition this is undesirable - since we are concerned with the identification of (say) local edge direction regardless of their amplitudes. The normalised scalar product metric is expressed as,

$$d(x,w) = \frac{\sum\limits_{i=1}^{N} x_i w_i}{\sum\limits_{i=1}^{N} x_i^2 \cdot \sum\limits_{i=1}^{N} w_i^2} \tag{9}$$

In effect, this means that the synaptic weight vectors are constrained to lie on the surface of a unit sphere.

RELATIONSHIP WITH OTHER PATTERN CLASSIFICATION TECHNIQUES

Self-organising maps possess functional properties similar to a number of classical clustering techniques, in particular the K-means algorithm. A discussion on how these maps act as principal component analysers is given by Oja[6].

Within the neural computing field, they are related to the general network types that employ competitive learning, and in particular the adaptive resonance theory of Grossberg[7]. The counter-propagation network of Hecht-Nielsen[8] is a combination of self-organising maps and the *outstar* structure of Grossberg.

APPLICATIONS

Self-organising feature maps are one of the most useful of artificial neural networks. Their abilities to perform, in an unsupervised manner, dimensionality reduction and topological organisation means that they have been employed in a number of application areas. They can be used as vector quantisers, that is the statistical encoding of data vectors in order to quantise and compress data. For example, Naylor and Li[9] have used them to construct codebooks for speech application and Nasrabadi and Feng[10] for image coding.

Speech recognition studies have been undertaken by Kohonen[11] and Tattersall[12]. If a two-dimensional array is trained on spectral vectors that represent different speech sounds, in particular the vowel sounds, then the adapted network reproduces the well-known vowel trapezium. Johnson and Allinson[13] have demonstrated their application to image processing, including character recognition and reconstruction. Luckman and Allinson[14] have combined a stack of resolution pyramids, each with its associated network, for the location and recognition of facial features.

The self-organising feature of these maps has been used to tackle the classical Travelling Salesman Problem and to provide quasi-optimal solutions[15].

REFERENCES

1. Kohonen T. Self-Organization and Associative Memory. Springer Verlag, Heielberg, 1984

2. Kohonen T. Biol Cyb 1982; 44:135-140

3. Cotterall M and Fort J C. Ann Inst Henri Poincare 1987; 23:1-20

4. Tattersall G D, Linford P W and Linggard R. Brit Telecom Tech J 1988; 6:140-163

5. Duda R O and Hart P E. Pattern Classification and Scene Analysis. Wiley, New York, 1973

6. Oja E. Int J Neural Systems 1989; 1:61-68

7. Grossberg S. Cognitive Science 1987; 11:23-63

8. Hecht-Nielson R. Counterpropagation networks. In Proc 1st int conf on neural networks. IEEE San Diego, 1988, pp 19-32

9. Naylor J and Feng Y. Analysis of a neural network algorithm for the vector quantization of speech parameters. In Proc 1st ann INNS meeting. Pergamon Press New York, 1988, p 310

10. Nasrabadi N M and Feng Y. Vector quantization of images based upon the Kohonen self-organising feature maps. In Proc 1st int conf on neural networks. IEEE San Diego, 1988, pp 1101-1108

11. Kohonen T. Speech recognition based on topology-preserving neural maps. In Aleksander I (ed) Neural computing architectures. North Oxford Academic London, 1989, pp 26-40

12. Tattersall G D. Neural map applications. In Aleksander I (ed) Neural computing architectures. North Oxford Academic London, 1989, pp 41-73

13. Johnson M J and Allinson N M. Digital realisation of self-organising maps. In Touretzky D S (ed) Advances in neural information processing systems. Morgan Kaufmann San Mateo, 1989, pp 728-738

14. Luckman A J and Allinson N M. Proc SPIE 1990; 1197:68-75

15. Angeniol B, de la Croix Vaubois G and Texier J-Y. Neural Networks 1988; 1:289-293

CONTRIBUTED
PAPERS

THE APPLICATION OF TOPOLOGICAL MAPPING IN THE STUDY OF HUMAN CEREBRAL TUMOURS

G. SIEBEN, L. VERCAUTEREN, M. PRAET, G. OTTE,
L. BOULLART, L. CALLIAUW, L. ROELS

INTRODUCTION

This study is part of a larger work in which we try to determine the prognosis and eventually optimised therapeutical guidelines in patients with cerebral tumours. Presented here are the neuropathological findings in cases of these tumours. However determining the prognosis of a patient with a cerebral tumour is a complicated multifactorial problem where the answers depend not only on the pathological data but also on clinical findings (age, sex, localisation, initial symptoms, functioning level...,) therapeutical strategies (type of operation, whether steroids are administered, chemotherapy), and some experimental data such as DNA distribution, behaviour in culture, the presence of immunological markers.

The aim of this study was to:
1° evaluate the potential of the topological mapping technique as described by Kohonen in the ordering of cerebral tumours.
2° examining the classification power of the map.
3° test the ability of the system to recognize new examples : this means using and evaluating the map as an expert system.

MATERIALS AND METHODS

A total of 200 cases of human cerebral tumours (table I) were investigated. Parafin embedded biopsy specimens were stained with hematoxilin-eosin and examined microscopically. Data were collected by a trained neuropathologist who was asked to score his findings on14 features in the preparation (border , necrosis , homogeneity , fibrillarity , rosettes , perivascular rosettes , vascular proliferation , epithelial configuration , mitosis , hyperchromasia , nuclear cytoplasmatic ratio , halos , cell density , abundance of cytoplasm) on a continuous scale ranging from 0 to 100.

A 14 - dimensional vector representation was created for each case while the collection of all labelled cases formed the learning set. The tumours were randomly chosen and presented to the map sequentially during 40.000 learning cycles. Each case was presented to all the neurons. The probability of selection was independent of the frequency of the tumour in the learning set .The dimensionality of the map was 2 dim :15 x 15 neurons on a square grid .

The networks training process consisted initally of a non-supervised learning algorithm ,described by Kohonen in order to select he winning unit (shortest Euclidian distance) and to adapt the weights of that unit and its neighbours .

A linearly decreasing learning rate was used (alfa .t = 0,7 -t. 0.001). The neigbourhood C was defined as C=(0.7 . alfa)/ 0.9.

From T> 10.000 a linear vector quantisation algorithm was applied with neighbourhood 0 while the learning rate was kept constant at 0.005.

The learning algorithm was implemented on a T800
transputer platform in the Occam II language. The user interface for application and expert system was programmmed Turbo pascal in a 80386 (with 80387 mathematical coprocessor) environment .

TABLE 1 :TUMOURS PRESENT IN LEARNING SET

Astrocytoma I (Q):	3	Astroblastoma (F):	2
Fibrillary Astrocytoma (A):	37	Medulloblastoma (E):	5
Gem. Astrocytoma (J):	12		
Oligodendroglioma (C):	20	Ectopic pinealoma (R):	2
Ependymoma (K):	12		
Anaplastic Astrocytoma (B):	30	Schwannoma (P):	2
Anaplastic Oligodendroglioma (M):	6	Plexus Papilloma:(I)	5
Anaplastic ependymoma (L):	7	Meningioma (G):	8
Glioblastoma (D)	29	Craniopharyngeoma (O):	2
		Angioma (N)	6
		Metastasis (H):	12

RESULTS

1° The topological map is shown in table 2. Each unit is labeled with the name of the tumour by which it is most activated. Tumours with the highest malignant potential (glioblastoma multiforme, astroblastoma, medulloblastoma, metastasis) are found in the left upper region of the map. Tumours with a less malignant potential (anaplastic astrocytoma, anaplastic oligodendroglioma, anaplastic ependymoma) are found lying as a rim around the more malignant tumours. Neuroepithelial tumours

TABLE 2. Label representation of the topological map.

Each unit is labeled with the tumor for which it is most sensitive.

	1	2	3	4	5	6	7	8	9	10	11	12	13	14	15
1	D	D	D	D	D	B	B	L	K	O	N	N	N	N	N
2	F	D	D	D	D	B	M	B	A	O	N	N	N	N	N
3	F	D	D	D	D	B	B	B	A	O	N	N	N	N	N
4	D	D	D	D	D	L	L	B	A	O	O	O	O	O	O
5	H	F	F	F	L	L	L	B	A	A	A	A	C	C	C
6	F	F	F	F	E	L	L	K	I	I	I	I	I	I	I
7	E	E	E	E	L	L	L	B	J	I	I	I	I	I	I
8	E	E	E	E	A	A	A	J	C	C	C	C	I	I	I
9	L	L	L	E	A	A	A	J	C	C	C	C	I	I	I
10	E	E	B	B	A	A	A	A	A	Q	Q	Q	I	I	I
11	E	B	B	B	A	A	A	G	A	Q	Q	Q	I	I	I
12	E	B	B	B	A	A	A	A	Q	Q	Q	Q	I	I	I
13	B	B	B	B	A	A	A	A	A	Q	Q	Q	I	I	I
14	B	B	B	A	A	A	A	A	A	Q	Q	Q	I	I	I
15	B	B	B	A	A	A	A	A	A	Q	Q	Q	I	I	I

with the lowest degree of malignancy (fibrillary astrocytoma, oligodendroglioma, ependymoma) are found to the right adjacent to the more malignant tumours. This ordering of the map was obtained without any prior knowledge of the degree of malignancy of the tumours.

Finally at the right side of the map the benign non - neuroepithelial tumours are found. Two tumours (Schwannoma and ectopic pinealoma) are not represented in this label map. When studying the examples in the learning set and the corresponding unit they activated mostly these two tumours were found on a unit that had as label plexus papilloma.

2° Before using the topological map as a full-blown expert system we tested its ability to recognise and label examples from the learning set by presenting it with a subset of degraded samples.

After each parameter (parameters were presented sequentially to the map) a selection was made of the set of remaining units. This yielded a 96% score of correct classifications. In each presentation only partial datasets was sufficient to establish the correct diagnosis. When confronted with new tumours only 90% of the cases were classified (the total number of new cases presented to the net was 50).

CONCLUSIONS

The topological mapping technique behaves as an important dimensionality reducing operator that is able to generate from the multidimensional data in our learning set a well ordered 2D-representation map. As such it is considered a useful tool for ordering the cerebral tumours. All tumours with identical labels are found grouped. Neuro-epithelial tumours are grouped as are non-epithelial tumours. At the same time a gradient from the more malignant to more benign tumours can be observed to emerge clearly from the representationmap.

No misclassifications were observed. However in this experiment two labels were not represented in the labeled map.

As an expert system tested on its own learning set (partial vectors) the map performed well with 96% correct classifications. The tumours the net was unable to classify correctly were the tumours that were not represented in the label map.

During the presentation of new tumours the performance of the map decreased to 90% of correct diagnoses.

The main difficulties that arose during this experiment could be considered partly user defined, partly map defined.
The pathologist using the system needs to adapt to the use of a "fuzzy measurement system" in describing his microscopical findings.

Map dependant factors were the lack of specific knowledge of some units i.e. the presence of best knowledge of Schawonoma, ectopic pinealoma and plexus papilloma on one unit and of course the fact that two tumours were not found in the labeled representation of the map. One of the reasons of this problem might be found in the fact that the present parameter space is not sufficient in order to differentiate these tumours. On the other hand further studies indicate that optimising the learning parameters in our algorithm might be usefull to avoid these difficulties.

Reliable Memory from Unreliable Components

P. Whittle

ABSTRACT

We return to the antiphon structure considered in earlier papers, and present exact results for its memory capacity. However, for this structure it is supposed that one set of nodes (the α-nodes) behaves reliably and can realise a perfect cut-off. We consider the effect of relaxing this unrealistic assumption.

1. CAPACITY RESULTS FOR THE ANTIPHON

We consider the antiphon structure proposed in Whittle (1989a, 1989b). This was based on the analogy of circulating a message around a noisy communication loop, and functioned by reverberating a pattern of excitation between two sets of nodes. There are M α-nodes and N β-nodes, denoted respectively by α_j and β_k ($j = 1, 2, \ldots, M$; $k = 1, 2, \ldots, N$). At time t the α-nodes hold a pattern $\xi(t) = (\xi_j(t))$ where the elements $\xi_j(t)$ adopt values 0 or 1; these patterns are the possible memory values. The node β_k receives an input

$$u_k(t) = \sum_j \xi_j(t) c_{jk} \tag{1}$$

where c_{jk} is the capacity of the arc between α_j and β_k, assumed to be 0 or 1. The β-node is the unreliable elements; β_k yields an output y_k with probability distribution

$$P(y_k(t) = y | u_k(t) = u) = p(y|u) \tag{2}$$

independent for different k conditional on the inputs u. From these outputs an input

$$x_j(t+1) = \sum_k c_{jk} y_k(t) \tag{3}$$

is formed, which is then normalised to

$$\xi_j(t+1) = f(x_j(t+1)) \tag{4}$$

where $f(x)$ is a threshold response function, taking values 0 or 1 according as x is less than or not less than a threshold value h.

The antiphon allows several interpretations. As well as its motivating interpretation of a closed communication loop, it reduces to the deterministic Hopfield net in the deterministic case $p(y|u) = \delta_{yu}$. This is a welcome indication that proposals made from very different starting points seem to lead to very similar structures, and so afford a degree of mutual confirmation. Note, however, that the stochastic antiphon model formulated above is rather different to the other stochasticisation of the Hopfield net: the spinglass model.

We shall take N, the number of unreliable elements, as defining the *size* of the system. Let us define the error probability ϵ as $P(\xi(t+1) \neq \xi(t))$, this taking account of the randomness of the network (c_{jk}) as well as of the β-output y. We shall say that a given mode of operation is *reliable* if $\epsilon \to 0$ as $N \to \infty$. Suppose this procedure distinguishes $R(N)$ memory values for a system of size N, and so has a memory size of $\log R(N)$ nats. We shall say the system stores information at *rate* K if $(1/N) \log R(N) \to K$ as $N \to \infty$; the *capacity* of the system is the supremum of reliable rates.

Capacities are evaluated over a class of random networks. We suppose that the c_{jk} independently take values 0 and 1 with probabilities $\phi = 1 - \theta$ and θ. Let $C(s, \theta)$ be the capacity for a given value of θ under s-fold excitation, so that the possible memory traces correspond to configurations in which exactly s of the ξ-components are non-zero. Define

$$\bar{p}_i(y) = \sum_u \binom{s-1}{u} \phi^{s-u-1}\theta^u p(y|u+i), \quad \bar{p}(y) = \sum_u \binom{s}{u}\phi^{s-u}\theta^u p(y|u).$$

Then it is shown in Whittle (1990a) that

$$C(s, \theta) = s \sup_{z \geq 1} \sum_y [\theta \bar{p}_1(y)\log z - \bar{p}(y)\log(\phi + \theta z^y)]. \tag{5}$$

The derivation of this result is interesting, in that one must appeal to large deviation theory. In the binary case, when y takes only the values 0 or 1, (5) reduces to

$$C(s, \theta) = s(-\bar{p}\log\bar{p} + \phi\bar{p}_0\log\bar{p}_0 + \theta\bar{p}_1\log\bar{p}_1) \tag{6}$$

where $\bar{p} = 1 - \bar{q} = \bar{p}(1)$, etc.

Suppose that, instead of the antiphon decoding rules (3) and (4), one used optimal inference methods on the 'observations' y to estimate ξ. It is shown in Whittle (1990b) that the capacity evaluation corresponding to (5) then becomes

$$C'(s, \theta) = H[\bar{p}(\cdot)] - \sum_u \binom{s}{u}\phi^{s-u}\theta^u H[p(\cdot|u)] \tag{7}$$

where $H[p(\cdot)]$ is the Shannon information $-\sum_y p(y)\log p(y)$ associated with a distribution $p(\cdot)$.

Comparison of (5) and (7) is most striking in the binary case with $s = 1$, when we have

$$C(1, \theta) = -\bar{p}\log\bar{p} + \phi p_0\log p_0 + \theta p_1\log p_1 \tag{8}$$
$$C'(1, \theta) = C(1, \theta) - \bar{q}\log\bar{q} + \phi q_0\log q_0 + \theta q_1\log q_1. \tag{9}$$

The effect of antiphon decoding is then to strip all the q-terms from (9), leaving only the p-terms (8).

These capacities are all realised with M exponentially large in N. However, by letting θ and s vary with N appropriately (θ of order s^{-1} and s of order $N/(\log N)$) it is possible to achieve positive capacity with M of order N. Details are given in Whittle (1990a).

2. THE EFFECT OF TOTAL UNRELIABILITY

If the intention of the investigation is to see how an assembly of unreliable elements can be made to achieve reliable operation at a positive rate per element, then there is one unacceptable feature in the antiphon model. This is the assumption that the unreliability is confined to the β-nodes, and that the α-nodes not merely behave reliably, but can also realise the perfect cut-off of the threshold function $f(\cdot)$. One sees how this assumption came about: the α-nodes represent the phase of hypothesis-testing in the operation of the device, when an effective test is being performed for which memory traces are active. In general, one has a dilemma with unreliable systems: if they are *totally* unreliable, how can any output which has been reduced to a few figures (e.g. a 'yes/no' output) be reliable? However, if we disregard this point, and require merely that the system have clear metastable regimes ('memory states') despite unreliability of all components, then we certainly need to realise the function of the α-nodes and their threshold operation from unreliable elements.

Note that an α-node and the set of β-nodes to which it is connected constitute a bistable unit, which can either be excited or unexcited. It can thus store one bit of information. The more β-nodes associated with a given α-node, the more reliably is this information stored. Economy forces the different α-nodes to share their β-nodes, and the capacity results deduced for the antiphon show that this sharing can be compatible with reliability if the parameters of the structure are chosen appropriately.

Suppose that one has as element for one's structure only one type of stochastic 'neuron', whose output (a stream of pulses of excitation) is, stochastically, a sigmoid function of its input. Such behaviour can readily be realised by a simple and natural model; see Whittle (1990c). An assembly of such neurons which incorporates feedback, in that a proportion of neuron outputs is led, by random paths, to provide inputs for other neurons of the assembly, also shows bistable behaviour. That is, its distribution of total excitation shows two peaks, at levels of low and high excitation. The larger the assembly, the more distinct these two peaks, and so the more reliably will the assembly store an information-bit.

Again, if one has M such assemblies (and so the possibility of storing M bits of information) then one must achieve economy by sharing neurons between the assemblies. However, one now encounters a difficulty not arising previously. In the case of the antiphon, the hard nature of the cut-off function meant that unexcited assemblies had zero output. The only 'background noise' that a given assembly suffered was thus from the excited assemblies, and this could be kept tolerable if not too many assemblies were excited.

However, in the totally unreliable alternative we now consider, the effective cut-off function is 'soft', so that even unexcited assemblies have an output. While this output is small, there are many unexcited assemblies, and the total background noise thus generated is seriously disturbing to any given assembly. The outcome is, that for a system of N neurons it seems possible to store reliably only $O(N/\log N)$ bits of information rather than $O(N)$.

It is possible that $O(N)$ behaviour can be restored by the appropriate use of inhibition as well as excitation; work continues on this point.

ACKNOWLEDGEMENT

This work was carried out during the author's tenure of a Science and Engineering Research Council Senior Fellowship.

REFERENCES

1. Whittle P. The antiphon: a device for reliable memory from unreliable components. Proc Roy Soc A 1989; 423:201-218.

2. Whittle P. The achievement of memory by an antiphon structure. In: Taylor, JG and Mannion CLT (eds) New developments in neural computing. Adam Hilger, Bristol New York, 1989, pp 119-124.

3. Whittle P. The antiphon. II: The exact evaluation of memory capacity. To appear Proc Roy Soc A (1990a).

4. Whittle P. Neural nets and implicit inference. Submitted Ann Appl Prob (1990b).

5. Whittle P. A stochastic model of an artificial neuron. Submitted J Appl Prob (1990c).

POSSIBLE STRATEGIES FOR USING SLEEP TO IMPROVE EPISODIC MEMORY IN THE FACE OF OVERLAP

A.R. Gardner-Medwin. Department of Physiology, University College London, Gower Street, London WC1E 6BT, UK & The Physiological Laboratory, Cambridge CB2 3EG, UK

It is not known what biological benefits may derive from information handling during sleep. Several facts about sleep suggest that information handling does take place, in different fashions in the two principal phases of sleep ('Slow Wave' and 'Paradoxical' or 'Rapid Eye Movement' (REM) Sleep). This paper seeks to identify benefits that could arise from such 'off-line' information processing, in relation to one of the simpler, but neurally potentially important, forms of memory: auto-association. One of the interesting outcomes is that the constraints of the theory lead naturally to an algorithm that requires two stages for its implementation, resembling in some respects the two phases of sleep [1].

In both phases of sleep the nervous system is cut off from its sensory and motor systems. Bizarre forms of recall and lines of thought take place, often driven substantially by association. Memory is poor. Activity and internal experiences during sleep can be remembered in some detail, especially on immediate rehearsal after awakening from REM sleep. Nevertheless, memory performance is in no way comparable to what it would be like for similarly unusual, vivid and often emotionally charged experiences in waking life. Physiological evidence indicates synchronous fluctuations of threshold in cortical neurons during Slow Wave Sleep, and activity in the visual pathway during Paradoxical Sleep that arises from the brainstem rather than from the eyes, so-called 'PGO' waves.

Theoretical approaches to the handling of information by neural networks may be able to prompt testable suggestions about benefits from information processing during sleep. Several suggestions already exist in the literature, either arising within specific theoretical models [e.g. 2] or within a more general theoretical framework [3,4]. The approach adopted here is to examine one of the simpler types of memory (auto-association) as rigorously and quantitatively as possible, and to see how algorithms can be applied to relax the constraints that normally would limit performance. Such processing might or might not require the isolation and the poor memory registration that are characteristic of sleep. As it turns out, not only are both these features necessary for some of the major benefits, but also a separation of the algorithm into two interdependent phases seems to be required, with possibly significant similarities to the two phases of sleep. This is consistent with the thesis of Giuditta [5], who argues that hypotheses about sleep function should take account of the interdependence of two sleep phases.

Auto-Association

Auto-association is the development of strong excitatory interactions within a population of nodes, between nodes that have been active together. It permits previously active patterns to be re-elicited on presentation of a subset of the active nodes or a set resembling the previously active set. It is not obvious that it should always be desirable to 'complete' previously experienced patterns in a neural system in this way. Early in a sensory pathway it is probably not desirable to do so. At higher perceptual levels completion seems to be a part of gestalt perception, in relation to which auto-association was probably first proposed as a neural mechanism [6]. Triggered evocation of episodic memory is commonplace in human memory, where it is usually beneficial but may sometimes cause trouble (as for example with victims of horrific experiences). Performance in this area of 'content-addressable memory' is one of the skills at which the human brain seems to excel.

Auto-association can be implemented with a Hebbian modification rule [7, 8], rules involving decreases as well as increases of weights [9, 10] or rules involving both positive and negative activity parameters and weights [11]. Only the first and simplest rule is considered in this article. The same issues in relation to overlap and confusion will arise, at least qualitatively, with any strategy for episodic recall. Therefore it is at least plausible that the principles that arise in the present analysis may have application in more complex settings with other primary algorithms.

In some respects auto-association can be treated analytically as a special case of 'cross-association', in which connections are strengthened between active cells in two separate populations [7]. Unlike cross-association however, auto-association can be carried out iteratively to improve performance by growing full patterns from a seed [8, 12]. This has been termed 'progressive' recall, requiring careful management of neural thresholds by recurrent inhibition [8]. Auto-associative storage can also be used to provide a measure of the familiarity of a pattern: a form of 'recognition' memory [1].

Auto-association permits storage and retrieval of the content of a pattern, after what may be simply a one-trial learning situation. Episodic memory requires such an algorithm: it is the features that are specific to a particular, possibly unique, experience that are important. The identification of features that may commonly be grouped together within patterns (adaptive recoding), or that correlate with external signals (classification learning), are different forms of memory requiring, by definition, presentations of many related patterns (often many times over). These are equally important forms of learning, but they are not considered here. It is envisaged that auto-associative learning of pattern content may contribute to the plasticity of the nervous system at each of many levels of representation (Fig. 1). The projections for recoding and classifying patterns, for seeding the content of patterns at higher levels, and for 'top-down' influences (hatched arrows in Fig. 1) will be subject to their own plasticity according to separate algorithms.

Auto-associative memory employing the Hebb conjunctive rule [6] (i.e. strengthening that occurs when a synapse is active in a situation in which its activity contributes to the firing of a postsynaptic neuron) is subject to two broad constraints. If M patterns are to be learned on N cells, each comprising activity in a fraction α of the neurons, then to avoid serious saturation effects the relation:

$$\alpha \ <\approx \ 1/\sqrt{M} \qquad\qquad (1)$$

must hold [7]. It is not necessary for each cell to be connected to every other cell, and in general if the number of connections per cell is R, the relation

$$\alpha R \ \approx \ 30 \qquad\qquad (2)$$

must hold for a good compromise of performance and efficiency. The quantity αR is the mean number of inputs received by individual cells in an active pattern from the other active cells in the pattern. The critical value of order 30 arises because the mean number of inputs must be large enough to ensure that on the basis of a Poisson distribution the actual number is not only reliably non-zero, but reliably greater than the number of inputs onto a typical spurious cell, which is a Poisson variable typically around $0.5\alpha R$ at saturation. If αR greatly exceeds 30, then there is unnecessary redundancy in the connections and the efficiency (i.e. the information capable of being stored and recovered per synapse) is less than maximum [8].

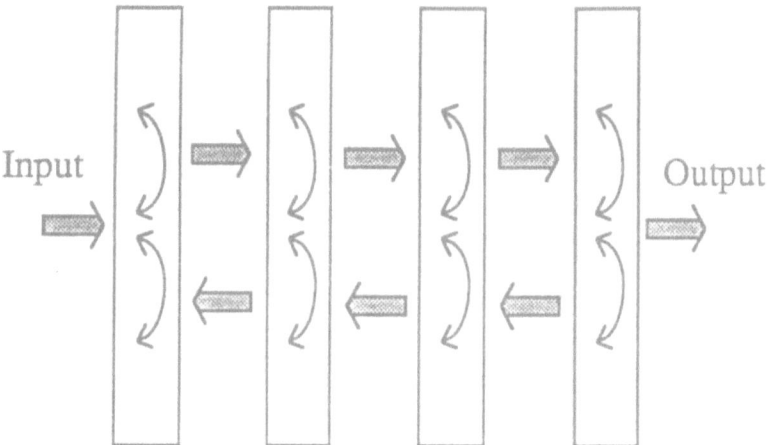

Fig. 1. Schematic representation of the nervous system. Shaded arrows are forward and backward projections reponsible for recoding, pattern classification (feature detection) and for the seeding of learned output patterns. Line arrows are auto-associative connections responsible for completion and correction of the content of patterns experienced at each level of representation.

It follows from Equation (1) that storage of a large number of patterns in these models requires that the patterns be coded into a sparse representation, with a low activity ratio α. Examples of statistics of patterns with different activity ratios and essentially the same information content are given in Table I. In principle it is possible to recode information reversibly from one such form to another, and indeed at early stages in visual processing there are known mechanisms that have the effect of reducing activity ratios (e.g. lateral inhibition, feature detection).

It follows from Equation (2) that in large networks storing patterns with a substantial information content (>>30 active cells per pattern), the optimal number of connections of any one cell can be substantially less than the number of cells (R<<N). Thus an efficient large auto-associative network in general requires both sparse coding (α<<1) and sparse connectivity (R/N <<1). Both conditions are plausibly realistic in relation to what is known about at least some parts of the cerebral cortex [8].

Table 1. Representation of information at different activity ratios (α). The same amount of information (100 ±5 bits) is required to specify each pattern of W active cells from a total of N. The information content is calculated on the basis of two slightly different assumptions: I_1 is for uniform independent probabilities α, giving rise to W as an expectation value: $I_1 = -N(\alpha \log_2(\alpha) - (1-\alpha)\log_2(1-\alpha))$. I_2 is calculated for fixed (integer) values of W (= αN) giving rise to probabilities of activation (α) that are not strictly independent: $I_2 = \log_2(N!/(W!(N-W)!))$. I_1 and I_2 differ by at most 4% over the indicated range.

No. Cells	No. Active	Activity Ratio	Information Content	
N	W	α	I_1	I_2
100	50	0.5	100	96
200	22	0.11	100	97
400	17	0.0425	101	98
1000	13	0.013	100	97
2000	11	0.0055	98	95
4000	10	0.0025	101	98
10000	9	0.0009	104	101

The overlap problem

Auto-association provides an algorithm for one-trial storage of patterns. The statistical constraints and handling techniques for sparsely connected nets have been analysed [8] and simulated [1] for simple situations. One of the fundamental limitations on performance arises through overlap between stored patterns (i.e the existence of active elements that are common to two or more patterns). This is illustrated in Fig. 2. The result of overlap is that recall of a pattern P_1 readily leads to activation of elements that do not belong to P_1, but are part of an overlapping pattern P_2. These are called 'intrusion' errors. The recalled pattern can readily become some sort of hybrid or intermediate between P_1 and P_2, even though the disparate elements of P_1 and P_2 may never have been experienced together.

In other contexts, the behaviour of neural networks in response to overlapping patterns can be an advantage. In classification tasks, a closely related phenomenon is that of generalisation, whereby learned responses can transfer to patterns that have never been experienced, but are similar to (i.e. overlap with) ones experienced in the training set.

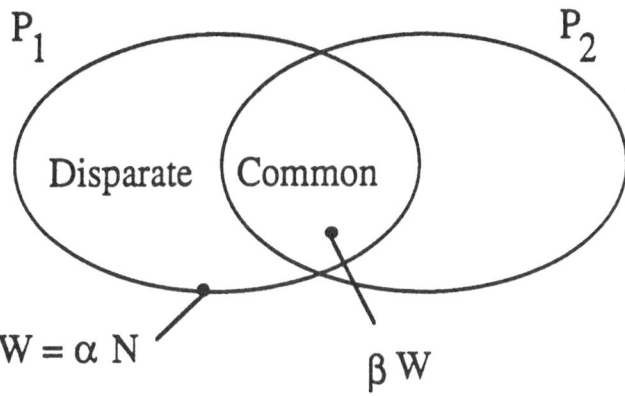

Fig.2. Patterns P_1 and P_2 each consist of W active cells with an overlap fraction ß. The cells active in P_1 and P_2 fall into categories called common and disparate, with the latter comprising cells that are specific to P_1 and specific to P_2.

When the task is to recall and re-evoke an experienced pattern, the consequences of overlap are often undesirable. Note that this is an observation about the way in which recall memory is used, not about the fundamental statistical issues underlying what one may variously call intrusion errors or generalisation. For example, if one visits the Georgian city of Bath, and then tries to recall details of a particular building in Bath, one may generate a sketch that is useless as a representation of the specific prompted building because of numerous intrusion errors from other buildings. It might nevertheless encapsulate the spirit of Georgian architecture even better than any single building might have done. The problem of overlap arises specifically where recall memory is used in an episodic fashion, to identify details of a specific episode or pattern. To pursue the example, it is useless, and indeed positively confusing, to have picked up a general appreciation of the preferred symmetry of Georgian architecture if one is trying to direct someone how to enter a building that happens to have its entrance on the left.

Given that intrusion errors from overlap are a problem in episodic memory, how can one reduce these errors? There are at least three distinct strategies:
1. It may be possible to use classification and pattern recognition techniques at a higher level of representation to identify probable or improbable combinations of elements in the recall of P_1 or P_2. For example, in the illustration, one might use knowledge of the general constraints on the positioning of building entrances.
2. It may be possible to reduce overlap in the representation. In episodic memory, after initial learning, it is too late to reduce overlap in the primary engram. Two things can happen, however:
i) Current experience may lead to alterations in the representation of future inputs so as to reduce overlap for these inputs. For example, once one has learned to classify the stereotypes of Georgian architecture one may on future occasions be able to represent new buildings in terms of combinations of these stereotypes and particular

departures from them. This is a form of 'feature detection', through which inputs may be represented with minimum use of information channels (minimum entropy coding [13]).

ii) It may be possible to generate recoded versions of the current patterns P_1 and P_2 with less overlap. For example, by surmising (either correctly or incorrectly) that minor differences in building style relate to different periods or different personalities, it may be possible to build up coherent networks of associations containing P_1 and P_2 with less overlap. Such a strategy has both benefits and risks: it may reduce intrusion errors due to overlap between P_1 and P_2 while generating errors due to the specific form of recoding.

3. It may be possible to adjust the relative weights of associations between elements of P_1 and P_2 to reduce the effects of the overlap.

Strategies 2ii and 3 both require that episodic memories be held in a temporary robust form that allows algorithms for reducing effects of overlap to operate. The potential for performing such operations is just one of the benefits that can arise from having temporary as well as long term (LT) memory stores with flexible consolidation processes for transfer from one to the other [1]. Strategy 3 is developed here because it is prima facie the simplest, and need relate only to the current representation and to a single, potentially homogeneous, set of cells.

Strategies for adjusting relative weights to reduce the overlap problem

Within a pair of overlapping patterns there are two distinct categories of cells described as 'common' (c) and 'disparate' (d). Between these cells there are 4 categories of associative connection that contribute to recall performance on P_1 and/or P_2 (c→c, c→d, d→c, d→d). Each has its own significance in relation to the overlap problem. Before discussing them individually, it is helpful to consider briefly the dynamics of recall in the face of overlap.

If recall is prompted by activation of a seed of active cells specific to P_1, then iterative recall may lead to recruitment of other cells specific to P_1, common cells, incorrect cells specific to P_2 (intrusion errors), and possibly spurious cells present in neither P_1 nor P_2. There are actually two inter-related problems arising from overlap:

1. If we suppose that P_1 has been successfully recalled with near total accuracy, then the mean excitation onto specific P_2 cells (from the common cells) may be nearly as great, with substantial overlap, as the mean excitation onto P_1 cells. The statistical separation of the excitation onto the two categories is poor because of the overlap, and intrusion errors are likely. It is the relative strength of d→d and c→d connections that is relevant in this situation. Improvements can be made if the d→d connections can be strengthened relative to c→d.

2. The second problem arises earlier in the progressive recall process. If the common cells are relatively numerous within P_1, then both by simple probability and by virtue of the strong interactive support that they provide for each other once activated, common cells will tend to be recruited in early iterations of the recall process. This contributes to the excitation of P_2 cells as well as P_1 and diminishes the statistical weighting in favour of recruitment of P_1 rather than P_2 that existed at the start by virtue

of the specific seed from P_1. To reduce the preference for early recall of common cells it is necessary to increase the strength of d→d connections relative to d→c and c→c connections.

The identified changes of relative connection strengths can be achieved for problem (1) either by increasing d→d weights or by reducing c→d. For problem (2) it is necessary to increase d→d weights or reduce d→c and/or c→c. The adjustment that helps with both aspects of the overlap problem is to increase the strength of d→d connections [1]. An alternative strategy proposed for helping with an analogous problem, that of too ready elicitation of spurious 'parasitic' states due to densely interconnected nodes in a network, is to decrease the strength of c→c connections [3]. In the present context this strategy diminishes the early recruitment of common cells, but fails to help with the problem of eliminating intrusion errors once recall is nearly complete.

To change the weights of a particular category of connections it is necessary somehow to identify these connections within the network. It is possible to identify the c→c connections by activating solely the c cells (which tend to be the most readily activated cells [3]). There is no such simple way of identifying directly the d→d connections in order to strengthen them. A two stage algorithm has been proposed, however, which achieves this automatically after storage of pairs of overlapping patterns [1].

In simulations the algorithm for d→d strengthening has been shown to have both of the desired effects: increase of stability of correctly recalled patterns with fewer intrusion errors, and early recall of the specifically correct cells in preference to the common cells. The average quality of recall elicited from a seed was increased substantially (Fig.3).

Implementation of this algorithm in a neural structure would require two stages in sequence, with a carry over of some form of temporary 'fatigue' within cells that are strongly activated in Stage 1 (which would be largely the 'common' cells) to Stage 2. Such a carry over of fatigue between the two phases of sleep is not known, but has probably never been sought experimentally.

Some of the other conditions necessary for implementation of the algorithm bear quite strong resemblances to known facts about sleep. For example, the first stage requires large threshold swings to activate firstly the hybrid union of cells that are within P_1 or P_2, then the common cells that recieve greatest excitation from this hybrid pattern. It is essential that memory traces should not be laid down for the hybrid patterns experienced at this time, since this would lead to associations between the disparate cells of P_1 and P_2 that would simply compound the problem of intrusion errors. Stage 2 (cf. Paradoxical Sleep) must always follow Stage 1 and requires recall from random seeds subject to the tight threshold control that is characteristic of normal recall (as presumably employed during waking). This ensures that coherent sets of disparate cells are activated together to permit enhanced strengthening of the d→d weights. Though there are striking parallels in these requirements to known facts about sleep, such parallels can be no more than suggestive of a true relation between the proposed optimisation procedure and sleep.

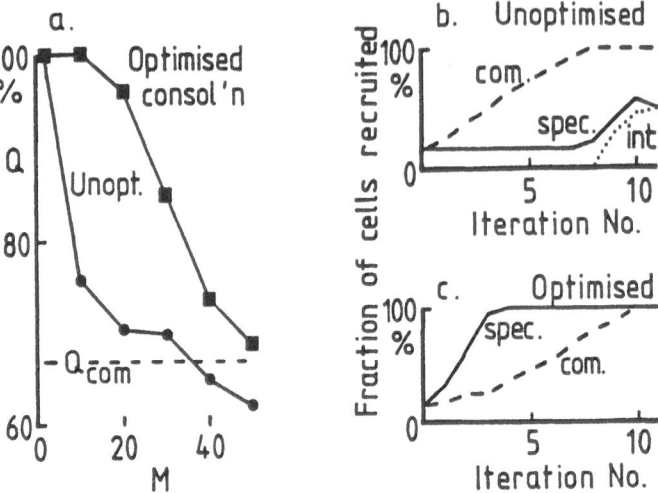

Fig.3. The effect on recall of overlapping patterns, of an algorithm for increasing d→d weights. Patterns were learned in pairs with overlap fraction ß=0.74 (Fig.2). (a) Quality of recall quality with and without the optimising algorithm. Q_{com}=quality corresponding to correct recall of common cells, with chance levels of discrimination between specifically correct cells and intrusion errors. M=number of learned patterns. (b,c) Recruitment sequence for common cells (com), specifically correct cells (spec) and intrusion errors (int) during iterative recall without (b) and with (c) the optimising algorithm. Simulation data from [1].

The advantages derived from specific strengthening of d→d connections can to some extent be analysed analytically rather than by simulation. An expression can be derived for the signal to noise ratio 't' for discrimination between excitation onto specific P_1 and specific P_2 cells once P_1 is correctly recalled. 't' is defined as the ratio of the difference between the mean excitation onto the two types of cells, to the sum of the standard deviations for the excitation onto the two types. A value t=2, for example, permits a threshold to be set between the two levels so as to give approximately 2.5% false positive and false negative rates. For a sparsely connected net with a fraction f of its synapses having been modified, an overlap fraction ß between a pair of patterns, and enhancement of d→d connections by a factor θ, the signal to noise ratio is given by:

$$t = \sqrt{(\alpha R)}\ (1\text{-}ß)\ (\theta\text{-}f)\ /\ \{\ \sqrt{(ß+\theta^2(1\text{-}ß))} + \sqrt{(ß+f(1\text{-}ß))}\ \}\ \qquad (3)$$

For ß=f=0.5, this gives t=0.13$\sqrt{(\alpha R)}$ for θ=1, t=0.31$\sqrt{(\alpha R)}$ for θ=2 and t=0.71$\sqrt{(\alpha R)}$ for θ→∞. This analysis assumes that enhancements of d→d connections for an overlapping pair of patterns are made on a background of uniform connection strengths for all the other synapses in the network at which modification conditions have been met. Much of the maximum benefit derived from arbitrarily large increases of d→d weights is obtained with θ=2.

There is a cost associated with increasing θ too far. The heavily weighted synapses affect adversely the performance in other recall situations, where their weight is inappropriate. Fig. 4 shows the results of analysis in which such effects are seen in the signal-noise ratio for different aspects of recall of a paired pattern. The entire experience of the network in this case has consisted of pairs of patterns with overlap fraction ß=0.5. All connections that have at some time in the net's experience been d→d connections (in this case a fraction 0.36 of those that have been modified generally) are taken to have a strength θ relative to the other modified synapses.

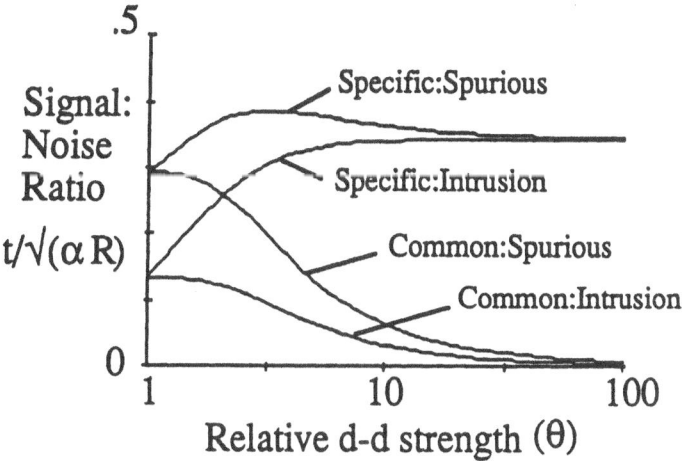

Fig. 4. Effect of enhancement of connections between cells in the disparate parts of overlapping patterns. The ordinate is the signal-noise ratio (in units of √αR) for discrimination between each of the two categories of correct cells (disparate and common) and each of the two categories of incorrect cells (intrusion errors from P_2 and spurious cells not part of P_1 or P_2). The abscissa is the factor θ by which d→d connections have been enhanced. Conditions are f=ß=0.5 as described in the text, and it is assumed that the entire experience of the net consists of pairs of patterns with equal overlap ß between pairs.

It can be seen in Fig.4 that the signal-noise ratio for the common cells falls with increasing θ throughout the range. For θ>≈3 it falls also for excitation of the disparate P_1 cells compared to spurious recruits. The signal-noise ratio for recruitment of the specific P_1 cells against intrusion errors rises continuously with θ. A reasonable compromise under these conditions would be achieved with θ=2-3: there are then substantial gains in the rejection of intrusion errors and relatively little loss in the signal-noise ratio for common cells. Precise optimisation would have to depend on the relative costs of errors associated with the different categories of cells.

Conclusion

It is possible to identify strategies for improving performance in auto-association through application of algorithms operating after the initial learning. In this way it may be possible to reduce confusions and intrusion errors resulting from overlap between similar patterns stored in episodic memory. Some of the potential improvements for a specific algorithm have been quantified by both analysis and simulation. The conditions that would be necessary for implementing such an algorithm neuronally are quite constrained and raise unresolved issues in relation to the experimental study of sleep.

Acknowledgement

I thank Horace Barlow, Graeme Mitchison and Peter Foldiak for comments on the ms.

References

1. Gardner-Medwin AR. Doubly modifiable synapses: a model of short and long term auto-associative memory. Proc Roy Soc Lond B 1989; 238:137-154

2. Marr D. A theory for cerebral neocortex. Proc Roy Soc Lond B 1970; 176: 161-234

3. Crick F, Mitchison G. The function of dream sleep. Nature, Lond 1983; 304: 111-114

4. Gardner-Medwin AR. Modifiable synapses necessary for learning. Nature, Lond 1969; 223: 916-918

5. Giuditta A. A sequential hypothesis for the function of sleep. In: Koella WP, Ruther E, Schulz H (ed.) Sleep '84. Gustav Fischer, Stuttgart, 1985

6. Hebb DO. The organization of behaviour. Wiley, New York, 1949

7. Willshaw DJ, Buneman OP, Longuet-Higgins HC. Non-holographic associative memory. Nature, Lond 1969; 222: 960-962

8. Gardner-Medwin AR. The recall of events through the learning of associations between their parts. Proc Roy Soc Lond B 1976; 194:375-402

9. Palm G. Local synaptic rules with maximal information storage capacity. In: Haken H. (ed) Neural and synergetic computers, Springer, Berlin, 1988

10. Willshaw D, Dayan P. Optimal plasticity from matrix memories: what goes up must come down. 1990; Neural Computation In Press

11. Hopfield JJ. Neural networks and physical systems with emergent computational abilities. Proc Natl Acad Sci USA 1982; 79:2554-2558

12. Lansner A, Ekeberg O. Reliability and speed of recall in an associative network. IEEE Trans. PAMI 1985; 7: 490-498

13. Barlow HB, Kaushal TP, Mitchison GJ. Finding minimum entropy codes. Neural Computation 1989; 1: 412-423

Curvature-Driven Smoothing in Backpropagation Neural Networks

C M Bishop

Abstract

The standard backpropagation learning algorithm for feedforward networks aims to minimise the mean square error defined over a set of training data. This form of error measure can lead to the problem of over-fitting in which the network stores individual data points from the training set, but fails to generalise satisfactorily for new data points. In this paper we propose a modified error measure which can reduce the tendency to over-fit and whose properties can be controlled by a single scalar parameter. The new error measure depends both on the function generated by the network and on its derivatives. A new learning algorithm is derived which can be used to minimise such error measures.

Acknowledgements

The author would like to thank I F Croall, K D Horton and I G D Strachan for a number of useful discussions relating to this work.

1 Introduction

Feed-forward neural networks, trained by error backpropagation, form one of the most widely used neural network architectures. If the network has hidden neurons, and non-linear activation functions, it can generate a large class of non-linear continuous mappings between multidimensional spaces (Funahashi, 1989; Hornik et al., 1989). The standard learning algorithm (Rumelhart et al., 1986) minimises an error measure which is the sum, over a set of training data, of the squares of errors for the output neurons. This form of error measure can lead to the problem of over-fitting of the data (sometimes called over-generalisation), in which the network 'stores' individual data points, but fails to generalise satisfactorily for inputs not included in the training set. An analogous problem arises when curve-fitting using high order polynomials (Tikhonov and Arsenin, 1977; Denker et al, 1987). Again, this problem is related to the minimisation of a mean-square error measure.

One approach for reducing this effect is to include a sufficiently large number of examples in the training set. This may not always be practical, however, particularly for problems with many degrees of freedom.

A closely related issue concerns the number of neurons in the network. The number of input and output neurons is generally determined by the dimensionality of the data itself. However, there exists no satisfactory theoretical basis for determining the number of hidden units, which must often be decided by trial and error. If the network has too few hidden neurons, the class of functions which it can generate is too restricted and it is unable to achieve the desired accuracy. Increasing the number of hidden neurons can, however, lead to the problem of over-fitting.

In this paper we propose the use of a modified error measure designed to reduce the tendency to over-fit, even for a network with many hidden neurons. To minimise this error measure a new learning algorthim is derived which generalises the standard back-propagation procedure. The modified error measure is described in section 2, and the learning algorithm is derived in section 3. Finally some conclusions are presented in section 4.

2 Curvature-Driven Smoothing

To begin with, consider mappings of a single variable x to a single variable y, so that the network has one input and one output neuron. The network has a feed-forward architecture in which each neuron generates a non-linear function of the weighted sum of its inputs:

$$z_i = f(\sum_j w_{ij} z_j),$$ (1)

where z_j is the activation of the jth neuron, w_{ij} is the connection weight between neurons i and j, and the function f is taken to be the standard sigmoid:

$$f(z) \equiv \frac{1}{1 + e^{-z}}.$$ (2)

There also exists a threshold for each neuron. Since, however, these are equivalent to weights from an extra neuron whose output is permanently set to +1, they are contained in the formalism of Eq.(1) and we need consider them no further. By construction, the function $y(x)$ will be continuous, single-valued and differentiable.

Suppose we have a set of data points $\{x_p, t_p\}$, $p = 1, ..., P$, where t_p is the target value for y corresponding to $x = x_p$. The standard learning algorithm minimises the error measure

$$E^S = \frac{1}{2} \sum_{\{p\}} (y_p - t_p)^2$$ (3)

where $y_p = y(x_p)$. The use of this error measure can result in the network function $y(x)$ over-fitting the data points, as shown schematically in Figure 1. We now seek to modify the error measure so as to generate smoother functions $y(x)$, as indicated in Figure 2. To achieve this we add to the standard error measure a regularising term which depends on the geometrical properties of the network function $y(x)$:

$$E = E^S + \lambda E^C$$ (4)

$$E^C = \frac{1}{2} \int_a^b \kappa^2 dx$$ (5)

where κ is the curvature of the line $y = y(x)$, and the interval (a, b) spans the range of values of $\{x_p\}$. Smoother curves will have a small value of E^C for a given internal (a, b). Note the use of κ^2 in Eq.(5) rather than κ, since κ carries a sign. Similar regularising functions have been discussed in the context of curve-fitting (Tikhonov and Arsenin, 1977; Denker et al., 1987). In terms of the network function $y(x)$ we can write (Korn and Korn, 1968)

$$E^C = \frac{1}{2} \int_a^b \frac{(y'')^2}{[1 + (y')^2]^3} dx$$ (6)

where primes denote d/dx. We now replace the integral in Eq.(6) by a sum over a discrete set of points $\{x_n\}$

$$E^C = \frac{1}{2} \sum_{\{n\}} \frac{(y_n'')^2}{[1 + (y_n')^2]^3} \Delta x_n \qquad (7)$$

where $y_n = y(x_n)$, and $\Delta x_n = x_n - x_{n-1}$. It will often be convenient to choose the points $\{x_n\}$ to coincide with the $\{x_p\}$ since this will make use of values for the neuron activations which need to be calculated anyway for the minimisation of E^S. If, however, the data points are too sparse in some regions for sufficient accuracy to be obtained, it is straightforward to include extra values of x. Equally, it may be acceptable to exclude a proportion of the data points from $\{x_n\}$ and so reduce the training time.

For a network with N input and M output neurons, the curvature term in the error measure can be generalised as follows:

$$E^C = \frac{1}{2} \sum_{i=1}^{N} \sum_{j=1}^{M} \int \kappa_{ij}^2 dx_1 \ldots dx_N, \qquad (8)$$

where $y_j(x_1, ..., x_N)$ is the activation of output neuron j. The curvature of y_j with respect to variations in the input x_i is given by

$$\kappa_{ij}^2 = \frac{(\partial^2 y_j / \partial x_i^2)^2}{\left[1 + (\partial y_j / \partial x_i)^2\right]^3}. \qquad (9)$$

3 Learning Algorithm

The standard mean-square error measure E^S is a function of the synaptic weights w_{ij} through the network function $y(x)$. For a given training set $\{x_p, y_p\}$ the error E^S can be minimised by gradient descent using the backpropagation training algorithm (Rumelhart et al., 1986). The curvature term E^C, however, contains derivatives of $y(x)$ and so the standard backpropagation procedure does not apply. We now derive a generalised form of backpropagation which can be used to minimise error measures containing derivative terms, and which therefore can be applied to the curvature function considered in the previous section.

As usual, the network is trained by gradient descent so that

$$\Delta w_{ij}(m) = -\eta \left(\frac{\partial E^S}{\partial w_{ij}} + \frac{\partial E^C}{\partial w_{ij}} \right) + \mu \Delta w_{ij}(m-1), \tag{10}$$

where m denotes the training step number, η is the learning rate, and μ is the momentum. The derivative $\partial E^S / \partial w_{ij}$ is calculated using the standard backpropagation algorithm. We now seek a procedure for calculating $\partial E^C / \partial w_{ij}$.

From Eq.(7) we have

$$\frac{\partial E^C}{\partial w_{ij}} = \sum_{\{n\}} \left\{ \frac{(y_n'')}{[1 + (y_n')^2]^3} \frac{\partial y_n''}{\partial w_{ij}} - \frac{3(y_n'')^2 y_n'}{[1 + (y_n')^2]^4} \frac{\partial y_n'}{\partial w_{ij}} \right\} \Delta x_n. \tag{11}$$

To calculate the partial derivatives in Eq.(11), we note that w_{ij} and x_n are independent variables, and so we can interchange the order of the derivatives:

$$\frac{\partial}{\partial w_{ij}} \left(\frac{dy}{dx} \right) = \frac{d}{dx} \left(\frac{\partial y}{\partial w_{ij}} \right). \tag{12}$$

We now introduce an 'error' term σ_i for each neuron:

$$\frac{\partial y}{\partial w_{ij}} = \sigma_i z_j, \tag{13}$$

$$\sigma_i = \frac{\partial y}{\partial z_i} z_i (1 - z_i), \tag{14}$$

where we have used Eq.(1) together with the relation

$$f' = f(1 - f). \tag{15}$$

From the chain rule for partial derivatives it follows that

$$\sigma_i = z_i (1 - z_i) \sum_k w_{ki} \sigma_k. \tag{16}$$

Using Eqs.(12) and (13) we can write

$$\frac{\partial y'}{\partial w_{ij}} = z_j \frac{d\sigma_i}{dx} + \sigma_i \frac{dz_j}{dx} \tag{17}$$

where

$$\frac{d\sigma_i}{dx} = z_i(1 - z_i) \sum_k w_{ki} \frac{d\sigma_k}{dx} + (1 - 2z_i) \frac{dz_i}{dx} \sum_k w_{ki} \sigma_k. \tag{18}$$

For the output neuron we have

$$\sigma_o = y(1 - y), \tag{19}$$

$$\frac{d\sigma_o}{dx} = (1 - 2y) \frac{dy}{dx}. \tag{20}$$

The partial derivatives z_i' can be calculated during the forward propagation phase using

$$\frac{dz_i}{dx} = z_i(1 - z_i) \sum_j w_{ij} \frac{dz_j}{dx}, \tag{21}$$

which follows from Eqs.(1) and (15). The quantities σ_i, $d\sigma_i/dx$ can then be found by backpropagation using the recursive formulae of Eqs.(16) and (18).

Analogous results for the second derivatives are easily obtained:

$$\frac{\partial y''}{\partial w_{ij}} = z_j \frac{d^2\sigma_i}{dx^2} + 2\frac{d\sigma_i}{dx}\frac{dz_j}{dx} + \sigma_i \frac{d^2 z_j}{dx^2}, \tag{22}$$

$$\begin{aligned}
\frac{d^2\sigma_i}{dx^2} = {}& z_i(1 - z_i) \sum_k w_{ki} \frac{d^2\sigma_k}{dx^2} \\
& + 2(1 - 2z_i)\frac{dz_i}{dx} \sum_k w_{ki} \frac{d\sigma_k}{dx} \\
& + (1 - 2z_i)\frac{d^2 z_i}{dx^2} \sum_k w_{ki}\sigma_k \\
& - 2\left(\frac{dz_i}{dx}\right)^2 \sum_k w_{ki}\sigma_k,
\end{aligned} \tag{23}$$

$$\frac{d^2\sigma_o}{dx^2} = (1 - 2y)\frac{d^2 y}{dx^2} - 2\left(\frac{dy}{dx}\right)^2, \tag{24}$$

$$\begin{aligned}
\frac{d^2 z_i}{dx^2} = {}& z_i(1 - z_i) \sum_j w_{ij} \frac{d^2 z_j}{dx^2} \\
& + z_i(1 - z_i)(1 - 2z_i)\left(\sum_j w_{ij}\frac{dz_j}{dx}\right)^2.
\end{aligned} \tag{25}$$

We can now summarise the learning algorithm as follows:

(1) Apply inputs $\{x_n\}$ and forward propagate to generate, layer by layer, the neuron activations z_{jn}, y_n using Eqs.(1) and (2), and the various derivatives dz_{jn}/dx_n etc. using Eqs.(21) and (25).

(2) Compute the error for the output neuron using Eqs.(19), (20) and (24) and back-propagate the errors using Eqs.(16), (18) and (23).

(3) Update the weights using Eqs.(10), (11), (17), and (22).

This algorithm readily generalises to networks having several input and ouput neurons, with a corresponding error measure given by Eq.(8), simply by keeping track of the indices labelling each neuron. For each term in the sum in Eq.(8) we have to consider the dependence of the ouput y_j on the input x_i with all other inputs held fixed. The learning algorithm equations derived above can then be applied to the function $y_j(x_i)$. Many of the heuristic procedures which have been developed to speed up conventional backpropagation can also be applied to this algorthim (Cater, 1987; Dahl, 1987; Hush and Salas, 1988; Jacobs, 1988; Stornetta and Huberman, 1987).

4 Summary and Discussion

In this paper we have proposed a new error measure for feed-forward neural networks which is intended to bias the network in favour of smooth solutions and thereby avoid the problem of over-generalisation. A learning algorithm for the minimisation of this error measure has also been described. This algorithm is also applicable to other error measures which are expressible in terms of the (multivariate) network function and its derivatives. For instance, the smoothing functional

$$\tilde{E} = \int \{y^2 + (y')^2\}dx \tag{26}$$

has been found useful in other contexts (Tikhonov and Arsenin, 1977; Farhat and Bai, 1989). In this case the smoothing term contains only first derivatives of $y(x)$, and so the learning algorithm is simplified.

The greater complexity of the learning algorithm described here, compared with the standard backpropagation procedure, will result in a significant increase in training time which in some situations will make this procedure inappropriate. It should be emphasised, however, that one of the great advantages of feed-forward networks, namely their speed of operation once trained, is unaffected. Detailed results from software simulations of networks using this new algorithm will be described in a subsequent publication.

A major outstanding problem with feed-forward networks is the determination of the number of hidden neurons. With the technique described in this paper it should be possible to use a network with a fixed number of neurons and to control the properties of the solution by varying a single scalar parameter λ instead of having to change the network architecture.

References

Cater J P (1987) Successfully Using Peak Learning Rate of 10 (and greater) in Back-propagation Networks with the Heuristic Learning Algorithm. *Proceedings of the IEEE First International Conference on Neural Networks*. San Diego, CA Vol II 645-651.

Dahl E D (1987) Accelerated Learning using the Generalised Delta Rule. *Proceedings of the IEEE First International Conference on Neural Networks*. San Diego, C A Vol II, 523-530.

Denker J, Schwarz D, Wittner B, Solla S, Howard R, Jackel L & Hopfield J (1987) Large Automatic Learning, Rule Extraction and Generalisation *Complex Systems* 1 877-922.

Farhat N H, and Fai, B (1989) Echo Inversion and Target Shape Estimation by Neuro-morphic Processing *Neural Networks* 2 No 2, 117-125.

Funahashi K (1989) On the Approximate Realisation of Continuous Mappings by Neural Networks. *Neural Networks* 2 No 3, 183-192.

Hornik K, Stinchcombe M & White H (1989) Mulitlayer Feedforward Networks are Universal Approxmations *Neural Networks* 2 No 5, 359-366.

Hush D R & Salas J M (1988) Improving the Learning Rate of Backpropagation with the Gradient Reuse Algorithm. *Proceedings of the IEEE International Conference on Neural Networks* San Diego, CA Vol I, 441-446.

Jacobs R A (1988) Increased Rates of Convergence through Learning Rate Adaptation. *Neural Networks* Vol I, No 4 295-307.

Korn G A & Korn T M (1968) *Mathematical Handbook for Scientists and Engineers* 2nd Ed 564.

Rumelhart D E & McClelland J L (1986) *Parallel Distributed Processing: Explorations in the Microstructure of Cognition* Vol 1: Foundations. Cambridge, MA MIT Press.

Stornetta W S & Huberman B A (1987) An Improved Three-Layer, Backpropagation Algorithm *Proceedings of the IEEE First International Conference on Neural Networks*. San Diego, CA Vol II, 637-643.

Tikhonov A N & Arsenin V Y (1977) *Solutions of Ill Posed Problems*. New York, Wiley.

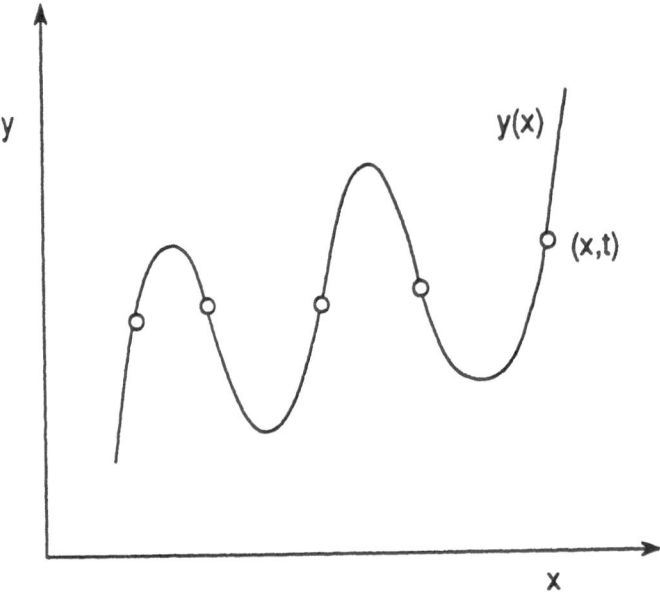

Figure 1. A schematic illustration of a set of data points $\{x_p, t_p\}$, together with an interpolating function $y(x)$ which over-fits the data.

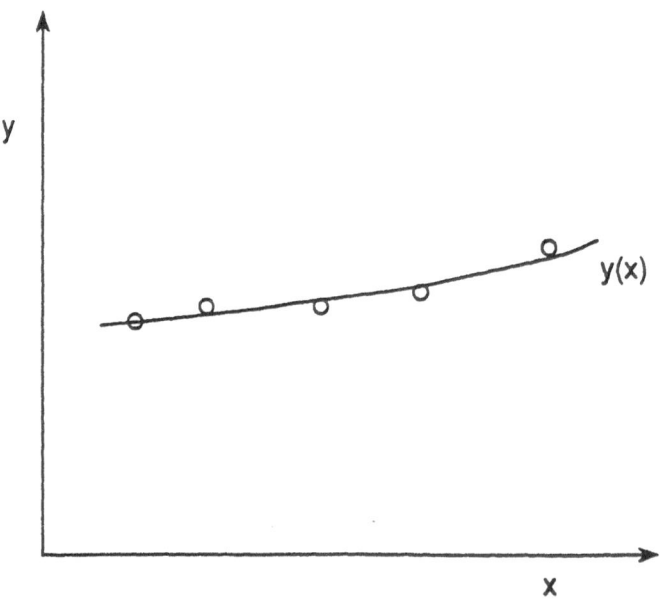

Figure 2. The same data points as in Figure 1, with an interpolating function $y(x)$ which gives a smooth representation of the underlying trend in the data.

A spontaneously growing network for unsupervised learning

Peter Fletcher

ABSTRACT

Connectionist research today is inhibited by two kinds of rigidity. Firstly, a rigidity in architecture: the connectivity of most networks is fixed at the start by the programmer. This limits the universality of learning procedures. Secondly, a mental rigidity: the widespread assumption that a node's activation must be a real number and that activations should be combined using weighted sums. This paper explores the consequences of relaxing these rigidities.

I describe a neural network for unsupervised pattern learning. Given an arbitrary environment of input patterns it grows into a configuration which allows it to represent the high-level regularities in the input. Like the Boltzmann machine, it runs in two phases: observing the environment and simulating the environment. It continually monitors its own performance and grows new nodes as the need for them is identified.

Simulating the environment involves repeatedly choosing states to satisfy many constraints. The usual method is to maximise a "harmony" function, which leads to a merging or blending of constraints: this lacks a clear semantics. My network uses logical inference to settle into a state consistent with as many as possible of the strongest constraints.

INTRODUCTION

The ideal learning algorithm works as follows. Given a collection of elementary processors ("nodes") and a population of input patterns, drawn from a fixed environmental probability distribution (I am not considering temporal patterns), the nodes observe the input patterns and spontaneously arrange themselves into the best configuration for learning the patterns. Most neural networks do not change their own connectivity during learning (two exceptions are [1] and [2]): this means that their learning simply consists of adjusting numerical parameters within a framework set up manually, and is not essentially different from the way a thermostat "learns" to maintain a constant temperature. It seems to me that this evades the real learning problem.

The goal of learning is to extract the "hidden structure" in the input – the "natural" high-level features which allow the input to be described "simply". The notion of a "natural" feature is, of course, philosophically suspect. It could be that what *we* call a "natural" feature is simply a feature which *we* would extract if presented with the patterns. According to this view, order is something we impose on the environment rather than something we discover in it: every learning system is predisposed to spot a certain class of regularities, which it then calls "natural". The alternative view is that an environment objectively contains certain natural features, in terms of which it is best described: e.g., an image is best described in terms of edges and regions. A universal learning system must search for those features, without preconceptions.

It is a long-term goal of my research to clarify this question. At present all I can do is give examples of what I consider natural features, and see how easy it is to devise a learning algorithm which discovers them. Here is a simple example. An input pattern consists of 25 bits, each bit being the activation of a pixel in a 5×5 image. Each image depicts a horizontal line and a vertical line; since each line may be in five possible positions, there are 25 possible patterns, all of which are equally probable. The network has 25 "input" nodes for receiving the patterns, and nodes for higher-level features; initially there are no connections. It is bombarded with thousands of patterns, and has to connect its nodes in such a way as to (firstly) learn to analyse the image into the horizontal and the vertical line, and (afterwards) learn that there is always one and only one line of each type in each image. This is non-trivial in that it involves segmenting the image into two overlapping features. Note that the network has no fore-knowledge of the grid structure of the input, and therefore no predisposition to detect lines. It could, of course, memorise the 25 possible images as separate patterns, but this would be considered a failure to learn as it misses the line structure.

As will be seen later, the network succeeds in this problem.

DESIGN PHILOSOPHY

A neural network program should be designed like any other program. Each piece of information held in it should have a clear meaning; each processing step should represent a sound inference of new information from old; each node should have a function, justifying its existence; the global behaviour of the network should have a simple description (simpler, that is, than the algorithm producing the behaviour). All this forms the basis for a correctness proof, and should be specified before beginning implementation.

Other branches of computer science follow these principles; by and large, artificial intelligence, and particularly neural networks, do not. The usual justification is that this methodology is not appropriate to such an "exploratory" discipline. Still, most explorers decide where to go before setting out, carry a map, and think before they act in unfamiliar situations.

The consequence of ignoring these principles is that neural networks have developed an arbitrary set of conventions which limit thought and lack a clear semantics. It is usually assumed that a node's activation must be a real number, possibly restricted in some way ("it must be continuous or discrete" is the usual way of putting it). This real number is vaguely thought of as a probability, or possibly a degree of partial truth, or possibly a degree of confidence. There is nothing wrong with any of these meanings in themselves: what is wrong is the vagueness. A network which treated activations as probabilities and manipulated them correctly according to probability theory would be fine. Even more interesting would be a clarification of the notions of degree of truth and degree of confidence, and a network which calculated with them correctly (they might turn out not to be real numbers). However, as far as I am aware, no one has ever done this. There are deep philosophical difficulties here [3,4]; "fuzzy logicians" are inclined to skate over these and concentrate on the mathematical aspects of their theories [5].

Since the activations are ill-defined there is no criterion for *correctness* in the processing of them by the network. This leaves the programmer to choose the activation functions (used for calculating a node's activation from lower-level nodes' activations) arbitrarily; unfortunately, the activation functions chosen are almost invariably weighted sums, usually with a sigmoid or threshold function applied. Weighted sums have advantages. They make it possible to understand the behaviour of simple networks using linear algebra; they are easy to compute; and one can use them to build networks illustrating distributed knowledge representation, content-addressability, spontaneous generalisation, and so on [6], all in a very crude way. However, there is nothing inherently linear about cognition. To focus so narrowly on such an artificial device surely distorts our perspective and obstructs our progress towards an understanding of the essential nature of intelligence.

The network I describe in this paper has boolean activations. Each node is a feature detector: its activation indicates whether the current input pattern possesses the relevant feature (a *feature* is, formally, a predicate applicable to input patterns). This implies that the network is feedforward, so that any assignment of activations to the input nodes implies a unique consistent assignment of activations to all nodes – such an assignment to all nodes is called a *state*. Each node is either an input node or it receives its input from several lower-level nodes. In forward propagation, an input node's activation is set by the environment, whereas a higher-level node's activation is calculated from lower-level nodes' activations by the node's activation function. Forward propagation should be thought of as an inference process, in which truth values are supplied for the lowest-level features and are deduced for successively higher features.

THE OBJECTIVE OF THE NETWORK

I have said that the purpose of the network is to discover the natural features in the input patterns. However, this is too ill-defined a goal to guide the learning: the network doesn't know how to decide which of two features is more natural. I need a precise goal which will imply the real goal. The one I choose is that the network should be able to simulate the environment. It runs in two phases or states of consciousness: (this is like the two phases in the Boltzmann machine [7] and Harmony Theory [8])

1. waking, or observing the environment – an input pattern is received from the environment and activation propagates forward throughout the network;
2. dreaming, or simulating the environment – the input nodes are disconnected from the environment and the network chooses its own state.

The goal of the network is to dream in such a way that the probability of any state during dreaming should equal the probability during waking. This is a hard goal in that no node can see the entire state, let alone keep track of the probabilities of every possible state. However, each node keeps records of the observed probability distribution of its "local state" (the activations it *can* see) during each phase.

Learning to simulate the environment entails learning the environmental probability distribution, which involves representing environmental information in a suitably compressed form. I presume this cannot be done without discovering and using the natural features. But this objective has other advantages as well. If the network can simulate the environment then it can perform pattern completion, it can correct noisy patterns, it can act as a novelty detector – in principle it can do anything, since it knows everything there is to know about the environment. It no longer even needs the environment, since it can simulate it perfectly. Thus simulating the environment is a "universal" goal including all other goals.

DIVISION OF LABOUR BETWEEN NODES

Each node must have a reason for existing. Initially the network should just consist of the input nodes; other nodes should be connected to it one by one as they convince the network that they will contribute to its goal of simulating the environment.

To understand the role of a node we must ask how the network would be handicapped by its absence. Input nodes are necessary to receive the input patterns. Suppose there were no other nodes. The input nodes would observe the environment and each would keep a record of the probability of its activation being *true* during waking (this is $\frac{9}{25}$ for our example). In dreaming it would choose its activation in such a way as to be *true* $\frac{9}{25}$ of the time; since there are no connections the choices of the nodes would not interfere with each other. Thus waking and dreaming would agree as far as single input node probabilities are concerned.

Clearly this is inadequate since the network is blind to the correlations between input activations. To see the correlation between two nodes we need a higher-level node which receives input from both. So let us take a supply of "new" nodes and connect them at random to pairs of input nodes. Each new node observes the correlation between its two lower nodes. The new nodes compete with each other to be *established* – that is, incorporated permanently into the network. The one with the highest correlation is established, and the ones with the lowest correlations die and are recycled (this just means choosing new connections for them and starting again). When a new node is established, it chooses an activation function for itself; and its task thereafter is to enforce its correlation: that is, to influence the choice of future dream states so that the correlation in dreaming matches that observed in waking. In the example problem, two input nodes in the same row or column have a positive correlation; any other pair of nodes has a small negative correlation. So the first node to be established will be a *row detector* or a *column detector*.

Once nodes have been established they can act as inputs to new nodes, which may be established in turn, so that nodes of ever higher level become possible. However, there is a problem with the mechanism described in the last paragraph: simply observing correlations may lead to duplication of function or otherwise redundant nodes. Suppose the first node established, i, takes input from the highly correlated input nodes j and k. Now suppose another new node also takes input from j and k. Then because j and k are highly correlated the new node may well get established – so duplicating i's function. Or consider a new node taking input from i and j: these are probably highly correlated, but the correlation is an artifact of the network and says nothing about the input, so the new node should not be established. These problems are avoided if instead of simply looking at the waking correlation we compare the waking correlation with the dreaming correlation; or, more generally, the waking "local probability distribution" with the dreaming "local probability distribution", as measured at the new node. We then establish the new node with the largest difference and recycle the ones with the smallest (the difference would be 0 in the case of the two undesirable nodes above).

This amounts to establishing the node which would make the most difference to the choice of dream state, and so would do most to bring the waking and dreaming probability distributions close together.

Thus the network grows, a node at a time; each node added is the best addition. "Best" here means that the network plus the new node will simulate the environment better than the network plus any other new node.

Repeatedly establishing the best node will, I hope, lead to the best network. Here I am making an important assumption. Let B_n be the network with n nodes which best simulates the environment. I assume the following.

INCREMENTAL GROWTH ASSUMPTION: B_{n+1} is obtainable from B_n by adding a node.

This could be false. For some environments it may be that good networks can only be grown from bad sub-networks: if so, my learning procedure cannot learn them. For example, suppose the environment consists only of *even parity* patterns, with all even parity patterns being equally probable. To spot the parity constraint one needs a node which can see *all* the input nodes; but such a node must receive its input via lower-level nodes which see *some* of the input nodes, and these lower-level nodes will not be established since they see no correlation between their inputs. Indeed, it is hard to see how any learning system, lacking any fore-knowledge of parity, could solve this problem: to detect parity it has to build a calculating apparatus whose value is not apparent until it is completed.

I claim that any learning system is subject to some constraint similar to my incremental growth assumption (cf Martin's Law, "You can't learn anything unless you almost know it already" [9].) No doubt the consequences will vary in detail from system to system.

Finally, notice the vagueness in my formulation of "best new node" and "best network". Ideally I would like a precise (possibly numerical) criterion for deciding whether one network's dreaming probability distribution approximates the waking probability distribution better than another network's. Relative to that criterion, I could then hope to estimate the best new node using the local probability distributions. At present I simply compare the local distributions in a somewhat *ad hoc* way to decide for which new node the dreaming distribution "deviates most widely" from the waking distribution.

CHOICE OF DREAM STATES

Having specified the function of each node, we may now begin to think about its implementation. Suppose for simplicity that each non-input node, i, receives input from two lower nodes, j, k. Consider the knowledge available to i. In waking and dreaming it can only see the "local state": that is, the activations, a_i, a_j and a_k, of i, j and k. Since a_i is a function of a_j and a_k, there are only four possible local states. The node keeps records of the relative frequency of each local state in each phase, which it treats as estimates of probabilities. Thus it has eight probabilities:

$$p_W(a_j \wedge a_k), \quad p_W(a_j \wedge \neg a_k), \quad p_W(\neg a_j \wedge a_k), \quad p_W(\neg a_j \wedge \neg a_k),$$

$$p_D(a_j \wedge a_k), \quad p_D(a_j \wedge \neg a_k), \quad p_D(\neg a_j \wedge a_k), \quad p_D(\neg a_j \wedge \neg a_k),$$

from which it calculates four *deviations*:

$$d(a_j \wedge a_k), \quad d(a_j \wedge \neg a_k), \quad d(\neg a_j \wedge a_k), \quad d(\neg a_j \wedge \neg a_k),$$

where $d(a_j \wedge a_k) = p_W(a_j \wedge a_k) - p_D(a_j \wedge a_k)$, and so on. Thus a positive deviation for $a_j \wedge a_k$ indicates that there have been too few states satisfying $a_j \wedge a_k$ in past dreaming. Node i's responsibility is to put that right, so it *asserts* that the next dream state shall satisfy $a_j \wedge a_k$. Clearly this decision has implications for nodes j and k, and for higher nodes receiving input from i, and hence indirectly for other nodes; so it has to be propagated to all nodes to which i is connected, and hence throughout the network.

If we imagine every node generating assertions of this kind, we obtain a logical propagation process in which each node receives assertions from its neighbours, combines them with its own home-grown assertions (which I shall call *axioms*), deduces all "local" consequences, and propagates its conclusions to all its neighbours. When the process has settled down (that is, when nothing new is deduced) the network has chosen a dream state which satisfies all the axioms and so reduces all the deviations. The difficulty here is that in a sizeable network the axioms will almost always be inconsistent. Hence we need a criterion for resolving disputes between combinations of axioms.

It is intuitively reasonable that it is more important to reduce large deviations than small ones. I shall criticise this later, but let us assume it for the moment. Let us say that the *strength* of an axiom is the magnitude of its deviation. This now begins to look like a typical "constraint satisfaction" problem. The familiar neural network solution is to minimise the sum of squares of the deviations by propagating forces around the network, by analogy with a physical system. One may then try experiments to see how the system as a whole behaves and try to prove theorems about it: for example, one would be worried about local minima. However, this is the wrong order to do things: we ought to specify the desired logic for resolving disputes and then design an algorithm to implement it. Minimising the sum of squares would produce a state bearing no *logical* relation to the axioms. One could not guarantee, for example, that the strongest axiom would be satisfied. Two incompatible strong axioms might nearly cancel each other out, leaving the state to be determined by weaker axioms, possibly satisfying neither strong axiom: it would be better if the strongest one were satisfied, overriding the second-strongest.

The desired criterion is that whenever a set of axioms is inconsistent the weakest axiom should be overturned. For any positive real α let A_α be the set of all axioms of strength at least α. Let α be the greatest number such that A_α is inconsistent. Then there must be an axiom X of strength exactly α, and the other axioms in A_α must imply $\neg X$. Assume no two axioms have exactly the same strength; then clearly X should be overturned. We seek a consistent subset S of the axioms (the set of non-overturned axioms) such that for any axiom $X \notin S$ the axioms in S stronger than X imply $\neg X$. That is, an axiom is satisfied if and only if the axioms stronger than it which are satisfied do not contradict it. This is equivalent to saying that the dream state chosen must be optimal, where it is better to satisfy an axiom than not to do so, even if it means not satisfying weaker axioms. The $\twoheadleftarrow$ ordering defined below formalises this notion, and the theorem asserts that the algorithm always settles into the optimum state.

This criterion is implemented as follows. Each assertion is accompanied by a positive real number called its *strength*. The strength of an axiom has already been defined; the strength of any other assertion is the minimum of the strengths of the axioms from which it was deduced. This is enforced by the following rule: whenever several assertions combine at a node to imply a new assertion, the new assertion should be given a strength equal to the minimum of the strengths of the premises. An axiom is not used if it has been overturned; that is, if there is a stronger assertion at the node negating it.

This definition of strength has the following desirable property. Let p be the *inference state*, the set of all assertions at some stage in the propagation process; and let p_α be the set of all assertions of strength at least α. Let S be the set of axioms X for which p also asserts X with at least the same strength; and let S_α be the set of those with strength at least α. Then we have

$$\forall \alpha \quad S_\alpha \vdash p_\alpha.$$

This property asserts the soundness of the inference process. From the point of view of someone who can only see assertions of strength $\geq \alpha$ the network is a sound inference engine: it only contains assertions which are a consequence of the non-overturned axioms.

What is the inference state when the propagation process has settled? In general there will be contradictions in p. If there is a contradiction of strength α at a node then we may make the following observations:

1. there will be a contradiction of the same strength at all neighbouring nodes, and hence throughout that connected component of the network;
2. there will be no assertions of strength $< \alpha$ in the connected component, since a contradiction of strength α implies all possible local assertions, which swamp any weaker assertions (the component of the network is "clogged" with the contradiction);
3. S_α is inconsistent; or, more strongly, there is a subset $X, Y, \ldots Z$ of S_α, all in this connected component, such that X has strength α, $Y, \ldots Z$ are stronger, and $Y, \ldots Z \vdash \neg X$;

and hence, combining 1. and 3.,

4. the axiom which should be overturned (X) is the one whose strength equals the strength of the local contradiction.

This gives a local test for whether an axiom should be overturned. After settling, each node decides independently whether any of its axioms should be overturned (there will be one per connected component in which there is a contradiction). Each node also removes from p the contradictions and all assertions

156

of the same strength: the justification for this is to preserve the $S_\alpha \vdash p_\alpha$ property. When an assertion is overturned it ceases to belong to S, so all its consequences must be removed from p. A consequence of an axiom of strength α has strength $\leq \alpha$, so we must remove all such assertions in the same connected component. However, the only such assertions are of strength exactly α, by 2. above. Hence if we remove everything of strength α then soundness will be preserved (this process is called *unclogging*).

Now the whole thing (settling and unclogging) is repeated until the time comes when settling produces no contradictions. The final inference state determines the chosen dream state.

Does this work? Not quite, as it stands. Suppose the axioms $X_1, \ldots X_n$ yield a contradiction, where $X_1, \ldots X_n$ are in decreasing order of strength; let the strengths be $\alpha_1, \ldots \alpha_n$. Then there is a contradiction of strength $\alpha = \alpha_n$, so in particular p_α contains $\neg X_n$, indicating that $S_\alpha \vdash \neg X_n$. If the strength of $\neg X_n$ is no more than α then the unclogging process will remove it (reasonably enough, since it is a consequence of X_n), and so X_n is not really overturned: it is free to yield the same contradiction next time. One might point out that in fact $X_1, \ldots X_{n-1} \vdash \neg X_n$, so $\neg X_n$ should be deduced with strength α_{n-1}, which is greater than α: then $\neg X_n$ will survive unclogging, and X_n will be suppressed, as desired. However, there is no guarantee of this. The logical propagation process is sound but not complete: it will not discover all logical consequences, since it is limited to local inferences. Thus it is possible that $\neg X_n$ will only be present in p with strength α.

To correct this, we need a "correction" mechanism which, at the same time as unclogging, detects such situations (where there is an axiom X, and assertions X and $\neg X$ in p, all of the same strength, at a node), and inserts $\neg X$ in p with a suitable greater strength.

When this is done, the algorithm is provably correct. This should be informally clear, although I have fudged a few details in this explanation for simplicity. To state the correctness theorem we need to be a little more formal.

An *assertion* is a pair (X, α), where X is a proposition and α is a positive real number.

A *state* is an assignment of boolean values to all activations, consistent with the activation functions.

Let A be the set of axioms. Two states, $\mathbf{a}$ and $\mathbf{a}'$, may be distinguished by which of the axioms they satisfy: I shall write $\mathbf{a} \models X$ to mean the proposition X is satisfied by the state $\mathbf{a}$. State $\mathbf{a}$ is "better" than state $\mathbf{a}'$ if $\mathbf{a}' \lll \mathbf{a}$, where $\lll$ is the following ordering on states.

$$\mathbf{a}' \lll \mathbf{a} \iff \exists \alpha \ \forall (X, \beta) \in A \ \beta > \alpha \Rightarrow (\mathbf{a}' \models X \iff \mathbf{a} \models X)$$
$$\wedge \ \forall (X, \alpha) \in A \ (\mathbf{a}' \models X \Rightarrow \mathbf{a} \models X)$$
$$\wedge \ \exists (X, \alpha) \in A \ (\mathbf{a}' \not\models X \wedge \mathbf{a} \models X).$$

This says that **a'** and **a** agree on which axioms of strength $> \alpha$ they satisfy, but **a** satisfies more axioms of strength α than **a'**.

I assume that no two axioms have the same strength, and that for each input node i either a_i or $\neg a_i$ is an axiom (that is, the deviation for a_i is non-zero). Then we have the following theorem.

THEOREM. The algorithm halts in the $\prec$-maximum state.

The proof is too long to include here; it will be published shortly (together with a precise account of the algorithm). The $\prec$-maximum state satisfies the strongest assertion, and also the second-strongest (if this is consistent with the strongest), and the third-strongest (if this is consistent with the strongest two, assuming they are both satisfied), and so on. Note that the final state depends only on the axioms and not on the order in which nodes are updated during propagation.

The theorem asserts the correctness of the algorithm relative to the $\prec$ criterion. Dreaming consists of repeatedly choosing the $\prec$-maximum state; after each choice the dreaming probability distribution is updated, giving a new set of deviations, and hence a new $\prec$-maximum state next time. However, recall that the objective in dreaming is not to $\prec$-maximise each state but to reduce the deviations. I make the following conjecture.

CONJECTURE. If we repeatedly choose the $\prec$-maximum state, then the resulting sequence of states reduces all the deviations to near 0 and maintains them there.

This seems reasonable. The natural way to reduce the deviations is to concentrate on reducing the largest ones. Smaller deviations may rise, but if they rise too far they will become the largest and be reduced themselves: thus the deviations will take it in turns to be reduced. It seems plausible that they will all go to 0 by this method, provided there is *any* choice of states which has this effect (and there *is* such a choice – choosing states according to the waking probability distribution would work).

However, I have been unable to prove this in general. One may imagine a case where several deviations rise together indefinitely. Each takes it in turns to be reduced, but when one is reduced the others rise, with more harm than good being done each time. Whether this is actually possible I have been unable to ascertain.

Notice, however, that if deviations did remain persistently large then the new nodes would detect the fact, and a new node would be established which would correct the situation.

I have implemented many versions of the network, or rather simulated them, on a sequential computer, in Pascal. The dreaming mechanism should really be a parallel process in which which nodes are updated asynchronously (there is little need for locking mechanisms to prevent deadlock or inconsistent states: a node must only be prevented from reading a value while another is in the process of changing it, which could lead to hardware-dependent errors); however, my Pascal program simply sweeps backwards and forwards through the nodes in a fixed order. The order makes no difference to the result; any order would lead to the ⤝-maximum state, provided no node is indefinitely deprived of update.

The program runs in phases of waking and dreaming, and periodically pauses to examine the new nodes and recycle or establish them. This is an approximation to the real situation, where the new nodes would be perpetually competing with each other, sending each other inhibitory messages in proportion to their strength, via the established nodes. However, the effect is much the same: the weakest nodes die and the strongest ones are established.

Using the test problem described at the end of the introduction, I tried networks in which each non-input node received input from *two* other nodes, and also networks with *three* inputs to every non-input node. To take the two-input case first: the network started to establish a sensible sequence of nodes (that is, row detectors and column detectors), and the dream patterns began to show some line structure. With 24 established nodes it dreamed its first correct pattern; the proportion of correct patterns then steadily increased. As the network became larger and more tangled it was no longer possible to understand the role of the individual nodes. A crucial question is whether the knowledge representation was local or distributed: that is, was there a cluster of nodes for each of the 25 possible correct patterns, or were there nodes to represent individual columns, the mutual exclusivity of different columns, and so on? We can throw some light on this by looking at the incorrect patterns it produced. Some of them were merely noisy versions of correct patterns (an extra or displaced pixel, say), and some were gibberish. However a large number were other line pictures – a single line, two parallel lines, an H or U shape, and so on. This suggests strongly that the network *was* thinking in terms of individual lines, that it produced pictures by choosing approximately two lines and superimposing them.

As learning continued performance gradually improved. With 280 established nodes, 98% of the patterns were correct and nearly all the rest were correct but for a single unwanted pixel. 280 is far from optimal: I believe there is a network of 84 established nodes which would do the job, but my algorithm is unlikely to discover it because it depends on correlations between triples of nodes.

With this thought I tried a network of three-input nodes. The results were just the same except that it needed about half as many established nodes for the same level of performance as the two-input network. Since a three-input node does about twice as much work as a two-input node, this means there is no real difference.

I am now trying the same problem with a 10 × 10 picture instead of 5 × 5. Learning is very much slower; at present my two-input network has 450 established nodes and still has a low, but gradually increasing, success rate. It seems here that the three-input network does substantially better.

One very general conclusion is that the algorithm is feasible on large networks. The size of the deviations shows little or no tendency to rise as the network grows, nor does the number of sweeps through the nodes required to choose a dream state (which is a measure of the time the parallel algorithm would take); however, both are higher for the 10 × 10 problem than for the 5 × 5.

FUTURE WORK

Assuming the network eventually learns the 10 × 10 problem, I would like to try it on others, such as detecting squares or arbitrary line drawings (detecting corners and line segments, developing a sense of neighbourhood, and so on), preferably with a larger image grid.

I would also like to make a determined effort to understand the role of the individual nodes in the existing networks. In particular, what happens if one inflicts brain damage by disabling a few nodes? I would expect only a slight general degradation of performance, perhaps with some recovery as the deviations readjust themselves.

The dreaming algorithm is not entirely local: the transition from one phase to another requires global coordination. Ideally, this would be changed. Also, the propagation process could probably be optimised, as it involves some redundant processing. The "correction" mechanism mentioned at the end of the account of dreaming, in which some axioms must be denied with a greater strength than they would otherwise be, is imperfectly implemented at present: the problem is knowing exactly what strength to choose. I don't know whether this significantly affects performance. There are ways around this, but I do not yet know whether they are worth the trouble.

The deviations do not tend to 0, but stabilise at small values (typically 0.002-0.012). I do not know whether this is harmful or why it happens: it could be the faulty "correction" mechanism or it could reflect the limitations of this approach to constraint satisfaction. If the latter, I can think of two answers. One is to kill the node with the worst deviation, thus breaking up the deadlock which is causing the problem. The second is to choose two dream states at a time: this would be a constraint satisfaction problem of twice the size, probably taking longer to settle, but allowing more elbow-room for reducing as many deviations as possible.

Another source of worry is the definition of "strength" of new nodes, which is used to pick out the best one to establish, and the choice of activation function for a newly established node. Both these are done in an *ad hoc* way at present.

My impression is that 280 established nodes is a bit too many for the 5×5 problem, and that learning is far too slow in the 10×10 case. This may reflect the restrictive framework within which I have forced the nodes to learn and work. The network is not very good at enforcing the rule that a pixel is *false* unless some higher-level node forces it to be *true*. It would help if a node could see not just the activations of the lower-level nodes connected to it but also the higher-level nodes to which it is connected.

Clearly there are many ideas here to try. However, I think it would be a mistake to be diverted into an "experimental" approach, spending a lot of time collecting statistics on the performance of different versions of the algorithm. For fundamental epistemological reasons, computing is not an empirical science. What is most needed is a theoretical argument justifying the choice of nodes to establish, and another one linking the goal of matching the two global probability distributions with the goal of choosing the ⧏-maximum state: at the moment I have only the most sketchy justification.

CONCLUSIONS

I am not aware of any other network which can arbitrate between hundreds of entangled and conflicting constraints, as mine does. It owes its success to its strictly logical semantics. It makes no concessions to fuzzy logic (the notion that a proposition has a numerical degree of truth or degree of confidence). Superficially this claim seems false: after all, I do assign numbers to propositions and combine the numbers using a minimising rule. However, the numbers are not degrees of truth or degrees of confidence. There is a purely logical semantics, given by

$$\forall \alpha \quad S_\alpha \vdash p_\alpha,$$

which says that everything in p of strength at least α follows from those axioms in S of strength at least α: $\vdash$ is classical logical consequence. Fuzzy logic systems, by contrast, presuppose a theory of uncertain reasoning; since no one has such a theory (apart from probability theory) the inference procedures used are arbitrary, and there is no guaranteed relation between the conclusion of a long inference process and its premises.

My logical propagation mechanism could be applied to other constraint satisfaction problems. Roughly speaking, all that is necessary is that

1. the assertions must be expressed in propositional logic and must be local to a node (they involve only propositional constants associated with that node);
2. the axioms must have "strengths": these need not be numbers, but they must be elements of a totally ordered set, indicating which axioms take priority over others when there is a conflict;

3. whenever the entire inference state is inconsistent the network must be able to deduce a contradiction.

Then the algorithm will settle into the $\prec$-maximum state.

The self-configuring property of my network is also novel. The usual approach is to organise nodes into layers, with fixed connections between each node and all or some of the nodes in the next layer, and to confine learning to weights or other transmission properties. In an image analysis problem, involving many pixels and many layers, one would need an enormous number of nodes and connections to ensure that appropriate high-level features could be detected, unless one wired in the right connectivity by hand. In a 625×625 image, a network should learn for itself which pixels are close to other pixels by observing the correlations between their activations. Since it cannot afford 625^4 second-level nodes to observe all these correlations it must use adaptable nodes which search for correlated pairs and establish themselves when they find one. Similarly it needs nodes which search for correlations between second-level nodes – in cursive pictures these indicate a short line segment. Unexpected correlations indicate natural structure. If one accepts this then my node growth mechanism seems to follow.

I have criticised the arbitrariness of some neural network conventions (fixed connectivity, real activations, weighted sums, and sums of squares). I hope this paper illustrates the benefits to be gained from transcending them.

References

1. Mozer MC, Smolensky P. Using relevance to reduce network size automatically. Connection Science 1989; 1:3-16

2. Geman S. Notes on a self-organising machine. In: Hinton GE, Anderson JA (eds) Parallel models of associative memory (updated edition). Lawrence Erlbaum Associates, Hillsdale, New Jersey, 1989, pp 277-303

3. Fine TL. Theories of probability: an examination of foundations. Academic Press, New York, 1973

4. Gillies DA. An objective theory of probability. Methuen & Company, London, 1973

5. Goguen JA. The logic of inexact concepts. Synthese 1969; 19:325-373

6. McClelland JL, Rumelhart DE, Hinton GE. The appeal of parallel distributed processing. In: Rumelhart DE, McClelland JL, the PDP research group. Parallel distributed processing: explorations in the microstructure of cognition, vol 1, Foundations. MIT Press, Cambridge, Massachusetts, 1986, pp 3-44

7. Hinton GE, Sejnowski TJ. Learning and relearning in Boltzmann machines. In: Rumelhart DE, McClelland JL, the PDP research group. Parallel distributed processing: explorations in the microstructure of cognition, vol 1, Foundations. MIT Press, Cambridge, Massachusetts, 1986, pp 282-317

8. Smolensky P. Information processing in dynamical systems: foundations of harmony theory. In: Rumelhart DE, McClelland JL, the PDP research group. Parallel distributed processing: explorations in the microstructure of cognition, vol 1, Foundations. MIT Press, Cambridge, Massachusetts, 1986, pp 194-281

9. Winston PH. Artificial Intelligence (2nd edition). Addison-Wesley, Reading, Massachusetts, 1984

Virtual Connectivity through Structural Dissipation; Parallel Distributed Computation with Local Connectivity

R. W. Taylor

1   Abstract

This paper introduces the application of locally connected computing cells for distributed parallel processing. Cellular Automata are presented as a model of ultra fine grain parallelism, and a brief introduction to their notation and application provided. A machine architecture developed at the University of York, the *Fuzzy Automata Machine (FAMe)* is presented, and its application to Cellular Neural Networks discussed.

2   Introduction

The rapid growth in the application of large scale distributed parallel processing has highlighted a number of significant problems including complexity (hardware and software), scaleability and fault tolerance. Attempts have been made to develop robust, self-organising structures of many types although much of this work relies on conventional message passing mechanisms and high connectivity schemes. Cellular Automata (CA) systems take a different approach to the problem, applying large numbers of homogeneous local programs (or rules) to the problem space. The application of these very simple local rules can produce complex global behaviour, capable of many different computations [1].

The principle component of a CA machine is the *cell*. This is an independent computing element, capable of a restricted range of computations based upon its own state, the state of a select group of near neighbours, and a finite number of previous states (self and neighbours). The machine may be considered to be an "ultra-fine grain" Single Instruction Multiple Data (SIMD) machine, with static "read only" communication links between neighbours. CA have a long pedigree, starting from the theoretical work by von Neumann[1] in the late 40's, to practical VLSI implementations in the late 70's onwards[2]. A number of machines, both experimental and commercial have been based upon some form of cellular model, and fine grain SIMD systems such as the CAM6[3] and the Connection Machine[4] are well known in the academic community at least.

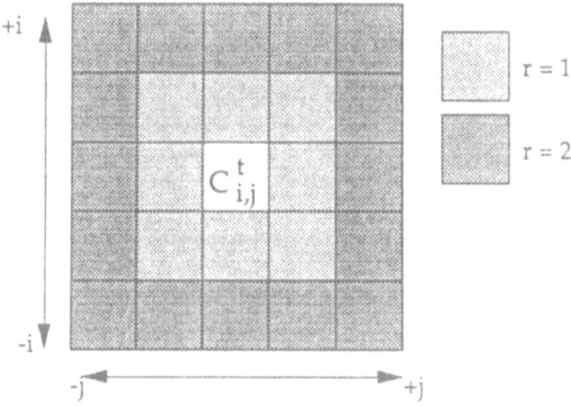

Figure 1: The cell processor and its neighbourhood in 2 dimensions

A mechanism of this form has many advantages over the more complex multi-processor approach; complexity is reduced, scaleability and fault tolerance increased. The applications of automata based machines are extremely varied, taking in physical models of systems which consist of large groups of simple, locally interacting particles such as crystal growth [5] and hydrodynamics[6], through alternative mechanisms for modelling conventional physical systems [7], high speed image acquisition and processing [2] and neural computation [8, 9].

2.1 CA properties

A cellular processor array can be informally characterised as follows

1. The array is made up of logically discrete cells (that may be implemented as spatially discrete);

2. Each cell computes at discrete time intervals;

3. There are a finite number of states per cell;

4. The array makes use of identical cells;

5. The cells are arranged in a regular array;

6. All cells update synchronously and update by fixed rules (that is rules can not alter dynamically);

7. All cells state transitions are dependent on the values of a fixed group of local cells and a fixed number of preceding values;

A machine constructed in this way has a number of very pleasing features;

- simple local behaviour (all cell behaviour is defined in terms of local properties : that is the behaviour of surrounding sites)

- complex global properties (many simple local systems may exhibit complex global behaviour when combined)

- homogeneity (the properties of cells does not vary with space)

- virtually infinite scaleability (the absence of global connectivity makes expansion a simple process)

The CA may be considered from either a formal mathematical standpoint as information processing systems - data is represented by the initial state of the machine and results by the final (and/or intermediate) result/s. If considered in this way a 1d automata presents a regular formal language after any finite number of steps. Alternatively they may be treated as discrete dynamical systems whose global properties are categorised by considering the time evolution from all possible initial conditions : as most automata are irreversible this will contract with time to provide some dominant asymptotic behaviour.

The large numbers of elements generally present in any cellular system make it difficult to describe the behaviour without treating it as a pseudo-continuous system. In practice, this means that characterisation of the system behaviour is often best achieved through techniques developed for describing continuous physical systems. Power spectra and Fourier transforms provide some information on the steady state behaviour of the system, although the use of zeta transforms (which measure the densities of periodic sequences in CA configurations) are of more value in determining overall data transfer characteristics. Other measures of use include

- spatial topological entropy (given by $lim(x \rightarrow \infty)(1/x) \log_k N(x)$ - there are in general $N(X) \leq kx$ (where k is the number of states per cell) possible sequences for a block of x sites in the set of configurations) - reflects the possible configurations of the system;

- spatial measure entropy (formed from the probabilities of each sequence) - reflects the configurations of a system that are most probable - proving insensitive to low zero probability phenomena.

CA behaviour can be broadly characterised as being in one of four categories (after Wolfram[10])

1. those which evolve to a homogeneous state : these demonstrate zero spatial and temporal measure entropy and are relatively perturbation insensitive (perturbations in the field die out quickly);

2. those which evolve to simple periodic structures demonstrating zero temporal measure entropy (since periodic structures become evident), positive spatial measure entropy and in which perturbations persist but remain localised;

3. those which evolve to chaotic aperiodic patterns, demonstrating strange attractors, positive temporal and spatial measure entropies and in which perturbations expand at an asymptotically constant rate. The rate of this expansion provides a measure of information transfer through the machine;

4. those which evolve complex patterns of localised structures, in which perturbations expand irregularly with time;

3   CA and the neural connection

The behaviour of classes 3 and 4 above are worthwhile examining in more detail. Making use of Wolfram's notation[10], we allow each cell to take on k possible values, updating the cell at each time interval according to a rule Γ. The value c_i^t of a cell in a one dimensional lattice (at position i, time t) is given by

$$c_i^t = \Gamma[c_i^{t-1} - r, c_{i-r+1}^{t-1} \ldots c_i^{t-1}, \ldots c_{i+r}^{t-1}] \tag{1}$$

where r is the "range" of the function Γ. In this case, the next state of the cell depends at the most on the last states of $2r + 1$ other cells. This may be further extended to permit "last but one" etc... to be used, generating functions of the form

$$c_i^t = \Gamma[c_i^{t-1} - r, c_{i-r+1}^{t-1} \ldots c_i^{t-1}, \ldots$$
$$c_{i+r}^{t-1}, c_i^{t-2} - r, c_{i-r+1}^{t-2} \ldots c_i^{t-2}, \ldots c_{i+r}^{t-2}] \tag{2}$$

for a second order rule (with $t - 3$ for a third...). From this model we can see that any one site will have an effect on at most $2r + 1$ other cells, and that in any direction, the effected region will grow by no more than r sites at each iteration. After t time steps, a maximum of $1 + 2rt$ cells will be effected.

The relation described in 1 above is a discrete analogue of a partial differential equation of order $2r + 1$ at most in space and first order in time. The form given in 2 is of second order in time. Arbitrary order equations can be constructed in this manner.

If we arrange our array as a surface (or hypersurface for dimensions greater than 2) then we introduce the periodic boundary conditions necessary for absolute homogeneity. If we make use of a system with N cells, then it will possess at most k^N possible states. These can be represented by finite state transition diagrams with each node representing a state and arcs representing the transitions from one state to another. After a sufficiently long time (at most k^n time steps) the system will enter a cycle. The cycles represent the equivalent of attractors for the CA evolution.

Not surprisingly, the most interesting and applicable behaviour occurs in class 3 and 4 systems.

CLASS 3 CA Class 3 automata evolve to aperiodic patterns from almost all initial states. After a sufficient number of time steps, the statistical properties of these states will be the same for almost all initial states. Since CA are local, they possess no intrinsic scale beyond that of the neighbourhood. In practice, many rules develop to self similar patterns across the array. Irregular patterns only develop correlations over a limited range (due to the connectivity) and achieve the scale invariance over large distances through uniformity.

As the automata develops, many (if not all) initially disordered states evolve into stable patterns and relatively large number of rules evolve to closely packed attractive cycles. It is these cycles that can be exploited to categorise and order initial states.

CLASS 4 CA Class 4 systems are seen to develop stable and/or periodic structures within the array which may propagate at irregular intervals. It has been speculated, though not proven[10] that this class of automata possess the capability of universal computation - that is, suitable initial conditions can specify arbitrary algorithms. Given a suitable coding scheme therefore, the CA may simulate any other system. This places a very important limit on the predictions that may be made for the behaviour of such machines. In general the specific behaviour may only be modeled by directly simulating the CA. No finite algorithm can in general be used to predict the detailed behaviour of such an automata.

3.1 Cellular Neural Networks

The attractors and propagating structures found in class 3 and 4 systems may be crudely likened to "classifier" and "memory" mechanisms. A system with a number of attractors may be used to classify initial conditions (input data), and the propagating structures to represent active memory units[1]. In combination (possibly though multiple layers (figure 2)) these may be used to drive other automata.

Chau and Yang[9] have proposed a cellular neural network (CNN) based upon analogue components. In their model, each cell is constructed from a linear capacitor, a nonlinear voltage controlled current source, and a number of resistive linear circuit elements. This system has a number of advantages over digital implementations, in that computation is continuous, and high density systems may be developed using existing silicon technology.

The major disadvantage with the CNN as proposed is that it makes use of non programmable devices - the system is hardwired to implement a specific algorithm. Adding flexibility with programmable analog components increases the complexity of the device to such an extent that it becomes non competitive when compared to its digital sibling. Other potential advantages of the digital implementation include the ability to make use of multiple neighbourhoods and multi level computations (figure 2).

---

[1]to place my neck in an awkward position

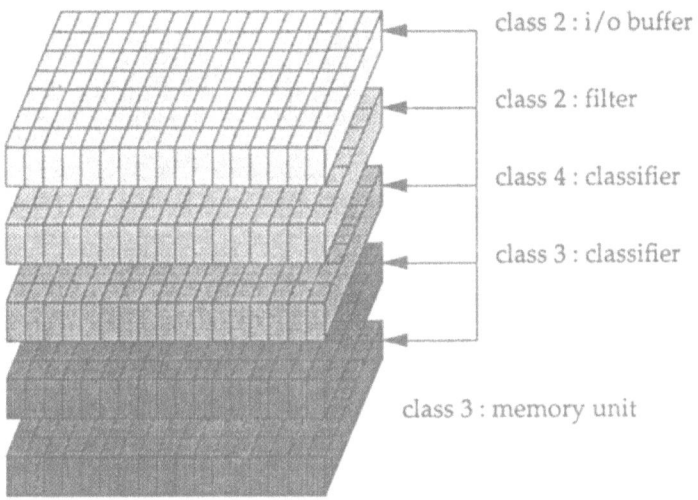

class 2 : i/o buffer

class 2 : filter

class 4 : classifier

class 3 : classifier

class 3 : memory unit

Figure 2: multi level directed computation

4 The Fuzzy Automata Machine (FAMe)

Although conventional processors (serial and parallel) may be used to implement CA algorithms, they are generally unsuitable for the development of large cellular systems for two reasons

- although automata based computation is sympathetic to a CSP based mechanism (we make use of Transputer networks and the Occam language for hardware design, verification and simulation) Transputers do not have the connectivity to provide either flexible expansion into three dimensions, the necessary data visualisation facilities nor the communications bandwidth for global test and set operations.

- specialised SIMD machines such as the DAP and the Connection Machine need a very high investment in equipment, with specialised support facilities and an unsuitable development environment.

- The very demanding data visualisation system is best suited to purpose built display hardware to provide a fast, cost effective solution

The Cellular Array is close to the ideal for VLSI implementation. Taking Kungs' design criteria[11] we may relate them to the basic characteristics of CA (section 2.1).

- *design complexity;* low in the typical CA - the bulk of any computation consists of logical (or fuzzy logical) operations.

- *modularity and effective utilisation of tools;* - the regularity of the CA means that once a cell has been developed, it is duplicated along with its communication links to produce the array.

- *simplicity and regularity of data and control paths;* as above, the CA is regular by definition.

- *localised or reduced connections;* all connections are regular, most, if not all will be local within two/three cell radii.

- *balance between input/output and computation;* the relationship between cells is read-only, and the very fine grain allows a precise balance to be achieved between communications and computation.

- *extensive concurrency;* local dependencies permit asynchronous hardware and concurrency as fine grained as the logical array.

- *fault tolerance;* conventional array recovery techniques for overcoming cell defects may be applied with little modification.

Previous work on hardware and software automata systems [12, 13] resulted in the specification of an automata mechanism which applicable as a production tool and of value for further research into highly distributed parallel processing.

1. a local system capable of supporting a hexagonal grid structure, and plane to plane connectivity with an individual four bit weight application on each connection

2. a minimum of eight planes, each of which is represented by an eight bit multi valued logic word

3. simple boolean and fuzzy (fuzzy) logic operations upon neighbours

4. capable of video rate computation

5. extensible in four dimensions (to provide 2nd and 3rd order structures)

6. complete data visualisation during computation

7. video rate i/o bandwidth for display/data acquisition

8. global test and logical operations

9. hosted by a readily available machine

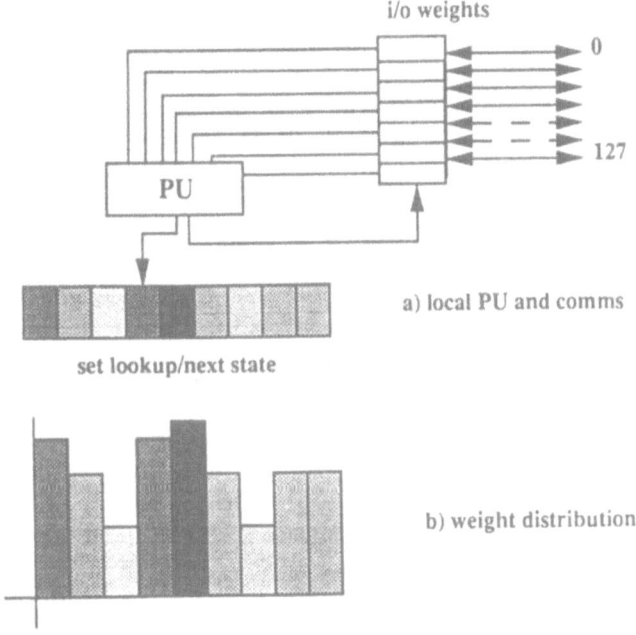

a) local PU and comms

set lookup/next state

b) weight distribution

Figure 3: A Block diagram showing the logical design of the York FAMe

There are a number of machines available which might at first sight seem very suitable for the implementation of cellular neural networks, including the Connection Machine[4], the DAP[14] and the Megacell[15]. In practice, these machines are expensive (the basic hardware + the operating environment and support) or lack the high i/o bandwidth required for video processing and interactive display. Machines such as the CAM6[3] that do have the i/o bandwidth lack a suitable instruction set for fuzzy operation, and insufficient memory for anything more than experimental work.

The York Fuzzy Automata Machine (FAMe) is a video rate Automata Array. The system has been developed primarily in ASIC based components, with the bulk of processing performed through a set of overlapped pipelines. Physical connectivity is limited to 128 nodes (in three dimensions, although higher 'virtual connectivities' are possible. Individual operations permitted at cellular level include binary and 'fuzzy' logic, plus simple weighted arithmetic. To complement the processor configuration, high bandwidth i/o and display units are currently under development, allowing arbitrary mappings of data i/o onto three dimensional surfaces within the unit.

4.1 The Instruction Set

The system has a very basic instruction set, allowing

1. standard simple arithmetic operations on 8 bits $(+, \times, /, -)$

2. extended arithmetic operations on a restricted set of neighbours with 4 bit weights (which may be modified at each node)

3. standard boolean operations (AND, OR, NOT, XOR)

4. fuzzy logical operations (FUZZY BOOLEAN [16])

5. 16 element set selection on each node

The simplicity of the instruction set permits the use of a very compact, hardwired cell processor. A number of instructions and the resulting state changes can be coded directly in lookup tables, as are the set selection operators. The language has been designed to be compact, easy to parse and optimise.

Two levels of instruction set are provided, master and slave. The master unit is responsible for loops, tests (group, cell and events) and local/global state initialisation. The slave units (representing groups of cells) describe the state changes. No loops exist within a slave, permitting a maximum clock cycle to be computed at compile time. This is important if the necessary video synchronisation is to be maintained.

4.2 The Architecture of the FAMe

A number of architectures were investigated for this system. The use of a totally parallel architecture, with each node on FAMe operating as an independent unit looked to be the most promising, although this turned out to not be so - the very large interconnection and global access required by the rule structure and display mechanism was prohibitive in silicon. Eventually a pipelined architecture was developed, with small numbers of *logical* cells being represented by physical processors. This makes use of fast static memory for rule and weight tables, compilation of sections of the code and special routers for address generation within the fetch and place cycles of operation.

4.2.1 The Processor Pipeline

Each processor has a small amount of fast static memory, local to itself which is used to hold the pre-computed lookup tables (where they can be generated), the set tables (for fuzzy selection) and the rule to be executed on each cell.

Data is held in a single memory unit, access of which (address generation) is controlled by a micro sequencer. The use of a fast (30MHz) sequencer is made possible by the regular cell structure. The sequencer may have its address generation modified via a memory mapped port.

The sequencer feeds data to each unit in the overlapped pipeline of processing units via the units co-processor interface. As each processor computes the new value for its cell, this information is multiplexed back into a single video rate data stream. This single stream fed through the global controller (capable of counting events and assessing areas) and then duplicated, partially feeding a multi ported memory system for the visual display, partially being fed back to the cell memory unit.

A controlling processor[17, 18] (which doubles as the global manager) is responsible for data display, this is performed by use of a hardwired video controller. Use of this pipelined system has a number of advantages

1. although individual timing is important, the system is relatively timing insensitive - there is considerable latitude on component tolerances capable of maintaining the data throughput

2. the overlapped architecture makes it possible to implement the system using relatively slow dynamic memory (120 ns units), since the memory may be driven at full speed continuously - small amounts of fast static memory provide the processors instruction cache

3. the overlapped architecture make the use of cheap, fast computing components possible.

4. extension of the system spatially can be performed since the data stream is available at one point on the board at a specific point in time - enlargement requires a sequencer capable of picking out the edge bit stream and integrating it into its own stream.

5. extension of the system by dimension may be performed in a similar manner .

6. visualisation on a single board is all handled by the global processor. This is capable of displaying data on a 512^2 display and also of tessalating the data to provide a 512^2 machine from four 256^2 planes. Since the data is gathered at one point for distribution to neighbouring boards, a multidimensional visualisation scheme may be integrated using a chipset such as the TR modulation set [19]. This allows bits from a serial stream to be selected under program control at video rates, any extrapolation required is automatically computed and displayed.

4.2.2 The Video-Resequencer

The video resequencer, currently being prototyped is based upon the TRW 3D sampler[19] for generating the X, Y, Z signals necessary to re-map some surface within the three dimensional physical unit onto a two dimensional plane (figure 5). This image is controlled from the master unit shown in figure 5. Currently this only permits the selection of the 'nearest' point within the surface - obviously a limitation when a noisy surface has been selected. We are designing an improved control and selection mechanism that permits either a nearest neighbour mapping (through a simple spiral algorithm) or a site average operation over a variable neighbourhood.

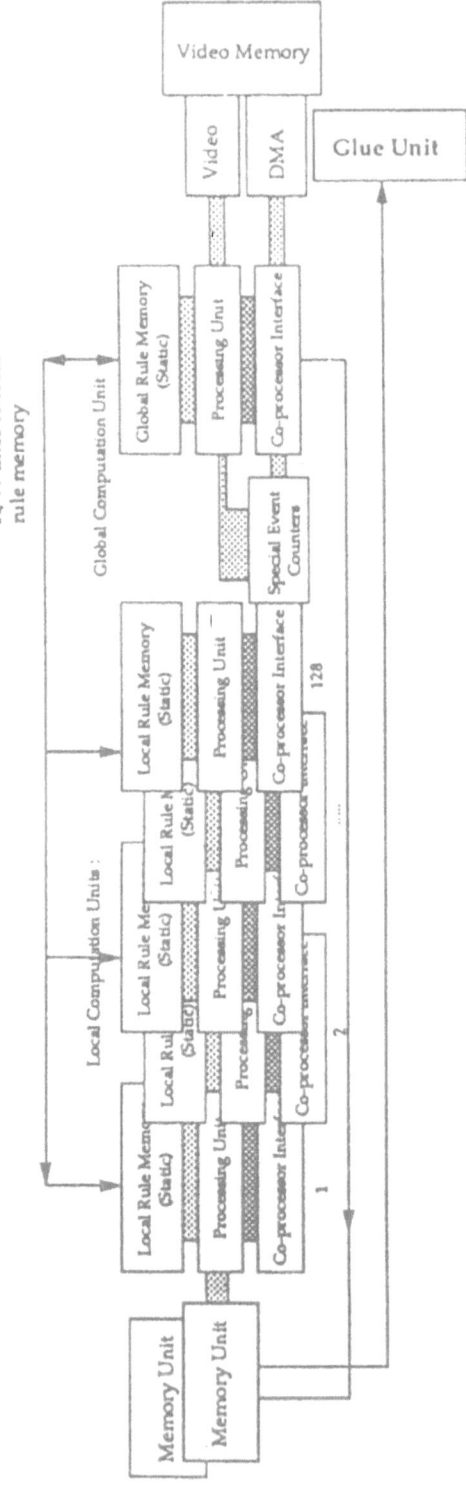

Figure 4: The Overlapped Processor Pipeline

174

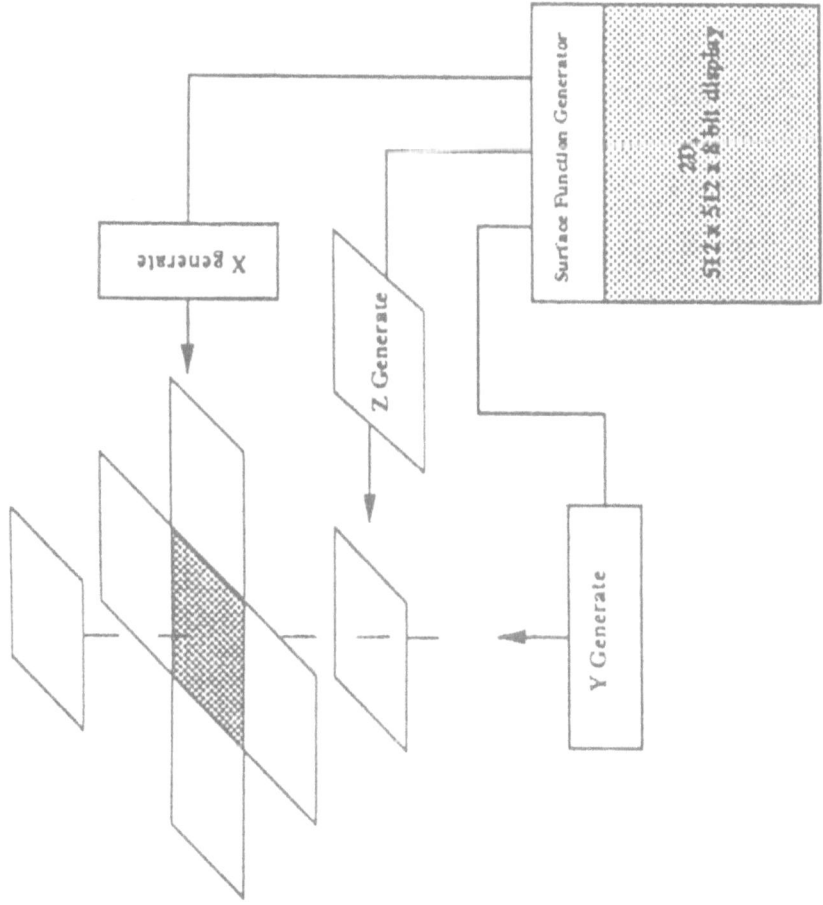

Figure 5: The 3D Video Resequencer

175

5 Software Development

5.1 The Programming Language

The Instruction set for the slave processor has been defined in a high level language based upon CSP (Communicating Sequential Processes [20]) which resembles a limited subset of the *occam* [21] language. The master processor implements an extended version of occam, providing loops, tests and event traps.

There were three main reasons for basing the system around the occam standard

1. the parallel processing community in the UK and Europe is familiar with the *CSP* model of parallel processing, and users at York have a considerable amount of experience with *occam* and its related languages.

2. support environments are currently available for the *occam* language and these required very little modification to allow the symbolic debuggers and profilers to be applied to FAMe

3. FAMe is intended to be of value as a development environment for CA algorithms; after development, these may be ported to an alternative architecture. *CSP* provides a convenient, architecture independent model of parallel processing.

5.2 The Programming Support Environment

Support for FAMe is based around the Parasol programming environment[22], an X/Unix program support system. This allows FAMe programs to be developed on an X Display system (currently hosted by either SUN, MIPS or DEC file servers) and then downloaded to the target architecture (figure 6). The host that is selected by the user determines the object code generated. We currently support both the FAMe (hosted by a 386 based PC running Unix and TCP/IP) and a network of Transputer[23] based nodes. The code that is written for both architectures does not differ, instructions for distributing the processes across the available nodes on the networks are generated automatically.

6 Conclusions

The CA paradigm of parallel distributed processing is powerful, but simple. It provides a means by which the behaviour of PDP systems may be analysed and the effectiveness of local connectivity investigated. The FAMe unit has been developed and optimised to provide an environment for experimentation, and some "production" work. The techniques developed are applicable to a wide range of machine architectures, and the FAMe programming system runs efficiently on both single processor RISC architectures and multi-processor Transputer based systems..

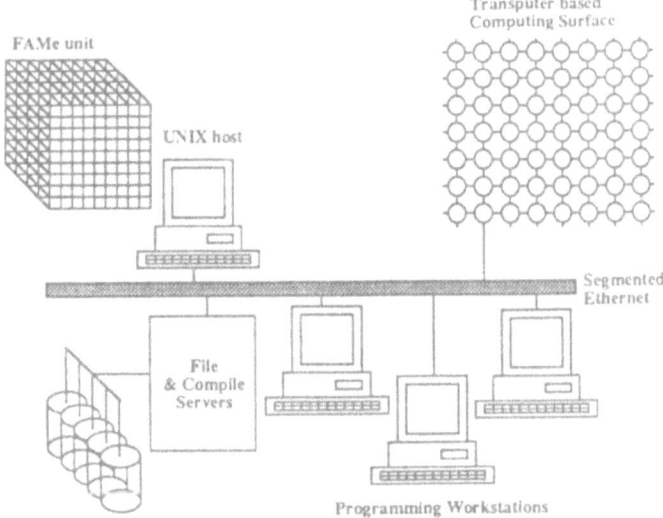

Figure 6: FAMe development environment

In conclusion, understanding the behavior of ultra fine grain SIMD systems (in terms of fault tolerance, noise immunity and communications) is essential if we are to exploit the very high levels of integration available through modern silicon. The model provided by the CA is a powerful tool in our effort to understand and exploit parallel distributed processing.

References

[1] J von Neumann. *Theory of self reproducing automata.* University of Illinois Press, Illinois, 1966.

[2] K Preston and M Duff. *Modern cellular automata.* Plenum, London, 1984.

[3] Toffoli and Margolus. *CAM a new environment for modelling.* MIT Press, Cambridge, Mass., 1986.

[4] W D Hillis. *The Connection Machine.* MIT Press, Cambridge, Mass., 1985.

[5] G M Crisp. A cellular automaton model of crystal growth : I) anthracene. Technical report, Crystallography Unit, University College, London, 1985.

[6] U Frisch, B Hasslacher, and Y Pomeua. Lattice gas automata for the navier-stokes equation. *Physics Review Letters,* 56, 1986.

[7] T Toffoli. Cellular automata as an alternative (rather than an approximation to) differential equations in modelling physics. *Physica,* 10D, 1984.

[8] J Rothstein. Bus automata, brains and mental models. *IEEE Transactions on Systems, Man and Cybernetics,* 18, 1988.

[9] L O Chua and L Yang. Cellular Neural Networks: Theory. *IEEE Transactions on Circuits and Systems,* 35 no 10.:1257,1272, 1988.

[10] S Wolfram. *Theory and Applications of Cellular Automata.* World Scientific Publishing Co., 1986.

[11] S Y Kung. VLSI Array Processors. In *Systolic Arrays.* Adam Hilger, 1987.

[12] R Taylor. The use of structural dissipation and replication to provide high virtual connectivity within local automata algorithms. *IEEE Transactions on Computers,* submitted.

[13] M J Johnson, N M Allinson, and K Moon. Digital Realisation of Self Organising Maps. In *Advances in Neural Information Processing Systems.* Morgan-Kaufmann, 1984.

[14] D Parkinson. The Distributed Array Processor (DAP). *Computer Physics Communications,* 28:325-336, 1983.

[15] T Legendi, E Katona, J Toth, and A Zsoter. Megacell machine. *Parallel Computing,* 8, 1988.

[16] L Zadeh. Fuzzy logic. *IEEE Transactions Computers,* April 1988.

[17] Acorn. *ARM Datasheet.* Acorn Computers Ltd, Cambridge, 1987.

[18] D M Goodeve and R W Taylor. A communications co-processor for the Acorn RISC Machine. *Journal of Microprocessor and Microsystems*, pages 301–305, July 1990.

[19] TRW LSI Products. *CMOS Image Resampling Sequencer*. TRW LSI Products, PO Box 2472, La Jolla, CA 92038, 1989.

[20] C A R Hoare. Communicating Sequential Processes. *Communications of the ACM*, 666, 1978.

[21] Inmos. *occam Reference Manual*. Prentice Hall, London, 1987.

[22] R W Taylor and S Ghatak. Parasol : an interactive parallel development and debugging environment for the SUN workstation. Technical Report YEE-1/89, Department of Electronics, University of York, 1989.

[23] Inmos. *The Transputer Reference Manual*. Prentice Hall, London, 1989.

TEMPORALLY PROCESSING NEURAL NETWORKS FOR MORSE CODE RECOGNITION

Darrin Hill[1]

ABSTRACT

Methods suggested for temporally processing neural networks
include recurrent multi-layer perceptrons, the use of
capacitive nodes, time dynamic networks and windowing
networks. These, along with self-organising temporal
neurons suggested by the author, are applied to the problem
of morse code recognition and their performances compared.
Experimental results show the inadequacy of error
back-propagation. The methods of feedback and windowing for
temporal recognition are shown to be inferior to neurons
that explicitly involve time. It is concluded that further
investigation into self-organising temporal neurons should
be made.

INTRODUCTION

Several methods have been suggested for neural networks
that will recognise temporal sequences. These include
recurrent networks [1], [2], [3], networks that use
capacitive nodes [3], [4], time dynamic networks [5], and
windowing networks [6]. These methods have been applied to
different problems. The purpose of this work was to compare
these methods along with a self-organising method produced
by the author [7] on the small problem of morse code
recognition.

---

[1]Supported by Smiths Industries Aerospace and Defence
Systems, Bishops Cleeve, Cheltenham. GL52 4SF.

Morse code is the encoding of letters and ultimately words by symbols given by the length of time a binary pulse is on or off. Two possible symbols are encoded when the pulse is on, either a dot or a dash. Likewise the length of time that the pulse is off encodes information. The important feature is that it is necessary to distinguish between patterns that differ only in the length of time that they are presented to the network. Thus the network is required to have memory of previous inputs. Also, the lengths of symbols are allowed to vary , this introduces the concept of non-linear time warping in the pattern. This is the feature of speech that makes recognition difficult and results in templates for the spoken word performing very poorly at recognition [8].

A structure for the recognition of morse code is shown in figure 1. This uses the same mechanism for symbol and space recognition and translates the time warped morse code input to an time-independent encoding of types of symbols and spaces. Thus the symbol detection unit has to remove time-warping and recognise different time lengths. It is this mechanism that the temporal neural network models have to achieve.

Problem Specification

Dot lengths are uniformly distributed on the interval $[\mu_1, \mu_1 + \sigma]$, similarly dash lengths on the interval $[\mu_2, \mu_2 + \sigma]$

The network has two output neurons producing (00) corresponding to no recognition until a symbol ends and then (10) or (01) corresponding to a dot or dash respectively. If the input length corresponds to neither (a non-symbol) then (00) is output. Recognition at the end of a symbol is necessary since a dot is contained within a dash, it is thus not possible to tell the difference between the two until the end of the symbol. Any other specification of output can lead to contradictions for the learning rule.

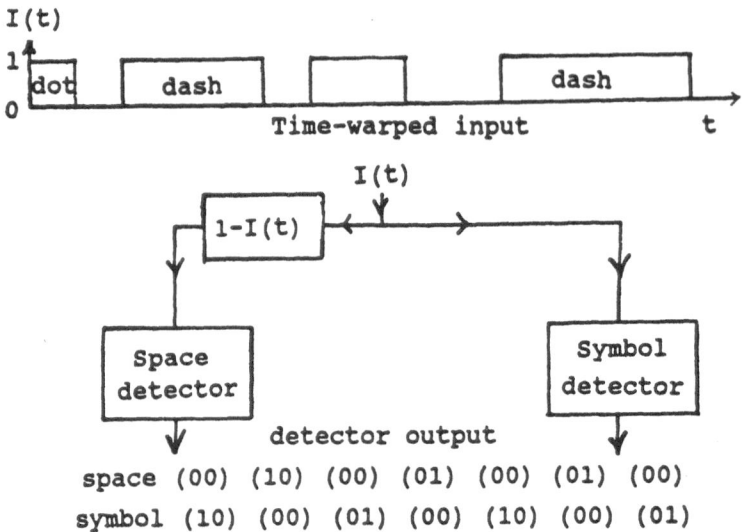

Fig. 1. Structure for recognition of morse code, showing
example time-warped input and output.

EXPERIMENTAL METHODOLOGY

The models were tested over three problems of increasing
difficulty. Poor performance on one problem resulted in the
method not being tested further. In each case robustness of
the learning algorithm to variation of μ_1, μ_2 and σ was
required. These problems were as follows-

1. The network was reset at the beginning of each
   symbol. Only the correct output during and at the
   end of each symbol was required. $\sigma=0$.
2. The network was reset at the beginning of each
   symbol. The Correct output for all binary pulses of
   length 1 to $\mu_2+2\sigma$ was required.
3. As 2. except that the network was not reset,
   instead spaces of length 5 were input. This
   corresponds to performance with a continuous input.
   The testing set was a fixed sequence of symbols and
   spaces.

Testing the performance of a network on each problem
was achieved under the following conditions.-

1. Before testing of networks the existence of a
   solution was tested by hand.
2. For particular values of μ_1, μ_2, σ the learning
   parameters were varied to find the values
   for optimum performance. For Multi-layer Perceptrons
   (MLPs) the learning rate, η, and momentum, α, as in
   Rumelhart et al [1] were varied.
3. Each experiment was repeated 10 times with different
   random seeds, giving the rate of successful
   learning, ϕ.
4. Symbols and non-symbols were presented randomly
   with equal probabilities. Non-symbols were required
   in the training set on problems 2 and 3 for all
   methods but self-organisation.
5. If ϕ did not improve within 10,000 runs then it
   was assumed that optimum performance had been
   achieved.

MLP WITH FEEDBACK

The use of feedback of output nodes to the input layer has
been suggested by many authors. Originally it was suggested
by Rumelhart et al [1] for the production of sequences.
Robinson and Fallside [2] applied this technique to speech
coding with an activation function given by

$$f(x) = \frac{2}{1+e^{-2x}} - 1 \tag{1}$$

Other applications have used the normal MLP activation
function (2) as in [1].

$$f(x) = \frac{1}{1+e^{-x}} \tag{2}$$

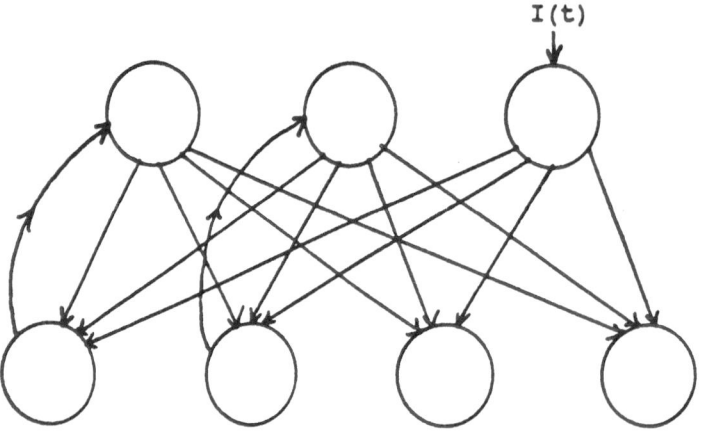

Fig. 2. MLP with 2 feedback nodes. Feedback arcs are direct
mapping of time delay 1.

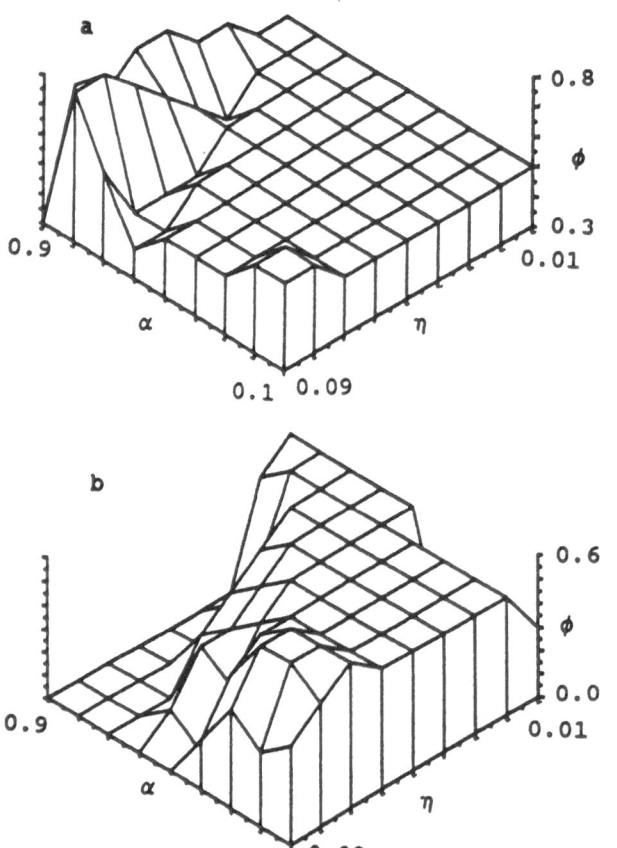

Fig. 3. MLP with 1 feedback node, activation function (1).
Variation of ϕ with α, η. 50,000 runs. a. $\mu_1=1$, $\mu_2=6$, $\sigma=0$.
b. $\mu_1=1$, $\mu_2=5$, $\sigma=0$.

Application of the learning rule has only proved successful on small problems as discussed in [3].

The approach of these mechanisms was applied to problem 1 using the network in figure 2 with a variable number of feedback nodes. The feedback arc is a direct mapping of the activity of the output node to the input node with a delay of one unit of time. Learning is achieved by the normal error back-propagation rule with feedback of the delta values calculated in the generalised delta rule [1] back through the feedback loop. The changes in the weights required for one symbol are calculated and averaged. This form of learning was used by [2].

This technique was applied to problem 1 with the activation functions (1) and (2). Figure 3 shows the results used to find the optimum parameters for a network with one feedback node using activation function (1). Comparison resulted in the choice of $\alpha=0.2$, $\eta=0.08$. Further experiments were run with larger values of η, but ϕ was 0 with $\mu_1=1$, $\mu_2=5$. Figures 4 and 5 show the results of performance as μ_1, μ_2 were varied with 1-3 feedback nodes.

The results for these networks show that the addition of one extra feedback node increases the length of symbols that can be learnt by one time unit. However, performance decays rapidly. Approximately 50,000 runs were required.

The activation function (1) has better performance than (2). For one or two encoding nodes the network performs better on odd values of $\mu_2-\mu_1$ than even values, this is due to the possible negative output of the activation function. Examination of these solutions showed that the feedback node oscillated between 1 and -1. Despite this, performance still falls off as μ_1 increases.

Examination of the incorrect solutions achieved by these methods showed that either the incorrect coding was such that gradient descent steps were too small to have any effect or steps calculated for each pattern summed to zero over a sequence of patterns. Degradation of feedback errors was not seen, in disagreement with McCulloch [9].

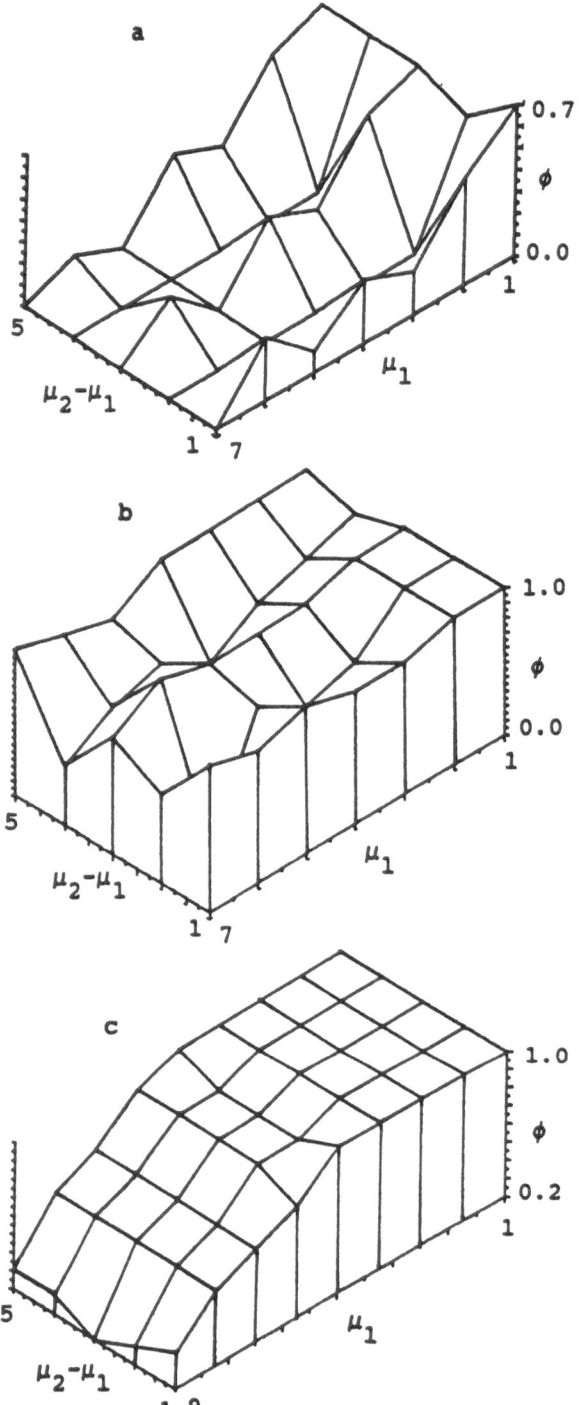

Fig. 4. MLP with feedback, activation function (1).
Variation of ϕ with μ_1, μ_2. 50,000 runs, $\sigma=0$. a. 1 feedback
node, $\alpha=0.2$, $\eta=0.08$. b. 2 feedback nodes, $\alpha=0.8$, $\eta=0.1$.
c. 3 feedback nodes, $\alpha=0.1$, $\eta=0.01$.

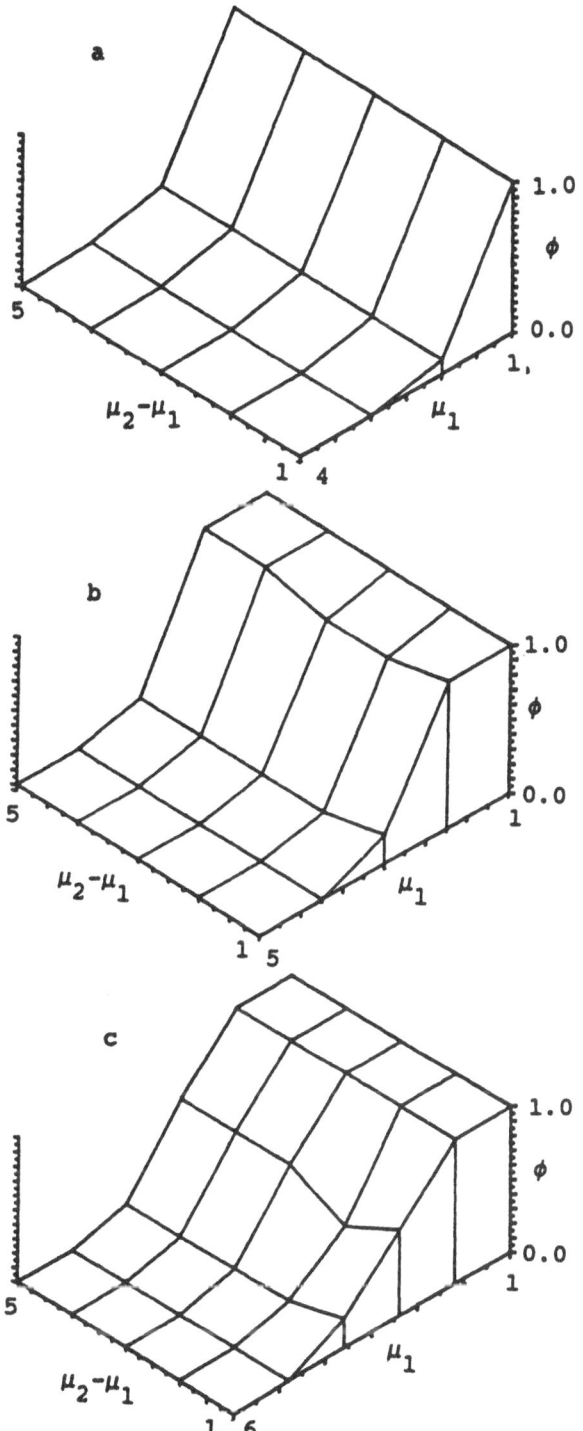

Fig. 5. MLP with feedback, activation function (2).
Variation of ϕ with μ_1, μ_2. 50,000 runs, $\sigma=0$. a. 1 feedback
node, $\alpha=0.6$, $\eta=0.5$. b. 2 feedback nodes, $\alpha=0.2$, $\eta=0.09$.
c. 3 feedback nodes, $\alpha=0.5$, $\eta=0.08$.

TIME-DYNAMIC NEURAL NETWORK (TDNN)

The structure for a TDNN has been applied to phoneme recognition [5]. The network is similar to a MLP with a sliding window input, except that copies of nodes with restricted connectivity are used to process previous inputs in the lower layers. Learning is achieved by error back propagation, but because of the repeating of hidden nodes the weight changes have to be averaged for the hidden layer. The network is updated at each stage of the input. Figure 6 shows the network used in this work. Figure 7 shows the results for problem 2. Further changes in the structure of the network have not been tried since the performance is very poor in comparison with the normal windowing technique.

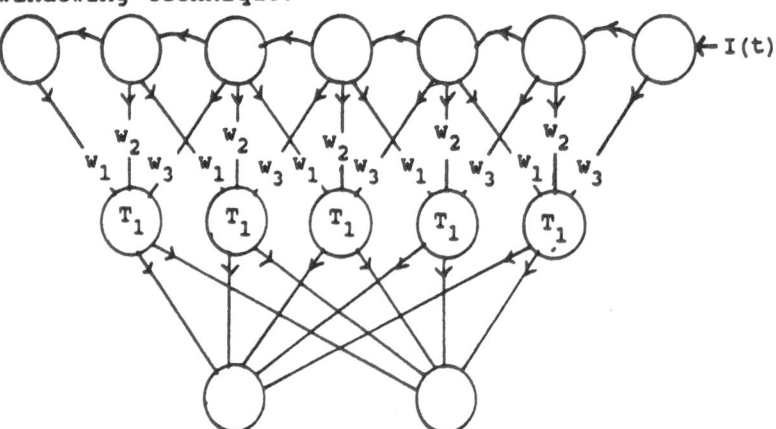

Fig 6. TDNN used for problem 2.

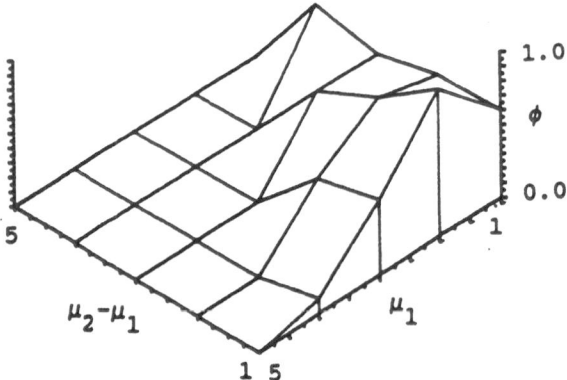

Fig. 7. TDNN on problem 2. Variation of ϕ with μ_1, μ_2, 50,000 runs, $\sigma=0$, $\alpha=0.2$, $\eta=0.7$.

The use of capacitive nodes in networks has been suggested by Norrod et al [3] and Stornetta et al [4]. They suggested it to overcome the problems of feedback networks. It has been applied to the detection of motion of a gaussian pulse [4].

In this example a capacitive node activity, x_t, at time t obeys

$$x_{t+1}=(1-b)I(t) + bx_t \qquad x_o=0 \qquad (3)$$

Thus the capacitive node builds up potential as the input pulse is on (4), the maximum activity is 1 for consistency with the remainder of the network. Learning with this network is by error back-propagation, but b is a chosen fixed value. Throughout these experiments b=0.875. The weights are altered throughout the processing of an input symbol.

The network for solution of problem 1 is shown in figure 8. This network was entirely successful for problem 1 with μ_1=1 to 10, $\mu_2-\mu_1$=1 to 5.

To solve problem 2 one layer of hidden nodes has to be added. Figure 9 shows the results for this structure.

Again increasing the number of hidden nodes by 1 increases the length of symbols that can be recognised by 1 unit of time. Learning was slow with approximately 80,000 runs required.

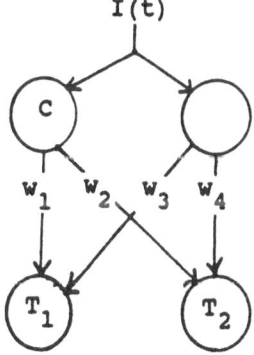

Fig. 8. MLP using capacitive node C for solution of problem 1.

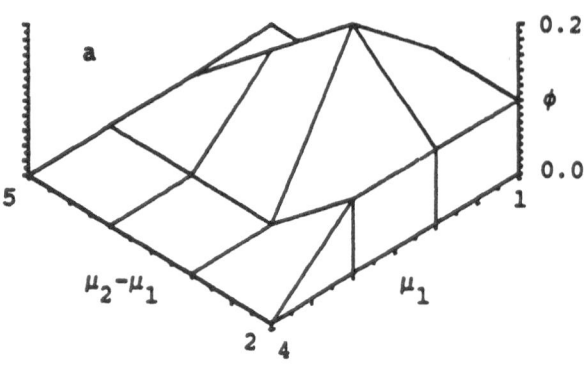

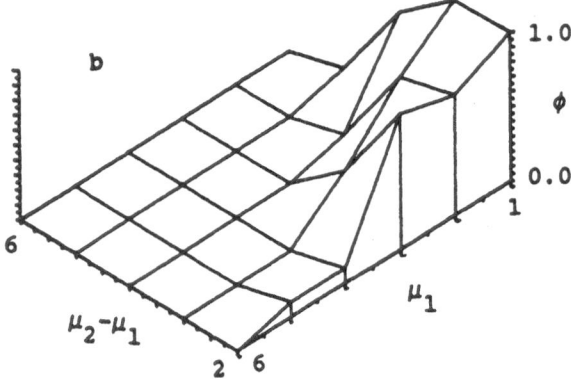

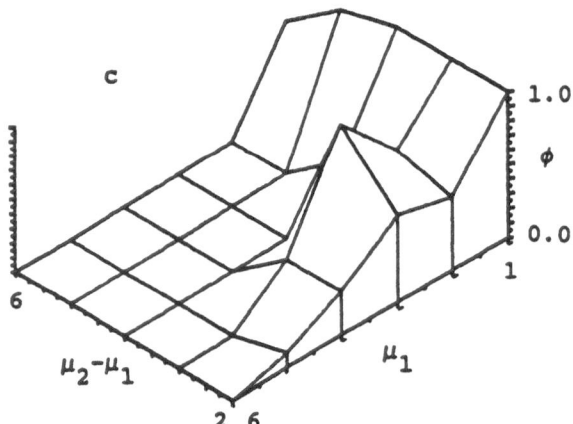

Fig. 9. MLP with capacitive node. Problem 2, variation of ϕ with μ_1, μ_2, 80,000 runs, $\sigma=1$. a. 4 hidden nodes, $\alpha=0.4$, $\eta=0.4$. b. 5 hidden nodes, $\alpha=0.7$, $\eta=0.2$. c. 5 hidden nodes, $\alpha=0.9$, $\eta=0.5$.

Study of neurophysiology has suggested a network with temporally processing neurons that self-organises to recognise dots and dashes, see [7]. The structure of this network is shown in figure 10. The nodes have a potential p_i governed by (5)

$$\frac{dp_i}{dt} = -\theta p_i + w_i I(t) \qquad \theta > 0, \; w_i > 0 \qquad (5)$$

The node fires at time τ with $p_i(\tau) = T$, $\frac{dp_i(\tau)}{dt} > 0$ and for subsequent time period if $p_i(t) \geq T$ and $t - \tau \leq r_i$. This rule is based on the principle of neurons building up potentials capacitively and firing once a threshold is passed. Here r_i is the time period for which a node can fire before tiredness prevents further firing. The node recovers once the potential has dropped below threshold. Figure 11 illustrates how the input affects the node. Thus the node for recognising a dot will fire during a dash, but the output is stopped by the inhibitory contact from the input. This also restricts output to occur only at the end of a symbol. Learning is by self-organisation governed by equation (6) and was based on work by Kohonen [10] and Rumelhart and Zipser [11] and occurs at time t when symbol input ends. If a node fires then there is no learning.

$$\left. \begin{array}{ll} \Delta w_j = \alpha(Tw_j/p_j(t) - w_j) & \forall j \text{ st } |p_j(t) - T| = \min_i |p_i(t) - T| \\ \Delta w_i = \beta(Tw_i/p_i(t) - w_i) & \forall i \neq j \qquad 1 > \alpha \gg \beta > 0 \\ r_i = t - \tau_i & \forall i \text{ st } \gamma \geq t - \tau_i - r_i \geq 0 \end{array} \right\} \quad (6)$$

Experiments on performance as the learning parameters α, γ are varied were not required as a mathematical analysis exists to choose the best parameters [7].

This network performed extremely well on all problems. Table 1 shows an example of learning results for problem 2. As can be seen convergence occurs within approximately 2000 runs.

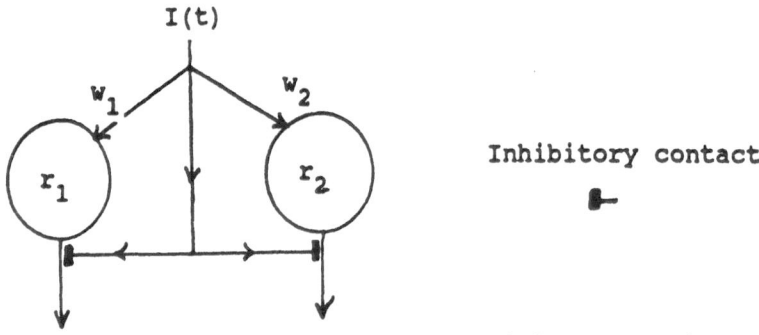

Inhibitory contact

Fig. 10. Structure for self-organising potential nodes to recognise morse code.

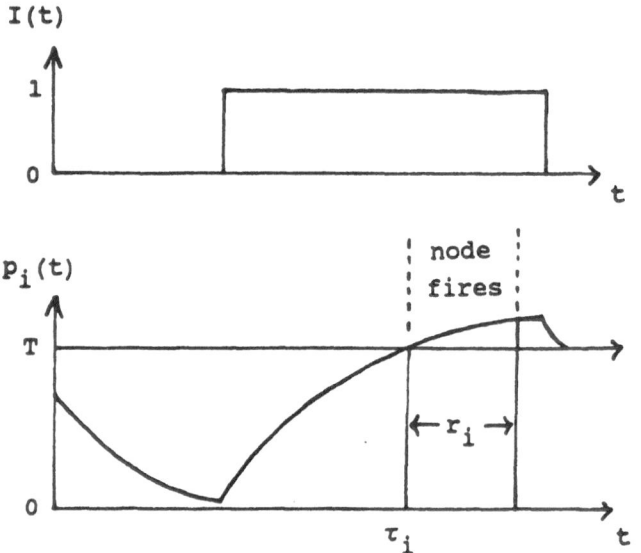

Fig. 11. Example activity of node due to input $I(t)$.

$\mu_1 \backslash \kappa$	3.0	4.0	5.0	6.0	7.0	8.0
1	1.0	1.0	1.0	1.0	1.0	1.0
	1881	1945	1945	1899	1752	1912
2	1.0	1.0	1.0	1.0	1.0	1.0
	2081	1950	1797	1797	1882	2013
3	1.0	1.0	1.0	1.0	1.0	1.0
	1974	2147	2063	2001	2012	2011
4	1.0	1.0	1.0	1.0	1.0	1.0
	1984	2226	2197	2189	2094	2141
5	1.0	1.0	1.0	1.0	1.0	1.0
	2063	2226	2243	2179	1976	1880
6	1.0	1.0	1.0	1.0	1.0	1.0
	2063	2273	2165	2011	1912	1871
7	1.0	1.0	1.0	1.0	1.0	1.0
	2000	2273	2264	2027	1944	1880

Table 1 Self-organising performance showing ϕ and average runs to convergence. $\kappa = \mu_2 - \mu_1$. $\sigma = 1$, $\alpha = 1$, $\gamma = 0.2$, $\beta = 0.001$, $T = 8$, $\theta = 0.3$.

This mechanism consists solely of an input layer that accumulates the last 10 inputs and feeds the current window contents forward through a normal MLP. The learning algorithm is applied at each output required. In this case 10 input nodes were chosen and two output nodes. There were no hidden nodes and the network was totally connected. Figure 12 shows this network. This mechanism has been applied to isolated digit recognition [6].

Due to the size of the window the maximum length of a dash to be learnt correctly for problems 2 and 3 is 8-σ. This is due to the requirement that non-symbols longer than a dash produce output (00). For problem 1 the maximum dash length for recognition is 9. For problems 1 and 2 the network learnt successfully for all dots and dashes within these ranges. Figure 13 shows the results for problem 3 where it can be seen that ϕ decays before μ_2=8-σ. However, this problem can be overcome by increasing the window size. Learning took approximately 2,000 runs.

The self-organising nodes have an advantage over windowing and the other methods, in that to accommodate for longer dots and dashes it is only necessary to alter the parameters θ and T. The other methods either require explicit addition of nodes as for windowing or addition of further hidden nodes as experimental results have shown.

COMMENTS

Apart from the self-organising method all the mechanisms process in steps at discrete time intervals. The smallest unit of which is the time period of a delay line or update of a capacitive node. The self-organising method uses a continuous input.

For the MLP methods learning was assumed to have occurred once the total error over all testing patterns was less than 0.2.

The self-organising method was assumed successful on

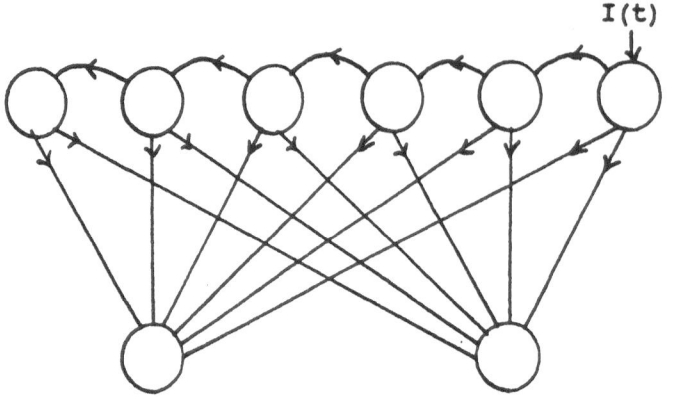

Fig. 12. Example MLP with 7 node input window.

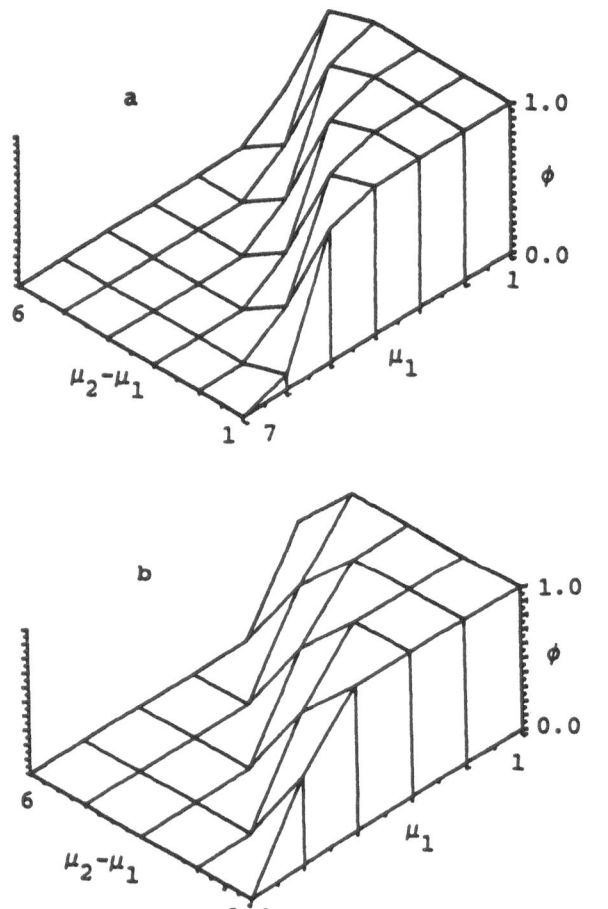

Fig. 13. MLP with 10 node input window. Variation of ϕ with μ_1, μ_2, 10,000 runs. a. $\alpha=0.3$, $\eta=0.7$, $\sigma=0$. b. $\alpha=0.5$, $\eta=0.5$, $\sigma=1$.

problems 1 and 2 if it responded to pulses within the range $[\mu_1+0.1, \mu_1+\sigma-0.1]$ and not to pulses outside of the range $[\mu_1-0.25, \mu_1+\sigma+0.25]$ for dots and similarly for dashes. This variation was allowed so that it was not necessary to wait for final convergence and since the discrete time nature of the other methods will immediately lead to similar errors in encoding of continuous values. In the case of problem 3 the network responses to the testing sequence were considered.

CONCLUSIONS

The self-organising potential node and MLP with input window perform much better on the morse code problem than the other methods tried. The self-organising method has advantages in that for large values of μ_1 and μ_2 the structure of the network does not have to be altered but only parameters changed. Further, capacitive nodes aid the MLP in solving the problem. Thus the use of temporal nodes aids solution of the morse code problem. The application of temporal nodes to more difficult problems should be explored.

Production of the self-organising potential node has been based on neurophysiology which has provided useful inspiration. As the resulting network performs well the application of neurophysiological mechanisms should be considered when constructing a network.

The self-organising method was constructed specifically for morse code recognition. As such it has been structured to solve the problem. Its performance demonstrates the advantage in structuring a network for a particular problem.

ACKNOWLEDGEMENT

I would like to thank Smiths Industries Aerospace and Defence Systems for their support during this project and my supervisor Dr C K Wright for his encouragement.

REFERENCES

[1] Rumelhart DE, Hinton GE, Williams RJ. Learning
     internal representations by error propagation. In:
     Rumelhart DE, McClelland JL, PDP Research Group.
     Parallel distributed processing. Explorations in
     the microstructure of cognition. Vol 1
     Foundations. MIT Press, 1986, pp318-362.

[2] Robinson AJ, Fallside F. Static and dynamic error
     propagation networks with application to speech
     coding. In: Proceedings of the IEEE conference on
     neural information processing systems: Natural and
     synthetic, 1987.

[3] Norrod FE, O'Neill MD, Gat E. Feedback-induced
     sequentiality in neural networks. Proceedings of the
     IEEE first international conference on neural
     networks, 1987.

[4] Stornetta WS, Hogg T, Huberman BA. A dynamical
     approach to temporal pattern processing. In:
     Proceedings of the IEEE conference on neural
     information processing systems: Natural and synthetic,
     1987.

[5] Waibel A, Hanazawa T, Hinton G, Shikano K, Lang K.
     Phoneme recognition using time-delay neural networks.
     Technical Report TR-1-0006, ATR Interpreting
     Telephony Laboratories, 1987.

[6] Peeling SM, Moore RK, Varga AP. Isolated digit
     recognition using the multi-layer perceptron. In:
     Proceedings of NATO ASI Speech Understanding, 1987.

[7] Hill D. A self-organising temporally processing
     network for recognition of morse code. In preparation.

[8] Moore R. Computational techniques. In: Bristow G (ed)
     Electronic speech recognition techniques,
     technology and applications. Collins, London,1986,
     pp130-157.

[9] McCulloch N. Personal communication. 1989.

[10] Kohonen T. Self-organizing feature maps. In: Kohonen T
     Self-organization and associative memory, 2nd Edition,
     Springer-Verlag, 1987, pp119-157.

[11] Rumelhart DE, Zipser D. Feature discovery by
     competitive learning. In: Rumelhart DE, McClelland JL,
     PDP Research Group. Parallel distributed processing.
     Explorations in the microstructure of cognition. Vol 1
     MIT Press, 1986. pp151-193.

Dynamics of Binary Networks with Extended Time-Summation.

P. C. Bressloff

ABSTRACT

A model of a binary network with extended time-summation is derived by considering a leaky integrator shunting network in which the output of each neuron is taken to be a sequence of impulses or spikes. The nature of the extended time-summation involves keeping a record of the network output activity that reaches back to some chosen initial time. It is therefore no longer possible to specify the state of the network at any particular time in terms of the discrete space of binary outputs $\{0, 1\}^N$. The appropriate description of the network dynamics is now in terms of the continuous space of internal activations R^N. Neural networks with extended time-summation can exhibit various forms of complex dynamics including phase-locking and chaos, in contrast to standard binary networks whose dynamics is necessarily recurrent; this is illustrated in the case of a single neuron. The effects of noise in such networks are also briefly discussed.

1. BINARY NETWORKS

Consider a network of N standard binary threshold neurons [1] and denote the output of neuron i at time t by $a_i(t) \, \varepsilon \, \{0, 1\}$. Assume that the network is fully-connected with w_{ij} being the connection weight from neuron j to neuron i. Then the system evolves in discrete time $t = 0, 1, \cdots$ according to the equations [2]

$$a_i(t+1) = \theta(\sum_{j=1}^{N} w_{ij} a_j(t) - h_i), \quad i = 1, ..., N \tag{1.1}$$

where h_i is the threshold of neuron i and θ is the step-function,

$$\theta(x) = \begin{cases} 1 & \text{if } x \geq 0 \\ 0 & \text{if } x < 0 \end{cases}$$

The state of the network at time t is given by the binary vector $\mathbf{a}(t) = (a_1(t), ..., a_N(t)) \, \varepsilon \, \{0, 1\}^N$. Since the number of possible states for finite N is itself finite, being equal to 2^N, the network dynamics is recurrent. That is, in a finite number of time-steps ($\leq 2^N$) the network returns to a state previously visited. This implies that the long-term behaviour of the network is cyclic. It is difficult, in general to derive properties of the cycles (such as typical cycle length) from details of the connection weights. An exception is in the case of symmetric weights, $w_{ij} = w_{ji}$, for which it may be shown that the network either converges to a fixed point (cycle of period one) or to a cycle of period two.

We conclude that binary networks (for finite N) cannot exhibit any form of long-term aperiodic behaviour. In particular, they cannot exhibit stimulus-induced synchronisation or phase-locking (i.e. switching from an aperiodic state to a periodic one) nor chaos. From observations of real neurons, it has been suggested that the former might play a role in feature linking [3], [4] and the latter in providing a mechanism of attention and novel feature detection [5]. Therefore, it is of interest to try to extend the binary neuron model in such a way that more interesting dynamics may be generated without losing the inherent simplicity of the original model.

Another feature of the binary neuron is that it is based upon a very simplified model of a real neuron. To make the analogy more explicit, it is useful to rewrite equation (1.1) in the form

$$V_i(t+1) = \sum_{j=1}^{N} w_{ij} a_j(t) \tag{1.2}$$

$$a_i(t+1) = \theta(V_i(t+1) - h_i) \tag{1.3}$$

so that the internal activation $V_i(t)$ represents the membrane potential of neuron i and the binary output $a_i(t)$ indicates whether or not the neuron fires at time t. Then equation (1.2) describes in idealised form the summation of post-synaptic potentials (PSP's) arising from synaptic inputs and (1.3) gives the condition for firing. In this paper we show how a slightly more detailed account of the mechanism of PSP summation in real neurons (as expressed by leaky integrator equations) leads to a model of a binary neuron with extended time-summation which exhibits the range of dynamics mentioned above and hence provides a basis for developing simple but computationally powerful networks. The model is derived in section 2, its dynamics at the single neuron level analysed in section 3 and the effects of noise discussed in section 4.

2. NETWORKS WITH EXTENDED TIME-SUMMATION.

A leaky integrator shunting network models the dynamical evolution of the membrane potential $V_i(t)$ according to the differential equation

$$\frac{dV_i}{dt} = -\frac{V_i(t)}{\tau_i} + \sum_{j \neq i} \Delta g_{ij}(t)[S_{ij} - V_i(t)], \quad i = 1, ..., N \tag{2.1}$$

Here Δg_{ij} is the change in conductance at synapse ij, with membrane reversal potential S_{ij}, due to incoming activity from neuron j. In the absence of any inputs the membrane potential decays at the rate τ_i^{-1} to an equilibrium level which is taken to be zero. The term Δg_{ij} may be written as

$$\Delta g_{ij}(t + t_d) = g_{ij} \frac{dN_j}{dt}(t), \quad g_{ij} \geq 0 \tag{2.2}$$

where g_{ij} is the change in conductance induced by the arrival of a single action potential from neuron j and dN_j/dt is the firing rate. (We are ignoring temporal features such as the time courses of ionic channels). Since the change in conductance is positive, the effect of each shunting term $\Delta g_{ij}[S_{ij} - V_i]$ is for V_i to tend towards S_{ij}. Thus, positive and negative S_{ij} correspond, respectively, to excitatory and inhibitory inputs. Note that a time delay t_d has been included in equation (2.2) to take into account of the fact that there is a finite time interval between the arrival of an action potential at a synapse and the occurrence of a corresponding PSP in the post-synaptic neuron. (For more details of neurophysiology see references [6], [7])

Equation (2.1) must be supplemented by conditions determining the firing rates dN_j/dt. A simple choice, neglecting the pulse-shape of action potentials, is to take each dN_j/dt to be a linear sum of delta-functions representing a neuronal spike-train,

$$\frac{dN_j}{dt}(t) = \sum_{n \geq 1} \delta(t - T_j^n) \tag{2.3}$$

where T_j^n is the time at which neuron j fires for the nth occasion since $t = 0$. The firing times are then determined by the iterative threshold condition

$$T_j^n = \inf \{t \,|\, V_j(t) \geq h_j; \, t \geq T_j^{n-1} + t_R \}, \quad j = 1, ..., N \tag{2.4}$$

where t_R is the absolute refractory period. Equation (2.4) may be understood as follows. Suppose that neuron j last fired at time T. Then for $T \leq t < T + t_R$ the neuron is incapable of firing again, although $V_j(t)$ continues to evolve according to equation (2.1); for $t \geq T + t_R$ the neuron fires as soon as $V_j(t)$ is above the threshold h_j. Using a special choice of initial conditions it can be shown that equations (2.1)-(2.4) reduce to a discrete time model describing a binary network with extended time-summation [8]. We shall indicate the steps in this derivation below.

To proceed, equation (2.1) is integrated with $V_i(0) = 0$ such that for $t > 0$

$$V_i(t) = \int_0^t dt' \; [\sum_{k \neq i} S_{ik} g_{ik} \frac{dN_k}{dt'}(t'-t_d)] \exp(-[t - t']/\tau_i)$$

$$\times \exp(-\int_{t'}^t dt'' \sum_{j \neq i} g_{ij} \frac{dN_j}{dt''}(t''-t_d)) \tag{2.5}$$

Impose the conditions that T_j^n, $n \geq 1$, $j = 1, ..., N$ are integer multiples of the delay and $t_R = t_d$; the former condition is satisfied provided the initial firing times T_j^1 are chosen to be multiples of t_d. Then equation (2.5) reduces to [8]

$$V_i(t) = [\sum_{m=1}^{[t]} \sum_{k \neq i} S_{ik} g_{ik} \Delta N_k(mt_d - t_d)] \exp(-[t - mt_d]/\tau_i)$$

$$\times \exp(- \sum_{n=m}^{[t]} \sum_{j \neq i} g_{ij} \Delta N_j(nt_d - t_d)), \quad t > 0 \tag{2.6}$$

where $[t]$ is the largest integer less than or equal to t/t_d. Here $\Delta N_j(mt_d)$ is the number of times neuron j fires in the interval $[mt_d, (m+1)t_d)$. Thus, since the T_j^n are integer multiples of t_d, $\Delta N_j(mt_d)$ satisfies the threshold condition (cf. equation (1.3))

$$\Delta N_j(mt_d) = a_j(m) = \theta(V_j(mt_d) - h_j) \qquad (2.7)$$

From equation (2.7) it follows that the dynamics of $V_i(t)$ is determined completely by solving (2.6) at the times $t = mt_d$, $m \geq 0$. Hence, restricting t to the discrete times $t = 0, 1, \cdots$ (with $t_d = 1$ for simplicity) and substituting $r = t-m+1$, $s = t-n+1$ we have the difference equation

$$V_i(t) = \sum_{k \neq i} \sum_{r=1}^{t} w_{ik} a_k(t-r) \gamma_i^{r-1} \exp(-\sum_{j \neq i} \sum_{s=1}^{r} w_{ij} a_j(t-s)/S_{ij}), \quad t = 1, 2... \qquad (2.8)$$

where $\gamma_i = e^{-\tau_i}$, $w_{ij} = g_{ij} S_{ij}$. Combining equation (2.8) with the threshold condition (2.7) finally gives

$$a_i(t) = \theta(\sum_{k \neq i} \sum_{r=1}^{t} w_{ik} a_k(t-r) \gamma_i^{r-1} \exp[-\sum_{j \neq i} \sum_{s=1}^{r} w_{ij} a_j(t-s)/S_{ij}] - h_i) \qquad (2.9)$$

which describes the dynamics of a network of binary neurons with extended time-summation and thresholding activity (membrane potential) which is nonlinear in weights.

Since equation (2.9) involves a time-summation over the complete past history of the network it is clear that the dynamical state of the network at any time t cannot be specified by the binary vector $\mathbf{a}(t)$, in contrast to the binary model, equation (1.1). However, the state of the network can be specified by the continuous vector $\mathbf{V}(t)$ since equation (2.8) may be rewritten in the form

$$V_i(t) = [\gamma_i V_i(t-1) + \sum_{k \neq i} w_{ik} a_k(t-1)] \exp(-\sum_{j \neq i} w_{ij} a_j(t-1)/S_{ij}) \qquad (2.10)$$

which is an iterative equation for $\mathbf{V}(t)$, (on replacing $a_j(t-1)$ by $\theta(V_j(t-1) - h_j)$ etc.). Thus the state space of a network with extended time-summation is given by the continuous space R^N rather than the discrete space $\{0, 1\}^N$. As the state space is no longer finite, the dynamics is not necessarily recurrent and aperiodic behaviour is possible; this will be illustrated in the case of a single neuron in the next section. Equation (2.10) extends equation (1.2) by incorporating certain qualitative features of the underlying leaky integrator model, equation (2.1). Firstly, the dynamics of the network is bounded. This is a consequence of the exponential factor in equation (2.10) which suppresses high activity levels in the network. To see this observe that $w_{ij}/S_{ij} = g_{ij} > 0$ for all $i \neq j$ and hence $\exp(-\sum_j w_{ij} a_j(t-1)/S_{ij}) < 1$. Thus, if the number of neurons active at time $t-1$ is large then the exponential tends to be small so reducing the value of each membrane potential at time t. Note that the exponential factor arises from the presence of shunting in the leaky integrator equation (2.1), and the latter ensures that solutions to (2.1) are bounded. In the limit $S_{ij} \to \infty$, $g_{ij} \to 0$, such that w_{ij} is constant, the exponential approaches unity; this limit corresponds to dropping the term $-\sum_{j \neq i} \Delta g_{ij}(t) V_i(t)$ in (2.1). Secondly, changes in the membrane potential V_i are not determined solely by the synaptic inputs but also depend on the membrane potential itself; in the absence of any inputs, V_i decays to zero at a rate γ_i.

It is the presence of the term $\gamma_i V_i$ in equation (2.10) which leads to the sum over histories in equation (2.9); in the limit $\gamma_i \to 0$ (or $\tau_i \to 0$) equation (2.9) reduces to the simpler form

$$a_i(t) = \theta(\sum_{k \neq i} w_{ik} a_k(t-r) \exp[-\sum_{j \neq i} w_{ij} a_j(t-s)/S_{ij}] - h_i) \qquad (2.11)$$

in which a(t) depends only on a($t-1$) at the previous time step.

3. DYNAMICS OF A SINGLE NEURON.

Let $V(t)$ be the activation state of a single neuron at time t and consider the leaky-integrator equation

$$\frac{dV}{dt} = -\frac{V(t)}{\tau} + \Delta g(t)[S - V(t)] + I(t) \qquad (3.1)$$

where $\Delta g(t)$ is the change in conductance,

$$\Delta g(t + t_d) = g\frac{dN}{dt}(t) = g\sum_{n \geq 1} \delta(t - T^n) \qquad (3.2)$$

and $I(t)$ is an external input. The neuron's firing times T^n, $n \geq 1$ are assumed to satisfy a threshold condition of the form (2.4) with $t_R = t_d$. We shall not impose any restrictions on the value of S and g. However, when $g > 0$, $S < 0$ the feedback term in (3.1) may be interpreted as a representation of the effects of relative refractory period [8]. For if the neuron fires at time T then it receives an inhibitory impulse at time $T + t_R$ which reduces the likelihood of subsequent firing; the effect of the inhibition decays with time constant τ. Note that such feedback may be incorporated into the full network model of section 2 by extending the summation on the right-hand side of equation (2.1) to include a diagonal term $\Delta g_{ii}[S_{ii} - V_i(t)]$

If the T^n are taken to be multiples of t_d and $I(t)$ is of the form

$$I(t) = I\sum_{m \geq 0} \delta(t - mt_d) \qquad (3.3)$$

then the analysis of section 2 leads to the difference equation

$$V(t) = [\gamma V(t - 1) + wa(t-1) + I] \exp(-ga(t-1)) \qquad (3.4)$$

where $\gamma = e^{-\tau}$, $w = gS$ and $a(t-1)$ satisfies the threshold condition

$$a(t-1) = \theta(V(t-1) - h) \qquad (3.5)$$

Note that in the limit $g \to 0$, $S \to \infty$, for fixed w, equation (3.4) reduces to the Nagumo-Sato model [9], [10]. Substituting equation (3.5) into (3.4) and setting $x_t = V(t) - h$ we obtain the one-dimensional map [11]

$$x_t \equiv f(x_{t-1}) \tag{3.6}$$

$$= \begin{cases} \gamma e^{-g} x_{t-1} + A - B & \text{if } x_{t-1} \geq 0 \\ \gamma x_{t-1} + A & \text{if } x_{t-1} < 0 \end{cases}$$

with

$$A = I - (1-\gamma)h$$

$$B = A(1-e^{-g}) - we^{-g}$$

The function f describes a piece-wise linear map with a single discontinuity at $x = 0$ where $f(0^-) = A$ and $f(0^+) = A - B \equiv C$. The parameters $-g$, γ determine the slope of the two halves of the graph of $f(x)$ to be $\gamma_+ = \gamma e^{-g}$ for $x > 0$ and $\gamma_- = \gamma$ for $x < 0$. We shall illustrate the different types of dynamical behaviour of the map f by considering different regions of the parameter space $\{A, C, \gamma_+, \gamma_-\}$; the only restrictions are that $0 < \gamma_- < 1$ and $\gamma_+ > 0$. (see figures 1-4).

(a) $A < 0, C > 0, \gamma_+ < 1$ (figure 1). There are two stable fixed points

$$x_- = A/(1 - \gamma_-), \quad x_+ = C/(1 - \gamma_+) \tag{3.7}$$

All trajectories with $x_t < 0$ for some t converge to x_-, whereas all trajectories such that $x_t > 0$ for some t converge to x_+. Note that the fixed points x_+ and x_- correspond, respectively, to the neuron being active and inactive at every time step.

(b) $C > 0, \gamma_+ > 1, A > 0$ (figure 2). All trajectories escape to infinity. This divergent behaviour reflects the presence of positive feedback in the original leaky integrator model (3.1) when $g < 0$.

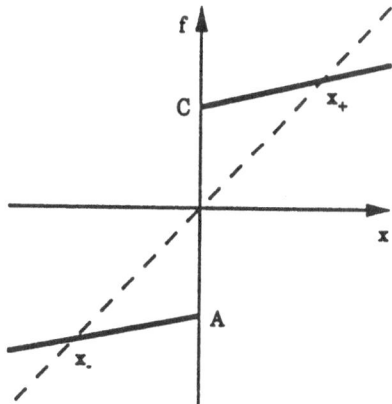

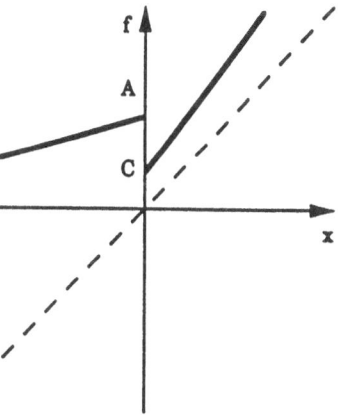

Fig. 1. Map f for $A < 0, C > 0$; two stable fixed points x_+ and x_-.

Fig. 2. Map f for $A > 0, C > 0$, $\gamma_+ > 1$.

(c) $A > 0$, $C < 0$, $\gamma_+ < 1$ (figure 3). All trajectories converge to the bounded interval $\Sigma = \{x : C \leq x \leq A\}$. The dynamics on the interval Σ is qualitatively the same as that of the Nagumo-Sato model [9], [10] which corresponds to the case $\gamma_+ = \gamma_-$. That is, for almost all inputs A the dynamics is phase-locked so that all trajectories are attracted to a unique periodic orbit whose cycle length depends on the value of A; in the exceptional cases the behaviour is aperiodic and the corresponding attractor is a unique Cantor set. This is illustrated in the bifurcation diagram of figure 5 which displays the long-term behaviour of equation (3.6) for a fixed starting point and $B = 1$, $\gamma_+ = \gamma_- = 0.8$, $0 < A < 1$. Note for example, that when $A = 0.5$ there is an orbit of period two in which the neuron fires at alternate time steps whereas when $A = 0.3$ there is an orbit of period three in which the neuron fires once every three time-steps etc.

(d) $A > 0$, $C < 0$, $\gamma_+ > 1$ (figure 4). There is an unstable fixed point at $x = x_+$ and all trajectories such that $x_t < x_+$ for some t converge to the bounded interval Σ provided the fixed point lies outside Σ, i.e. $A < x_+$ (otherwise the trajectories escape to infinity). For a certain range of values of the input A the dynamics is chaotic as shown in the bifurcation diagram of figure 6 for $B = 1$, $\gamma_+ = 4.0$, $\gamma_- = 0.8$.

For a more detailed analysis of equation (3.6) see reference [11] where it is shown how the behaviour exhibited in cases (c) and (d) may be understood in terms of the dynamics of discontinuous circle maps. Having discussed the dynamics of a single neuron, we may view the full network model of section 2, with diagonal feedback terms included, as a dynamical system of coupled maps based upon equation (3.6). The dynamics of such a system has certain similarities with that of coupled nonlinear oscillators [11] and might be useful as a basis for developing networks which exhibit stimulus-induced oscillations.

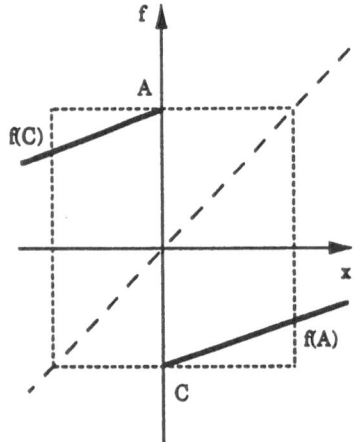

Fig. 3. Map f for $A > 0$, $C < 0$, $\gamma_+ < 1$. Dotted rectangle indicates map on interval $C < x < A$.

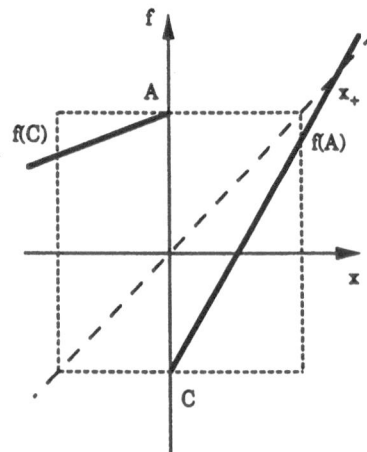

Fig. 4. Map f for $0 < A < x_+$, $C < 0$, $\gamma_+ > 1$. Unstable fixed point at x_+

204

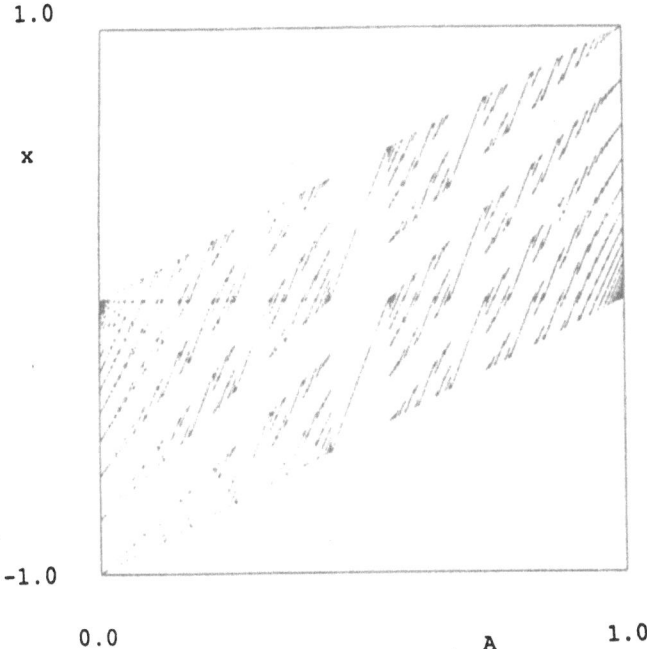

Fig. 5. Bifurcation diagram of the map f with respect to an external input A where $B = 1.0$, $\gamma_- = \gamma_+ = 0.8$.

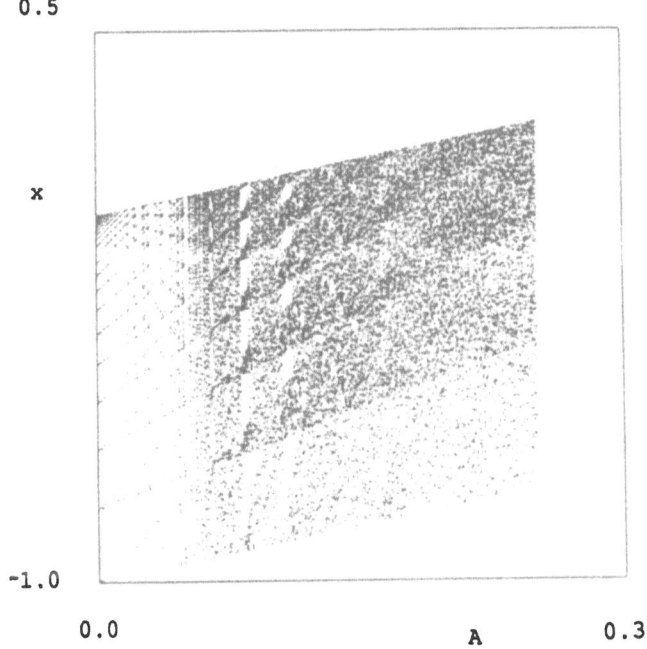

Fig. 6. Bifurcation diagram of the map f with respect to an external input A where $B = 1.0$, $\gamma_- = 0.8$, $\gamma_+ = 4.0$.

4. NOISE.

In this final section we consider the issue of noise in networks with extended time-summation. The simplest way to incorporate noise into such networks is to replace equation (2.10) by the stochastic equation

$$V_i(t) = F_i(\mathbf{V}(t-1)) + \eta_i(t-1)$$

$$= [\gamma_i V_i(t-1) + \sum_{k \neq i} w_{ik} a_k(t-1)] \exp(-\sum_{j \neq i} w_{ij} a_j(t-1)/S_{ij}) + \eta_i(t-1) \quad (4.1)$$

where $a_j(t-1) = \theta(V_j(t-1) - h_j)$ and η_i is an additive white noise term. In particular, each sequence $\{\eta_i(t), t \geq 0\}$, $i = 1, ..., N$, is an independent stochastic process with a smooth time-independent probability density $\rho_i(\eta)$. Thus, denoting averages with respect to these densities by $<...>$, we have

$$<\eta_i(t)> = \overline{\eta}_i \quad (4.2)$$

$$<[\eta_i(t) - \overline{\eta}_i][\eta_j(t') - \overline{\eta}_j]> = \delta_{ij} \delta_{tt'} \sigma_i^2 \quad (4.3)$$

where $\overline{\eta}_i$ and σ_i^2 are, respectively, the mean and variance of the density ρ_i.

The additive noise η_i may be considered as a random fluctuation of the threshold h_i. Note, however, that in real neurons a more significant source of noise is associated with the quantal release of chemical transmitters at synapses [12]. This may be incorporated into equation (4.1), in the form of multiplicative white noise, by taking each weight w_{ij} to be a random variable $w_{ij}(t)$ which is independently updated at every time-step from a fixed probability density along similar lines to $\eta_i(t)$ [8]. The resulting stochastic network model is an extension of the random iterative network model analysed extensively elsewhere [13], [14]. In the following we shall consider the simpler case of additive noise.

Deterministic dynamical systems with applied stochastic perturbations have been considered by Kifer [15] and in the physical context by Feigenbaum and Hashler [16]. More specifically, a useful way of studying such systems is to consider the time evolution or flow of probability densities in state space. This flow is generated by picking a large number of initial states of the system and following the ensemble of trajectories associated with these states. The probability density at a particular point in state space and at a time t determines the likelihood of a trajectory of the ensemble passing through an infinitesimal neighbourhood of that point at time t. Let u_t denote the probability density on the space of membrane potentials $\mathbf{V}(t)$. For a fixed vector $\eta = (\eta_1, ..., \eta_N)$, the density of the (deterministic) system (4.1) evolves according to the linear operator equation $u_{t+1} = P_\eta u_t$ where

$$u_{t+1}(\mathbf{V}') = [P_\eta u_t](\mathbf{V}') = \int_{R^N} \delta(\mathbf{V}' - \mathbf{F}(\mathbf{V}) - \eta) u_t(\mathbf{V}) \, d\mathbf{V} \quad (4.4)$$

The delta-function in equation (4.4) restricts the integral on the right-hand side to points $\mathbf{V}$ which satisfy $\mathbf{F}(\mathbf{V}) + \eta = \mathbf{V}'$. When η is a random variable, the density of the corresponding stochastic system evolves according to the modified linear operator equation $u_{t+1} = \overline{P} u_t$ where

$$u_{t+1}(V') = \bar{P}u_t(V') = \int_{R^N} \rho(\eta) [P_\eta u_t](V') \, d\eta$$

$$= \int_{R^N} \rho(V' - F(V)) u_t(V) \, dV \tag{4.5}$$

and $\rho(\eta) = \prod_i \rho_i(\eta_i)$.

It can be shown [17] that the sequence of densities $\{u_t; t \geq 0\}$ satisfying equation (4.5) converges to a unique limiting distribution u_∞ provided the smooth density ρ satisfies

$$\int_{R^N} \rho(\eta) |\eta| \, d\eta < \infty \tag{4.6}$$

and $\rho(\eta) > 0$ almost everywhere. Then,

$$\lim_{t \to \infty} ||u_t - u_\infty|| = 0 \tag{4.7}$$

where $||...||$ is the L_1 norm [18]. One consequence of equation (4.7) is that time averages are independent of initial conditions and may be replaced by ensemble averages over the limiting distribution u_∞. Therefore, for any integrable function f,

$$\lim_{T \to \infty} \frac{1}{T} \sum_{t=0}^{T} f(V(t)) = \int_{R^N} f(V) u_\infty(V) \, dV \tag{4.8}$$

As in the deterministic case (section 2), the stochastic dynamics of a network with extended time-summation is formulated on R^N rather than $\{0, 1\}^N$. Define $P_t(\mathbf{a})$ to be the probability that the output of the network at time t is $\mathbf{a}$. Then $P_t(\mathbf{a})$ may be obtained from $u_t(V)$ by the projection,

$$P_t(\mathbf{a}) = \int_{R^N} u_t(V)\Theta_{\mathbf{a}}(V) \, dV \tag{4.9}$$

where

$$\Theta_{\mathbf{a}}(V) = \prod_{i=1}^{N} [a_i \theta(V_i - h_i) + (1 - a_i)(1 - \theta(V_i - h_i))]$$

Hence, the sequence of densities $\{u_t; t \geq 0\}$ on R^N induces, via equation (4.9), the sequence $\{P_t; t \geq 0\}$ on $\{0, 1\}^N$. Moreover, equations (4.7) and (4.9) imply that the latter sequence converges to a unique distribution P_∞ where

$$P_\infty(\mathbf{a}) = \lim_{t \to \infty} P_t(\mathbf{a}) = \int_{R^N} u_\infty(V)\Theta_{\mathbf{a}}(V) \, dV \tag{4.10}$$

In the limit $\gamma_i \to 0$, $i = 1, ..., N$ it can be shown that applying equation (4.9) to equation (4.5) leads to the Markov chain

$$P_{t+1}(\mathbf{b}) = \sum_{\mathbf{a}} Q_{\mathbf{ba}} P_t(\mathbf{a}) \tag{4.11}$$

where $Q_{\mathbf{ba}}$ is the probability of transition from $\mathbf{a}$ to $\mathbf{b}$, with [17]

$$Q_{\mathbf{ba}} = \int_{R^N} \prod_{i=1}^{N} \rho_i(V_i - [\sum_{k \neq i} w_{ik} a_k] \exp[-\sum_{j \neq i} w_{ij} a_j / S_{ij}]) \, \Theta_{\mathbf{b}}(V) \, dV \tag{4.12}$$

Hence, in this limit the sequence $\{P_t : t \geq 0\}$ can be determined directly. Note that if the exponential in equation (4.12) is dropped and

$$\rho_i(\eta) = \frac{d}{d\eta}[1 + e^{-\eta/T}]^{-1}, \quad i = 1, ..., N \qquad (4.13)$$

where T is a 'temperature' parameter, then $Q_{\mathbf{ba}}$ is precisely the transition matrix of the Little model [19] which has been studied extensively in the spin-glass approach to neural networks [20]. It is clear from the discussion of this section that in the presence of additive noise, standard binary networks and those with extended time-summation exhibit similar long-term behaviour, (convergence to a unique probability density); in the former case the stochastic dynamics on the space of binary outputs may be determined directly in terms of a Markov chain.

5. CONCLUSION

We conclude that the important dynamical variables of a network with extended time-summation are the continuous-valued internal activations or membrane potentials $V_i(t)$. This is true in both the deterministic and random cases. One feature that has not been considered here is the nature of learning rules for these networks. Learning rules for standard binary networks (section 1) are usually of the Hebbian form in which each weight w_{ij} is modified according to the output activities a_i, a_j on either side of the connection (ij). This learning rule does not depend on the particular values of the membrane potentials V_i, V_j and therefore may not be the most appropriate one for networks with extended time-summation. Such networks should have additional temporal pattern storage facilities as indicated by the presence of a memory of previous activity in equation (2.10) leading to the sum over histories in equation (2.9) (see for example reference [21]). In this paper we have only considered finite N; it is well known that the behaviour of a standard binary network can drastically alter when the size of a system becomes large, which is represented mathematically by the thermodynamic limit $N \to \infty$. In the stochastic case this leads to a breakdown of the ergodicity condition (4.8) and in the deterministic case can lead to chaotic dynamics [22]. The statistical dynamics on $\{0, 1\}^N$, when N is large, can be analysed using techniques from spin-glass theory [20]. However, such techniques cannot be applied to the study of the statistical dynamics of networks with extended time-summation since the analogy of magnetic spins is no longer appropriate. We hope to consider these issues further elsewhere.

ACKNOWLEDGEMENTS

The construction of the discrete time leaky integrator model was carried out in collaboration with Prof. John G. Taylor of the mathematics department, King's College, London. The single neuron model was analysed in collaboration with Dr Jaroslav Stark of the systems theory group at Hirst Research centre.

REFERENCES.

1. McCullogh WS and Pitts W. A logical calculus of the ideas immament in nervous activity. Bull. Math. Biophys. 1943; 5: 115-133

2. Caianello ER. Outline of a theory of thought processes and thinking machines. J. Theor. Biol. 1961; 1: 204-235

3. Gray CM, Konig P, Engel AK, and Singer W. Oscillatory responses in cat visual cortex exhibit inter-columnar synchronisation which reflects global stimulus response. Nature 1989; 338: 334-7

4. Eckhorn R, Bauer R, Jordan R,, Brosch M, Kruse W, Munk M, and Reitboeck H J. Coherent oscillations: a mechanism of feature linking in the Visual cortex. Biol. Cybern. 1988; 60: 121-30

5. Yao Y and Freeman W. Pattern recognition in olfactory systems. In; Proceedings IEEE INNS international joint conference on neural networks, vol. II, pp.167-174, 1989

6. Shepherd GH. The synaptic organisation of the brain, 2nd ed. Oxford University Press, Oxford, 1988

7. Kuffler SW, Niccols JG, and Martin AR. From neuron to Brain. Sinauer, Sunderland, Mass. 1984

8. Bressloff PC and Taylor JG. Discrete time leaky integrator networks with synaptic noise. HRC preprint, submitted to Neural Networks, 1990

9. Nagumo J and Sato S. Kybernetik 1972; 10: 155

10. Aihara K, Takabe T and Toyoda M. Chaotic neural networks. Phys. Lett. A 1990; 144: 333-341

11. Bressloff PC and Stark J. Neuronal dynamics based on discontinuous circle maps, HRC preprint, submitted to Phys. Lett. A, 1990

12. Katz B. The release of neural transmitter substance. Thomas, Springfield, 1969

13. Bressloff PC. Neural networks and random iterative maps. In: Taylor JG and Mannion CLT (eds) New developments in neural computing. Adam Hilger, Bristol, 1989

14. Bressloff PC and Taylor JG. Random iterative networks. Phys Rev A 1990; 41: 1126-1137

15. Kifer Y. Ergodic theory of random transformations. Birkhauser, 1986

16. Feigenbaum MJ and Hashler B. Irrational decimations and path integrals for external noise. Phys. Rev. Lett. 1982;49: 605-609

17. Bressloff PC. Noise in binary networks with extended time-summation, in preparation, 1990

18. Dunford N and Schwartz JT. Linear operators. Part I. General theory. Wiley, New York, 1957

19. Little WA. The existence of persistent states in the brain. Math. Biosci. 1974; 19: 101-120

20. Amit DJ. Modelling brain function. Cambridge University Press, Cambridge, 1989

21. Stornetta W, Hogg T and Huberman BA. A dynamical approach to temporal pattern processing. In: Proceedings of the IEEE conference on neural information processing. San Diego, Ca. 1988

22. Sompolinsky H. and Crisanti A. Chaos in random neural networks. Phys. Rev. Lett. 1988; 61: 259-262

Training Strategies for Probabilistic RAMs

D. Gorse and J.G. Taylor

ABSTRACT

Training algorithms for probabilistic RAMs (pRAMs) are discussed. In particular it is described how a form of gradient descent training may be implemented using spike train correlation analysis, and it is indicated how pRAMs may be applied to problems of associative search, using local reinforcement training rules which utilise synaptic rather than threshold noise in the stochastic search procedure.

INTRODUCTION

There are many learning algorithms for artificial neural nets, but none of them has yet proven to be easily implementable in hardware, either by analog or digital technologies. Recent developments in learning theory have indicated that stochastic activity in the neural units is important for allowing a fuller exploration of the state space, although such noise is usually introduced at the threshold level, which is biologically unrealistic. We have recently developed a hardware implementable stochastic model which uses probabilistic RAMs or pRAMs, and have shown that such a model develops in time identically to a corresponding net of synaptically noisy neurons [1]; this model can be extended considerably in the direction of greater neurobiological realism whilst retaining the potential for a straightforward hardware realisation [2]. We have investigated a range of training procedures for pRAM networks, and have found that the model has significant potential as an alternative to more conventional connectionist nodes.

THE pRAM MODEL

Networks of Boolean units (RAMs) were first studied by Kauffman [3] in the context of genetic nets, and were subsequently extensively used by Aleksander in pattern recognition applications (see, for example, Aleksander, Thomas and Bowden [4]). It was noted that such deterministic units could be regarded as having 'neuron-like' properties (in fact subsuming the category of McCullough-Pitts binary decision neurons (BDNs), since an N-input RAM can perform any of the 2^{2^N} possible functions of its inputs, whilst a BDN can perform only those which are linearly separable) but no attempt was made to closely model biological neurons.

The units mentioned above were constructed from conventional RAMs, with either 0 or 1 stored at a given address. Aleksander [5] extended the RAM model to that of a 'probabilistic logic node' (PLN): in addition to storing 0 or 1, a PLN memory location could be in a 'u' state, in which it was equally likely to output 0 or 1 when addressed. The PLN model has since been further extended by Myers [6] to include more internal states. The natural limit of these multi-state PLN models would be to let the 2^N memory contents α_u (where u is an N-bit binary address vector) take on a continuous range of values $\in [0,1]$: this condition defines the 'probabilistic random access memory' (pRAM) of Gorse and Taylor [1]. In this model the output $a \in \{0,1\}$ of the N-input pRAM A is 1 with probability

$$\Pr(a{=}1 \mid \underline{i}) = \sum_{\underline{u}} \alpha_u \prod_{j=1}^{N} (\, i_j u_j + \bar{i}_j \bar{u}_j \,)$$

dependent on the binary input vector u. The pRAM model can be extended to perform mappings from $[0,1]^N$ to $\{0,1\}$ (defining the *integrating pRAM* or *i-pRAM*) by an appropriate generalisation of the above expression.

SELF-ORGANISING pRAM NETS

pRAM nets have been shown to possess self-organising properties and to generate topographic maps [7]. The Kohonen learning rule can be adapted for an input pattern which is a distribution of probabilities P_u over the 2^N addresses u in each of n N-input pRAMs (we assume here that all inputs go to all pRAMs). The basic learning algorithm involves only the set of memory contents of the pRAM i for which the 2^N-vector α^i is closest to the 2^N-vector P (with respect to, say, the Euclidean distance) and its geographic neighbours, all of which are to be rotated some way toward P:

$$\Delta\alpha^i = \varepsilon(\underline{P} - \alpha^i)$$

Note that there is no requirement for normalisation here; probabilities are automatically conserved. Since the mean output of the ith pRAM is given by the scalar product $P.\alpha^i$ the learning rule above maximises the unit's output level, as in the Kohonen case, so it should be possible to single out those units whose memory contents are to be changed by a process of lateral inhibition.

SUPERVISED LEARNING

A supervised learning algorithm has been developed which is conventional insofar as it involves a supervisor and the reduction of an error function, but novel in its use of pRAM spike train correlation analysis to implement gradient descent. Consider an net of n L-input pRAMs, n_I of which receive one or more external inputs, n_O of which are designated 'output nodes'. The aim is to produce the pattern $\underline{O}_p$ on the n_O output lines whenever the n_I input lines deliver the binary pattern $\underline{I}_p$.

An error function for the pth input-output pair is defined by

$$E_p = \frac{1}{2n_O} \sum_{j=1}^{n_O} (O_{p,j} - <o_{p,j}>)^2$$

where $<o_j>$ is the actual firing rate of output unit j. The $n\times2^L$ memory contents $\alpha_{\underline{u}}^i$ (initially assigned random values $\in [0,1]$) are updated according to the rule

$$\Delta\alpha_{\underline{u}}^i = -\eta.\frac{\partial E_p}{\partial\alpha_{\underline{u}}^i}$$

$$= \frac{\eta}{n_O} \sum_{j=1}^{n_O} (O_{p,j} - <o_{p,j}>).\frac{\partial<o_{p,j}>}{\partial\alpha_{\underline{u}}^i}$$

where η is a small positive constant (training rate). Using the chain rule

$$\frac{\partial<o_{p,j}>}{\partial\alpha_{\underline{u}}^i} = \frac{\partial<a_{p,i}>}{\partial\alpha_{\underline{u}}^i}.\frac{\partial<o_{p,j}>}{\partial<a_{p,i}>}$$

where $<a_{p,i}>$ is the mean firing rate of the ith unit. For a training step consisting of R presentations of the input pattern $\underline{I}_p$ the above factors can be estimated according to

$$\frac{\partial<a_{p,i}>}{\partial\alpha_{\underline{u}}^i} \approx \frac{R_{\underline{u}}^{p,i}}{R} , \quad \frac{\partial<o_{p,j}>}{\partial<a_{p,i}>} \approx \frac{1}{R}\sum_{r=1}^{R} X(a_{p,i}(t-r),\, o_{p,j}(t-r))$$

where $R_{\underline{u}}^{p,i}/R$ is the proportion of times location $\underline{u}$ in the ith pRAM is addressed and X is a correlation function between the binary activities of a pair of nodes:

$$X(a_i(t),\, a_j(t)) = (\bar{a_i}\bar{a_j} + a_i a_j - a_i\bar{a_j} - \bar{a_i}a_j)(t)$$

$(\bar{a} \equiv 1-a)$. In the case that the network is required to learn a set of P associations, an overall error can be defined by $E = \frac{1}{P}\sum_p E_p$. If the training rate η is small

$$\frac{\partial E}{\partial\alpha_{\underline{u}}^i} = \frac{1}{P}\sum_p \frac{\partial E_p}{\partial\alpha_{\underline{u}}^i}$$

so that the method above implements a gradient descent in E.

In order to examine the role played by the training rate in the algorithm described above it is useful to consider the case $\eta \to \infty$, in which case the update rule reduces to

$$\Delta\alpha_{\underline{u}}^i \to 0 \ , \ \frac{\partial E_p}{\partial\alpha_{\underline{u}}^i} > 0$$

$$\to 1 \ , \ \frac{\partial E_p}{\partial\alpha_{\underline{u}}^i} < 0$$

with the memory contents quickly acquiring deterministic ($\in \{0,1\}$) values. However once the $\alpha_{\underline{u}}^i$ have deterministic values it is impossible to estimate $\dfrac{\partial E_p}{\partial\alpha_{\underline{u}}^i}$ using the 'spike train correlation' method above, since in this case no alternative information pathways are being exercised. Thus in the limit $\eta \to \infty$ the training algorithm performs no better than random guess. Since very small values of η will also lead to long training times, it is clear that for any given problem there will be a range of values for this parameter which will optimise training performance. These questions are explored further in the context of the 1-pRAM chain simulations described below.

1-pRAM Chains

Properties of the gradient descent algorithm were investigated using a particularly simple network structure, consisting of N 1-pRAMs arranged so that the output of the ith pRAM is the input of the (i+1)st (i = 1..N-1). The chain was trained to perform the identity function using batch mode training (no updates made until all the members of the training set have been seen) with $\eta = 2.0$, terminating when the overall error E fell below 0.001. Increasing R enabled a more reliable estimate of the error surface gradient,and hence decreased training times; this was particularly apparent for larger N. However, a large value of R is not necessarily appropriate at all stages of the training process. It was described above how increasing the training rate η would eventually result in increased training times, as the system became trapped in 'false minima' associated with sets of incorrect deterministic memory contents. The variation of A, the average number of training sets to solution for a 3-node chain with η, in the range $\eta \in [0.5, 3.5]$, was examined, and it was seen that A increased very rapidly for $\eta \geq 3.0$. In this simulation R was chosen to have the small value of 16 time steps. The reason for this choice was that it allowed escape from the false minima described above. Thus it can be seen that under some circumstances, typically in the initial stages of training, a small value of R (and the associated noise) might in fact be desirable. This raises the interesting possibility of a form of simulated annealing for pRAM nets, with R playing the role of an inverse temperature.

Training of pRAM Pyramids

Because the storage requirements for a Boolean unit rise exponentially with the number of inputs it is usually necessary to restrict the fan-in to the units. In particular Aleksander has proposed using pyramids of two-input nodes as the basic components of a PLN network. However, there is a problem with replacing an N-PLN by an N-input pyramid in that the pyramid (with 4(N-1) memory locations) is able to compute far fewer functions than the full N-PLN (2^N memory locations); it would thus be necessary to set up the network topology very carefully in order to ensure convergence of the PLN training algorithm.

The pRAM gradient descent algorithm can be used to train an N-pyramid to give a best approximation (in the sense of least squares) to any function which can be performed by an N-pRAM. The training scheme used in these simulations followed the same lines as the method described for the 1-pRAM chain above, but terminated after a fixed number of training steps rather than when the error function had fallen below some fixed value. The algorithm (with $\eta = 2.0$, $R = 256$) was applied to (a) the 4-bit parity problem and (b) the function $\{I_p \rightarrow 1$ if $\sum_{i=1}^{4} I_{p,i} = 2$, $I_p \rightarrow 0$ otherwise$\}$. The latter function is not deterministically realisable by a 4-pyramid, and this could be seen in the way that the output error converged toward a non-zero value.

REINFORCEMENT TRAINING

An alternative to fully supervised learning ('learning with a teacher') is reinforcement learning ('learning with a critic'), in which individual nodes only receive information about the quality of the performance of the network as a whole and have to discover for themselves how to change their behaviour so as to improve this. It is possible to extend the ideas of Barto and Sutton (see, for example, [8]) to pRAM nets, adopting an update rule for the memory locations which depends on global success ($r(t)$) and failure ($p(t)$) signals $\in \{0,1\}$ which are emitted with a probability dependent on the environmental input to the node at time t (context) and on its output action. When $r = 1$ (success) the memory contents change so as to increase the probability of the chosen action in the same context, whilst if $p = 1$ (failure) the probablity of choosing the other action increases. Note that the probabilities of reward and penalty are independent in this model; this allows the possibility of 'neutral' actions which are neither punished nor rewarded, but may correspond to a useful exploration of the environment. The pRAM version of reinforcement learning differs from that of Barto in that noise is introduced at the synaptic rather than the threshold level; it is well known that synaptic noise is the dominant source of stochastic behaviour in biological neurons.

The reinforcement rule discussed above has been investigated using a small pRAM net already realised in hardware [9]; simulations of larger systems have also been performed. It is of interest to compare the performance of the reinforcement rule with the gradient descent training scheme described above. The reward/penalty strategy was applied to the 1-pRAM chain identity problem, with an identical convergence criterion, and with reward and penalty probabilities given simply by

$$\Pr(r{=}1) = 1, \quad input_1 = output_N$$
$$= 0, \quad input_1 \neq output_N$$

$$\Pr(p{=}1) = 0, \quad input_1 = output_N$$
$$= 1, \quad input_1 \neq output_N$$

It was found that this much less computationally expensive stochastic search procedure outperformed the R = 32 gradient descent algorithm for N > 4, and compared well with the R = 256 implementation.

Landmark Learning

There are many interesting problems of adaptive control which require real-valued inputs. The reinforcement rule can be adapted to such situations, and i-pRAMs have been used very successfully in an associative search problem originally proposed by Barto and Sutton [10]. The task involves training a simulated "bug" to find its way to a particular spatial location, given certain (real-valued) location cues. The environment contains four neutral landmark generators N, S, E, W and a central attractant. In this formulation of the problem all five "odours" fall off in a Gaussian way with distance. The bug itself consists of four movement generating i-pRAMs, M_N, M_S, M_E, M_W, each of which has inputs from all four landmark generating i-pRAMs as well as from reward and punishment pRAMs R, P. Movement decisions are made according to the rule $\Delta X = m_E - m_W$, $\Delta Y = m_N - m_S$, where the $m_i \in \{0,1\}$ are the outputs of the four i-pRAMs. The reward r and punishment $p \in \{0,1\}$ are generated stochastically, according to the rule

$$Pr(r{=}1) = f(k.dA), \quad dA \geq 0$$
$$= 0, \quad dA < 0$$

$$Pr(p{=}1) = f(-k.dA), \quad dA \leq 0$$
$$= 0, \quad dA > 0$$

where dA is the change in sensed attractant associated with the move just made, and f is a sigmoidal function. Simulations have indicated that a 4×4-input i-pRAM net of this kind shows an excellent capacity for learning and generalisation: the trained "bug" is able to easily find its way to the central target region, through a region of its input space it has not visited in training, when the attractant itself is no longer present. Moreover training times are quite short (around 300 time steps), even when the initial values of the 4×2^4 memory contents are unfavourable (representing an effectively repellent central region).

DISCUSSION

The gradient descent training scheme presented here is of interest in that the algorithm is of very general utility, not requiring a detailed knowledge of network connectivity for its implementation, and able to deliver a 'best approximation' (in terms of mean firing rates) in cases where a Boolean function cannot be exactly realised by a given network. However it is somewhat expensive in its need to evaluate cross-correlations between a large number of output spike trains (this is necessary in order to establish the role played by each unit in determining the output error). The same criticism might be levelled at any supervised training scheme: such schemes are unattractive in their requirement for a centralised learning controller, and seem unsuited to 'on-line' learning applications. Thus we are most interested in developing reinforcement training strategies (possibly combined with some element of self-organisation). It seems likely that the quality of the performance in the reported simulations relates to the use of independent sources of synaptic noise, as well as to the higher functionality of the pRAM node. We are presently working on an extension of the i-pRAM model which will include the capacity to predict future reinforcement, and intend to apply this model to the cart-pole system [11] and to other problems of learning control.

References

1. Gorse D, Taylor JG. An analysis of noisy RAM and neural nets. Physica 1989; D34:90-114

2. Gorse D, Taylor JG. A general model of stochastic neural processing. Biol Cybern (to appear)

3. Kauffman SA. Metabolic stability and epigenesis in randomly connected genetic nets. J Theor Biol 1969; 22:437-467

4. Aleksander I, Thomas IV, Bowden PA. WISARD: a radical step forward in pattern recognition. Sensor Review 1984; July:120-124

5. Aleksander I: the logic of connectionist systems. In: Aleksander I (ed) Neural computing architectures. MIT Press, 1989, pp 133-155

6. Myers CE: output functions for probabilistic logic nodes. In: Proceedings of the first IEE international conference on artificial neural networks. IEE, 1989, pp 310-314

7. Gorse D, Taylor JG: hardware realisable learning algorithms. In: Proceedings of INNC 90, Paris (to appear)

8. Barto AG, Sutton RS, Brouwer PS. Associative search network: a reinforcement learning associative memory. Biol Cybern 1981; 40:201-211

9. Clarkson TG, Gorse D, Taylor JG: hardware realisable models of neural processing. In: Proceedings of the first IEE international conference on artificial neural networks. IEE, 1989, pp 242-246

10. Barto AG, Sutton RS. Landmark learning: an illustration of associative search. Biol Cybern 1981; 42:1-8

11. Barto AG, Sutton RS, Anderson CW. Neuronlike adaptive elements that can solve difficult learning control problems. IEEE Trans Syst, Man, Cyb 1983; 13(5):834-846

Computer Simulations of Recurrent Neural Nets for Temporal Recognition Problems

G.S.Cooper and T.M.Child

ABSTRACT

A number of approaches are presented to the use of neural nets with feedback to handle the recognition of temporal data and these are assessed with respect to resilience (ability to handle noisy or incomplete input) and performance in handling similar and overlapping patterns. Particular attention is given to the behaviour of the net on encountering sequences embedded within other sequences and certain hypotheses and conclusions are drawn regarding the nature of the abstract representations formed within the nets. A self-organizing recurrent net is investigated, which displays interesting and useful properties due to the creation of a fractal state space topology. It is shown that the net recognizes sequences effectively by means of a tree search backwards in time. Finally, an estimate is made of the theoretical maximum capacity of such a neural net.

1. INTRODUCTION

Various schemes have been put forward [1,2,3,4,5,6,7] to enable the handling by neural nets of patterns varying in space and time. Some of these models [2] have been applied to the relatively simple problem of getting a neural net to store and recall sequences of patterns such that each pattern in the sequence, when input to the network, causes the next pattern to appear on the output. Thus the sequence is stored as a series of associations linking pairs of consecutive patterns.

This paper is concerned with the problem of recognition of sequences rather than recall. The provision of memory in neural nets, along with some kind of time reference such as a clock or perhaps some characteristic relaxation time [6], allows the net implicitly to handle temporally changing inputs. Of the schemes that have been put forward to address this problem, the predominant ones appear to be the time-delayed neural net (TDNN) [4], schemes based on Kohonen's LVQ2 model [5] and schemes involving recurrence, or feedback [8, 9]. A number of these have been compared by Bourlard and Wellekens [10] and are shown to be equivalent in certain respects. In the first two cases, memory is provided explicitly by buffering patterns at the input by means of a shift register (which may or may not be neural in nature) and such schemes suffer a number of disadvantages as set out by Elman [8]. In the case of recurrent nets, memory is provided by allowing the network at time t_i to see, at its inputs, the output from time t_{i-1}. It has been suggested that such a feedback mechanism is employed in the hippocampus of the brain to provide storage of temporal patterns [11].

2. EMBEDDED SEQUENCE RECOGNITION (THE TASK)

Figure 1 illustrates the basic task to be performed by means of a neural net. The initial objective was for the net to be able to flag the occurrence of a previously learnt sequence of bit patterns and to identify which of a number of learnt sequences was encountered.

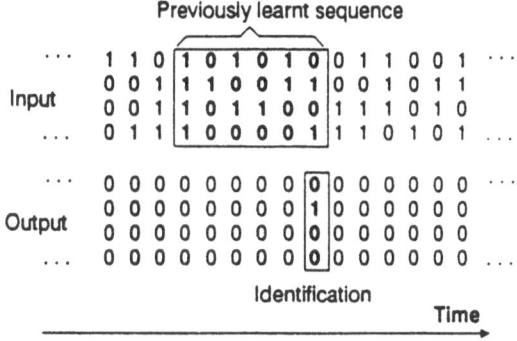

A minimum of constraints is placed on the nature of sequences and, in particular, the length of the sequences is variable, the sequence may be embedded within a continuous stream of patterns (the sequences are not delimited prior to

Fig.1 The embedded sequence recognition task.

presentation to the net), and the same pattern may appear any number of times in a given sequence. Indeed, one of our requirements has been that the net should distinguish between sequences containing the same patterns in a different order. Some of the work presented addresses the handling of corrupt input (noise and partial information) and resilience of the net when presented with test sequences containing additional embedded and repeated patterns or with patterns missing, and particular attention is given to cases in which one sequence is embedded within another.

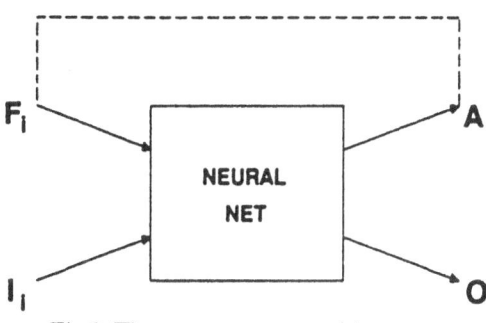

Fig.2. The recurrent net architecture.

Many of the above requirements have been determined with tasks such as speech recognition and temporal reasoning in mind, although neither the work nor this paper are addressed towards any particular application.

3. RECURRENT NETS

The basic architecture for the type of recurrent net considered in this paper is shown in figure 2. The primary function of the neural net is to perform some operation (denoted here by $*$) on vector I_i (of dimension N_I) and vector F_i (of dimension N_F) to form vector A_i (also of dimension N_F):

$$A_i = I_i * F_i \tag{1}$$

A_i is then fed back to the input:

$$F_{i+1} = A_i \tag{2}$$

The * operator needs to be defined so that, over time, the A output contains an abstract representation of all patterns previously seen since, from (1) and (2):

$$A_i = I_i * I_{i-1} * I_{i-2} * I_{i-3} * \ldots \qquad (3)$$

The O_i output provides an indication and identification of known sequences and is essentially trained to recognize those states of the net (ie. particular values of A_i), that approximate the abstract representations of previously learnt sequences.

The requirements defined in section 2 impact on the nature of the operator * of equations (1) and (3). In particular, it is important that this operator is non-commutative if the net is to distinguish between sequences containing the same patterns in different orders. It is also necessary for the net, on the one hand, to be able to "remember" having seen patterns early in the input stream in order to identify long sequences whilst, on the other hand, being capable of ignoring early patterns where required so that sequences may be recognized irrespective of their being embedded in a continuous stream of patterns. This may seem to be a contradictory set of requirements, but we shall see later how it may be achieved.

It is interesting to note that simply training the net to implement a "sum and re-normalize" operator, such that

$$A_i = I_i * F_i = \frac{1}{(1+a)} . (I_i + a.F_i) \quad (0 < a < 1) \qquad (4)$$

gives surprisingly good performance. The non-commutative nature of the operator, and the ability to forget or ignore earlier patterns, are achieved through the renormalization, since equation (3) becomes:

$$A_i = \frac{1}{(1+a)} . (I_i + b.I_{i-1} + b^2.I_{i-2} + b^3.I_{i-3} + \ldots) \qquad (5)$$

where
$$b = \frac{a}{(1+a)} \quad (< 0.5).$$

However, it would be surprising if the operator described by equation (4) were optimal for the requirements of section 2. The approach taken in this work is to allow the net, by means of an appropriately defined training task, to determine a suitable operator for itself. The precise nature of the operator actually implemented will, of course, depend on the method used to train the net both in terms of the learning algorithm employed (in this work, backward error propagation [11] has been used) and, more importantly, in terms of the training task assigned. The latter aspect will be addressed later in sections 4, 5 and 6.

4. BACKPROPAGATION IN TIME.

The recurrent net may be understood in terms of an equivalent feed-forward net as shown in figure 3. This immediately suggests a particular training algorithm, which has been referred to as backpropagation in time [12], in which a complete sequence is shown to the net and the states of the net and the outputs at each time step are recorded. When the complete sequence has been presented, backpropagation of errors is used to update the weights in the net for each of the time steps in reverse order, propagating the errors from the F_{i+1} input around to the A_i output. In this scheme, one is effectively training the equivalent feedforward net which is like a traditional feedforward net, except that links are constrained to be the same in each of the sections of the net shown in figure 3. This approach is very successful, at least for short sequences, since the equivalent feedforward net is effectively being trained to perform precisely the task described in section 2. However, it has the major disadvantage that it requires the state of the net at each time step of a sequence to be stored until the end of the sequence during training. Thus, the technique does not easily extend to long sequences.

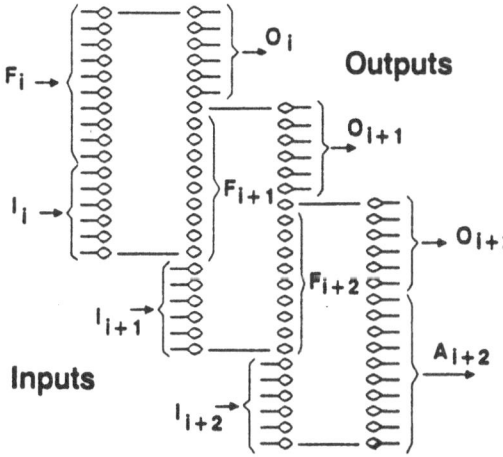

Fig.3. The equivalent feedforward net.

It is convenient, at this point to raise the issue of how to train the net to handle not only sequences, but sequences that are embedded within a continuous stream of patterns. Another way of expressing this requirement is that the net must be capable of recognizing a sequence regardless of the initial state of the F input (ie. regardless of the previous history). It is not sufficient merely to initialize the feedback inputs to 0.5 on the basis that this is half way between the normally expected input or output values of 0 and 1, since the neurons used are, in fact, analogue rather than binary devices. The authors have found that nets whose feedback inputs are initialized to 0.5 during training are only capable of recognizing the trained sequences if the F inputs are again set to 0.5 on playback. The approach taken, initially, in the current work was to prefix sequences with a number of randomly determined patterns (usually 2) during training on the basis that this would initialize the feedbacks to typical, but randomly changing values, thus training the net to *ignore* the F inputs when appropriate. This has been found to be quite successful in allowing the net to recognize sequences irrespective of the particular random prefix patterns applied during playback. Unfortunately, however, it is found that the net is still able to remember the *number* of random patterns that were prefixed to the training sequences even though it ignores the *actual* patterns that were seen, so that this training scheme still does not completely solve the embedded sequence recognition problem. This topic will be discussed further in section 6.

5. TRAINING TO A GLOBAL CONTEXT

In order to circumvent the problem of storing all the states of the net during each sequence, training schemes were next tried in which the connection weights are updated at each time step during the training of a particular sequence. The first of

221

these involves the net architecture shown in figure 4. This is, in fact, much closer to the architecture used by Elman [8] and Cleermans et al. [9], in which the net was trained to predict, at the output, the (i + 1)'th pattern in the sequence upon receiving, at the input, the i'th pattern in the sequence. In the work described in this section, however, the approach used is to train the net to produce a constant output (O) throughout the sequence (a "global context"), with the flag output trained to produce a "1" only on

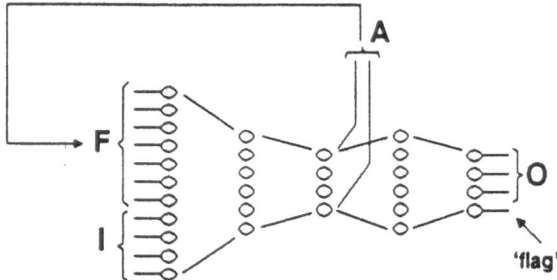

Fig.4. "Context limited" recurrent net.

receiving the last pattern of any recognized sequence. Because the required output is shown to the net throughout the sequence during training, effectively limiting in some way the abstractions that may be formed by the net, and for comparison with the architecture to be presented later, this net is referred to as the "context limited" net. Finally, the errors propagated back at the outputs are weakened in the later stages of training for all but the last pattern in each sequence for reasons that will be explained in the following section.

The following sections contain some of the more interesting results obtained using this net architecture with 8 input (I) units, 24 feedback (F) units, and 8 output (O) units.

The Training and Test Sequences

In order to test against the requirements set out in section 2, a training set and related test set were created as shown in figure 5, in which each of the letters A to I represents a particular eight bit pattern.

Sequence	Training set	Test set
1	A B	1 B
2	C D B	1 D 1
3	E F C D B	E F C ? D B
4	D C B	1 1 B
5	D C B E	1 1 B E
6	B D E F C D B C	B D E F F C D B C
7	C D B D E F B C	C 8 B D E F B C
8	B D C D E F B C	B D C D E F C C
9	G H I H I B E G A	G H I H I B E G A
10	H I B E G A	G H I B E G A

Fig.5. Training and test sequences used.

The figure has been laid out to expose some of the important features of the training set. In particular, note that: sequence 3 is sequence 2 with a prefix; sequence 5 contains an embedded sequence 4; sequence 6 contains an embedded sequence 3; sequences 6, 7 and 8 contain the same patterns in different orders with 7 and 8 differing only in the ordering of the first 3 patterns.

In the test set, various modifications (highlighted) have been made in order to test the resilience of the net to incomplete and noisy input. In this table, a 1 means that one bit of the pattern has been inverted, an **8** indicates that all the bits have been inverted, a line through a character indicates that the pattern was omitted from the test sequence, the **?** indicates that a previously unseen pattern was inserted into the sequence.

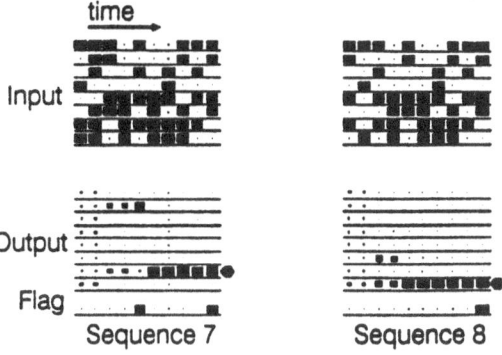

Fig.6. Response of the context limited net to sequences 7 and 8.

Notice that in, for example, sequences 4 and 5, where one of the trained sequences appears embedded within another, simply training the net by means of error backpropagation would result in failure, since the training target presented for sequence 4 would contradict the training target presented for the same sequence embedded within sequence 5. This contradiction would result in the net arriving at a compromise between the two targets so that the total error at the outputs would level out at a constant value rather than training towards zero. It is for this reason that the learning is weakened towards the end of the training on all but the last pattern in each sequence by multiplying the error propagated back to the outputs by a small factor (in this case, 0.1). In the example mentioned above, this results in the output vector defined for sequence 4 having significantly more influence than that defined for sequence 5 during the early part of the sequences.

Performance Using the Training Set

The performance of the net on replaying sequences from the training set is illustrated in figure 6, which shows the variation of the inputs and outputs over time for sequences 7 and 8, with the spots to the right of the output indicating the target pattern. The figure demonstrates the non-commutative nature of the * operator implemented by the net and the ability of the net to "remember" over time, since the sequences only differ in the exchange of the first and 3rd

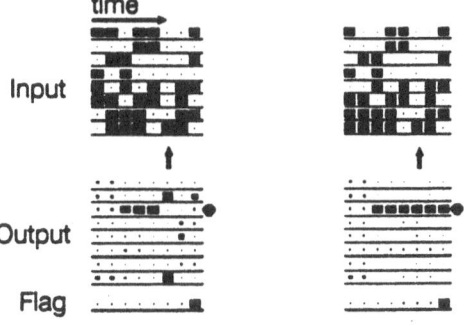

Sequence 3

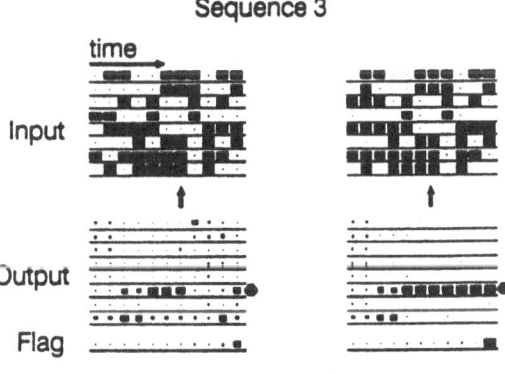

Sequence 6

Fig.7. Effect on test performance of random noise during training.

patterns. The first two patterns in each sequence are the randomly chosen prefix patterns. Notice that sequence 7 starts with an embedded sequence 2, which has successfully been detected by the net. The response of the net is equally good for all the sequences in the training set.

Handling of Noisy and Incomplete Data

If the net is straightforwardly trained using the training set, it is found that the performance is fairly poor when the test set is presented. This performance tends to worsen as the net is trained further and appears to be a consequence of the net's learning to recognize the precise patterns in the training set without making any generalizations. The performance is particularly poor in those cases where a pattern is removed, inserted or replaced, even though the net appears to be making a fairly good early hypothesis about the sequence being presented. In order to improve this performance, it was decided to *train* the net in the presence of noise, simply by introducing random bit inversions such that each bit in each pattern is randomly inverted with a probability of 0.1, at every presentation. As expected, this results in much greater resilience to bit inversions in the test set. More surprising, however, is that the performance is greatly improved in recognising sequences in which whole patterns have been inserted, replaced or removed. This effect is illustrated in figure 7, which shows the response to test sequences 3 and 6, of nets trained without random noise (left) and with random noise (right). The vertical arrows indicate the point at which the error was introduced into the test set as shown in figure 5.

The Nature of The Abstractions Created - A Conjecture

An analysis of the net's response to pairs of sequences such as 4 and 5, along with the earlier discovery that the net is sensitive to the number of random prefix patterns applied to the sequences, suggests that the net is organizing its analysis of the sequences in the form of a tree search. This conjecture is further borne out by the failure of the net to indicate the occurrence of a sequence 3 embedded within

sequence 6 when the training set is played back, as illustrated by figure 8. This "failure" occurs even though the weakened learning described earlier is employed. This situation may be better understood by considering the state space of the net, which represents all possible values of the vector A, to be represented by the 2-dimensional space of figure 9. In this diagram, the areas delimited by dotted lines

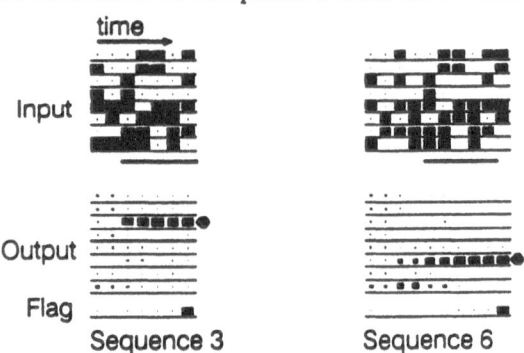

Fig.8. Failure of context limited net to detect sequence 3 embedded within sequence 6.

contain all the points corresponding to the abstractions for sequences 3 and 6 respectively. Here, the sequences 3 and 6 are represented by the two trajectories in the state space. If the net really is implementing a tree search, it will be impossible for the abstract representation to return to the branch representing sequence 3 once the branch representing sequence 6 has been chosen. Notice, also, that the path taken on receiving the two random patterns (R) forms the root of the tree and is shown as being the same (or similar) irrespective of the random patterns chosen. Whilst it must be emphasised that this is purely conjecture at this stage, the scheme shown does accord with the results of Elman [8] and Cleeremans et al. [9], who discovered a hierarchical clustering of the significant points in the state spaces of their neural nets (although this does not necessarily imply that a tree search was implemented). Further evidence in support of this conjecture will be presented in section 6.

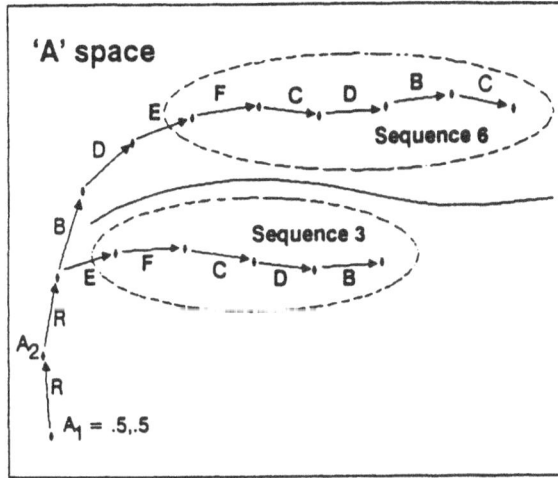

Fig.9. Schematic of the possible tree search arrangement for sequences 3 and 6.

Many of the limitations apparent in the context limited net are a result of the rather strict training task employed. In fact, the application of a constant target pattern throughout the presentation of each sequence during training, along with the weakened learning mentioned earlier in this section, is quite likely to encourage the implementation of a tree search "algorithm" by the net. The architecture and training approach presented in the next section are an attempt to move away from this situation.

6. A SELF-ORGANIZING RECURRENT NET

Figure 10 shows the final neural net architecture to be studied in this paper. This architecture is essentially divided into two separate neural nets. The large net at the top (the "sequence abstractor") is responsible purely for generating the abstract internal representations of the sequences. The smaller net below it (the "sequence classifier") is responsible for analysing the internal abstractions (states) and producing the output codes to indicate states corresponding to particular sequences. The abstractor net is trained as an auto-associator, to produce at

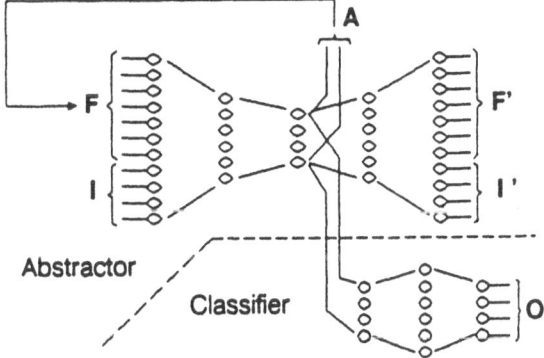

Fig.10. A self-organizing recurrent net.

its outputs an approximation, (I' | F'), of the input pattern, (I | F). In order to do this, it must generate abstract representations in A, of all combinations of the vector (I | F) presented during training, since the dimension of A is equal to the dimension of F [13].

The most significant feature of this net is that the recognition task does not constrain the abstractions formed during training in any way, since the errors in the classifier net are not propagated back into the abstractor net. In fact, once the abstractor net has been trained, the classifier may be trained independently to perform any task that might later be required. This feature is utilized in some of the examples that follow. It is important to recognize that the only purpose of the classifier net is to analyse the state space of the abstractor net in order to identify particular instantaneous states. Because of this, it is possible to train the classifier net to produce a pattern only when the whole sequence has been presented to the abstractor net. At all other times, the classifier is weakly trained to produce the zero vector, so that there is a general tendency for the outputs to drift towards zero. This technique is equivalent to the weakened learning employed in training the context limited net, and the same factor (0.1) is applied to the output errors. The only difference is that in this case the target pattern is the zero vector rather than a "global context" pattern.

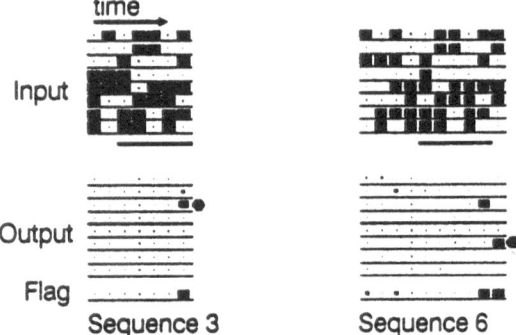

This net is able to perform all the tasks that the context limited net has carried out, to at least the same proficiency, with 8 input units and 24 feedback

Fig.11. The self-organizing net is able to detect sequence 3 embedded within sequence 6.

units, although an extensive study of its resilience to noisy or incomplete inputs has not yet been carried out. The following sections will describe some of the additional results that are obtained with the self-organizing net.

Handling of Embedded Sequences

The first result to be presented concerns the recognition of sequence 3 embedded within sequence 6, which the context limited net is unable to achieve. Figure 11 shows the performance of the self-organizing net when presented with the same task. (Note that the flag output is, in fact, redundant in this net.) It is important to stress that the classifier has been trained to recognize sequence 3 only as a separate sequence and not within the context of sequence 6, where the outputs are weakly trained to zero. This indicates that the abstractor net is using the same region of the A-space to represent sequence 3 irrespective of whether it is presented alone or embedded within another sequence. Notice also that the net still resolves sequence 3 from sequence 2, which itself consists of the last three patterns of sequence 3.

Another observation, which is closely related to the above, is the fact that the performance is unaffected by the initial value of the feedback inputs. It is not necessary to initialize the feedbacks in any particular way during training, and starting from all 0.5's is perfectly adequate.

Finally, since no particular recognition task is used during training of the abstractor, then if the net is to perform its task at all, it must organize its state space in a manner that allows it to learn (or form abstractions of) all sequences that are presented to it during training. If this is the case, it must be possible later to re-train the classifier to perform tasks that were not envisaged during the original training. In order to confirm this, and to probe the nature of the state space, the classifier was trained to recognize a sequence that only appeared embedded within another sequence during training. The task chosen is illustrated in figure 12. The classifier was trained, in the manner described earlier, to recognize sequences 7, 8 and 11 (a new sequence), with no additional training of the abstractor net. On testing with the training set, it was found that the classifier is able to recognize sequence 11 embedded within sequences 7 and 8, and still to resolve sequences 7 and 8 on the basis of the differences in the first three patterns.

11	D E F B
7	C D B D E F B C
8	B D C D E F B C

Fig.12.

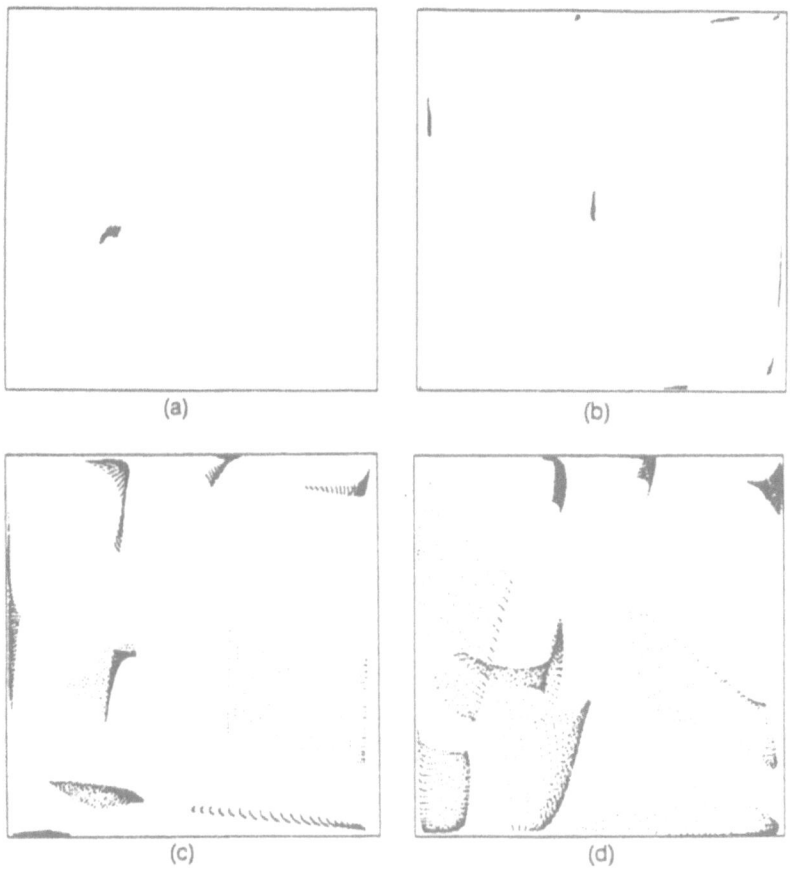

Fig.13. Maps of the abstraction space for the self-organizing recurrent net after: (a) zero; (b) 1000; (c) 4000; (d) 14000 training iterations.

227

It is clear from all the results presented above that the nature of the abstractions implemented by the auto-associator net is quite different to those of the context limited net, and it will be shown here that the net effectively analyses the incoming sequences by means of a tree search *backwards* in time. In order to understand this, it is helpful to discuss the form of the * operator implemented by this net.

The * operation performed by the net maps points in the space {I , F} into the space {A}. The auto-association task used to train the net causes this mapping to be such that all vectors (I | F) that have been presented during training are mapped onto vectors A that are at least mutually exclusive. (Further work is required to ascertain whether this mapping is unique.) The resulting vector A is mapped trivially back into {I , F} by feeding it around to the inputs (F) and concatenating it with a new I vector. The resulting (I | F) vector is again mapped into {A} by the net. Thus, at each iteration, the state space, {A}, is mapped into itself in a manner determined by the incoming I vector.

In order to understand the nature of this mapping in more detail, a new abstractor net was created with 8 sequence inputs and only 2 feedback inputs. This net does not perform the required tasks very well, but it is possible to produce a 2-dimensional map of the state space of the trained net. The maps shown in figure 13 were created by fixing the input I to one of the patterns used in the training set and plotting the A vectors produced by the net from a regular array of values in {F}, on the interval (0,0) - (1,1), applied at the feedback inputs. This was repeated for each of the nine patterns used in the training set. The four pictures show the map of the state space produced in this way for various stages of training, starting from the untrained net. Since each of the regions emerging is a smaller, distorted image of the whole area, the space has a self-similar topology which, when the net is trained on long sequences, is fractal in nature. The regions of overlap between and within

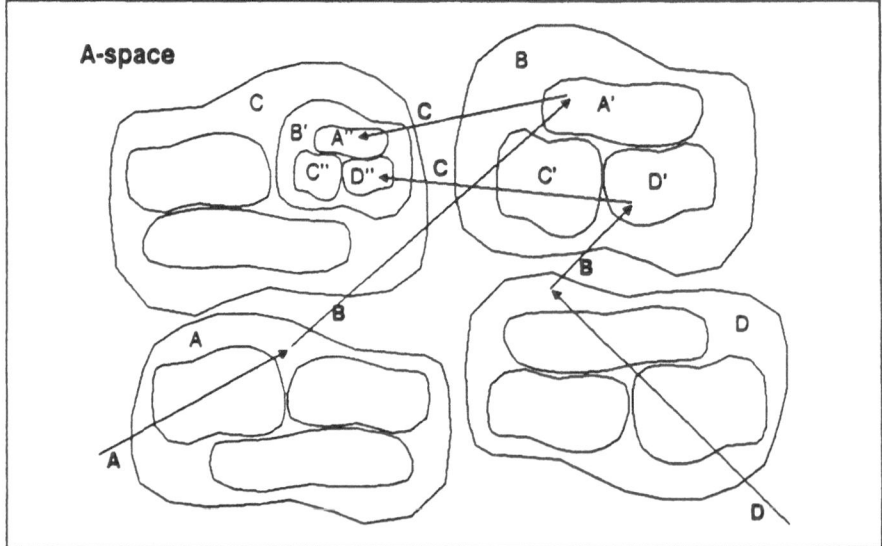

Fig.14. Trajectories of two similar sequences in the state space of the
self-organizing recurrent net.

the mapped images are the subject of further study, but the authors suspect that these correspond to mappings that are not required in representing the trained sequences. This type of hierarchical representation is often seen in self-organizing systems in which information of a high dimensionality is represented in a space of a lower dimension [7].

Figure 13 illustrates the type of trajectory that would be followed in the state space of the self-organizing net by two similar sequences, ABC and DBC, starting from arbitrary initial conditions. The primes indicate that a particular region represents a pattern having been presented one (A'), two (A"), ... time periods earlier than the current time. The highlighted characters indicate the pattern presented at each time step. The regions of the state space representing the learned patterns are arranged hierarchically in reverse order of presentation. The classifier learns to recognize states corresponding to particular sequences by partitioning the state space of the abstractor in an appropriate manner. The level of detail analysed (ie. the size of a particular partition) is determined by the length of the sequence to be detected, allowing earlier history, represented by the fine detail, to be ignored.

The question now arises as to whether this state space topology generalizes to nets with more than 2 feedback nodes. In order to address this question, figure 15 shows the time evolution of the "distance" between the states visited during two similar sequences (7 and 8). The results are shown for the context limited net and the self-organizing net, both with 8 input nodes and 24 feedback nodes. As in the input-output diagrams, the first two patterns are random prefix patterns. The graphs show both the Euclidean distance between the states, A_7 and A_8, and the angle subtended at the centre of the state space (ie. $\cos^{-1}(A_7 \bullet A_8 / |A_7||A_8|)$, where A_7 and A_8 are measured relative to the centre of the state space). The states in the self-organizing net converge as would be expected if the fractal state space topology is maintained. In the context limited net, the states remain separated, as would be expected for the tree search algorithm described in section 5. In a similar experiment

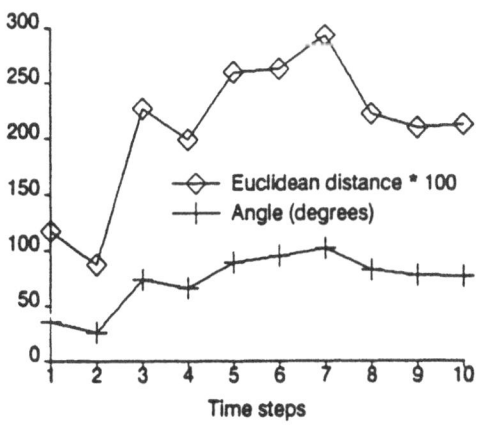

Context Limited Net

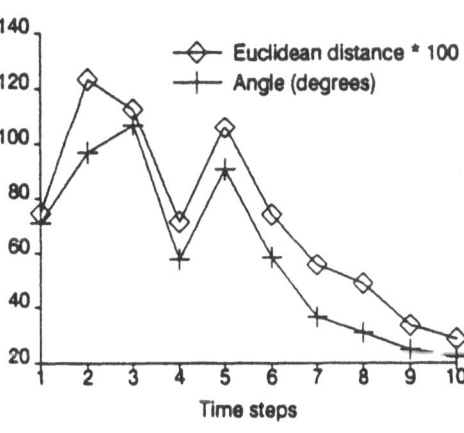

Self-Organizing Net

Fig.15. Separation between the states
visited during sequences 7 & 8.

carried out on the context limited net, involving two similar 15 pattern sequences, the states showed no sign of converging.

The Maximum Capacity of the Self-Organizing Recurrent Net

Because of the fractal nature of the state space, the capacity of the self-organizing net will be determined largely by the precision with which the states of the net may be resolved. Although the capabilities of the classifier net are extremely important in determining this, it is, nevertheless possible to estimate an upper limit for the capacity of the abstractor net, subject to certain assumptions, as follows:

Let the number of sequences stored = S, the number of distinct patterns used in the sequences = N, the minimum distance between separate states = p, the length of each sequence = L (uniform length) and the dimension of the state space (ie. the number of feedback nodes) = D . Referring to figure 14: if it is assumed that the net is able to optimize the use of the state space so that unnecessary mappings take up negligible space, then the number, K, of coarse sub-divisions (represented by A', B', ...) required in a particular region (say the A region) is determined by the number of different patterns that immediately precede the corresponding pattern (A) in the set of stored sequences. Assuming that all patterns occur with equal frequency, and assuming the worst case in which each pattern has the maximum number of different predecessors, two cases may be considered:

Case 1, $S.(L-1) < N^2$. In this case, K will be approximately given by $S.(L-1)/N$. In order to store sequences of length L, each of the regions must be sub-divided hierarchically to a depth L-1, so that the total number of partitions required is $N.(S.(L-1)/N)^{L-1}$. The minimum volume required for each separable partition is given approximately by p^D so that, since the total volume of the state space is 1, the number of available partitions is p^{-D}. Thus, the maximum number of sequences stored is given by:

$$S_{max} = \frac{(p^{-D}.N^{L-2})^{1/L-1}}{L-1} \qquad (6)$$

Notice that this theoretical capacity increases dramatically as the number of feedback nodes is increased.

Case 2, $S.(L-1) > N^2$. Here, K will be approximately equal to its maximum value, N. In this case, an estimate of the maximum length of the sequences is given by:

$$L_{max} = -D. \frac{\log p}{\log N} \qquad (7)$$

The maximum length of the sequences is, therefore, proportional to the number of feedback nodes.

For the small nets used in this paper, with the following data: D = 24, N = 10, L = 10, and assuming p = 0.1, equation (6) gives a maximum theoretical capacity of approximately 320 sequences, whilst equation (7) suggests a maximum length of L = 24.

REFERENCES

1. Hecht-Nielsen R. Nearest matched filter classification of spatiotemporal patterns. Appl.Optics 1987; 26:1892-1899

2. Kosko B. Bidirectional Associative Memories. IEEE Trans. on Systems Man & Cybernetics 1988; 18:49-60

3. Sejnowski T.J. and Rosenberg C.R. Parallel Networks that Learn to Pronounce English Text. Complex Systems 1987; 1:145-168

4. Waibel A., Hanazawa T., Hinton G., Shikano K. and Lang K. Phoneme Recognition: Neural Networks vs. Hidden Markov Models. Proc IEEE ICASSP 1988; 107-110

5. McDermott E. and Katagari S.: Shift Invariant, multi-category phoneme recognition using Kohonen's LVQ2. Pro. IEEE ICASSP 1989; 81-84

6. Sompolinsky H. and Kanter I. Temporal Association in Asymmetric Neural Networks. Phys.Rev.Lett. 1986; 57:2861-2864

7. Kohonen T. Self-Organization and Associative Memory, 3rd Edition Springer-Verlag, Berlin Heidelberg New-York, 1989

8. Elman J.L. Finding Structure in Time. CRL Technical Report 8801. Centre for Research in Language, UCSD 1988

9. Cleeremans A., Servan-Schreiber D. and McClelland J.L. Finite State Automata and Simple Recurrent Networks. Neural Computation 1989; 1:327-381

10. Bourlard H. and Wellekens C.J. Speech Dynamics and Recurrent Neural Networks. Proc IEEE ICASSP 1989; 33-36

11. Taylor J.G. and Reiss M. Does the Hippocampus Store Temporal Patterns? Preprint, King's College, London 1990

12. Rummelhart D.E., Hinton G.H. and Williams R.J. Learning internal representations by error propagation. In: Rummelhart D.E. and McClelland J.L. (Eds.) Parallel distributed processing: Explorations in the microstructure of cognition vol.1, MIT Press, Cambridge, Mass. 1986, pp.318-362

13. Hewitt P.D., Skitt P.J.C. and Witcomb R.C. A self-organizing feedforward network applied to acoustic data. In: Taylor J.G. and Mannion C.L.T. (Eds) New developments in neural computing. Adam Hilger 1989, pp 71-78

INVITED
PAPERS

Learning Vector Quantisation and the Self Organising Map

Teuvo Kohonen

1. INTRODUCTION

A multitude of detailed circuits for artificial neural networks has been suggested. The general modes of their operation, however, are still based on much fewer underlying philosophies. Some of the following three principles seem to be incorporated in any of the contemporary approaches:

1. In *feedforward networks*, patterns of input signals are transformed into patterns of output signals.
2. In *feedback networks*, input information defines the initial state, and successive state transformations the final state, respectively, which then represents the outcome of computation.
3. In *self-organising networks*, cells compete in their activities. The "winner", and eventually its topological neighbours develop into specific detectors of signal patterns. It is then not the exact value of the output response, but its presence vs. absence at a particular spatial location that interpretes (decodes) the input information.

The algorithms discussed in this work belong to the third category. They are also related to a classical methodology that has been used in signal processing and pattern recognition, namely, *vector quantisation* [1,2].

The objective in basic vector quantisation (VQ) has been to approximate continuous functions of vectorial variables, such as probability density functions of input signals, by a finite number of *codebook vectors*. The location of the codebook vectors in the signal space ought to be such that the discretisation error, i.e., the distance of the input sample from the closest codebook vector in some metric is minimised on the average. One may stipulate, for instance, that the rth power of the (eventually Euclidean) distance must be minimised. If $p(x)$ is the probability density function of input $x \in R^n$, dx is a volume differential in the signal space, and the codebook vectors are denoted by $m_i \in R^n$, $i = 1,2,...,c,...$, the minimum of the following error functional is then sought:

$$E = \int \|x - m_{c(x)}\|^r \, p(x) \, dx \, , \tag{1}$$

where $c = c(x)$ is the index of the codebook vector nearest to x. In general, closed solutions for the m_i do not exist, but their approximate values may be found, e.g., in the following discrete-time stochastic-approximation-type iterative process, which almost immediately follows from the steepest-descent gradient-step minimisation of E:

$$m_c(t+1) = m_c(t) + \alpha(t) \, [x(t) - m_c(t)] \, ,$$
$$m_i(t+1) = m_i(t) \quad \text{for } i \neq c \, . \tag{2}$$

Here we have $t = 0,1,2,...$ and $0 < \alpha(t) < 1$; usually $\alpha(t)$ attains small values, which also decrease monotonically in time during iteration.

It can be shown [3,4,5] that the point density function of the codebook vectors in VQ approximates to the expression $[p(x)]^{n/(n+r)}$. If $n \gg r$ as in most practical problems, it can be said that the point density function then approximates to the probability density function $p(x)$. We shall refer to this result in the sequel.

The above iteration in the basic VQ is an *unsupervised learning process*, and its main applications are in *signal approximation*. We shall now derive two new categories of VQ, which behave quite differently, and are used for different purposes. They are the *Learning Vector Quantisation (LVQ)* [6,7,8], which directly aims at *optimal classification* of signal pattern vectors, and the *Self Organising Map* [8,9], the purpose of which is to create "*internal representations*", i.e. various kinds of abstraction of the input signals, the images of which are confined to particular spatial locations in the network.

2. LEARNING VECTOR QUANTISATION (LVQ)

LVQ, which is further subdivided into three algorithms LVQ1, LVQ2, and LVQ3 is a *supervised* (decision-controlled) learning process. It is assumed that all input vectors fall into a fixed number of categories or classes. Similarly, every codebook vector is assigned to some of these classes, and each class is usually represented by a number of codebook vectors. During learning, the class-affiliation of input x is known, whereas during testing, x is assigned to that class, the codebook vector of which is nearest to x. The class zones in the signal space are thus demarcated by the midplanes (hyperplanes) of those codebook vectors that are mutually adjacent and belong to different classes. The class borders are piecewise linear, and the purpose is to place the m_i in such a way that the probability for misclassification of the test vectors is minimised on the average. With a sufficient number of codebook vectors to describe each class zone, the classification accuracy, in spite of the piecewise linear approximation of the borders, can be very close to that of the decision-theoretic Bayes classifier, as shown by many practical experiments already performed.

2.1. LVQ1

The basic idea in the first of the LVQ algorithms (LVQ1) is to repel those selected codebook vectors that cause a misclassification; codebook vectors that classify inputs correctly will be updated as in the basic algorithm, Eq. (2). It turns out that this strategy leaves a "depletion layer" of codebook vectors approximately in those regions where the decision-theoretic class borders are.

Consider the following modification of Eq. (2) where the direction of correction depends on the correctness of tentative classification (during learning):

$$m_c(t+1) = m_c(t) + \alpha(t)[x(t)-m_c(t)] \quad \text{if } x \text{ and } m_c \text{ belong to the same class },$$
$$m_c(t+1) = m_c(t) - \alpha(t)[x(t)-m_c(t)] \quad \text{if } x \text{ and } m_c \text{ belong to different classes },$$
$$m_k(t+1) = m_k(t) \qquad \text{for } k \neq c , \tag{3}$$

and $0 < \alpha(t) < 1$, whereby α is decreasing monotonically with time (e.g., linearly or exponentially, starting from a small value like 0.01 or 0.02).

That this algorithm pulls the codebook vectors away from the class borders can be deduced in the following way. The $p(x)$ in Eq. (1) implies with which statistical frequency the samples $x(t)$ occur in the sequence defined by Eq. (2). On the other hand, in Eq. (3) the minus sign in front of the brackets in the second equation may be interpreted as *to define corrections in the same direction as if Eq. (2) were used for the class to which m_c belongs, but the probability density function of the neighbouring (overlapping) class were subtracted from it.* In other words, we would perform a classical vector quantisation of the function $|p(x|C_i)P(C_i) - p(x|C_j)P(C_j)|$ where C_i and C_j are the neighbouring classes. The difference of density functions of the neighbouring classes, by definition, falls to zero at the Bayes border, inducing the above "depletion layer" of the codebook vectors.

Recently, LaVigna [10] has presented a mathematically rigorous analysis of LVQ1.

2.2. LVQ2

It may be generally known that if the optimal placement of the decision borders between the classes is based on the Bayes philosophy, i.e. on the average expected misclassification rate, then such borders lie at the crossing of the class density functions. An "optimal" LVQ also should be trained by samples picked up from the neighbourhoods of these borders only. As the location of the borders is unknown in the beginning, the idea followed in LVQ2 is to define the approximations of the borders dynamically, i.e., as midplanes of the codebook vectors during the process. The following algorithm reflects upon the above ideas. While in the LVQ1 only one codebook vector was updated at a time, this algorithm updates *two* vectors at each step, namely, the "winner" and the "runner-up". The purpose is to shift the midplane of these two vectors directly towards the place where the Bayes border is supposed to lie. An algorithm that can easily be seen to work in that direction is the following. First define a reasonably narrow "window" (cf. Fig. 1) around the midplane of neighboring codebook vectors m_i and m_j. Let m_i belong to class C_i and m_j to class C_j, respectively. The corrections are defined by

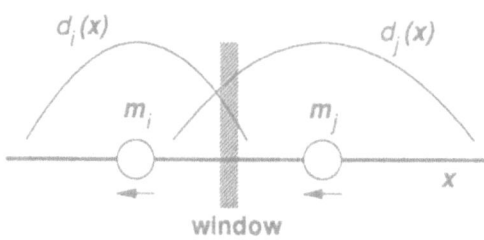

$$m_i(t+1) = m_i(t) - \alpha(t)[x(t)-m_i(t)],$$

$$m_j(t+1) = m_j(t) + \alpha(t)[x(t)-m_j(t)],$$

if m_i is the nearest codebook vector to x and m_j the next-to-nearest one, respectively, and x belongs to C_j but not to C_i; furthermore x must fall into the "window". $\qquad$ (4)

Fig. 1

2.3. LVQ3

The previous LVQ2 algorithm was based on the idea to *differentially* shift the decision borders towards the Bayes limits, whereas no attention was paid to what might happen to the location of the m_k in the long run if this process were continued. Although some researchers have reported good results, some have had problems, too.

Because the distance of x from m_j (correct class) has a larger magnitude than from m_i (wrong class) and corrections are proportional to distance, the $\|m_i-m_j\|$, during learning, decrease monotonically. Although this effect is not as severe with high dimensionality (where the corrections on m_i and m_j in general are not in the same direction) as when, e.g., $n = 1$ or 2, nonetheless it might be an improvement if the corrections on m_i and m_j had the same magnitude. A straightforward remedy would be to normalize the lengths of the corrections. However, this would make the learning computations significantly heavier and longer. An alternative is to compensate for the above effect, approximately at least, by the following means. The original assumption about corrections depending on *errors* only seems unnecessary, as already indicated by the LVQ1 experiments. We can accept *all the training vectors falling into the "window"*, and the only condition is that *one* of m_i and m_j must belong to the *correct* class, and *the other* to the *incorrect class*, respectively. Thus $\|m_i-m_j\|$ may increase, too. Another flaw in the original LVQ2 is that it only pays attention to the corrections of the codebook vectors perpendicular to the decision border, while there is still no control factor present that would prevent the vectors from drifting in the direction parallel to the border. Apparently some effect must be added that sustains some kind of "cohesion" within each class such that the m_k keep approximating the density functions; LVQ1 already contained this effect because it also corrected those codebook vectors that were not responsible for classification at the border. The simplest remedy is therefore to add such corrections to LVQ2, too, but multiplied by a small controllable parameter ε, since the size of this effect is not quite predictable.

Combining the above ideas, we now obtain an improved algorithm that may be called LVQ3:

$$m_i(t+1) = m_i(t) - \alpha(t)[x(t)-m_i(t)] ,$$

where m_i and m_j are the two closest codebook vectors to x, and if x and m_j belong to

$$m_j(t+1) = m_j(t) + \alpha(t)[x(t)-m_j(t)]$$

the same class, while x and m_i belong to different classes; furthermore x must fall into the "window";

$$m_k(t+1) = m_k(t) + \varepsilon\alpha(t)[x(t)-m_k(t)] \text{ for } k \in \{i,j\} , \text{ if } x, m_i, \text{ and } m_j \text{ belong to the same class.} \tag{5}$$

Here the optimal value of ε depends on the size of the window. With narrow windows ε must be small. In a series of experiments, a proper value of ε was in the range 0.1 to 0.5. After introduction of this extra "cohesion", the process seemed to become self-stabilizing even over extensive periods of learning (say, hundreds of thousands of learning steps).

2.4. Classification results with speech data

For this experiment we used 15-frequency-channel spectra of phonemes (from Finnish speech) picked up by our real-time microprocessor-based "Phonetic Typewriter" [11]. In Test 1, the first of the data sets (1550 samples) was used for training and the second (1550 samples) for testing, respectively; in Test 2 the order was reversed. Table 1 contains the recognition accuracies for the same test data using the Parametric Bayes Classifier (with assumed multivariate normal distributions), the kNN classification results (practically identical with $k = 5$ and 6 neighbours), and results obtained by LVQ1, LVQ2, and LVQ3.

Table 1 **Speech recognition experiments. Error percentages for isolated phonemes.**

	Parametric Bayes	kNN	LVQ1	LVQ2	LVQ3
Test 1	12.1	12.0	10.2	9.8	9.6
Test 2	13.8	12.1	13.2	12.0	11.5

3. SELF ORGANISING MAP

The algorithm known as Self Organising Map was never meant for pattern classification. Its original purpose was creation of abstractions from primary sensory signals, as it has been known for a long time that the brain has cells capable of responding to rather abstract qualities of sensory information. Moreover, such brain cells often seem to be organized in an orderly fashion, as if there existed coordinate systems for many important specific sensory feature dimensions over the cortex. Such abstract representations for features can then also be created by the artificial Self Organising Maps.

In order that ordered mappings are formed (in an unsupervised learning process like VQ), the neural cells, during learning, must be made to interact in the spatial domain. It has turned out to be a very effective strategy that if cell c is distinguished as the "winner", i.e., if its codebook vector m_c matches best with the input pattern x, then a similar updating operation must be applied *not only to cell c but to all the cells that lie in the topological neighborhood N_c of cell c.*

If we use, e.g., Euclidean distances to define the "winner" c,

$$\|x(t) - m_c(t)\| = \min_i \{\|x(t)-m_i\|\} \quad , \tag{6}$$

then the updating may be such that

$$
\begin{aligned}
m_i(t+1) &= m_i(t) + \alpha(t)[x(t)-m_i(t)] & \forall i \in N_c(t), \\
m_i(t+1) &= m_i(t) & \forall i \notin N_c(t).
\end{aligned}
\tag{7}
$$

If we start with randomly chosen initial values for the $m_i(0)$ and let the system converge towards an asymptotic equilibrium, then $\alpha = \alpha(t)$ ought to be a scalar parameter that during the course of the process decreases monotonically $(0 < \alpha < 1)$. The neighborhood set N_c also must be a function of time (for details, see, e.g., [8]).

The process defined by Eqs. (6) and (7) changes the codebook vectors m_i in such a coordinated way that their point density tends to describe the statistical density function of the input samples $x = x(t)$. At the same time they tend to be placed into the signal space *in an orderly fashion*, whereby *their topological order in the signal space becomes the same as that of the spatial locations of the cells in the network*. This result is too complicated to be proved in the present article; cf. the collateral reading [8,12,13,14,15,16]. One might simply state that the self-organising process defined by Eqs. (6) and (7) asymptotically tends to place the m_i into the signal space such that the "elastic net" formed of them nonlinearly projects the probability density function onto itself.

An example [17]
The components of the input pattern vector $x \in R^n$ may represent many different things. In the following example, more closely defined by Table 2, sixteen animals were described by thirteen attributes; the set of attributes in this example was selected heuristically and cannot be considered as complete. It is neither speculated here what mechanism might generate the observed attribute signals. It is only assumed that the presence (=1) or absence (=0) of an attribute can somehow be detected.

		dove	hen	duck	goose	owl	hawk	eagle	fox	dog	wolf	cat	tiger	lion	horse	zebra	cow
is	small	1	1	1	1	1	1	0	0	0	0	1	0	0	0	0	0
	medium	0	0	0	0	0	0	1	1	1	1	0	0	0	0	0	0
	big	0	0	0	0	0	0	0	0	0	0	0	1	1	1	1	1
has	2 legs	1	1	1	1	1	1	1	0	0	0	0	0	0	0	0	0
	4 legs	0	0	0	0	0	0	0	1	1	1	1	1	1	1	1	1
	hair	0	0	0	0	0	0	0	1	1	1	1	1	1	1	1	1
	hooves	0	0	0	0	0	0	0	0	0	0	0	0	0	1	1	1
	mane	0	0	0	0	0	0	0	0	0	1	0	0	1	1	1	0
	feathers	1	1	1	1	1	1	1	0	0	0	0	0	0	0	0	0
likes	hunt	0	0	0	0	1	1	1	1	0	1	1	1	1	0	0	0
to	run	0	0	0	0	0	0	0	0	1	1	0	1	1	1	1	0
	fly	1	0	0	1	1	1	1	0	0	0	0	0	0	0	0	0
	swim	0	0	1	1	0	0	0	0	0	0	0	0	0	0	0	0

Table 2

When the columns of Table 2, regarded as input vectors $x(t)$, were presented to the map algorithm, Eqs. (6) and (7) in a random order, certain cells in the network started to become specifically sensitive to representations of particular animals. This order is discernible from Fig. 2 where the cells whose codebook vectors match best with the attribute vectors of Table 2 have been labelled by the corresponding animal names. Very clearly the spatial organisation of the cells in this map reflects a natural taxonomy of the animals. As a matter of fact, the Self Organising Map frequently carries out some kind of taxonomy or hierarchical clustering of the input samples.

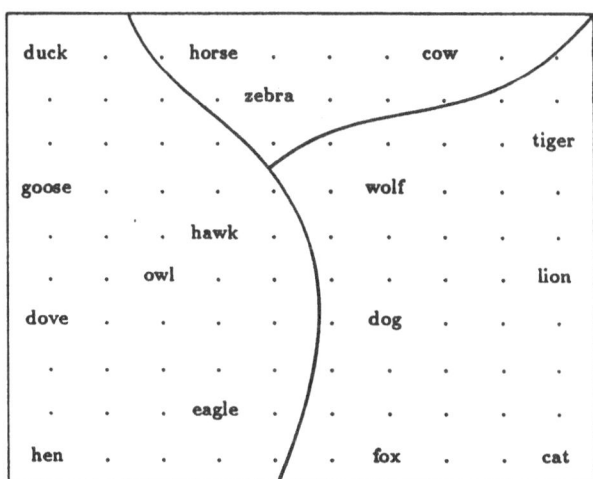

Fig. 2

4. CONCLUSIONS

To recapitulate, it may be proper to recall that the original vector quantisation was only meant for the approximation of signals using discrete codebook vectors. The Learning Vector Quantisation methods were designed for optimal statistical pattern classification. The main purpose of the Self Organising Map, on the other hand, has been creation of geometrically and topologically organised internal representations (abstractions) of input information similar to those encountered in the brain. The encoding of information is spatial and the logic relationships are reflected by the topology of the representations.

The maps, as such, do not yet classify patterns at optimal decision accuracy. However, if their codebook vectors are fine-tuned using the Learning Vector Quantisation algorithms, the maps classify patterns with *close-Bayesian accuracy* even in difficult cases. The LVQ algorithms can also be applied directly, without prior formation of topologically organised maps.

REFERENCES

1. Makhoul J, Roucos S, Gish H. Vector quantization in speech coding. Proc IEEE, Nov 1985, 1551-1588
2. Gray R M. Vector quantization. IEEE ASSP Mag 1984; 1:4-29
3. Max J. Quantizing for minimum distortion. IRE Trans Inform Theory 1960; IT-6:7-12
4. Gersho A. On the structure of vector quantizers. IEEE Trans Inform Theory 1979; IT-25:373-380
5. Zador P L. Asymptotic quantization error of continuous signals and the quantization dimension. IEEE Trans Inform Theory 1982; IT-28:139-149
6. Kohonen T. An introduction to neural computing. Neural Networks 1988; 1:3-16
7. Kohonen T. Learning vector quantization. Neural Networks 1988; Suppl 1:303
8. Kohonen T. Self-organization and associative memory. Springer, Heidelberg, 1984; 3rd ed 1989
9. Kohonen T. Self-organized formation of topographically correct feature maps. Biol Cybern 1982; 43:59-69
10. LaVigna A. Nonparametric classification using learning vector quantization. PhD thesis, University of Maryland, College Park, 1989
11. Kohonen T. The "neural" phonetic typewriter. Computer 1988; 21:11-22
12. Cottrell M, Fort J-C. A stochastic model of retinotopy: A self-organizing process. Biol Cybern 1986; 53:405-411
13. Cottrell M, Fort J-C. Étude d'un processus d'áuto-organisation. Ann Inst Henri Poincaré 1987; 23:1-20
14. Ritter H, Schulten K. On the stationary state of Kohonen's self-organizing mapping. Biol Cybern 1986; 54: 99-106
15. Ritter H, Schulten K. Convergency properties of Kohonen's topology conserving maps: Fluctuations, stability and dimension selection. Biol Cybern 1989; 60:59-71
16. Luttrell S P. Self-organization: A derivation from first principles of a class of learning algorithms. Proc IJCNN 89 Int Joint Conf on Neural Networks, Washington, DC, 1989, pp II-495 - II-498
17. Ritter H, Kohonen T. Self-organizing semantic maps. Biol Cybern 1989; 61:241-254

NATURE OF THE FUNCTIONAL LOSS IN AMNESIA: POSSIBLE ROLE FOR A HIGHLY STRUCTURED NEURAL NETWORK.

Andrew Mayes

INTRODUCTION

Organic amnesia is a condition in which brain damage to structures in the medial temporal lobes, midline diencephalon or basal forebrain impairs the ability to recall or recognize recently experienced facts or episodes (anterograde amnesia) and also the ability to recall and recognize facts and episodes, memories for which may have been formed normally up to decades before the onset of brain damage. Despite these impairments, which can be very severe in some patients, many amnesics show preserved intelligence and short-term memory. Amnesics therefore show an impairment that is specific to certain kinds of memory, leaving other kinds of memory and cognitive function intact. In this paper, the precise nature of the preserved and impaired functions will first be described in more detail in order to facilitate an appropriate characterization of the disturbed function(s) and to help determine whether patients are suffering from only one functional deficit or several independent functional deficits. Work that is concerned with identifying the structures, damage to which is critical in producing the syndrome, will then be briefly reviewed. The anatomy and physiology of the critical structures will then be outlined and the nature of their informational inputs and outputs briefly considered. Finally, the conditions that must be met by a neural network model that can produce the kinds of memory that are deficient in amnesics will be discussed.

The approach that will be adopted throughout the paper depends on viewing the brain as comprising a large number of modular systems that are connected both in series and in parallel. Each module consists of a specific set of neurons that perform a particular type of processing operation on a specified kind of informational input. The existence of such modules can be established with confidence when two sources of evidence have consistent implications. The first kind of evidence shows that lesions to a particular structure or set of structures impairs only one kind of processing for information of a specific kind. The second kind of evidence shows that the same brain structure or structures are selectively activated when the specified kind of information is processed in the relevant fashion by people with intact brains. Thus, for example, the structures that are damaged in amnesia should show increased activity in normal people when they are either acquiring new memories or retrieving old memories. The reason that amnesia is interesting is that the syndrome highlights what kinds of processing are necessary if old memories are to be recalled and recognized and new memories are to be created so that they can be later recalled and recognized.

Organic amnesia can be caused by damage to more than one brain region. Although these regions are interconnected, this fact raises the question of whether the syndrome is associated with damage to more than one processing system. If damage to more than one module is typically involved in the syndrome, then it should be possible to find patients who show more selective impairments, reflecting damage to a single module. It is, for example, well-established that damage to the left hemisphere can cause an amnesia that is specific to verbalizable information whereas damage to parts of the right hemisphere can cause an amnesia that is specific to non-verbalizable information. Nevertheless, it seems likely that the left and right hemisphere modules that have been damaged perform basically the same kind of processing operation albeit on somewhat different kinds of information.

Other proposed dissociations of the amnesic syndrome imply that many (if not all) patients have suffered damage to two or more modules that may process basically the same kinds of information in different ways. There are several such proposals and all are controversial and need more research to establish their validity. The one which is currently best supported claims that one kind of processing impairment generates severe retrograde amnesia whereas another processing impairment is mainly responsible for anterograde amnesia. In many patients it is well-known that severe anterograde amnesia can be accompanied by a mild retrograde amnesia that does not seem to affect memories acquired more than a few years before the onset of the amnesia. In other patients mild anterograde amnesia is accompanied by severe retrograde amnesia that affects memories acquired decades before the onset of amnesia. Recent research suggests, but has not yet proved, that when retrograde amnesia affects memories that were acquired decades before the critical brain damage, there is damage to temporal or frontal association cortex. For example, Squire and his co-workers have reported that a patient with medial temporal lobe damage, whose lesion did not extend into cortical structures, did not show a retrograde amnesia that was detectable by standard tests whereas patients with damage, that MRI has recently shown to extend into temporal association cortex (Press, Amaral and Squire, 1989), had retrograde amnesias that extended back for decades (Zola-Morgan, Squire and Amaral, 1986; Squire, Haist, and Shimamura, 1989).

It seems possible that many amnesics suffer damage to two modular systems that may be closely related to each other. Damage to the first causes an anterograde amnesia and a mild retrograde amnesia that extends back no more than a year or so (and possibly much less) before the onset of brain damage, whereas damage to the second primarily causes a retrograde amnesia that extends back for decades premorbidly. Support for this notion may be drawn from two further sources. First, there is evidence that retrograde amnesia can occur in the absence of anterograde amnesia (see Mayes, 1988). These cases are rare, however, and it still needs to be clearly established that the critical damage is to the association cortex of the temporal and/or frontal lobes. The second source of evidence is still preliminary and involved the use of a PET scanner to record metabolic activity in the brains of normal subjects, who were (a) learning and having their memories tested for some new faces, and (b) remembering faces that they had learnt many years before (Kapur, personal communication). When performing the first task the subjects showed increased metabolic activity in the hippocampus, which lies in the medial temporal lobes, but this increased metabolic activity was not seen in the hippocampus when the subjects performed the second task. As the hippocampus is damaged in amnesics who have suffered medial temporal lobe damage, this suggests that when the processing of this structure is disrupted, an anterograde amnesia will become apparent, but this may only be associated with a retrograde amnesia that extends back a short time before the onset of brain damage. Recall or recognition of remote memories may depend on activation of temporal and perhaps frontal association neocortex.

The possibility that amnesia comprises a salmagundi of disorders that can, in principle, be dissociated from each other makes it somewhat harder to discover what features, if any, are present in all cases of the syndrome. Work over the past twenty years has suggested, however, that many and perhaps all patients show (a) preservation of certain kinds of memory, (b) impairments of other kinds of memory, and (c) particularly severe impairments of yet other kinds of memory. It can be stated quite generally that patients show both anterograde amnesia and some degree of retrograde amnesia when they are required to recall or recognize events or facts. This kind of memory has been referred to as declarative, explicit or direct because it must be revealed directly either through a verbal statement or through a non-verbal gesture such as pointing. Tests of anterograde amnesia usually assess direct memory for information which was attended to during an initial learning session. This is referred to as target information. Recent work by Hirst and his colleagues (1986, 1988) indicates that amnesics are more impaired at free recalling target information than they are at recognizing it. Free recall is the uncued remembering of facts or events experienced on a particular occasion or which satisfy certain general conditions, and Hirst and his colleagues found that amnesics were disproportionally impaired at recalling words from a previously seen list. In order to avoid artefacts due to floor and ceiling effects and scaling effects, demonstrations such as this compare normal control subjects and amnesics under different conditions. The conditions are much harder for the controls in order to ensure that their levels of recognition of the target information can be equated to that of the amnesics. This can be achieved either by testing the control subjects after a much longer retention interval or after less learning opportunity, or both. When Hirst and his colleagues followed this procedure their amnesic subjects did as well as the normal controls at recognizing target words that they had been shown earlier, but were still impaired at recalling those words.

There is evidence that amnesics show preservation of four kinds of memory, which are not declarative, explicit or direct. The first of these is immediate memory for various kinds of information such as sequences of spoken digits or the spatial locations of identical shapes. This preserved ability indicates that the amnesic memory deficit only becomes apparent after attention has been temporarily withdrawn from encoded information and it also suggests that amnesics initially encode or represent the information for which they later show impaired direct memory. There is, in fact, good evidence that amnesics encode as much semantic and contextual information about complex events as do normal people (Shoqeirat, 1989). Immediate memory probably depends on the activity of association neocortex neurons that are undamaged in amnesics.

The second kind of memory for which amnesics show no impairment is classical conditioning. There is good evidence that amnesics are unimpaired at the acquisition and retention of simple forms of classical conditioning although they do show deficiencies with more complex conditioning phenomenona, such as blocking (Daum et al., 1989). There is evidence that the simple forms of classical conditioning, impaired in amnesics, are disrupted in humans as well as in other animals by cerebellar lesions (Lye, O'Boyle, Ramsden and Schady, 1988). Simple forms of classical conditioning probably depend, therefore, on very different neural systems to the ones affected in amnesics.

The third kind of memory for which amnesics show little or no impairment is the acquisition and retention of skills of various sorts. Patients have been shown to be normal at learning to trace the outline of a star while viewing the star through a mirror. They can also learn and retain other motor skills normally (see Shimamura, 1989). Patients have also been shown to learn and retain normally over a 13 week period the perceptuomotor skill of reading mirror-reversed words (Cohen and Squire, 1980). With all these perceptuomotor skills experience gained with certain instances is generalized to new instances. It has also been claimed that some amnesics can learn certain cognitive skills as well as control subjects. These skills less obviously involve generalization. One such task is the Tower of Hanoi puzzle, in which subjects move five wooden blocks from one peg to another, moving only one block at a time and never placing a larger block on a smaller one. The puzzle's solution depends on an iterative strategy that requires a minimum of 31 moves. There is evidence that although normal subjects improve with practice they are unable to articulate what it is that they are doing which has led to their improved performance. It remains to be shown whether all amnesics are normal at learning similar "intuitive" cognitive skills unless they have additional brain damage that is unrelated to their amnesic symptoms. Mishkin and his co-workers (1984) have argued that memory for skills depends on creating links between the neocortex and underlying striatum. If correct, skills, like simple classical conditioning, would be formed and stored in a very different brain system to the one that is damaged in amnesics. It seems likely that the modules involved in skill learning and classical conditioning deal with different inputs and process those inputs in radically different ways from the modules implicated in amnesia.

The fourth and most interesting form of memory that is believed to be preserved in amnesics is known as priming. Priming is present whenever information is processed differently or more efficiently as a result of having been recently perceived. Unlike recall and recognition it is an indirect form of memory, the presence of which is inferred from changes in behaviour rather than directly declared. But like direct memory priming is an item specific form of memory. A number of experiments have shown that amnesics can show preserved priming to the same items for which they show very impaired direct memory. For example, in one study, Jacoby and Witherspoon (1982) got amnesics and their control subjects to answer questions which contained the less common form of a homophone ("reed instead of "read"). Later the subjects were asked to spell homophones, which were presented to them orally. Both the normal subjects and the amnesics tended to spell the homophones in a way corresponding to its less common variant, which they had previously seen. The tendency was as strong in the amnesics as it was in their normal control subjects. Despite this the patients' direct memory of having seen the homophones earlier was very impaired. Similar demonstrations have been made with several kinds of priming at which amnesics were shown to perform normally despite showing very impaired direct memory for the same items to which they showed this normal priming.

The tasks that have most convincingly shown preserved amnesic priming of item-specific information have typically used verbal material. One feature of such material is that subjects usually have a pre-existing and well-rehearsed memory for the primed items. It is not necessary for the amnesics to create a new memory for which they show preserved priming. Instead it is plausible to argue that normal performance depends on activating a memory representation that already exists in the posterior association neocortex and that this activation may persist for some hours as is found with certain forms of familiar information priming. This kind of argument could not be used if amnesics showed normal priming of information that was novel before the priming exposure was given. In this case it would have to be conceded that a new memory has been created and that, under some conditions, amnesics are as good at retrieving this new memory as normal people.

There is some evidence that amnesics do show preserved priming for certain kinds of novel item although this evidence is more controversial than that concerned with priming of previously familiar information. For example, it is known that subjects read faster on the second exposure to verbal material than they do on initial exposure. This speed up effect depends in part on a memory for associations between words that would not have previously been related in people's minds. It has been shown that amnesics show this novel association speed up effect to the same extent as normal subjects (see Mayes, 1988) and we have recently found a similar kind of preservation in amnesics with lesions to each of the main brain regions damage to which produces the syndrome. Most studies that have examined novel information priming in amnesics have, however, produced somewhat more equivocal results. Typically, it has been found that some, but not all, amnesics show preserved priming in a particular paradigm. This could be because the patients, who do not perform normally, have additional damage, unrelated to amnesia, that prevents them from showing normal priming. Nevertheless, this has not been proved and it remains possible that the patients, who apparently perform normally, originally performed at a very high level and have merely dropped to a "normal" level as a result of the brain damage that caused their amnesia. The issue is not resolved, but on balance the evidence is slightly stronger that amnesics can show preserved priming for previously novel information when certain paradigms are used. It is also clear that the memories for the previously novel information can persist for long periods despite the absence of direct memory for the material. For example, even severely amnesic patients retain the ability to disambiguate unclear sentences such as "It was as well the haystack was there because the cord broke" after a delay of one week (see Mayes, 1988). This ability was retained despite the fact that there was little direct memory for the sentences within minutes of their presentation. Severe amnesics may therefore be able to create new memories, but only their indirect access to these memories seems to be preserved or nearly so.

Evidence has already been cited that although amnesics are impaired at recognition of target material, they are more impaired at free recalling the same target material. In contrast, the ability of patients to show cued recall for target items is no more impaired than their ability to recognize the items. There is, however, growing evidence that amnesics are more impaired at the cued recall of contextual information than they are at recognition of target material. Contextual information is what falls on the periphery of attention when a subject is concentrating on target material. It has been divided into two kinds. The first kind, referred to as independent context, includes information about the spatiotemporal location of target material and about the manner in which the target material is presented. This kind of context does not affect the meaningful interpretation of target material. The second kind of contextual information, referred to as interactive context, does affect the meaningful interpretation of target material. For example, if subjects are told to attend to the word "bank", but this word is shown to them at the same time that the word "river" is spoken to them, then their interpretation of the word "bank" is likely to be affected.

Amnesics have been shown to be more impaired at the cued recall of three kinds of independent context than they are at recognition of target material. First, there is evidence that, regardless of the precise location of their brain damage, amnesics are more impaired at the cued recall of several types of spatial information concerning the location of target items than they are at recognition of the target items themselves (Shoqeirat, 1989). They are equally impaired at using spatial locations to cue their recall of target items and at using the target items to identify the positions of the same target items. Second, amnesics, regardless of the precise location of their brain damage, are more impaired at identifying the sensory modality via which information was presented to them than they are at recognizing the information itself (Shoqeirat, 1989). Third, amnesics, regardless of the precise location of their brain damage, are more impaired at identifying in which of two sequentially presented lists words had occurred than they are at recognizing the words themselves (Shoqeirat, 1989). Amnesics may therefore be disproportionately impaired at a form of memory for the temporal location of target items. As well as showing particularly severe impairments in the cued recall of independent context we have recently found evidence that amnesics are more impaired at recognizing interactive context than they are at recognizing target material. This impairment was found in amnesics regardless of the precise location of their brain damage.

The interpretation of all of the above evidence is currently controversial for two reasons. The first reason is that the particularly severe deficits may not be an essential feature of amnesia, but could arise because of additional brain damage (most probably to the frontal lobes) that is unrelated to amnesia. There is, however, no evidence that frontal lobe damage causes impairments in memory for spatial location, the sensory modality via which items are presented, and interactive context, and although there is evidence that frontal lobe damage can cause deficits in certain kinds of memory for temporal order, some amnesics without obvious frontal lobe lesions seem to show disproportionately severe deficits for temporal order information. The second reason that the evidence is controversial relates to a number of subtle artefacts that could be operating with the procedure that is used to test for disproportionate deficits in the patients. There is, for example, a possibility that the particularly severe deficits arise because the context memory tasks are harder than the target recognition tasks. It is true that normal subjects make fewer correct responses in the context memory tasks than they do with the target recognition tasks. The notion of difficulty is nevertheless atheoretical so even if this artefact is operating, its significance requires a theoretical interpretation. This will be offered in the next section.

There are three rather different theories that attempt to characterize the deficit(s) that cause amnesia. These should be regarded as hypotheses that indicate what kinds of processing are performed by brain modules, damage to which causes organic amnesia. The first hypothesis is that amnesia is caused by a failure to consolidate novel information that should ultimately be stored in the posterior association cortex. If, as seems likely, novel memories about facts and episodes involve forming new links between attributes that are already represented in association cortex, then amnesics are impaired at consolidating such links into memory storage. There are several versions of this hypothesis. For example, in amnesics cortical storage may be impaired because it is no longer being facilitated by the damaged structures or in normal people, new information may be stored initially in the structures damaged in amnesics and only later transferred to connected storage systems in association cortex. This transfer will be greatly reduced in amnesics because they will store little information initially as well as having a reduced ability to transfer what little information they do store to association cortex.

All versions of the consolidation hypothesis are compatible with patients' usually preserved ability to encode information and can predict the preservation of priming for already familiar information that is found in amnesics provided such priming depends solely on the prolonged activation of already established memories. The hypothesis cannot explain preserved amnesic priming of any kind of novel information and must deny the validity of the evidence relevant to this claim. For example, it could be argued that novel information priming may occur in amnesics but at subnormal levels because such priming can operate at memory levels that are too weak for direct memory to be apparent. It can explain why amnesics show preserved intelligence, immediate memory, classical conditioning and skill learning in so far as these must depend on the operation of brain modules that are intact in amnesics. In the past, it has been assumed that poor consolidation should affect direct memory for different kinds of material equally. It is possible, however, that when the consolidation module is damaged it can operate relatively normally if only required to work at slow rate, but is grossly impaired if required to work at a fast rate. As both free recall and context memory are typically more difficult for normal people than is target recognition, it is not unreasonable to argue that they depend on a greater amount of consolidation. In other words, successful free recall and context memory need more features to be linked together in memory than does successful target recognition. If both these assumptions are true, then the consolidation view of amnesia would predict the pattern of disproportionate deficits that has been reported in patients. If amnesics fail to consolidate information at a normal rate, then it seems likely that they should forget faster than normal people. This prediction is vague and can only be adequately made if the hypothesis makes the features of consolidation more explicit. At present, it is unresolved whether amnesics forget faster than normal people because testing the issue is confounded with severe methodological difficulties. The consolidation hypothesis cannot explain retrograde amnesias that extend back for decades but does not have to if it is accepted that such prolonged amnesias are caused by damage to a different module probably located in the posterior association cortex. Nevertheless, even if the retrograde amnesia that is caused by the same modular damage that produces anterograde amnesia only extends back a few years, this creates a serious problem for the hypothesis because conventional accounts of consolidation confine it to a much shorter time scale. It is extremely important for research to be focused on identifying the minimal duration of retrograde amnesia that accompanies severe anterograde amnesia.

A second hypothesis of amnesia, discussed by Mayes (1988), is the context-memory deficit hypothesis. This postulates that amnesics have a consolidation problem (perhaps accompanied by a retrieval deficit) that is specific to independent and interactive context, and that this primary deficit causes a secondary, less severe deficit in the recognition of target information. Free recall of target information is more impaired in patients because this depends more than does target recognition on retrieving links between context and targets. This hypothesis can explain all the kinds of preserved function that the consolidation hypothesis can explain, and, in addition, it can predict that amnesics will show preserved priming for previously novel target information. It can do this if it is assumed that priming of novel target information does not require the retrieval of contextual information. This is plausible given that priming does not require the retrieval of specific episodes. Like the consolidation hypothesis, the context-memory deficit hypothesis should predict that amnesics should forget pathologically fast not only because they fail to consolidate contextual features normally, but also because their inability to associate targets with context makes them abnormally sensitive to interference in certain situations, and interference accelerates forgetting. The hypothesis can also account for retrograde amnesia of a few years duration provided one accepts that memories gradually become reorganized with the passage of time so that target information can eventually be retrieved without also having to retrieve its contextual markers. An important implication of the consolidation version of this hypothesis is that in intact people the brain regions damaged in amnesia are the sites in which contextual information is at least partially stored.

The third hypothesis is the least fully articulated and proposes that amnesia is caused by a disconnection between an intact fact and episode memory system and a cortically located conscious awareness system (Schacter, 1990). According to this hypothesis all aspects of facts and episodes are stored normally and can be retrieved indirectly, but patients show impaired direct memory for this stored information because it cannot gain access to consciousness normally. The hypothesis predicts that amnesics will show preserved priming not only for previously novel target information, but also for contextual information. This is a prediction that clearly distinguishes it from the context-memory deficit hypothesis. Currently, it is unknown whether amnesics show preserved priming for contextual information. The disconnection account does have great difficulty in explaining why patients appear to be more impaired at target free recall and context memory than they are at target recognition. It is also hard to see how it can explain why amnesics show preservation of immediate memory (which is direct) and direct memory for very remote and well-rehearsed facts and episodes because these forms of memory also depend on gaining access to the hypothetical conscious awareness system. The hypothesis correctly stresses that direct memory is conscious and depends on a feeling of familiarity for which neither of the other hypotheses offers an adequate theoretical account.

Amnesia can be caused by damage to structures in the medial temporal lobes, the midline diencephalon or the basal forebrain. There is still controversy about which structures in these regions have to be damaged to produce amnesia, but it need not be supposed that damage to the separate regions causes a different kind of amnesia because several structures in the three regions are quite strongly interconnected. Thus, the hippocampus in the medial temporal lobes receives a projection from the underlying entorhinal cortex and itself projects directly to the anterior nucleus of the thalamus via the fornix and also indirectly via the forniceal projection to the mammillary bodies. The anterior nucleus of the thalamus projects to the cingulate cortex, which projects back to the hippocampus via the entorhinal cortex. Similarly, the amygdala in the medial temporal lobes receives projections from a number of cortical regions that include the orbitofrontal, insular and anterior temporal cortices and itself projects both directly and indirectly to the dorsomedial thalamic nucleus and other midline thalamic nuclei, and the dorsomedial thalamic nucleus projects to the orbitofrontal cortex, which completes the circuit back to the amygdala. Both the hippocampus and amygdala project to and receive cholinergic projections from the basal forebrain, which also projects to association neocortex and midline thalamic structures.

Precise localization of the lesions that are critical in amnesia is made difficult in humans because the adventitious nature of brain damage means that structures unrelated to amnesia are usually also disrupted. The search for the location of the critical lesions has, however, been facilitated in recent years by the use of a monkey model of amnesia that has examined the effects of different lesions on the animals' performance on an analogue of a recognition task. Two views about the structures, damage to which causes amnesia, have emerged from this work using the monkey model of amnesia, and both views also receive some corroboration from the human literature.

The first view is that of Mishkin and his colleagues (see Mishkin and Appenzeller, 1987) and states that severe, permanent amnesia only occurs when there is damage to both the hippocampal and amygdalar circuits just described or to the parts of the cholinergic basal forebrain that modulates both the hippocampal and the amygdalar circuits. According to this view, severe temporal lobe amnesia only occurs if both the hippocampus and amygdala are damaged although a milder amnesia results if only one structure is disrupted. Similarly, a severe midline diencephalic amnesia only occurs either if there is conjoint damage to the anterior and dorsomedial thalamic nuclei (or thalamic projections to them) or to the dorsomedial thalamus and the mammillary bodies. Damage to diencephalic structures in only one of the circuit's has little or no effect on recognition memory.

The second view derives from recent work of Zola-Morgan and his colleagues that is critical of Mishkin's hypothsis (Zola-Morgan, Squire, Amaral and Suzuki, 1989, Zola-Morgan, Squire and Amaral, 1989). These researchers have found that lesions confined to the amygdala without damage to the underlying association cortex neither cause amnesia nor exacerbate the amnesia caused by hippocampal damage. In contrast, they have found that lesions confined to the perirhinal and parahippocampal cortex cause a more severe amnesia than lesions of the hippocampus alone. A possible interpretation of these results depends on a knowledge of the projections to the entorhinal cortex that then go to the hippocampus. The entorhinal cortex receives projections from polysensory association cortex that includes regions such as the orbitofrontal, insular and superior temporal cortices. But nearly two thirds of the projections come from the perirhinal and parahippocampal polysensory association cortices. Damage to these two regions therefore massively reduces the input of processed cortical sensory information into the hippocampus. Although the hippocampus does project to the diencephalon via the fornix, in primates, its projections back to polysensory association cortex via the entorhinal cortex probably assume a greater importance. The polysensory association cortices also project to midline thalamic nuclei that may be implicated in amnesia and these nuclei may work relatively independently of the hippocampus. The following view therefore emerges: damage to the hippocampus causes a moderate amnesia because this damage disrupts activity in a hippocampal-entorhinal-polysensory association cortex loop. Damage to certain midline diencephalic structures causes amnesia because this damage disrupts activity in a relatively independent diencephalic-polysensory association cortex loop. Damage to the basal forebrain causes amnesia because it disrupts activity in both these systems, but perhaps that in the hippocampal loop in particular. Finally, damage to polysensory association cortices and parahippocampal and perirhinal cortices in particular causes a more severe amnesia because it disrupts activity in both hippocampal and diencephalic systems.

It is currently not possible to rule conclusively between these two views. Although both groups agree that parahippocampal and perirhinal cortex lesions cause severe amnesia, the evidence is not conclusive that the amygdalar system plays no role in amnesia. It is not disputed that hippocampal lesions alone can cause a moderate amnesia in humans as several cases have been reported with lesions more or less specific to the hippocampus of which the best described is case R.B. (Zola-Morgan, Squire and Amaral, 1986). This patient, whose only appreciable bilateral damage was to the CA1 field of the hippocampus had a moderate anterograde amnesia and, at most, a very mild retrograde amnesia. Other patients with damage extending into polysensory association cortices seem to have more extensive retrograde amnesias either because these regions are more involved in the storage of factual and episodic memories or because they are more involved in the retrieval of such memories or both. More research also needs to be done to identify the critical diencephalic damage in amnesia and to work out the extent to which these structures receive hippocampal and polysensory association cortex projections. Mishkin and Appenzeller (1987) have argued that amnesia can result not only from lesions to the cholinergic basal forebrain, but also to other relatively non-specific systems that modulate association cortex and hippocampal processing. One such system is the noradrenergic pathway from the locus coeruleus, which is often disrupted in amnesics with an aetiology of chronic alcoholism (see Mayes et al., 1988), and which projects to medial temporal lobe structures as well as association cortex. A key question, not yet answered, is which kinds of damage have additive disruptive effects on memory? For example, are the effects of hippocampal and medial diencephalic lesions additive, and are the effects of either of these kinds of damage additive with locus coeruleus lesions?

Amnesics cannot learn to recall or recognize new facts and episodes and also have some degree of difficulty with recalling and recognizing facts and episodes learnt before their brain damage. It is therefore important that both the medial temporal and the diencephalic regions, damaged in amnesia, receive either directly or indirectly a massive input of highly processed sensory information from polysensory association cortex. Both regions must then perform some further processing on this complex input before feeding back an output to widely distributed association cortex neurons. Less is known about which diencephalic structures are involved and consequently about the nature of their processing and the precise nature of their feedback to cortex so these structures will not be considered further. Nevertheless, they must be performing an operation important for recall and recognition that could be somewhat different to that performed by the hippocampal-cortical loop. It also needs to be determined whether this operation involves any kind of information storage.

Not much is known about how the information, fed into the hippocampus via the perforant pathway from the entorhinal cortex, is encoded. This needs to be explored by recording from single neurons contributing to this pathway. The input is then processed through a well-known trisynaptic circuit running from the dentate gyrus to the CA3 field of the hippocampus proper to the CA1 field and then back to the entorhinal cortex via the subiculum or down to the midline diencephalon via the fornix. The perforant pathway input may divide into different medial and lateral components that project to different parts of the dendritic field of the dentate granule cells although the significance of this division is currently a matter for speculation (Morris, 1989a). In addition, the granule cells receive feedback inhibition from basket cells in the dentate, which would allow competitive learning to occur in this hippocampal region. The CA3 stage of the circuit is also interesting because the pyramidal neurons of this stage have a very extensive system of recurrent collaterals so that it is estimated that the contact probability of a CA3 neuron with another CA3 neuron is about 4.3% whereas the contact probability of a granule cell with a CA3 neuron is 0.008%. In humans, it is estimated that there are about 8.8 million neurons in the dentate gyrus, 2.5 million neurons in the CA3 field and 6.0 million in the CA1 field (interestingly, there is a greater increase in the number of CA1 neurons between monkey and humans than there is in the number of CA3 neurons).

Not only is the trisynaptic circuit concerned with transforming the input it receives from the entorhinal cortex, it also seems likely that it stores information. Long-term potentiation (LTP) seems to be easier to produce in the hippocampus than it does in association cortex. LTP is an increase in synaptic efficiency that is produced experimentally by rapid bursts of stimulation on the input pathway. It is long-lasting, develops rapidly, is synapse specific, and is associative (see Morris, 1989a). LTP seems to develop according to a quasi-Hebbian learning rule because it requires a conjunction of pre-synaptic activity with a critical level of post-synaptic depolarization. Cholinergic inputs from the basal forebrain and noradrenergic inputs from the locus coeruleus may facilitate the production of LTP because they increase the likelihood that depolarization thresholds are reached (Singer, 1990). There is also evidence that two forms of long-term depression can be produced in the hippocampus. Heterosynaptic depression occurs when there is a conjunction of postsynaptic activity and pre-synaptic inactivity whereas homosynaptic depression, for which there is less good evidence, occurs when there is a conjunction of presynaptic activity and post-synaptic hyperpolarization. Evidence also exists that an LTP-like plastic process in the hippocampus is necessary if certain kinds of learning are to occur. If hippocampal LTP is selectively blocked pharmacologically or if LTP-like processes are saturated experimentally, then spatial memory does not develop normally in rats (see Morris, 1989a). Interestingly, blocking LTP prevents the development of new spatial memories whereas it does not affect already existing spatial memories, although hippocampal lesions disrupt both new and old spatial memories (see Morris, 1989a). In these animals therefore hippocampal storage may be essential for memory of certain kinds of independent context and possibly other kinds of complex information.

Recordings from single neurons in the rat hippocampus show that many become selectively active when animals are in a specific location. But, in different situations, the same neuron may become active at specific locations within each situation. In other words, hippocampal neurons in the rat do not uniquely encode a particular spatial location, but participate in the encoding of several locations as well perhaps as other kinds of information. It is almost certain that these selective mapping responses are learnt rapidly (see Dudai, 1989). In monkeys, there is evidence that the responsivity of hippocampal neurons can be changed during learning so that they come to respond to specific conjunctions of object and location, or of object and response (see Rolls, 1989). There is also evidence that hippocampal neurons in humans show a relatively specific increased firing rate to particular words and faces (Heit, Smith and Halgren, 1988). The degree of selectivity should not be exaggerated and firing rate did not increase with further repetition so it is likely that the learning that underlay the response was largely acquired on the first trial. The authors argued that their results suggested that the hippocampus supplies association cortex with specific information rather than diffuse modulation relevant to the consolidation and subsequent recognition of memories. This may be so, but Squire, Shimamura and Amaral (1989) have argued that the marked convergence and divergence characteristic of several stages of the hippocampal circuitry make it improbable that specific point-to-point mapping of the source of the neocortical information is preserved through the system.

Some Preliminary Models of Amnesia

Although predictions can be derived from the three theories of the functional deficit(s) that underlies amnesia, these predictions lack precision and it is even uncertain that they can be made because the theories themselves are imprecisely formulated. If a plausible computer model of these theories could be generated, then it should be possible to derive more exact predictions including some that may be counterintuitive that could then be examined to test the validity of the theory. A preliminary model of this kind has been produced by McClelland and Rumelhart (1986) for the theory that the amnesia, resulting from medial temporal lobe damage, is caused by a failure to consolidate memories of facts and episodes into storage in the association cortex. The model makes certain rather biologically implausible assumptions about a putative consolidation process and then assigns values to this process based on the temporal extent of retrograde amnesia in patients who have received a course of Electroconvulsive Shock Therapy. There is currently no evidence that a consolidation process with such a long course exists. Even so, the modelling makes clear that a single consolidation process is incapable of accounting for a retrograde amnesia of several years duration and accelerated forgetting of new learning in anterograde amnesia that extends over a few days. If accelerated forgetting over a short period after learning is a fact of anterograde amnesia, then disruption of at least two consolidation processes with radically different time courses will be necessary to explain anterograde and retrograde amnesia. One possible interpretation of the consolidation process with the slower time course is that the hippocampus initially stores the memory, which is laid down via a rapid consolidation process, and then the memory is gradually transferred to association cortex structures through a process of automatic and voluntary rehearsal that continues for months or even years - the slow consolidation process. A slow consolidation process of this sort could obviously restart after a period during which it has not been working (as in the case of a reversible lesion) so the model predicts that when new learning and memory recover retrograde amnesia usually largely dissipates.

The modelling also shows that if the consolidation process is incorporated into a PDP network with backpropagation and the strength of consolidation reduced, then the system can produce normal or even supernormal learning of generalizable skills. It is highly unlikely, however, that memories about such skills are stored in the association neocortex so the assumption underlying this aspect of the model is probably wrong. Furthermore, it is unlikely that the model can produce normal priming of even previously familiar, let alone novel items, memories for which are almost certainly stored in association cortex. Nevertheless, the model indicates that the development of skills may occur at least as efficiently, in a system where consolidation increments connection strengths in very small steps rather than in the large ones which are postulated to occur in medial temporal lobes. In other words, it hints at a possible reason why skills may be stored in a different brain region from that concerned with memory for facts and episodes. In summary, the McClelland and Rumelhart model represents an advance in so far as it makes a theory of amnesia more precise, but it is unsatisfactory in paying insufficient attention to biologically constraints and the detailed psychological features of amnesia.

One model that pays more attention to biological detail is being developed by Rolls and his colleagues (see Rolls, 1989). This is a connectionist model of the hippocampus. As damage to the hippocampus produces at least a mild amnesia, then disruption of the functions performed by Rolls' model should produce the memory symptoms of amnesia. In simple terms, it is postulated that stage one of the trisynaptic circuit, the dentate gyrus, reduces the redundancy of the hippocampal input from the entorhinal cortex using a competitive learning algorithm that relies on the inhibitory feedback from basket cells onto granule cells. The less redundant input feeds forward via mossy fibres that connect only sparsely to the CA3 pyramidal neurons at the next stage of the circuit. The extensive collaterals operating between CA3 cells gives rise to the suggestion that this stage of the circuit performs an autoassociative function. In effect, components of an encoded episode that reach CA3 from widely distinct cortical areas are combined through the linked activity of cells at this stage. The information is then fed forward to the CA1 neurons of the third stage of the trisynpatic circuit where it is supposed to be subjected to further competitive learning so that the episodic information encoded at the CA3 stage can be represented on fewer neurons. Rolls proposes that the output of all this processing is then fed back to the deep layers of the entorhinal cortex and probably to the polysensory association cortex that projects to the entorhinal cortex where it guides long-term information storage. The model can then be seen to derive from a particular kind of consolidation hypothesis.

This model clearly pays great attention to the biological features of the hippocampus although it remains to be seen whether the currently known biology is sufficient for an adequate network model and whether Rolls gives a correct account of the function of known biology. For example, he suggests that homosynaptic depression plays a role in the normalization of the synaptic weight vector on each dendrite whereas heterosynaptic depression plays a role in increasing the effectiveness of stimulus categorization. A diametrically opposite view has been put forward by Morris (1989b). With respect to details of the circuitry of the hippocampus, it is known that the perforant pathway projects directly as well as indirectly to CA3 and CA1, which is consistent with these regions performing comparisons of their input with a transform of itself. A function of this kind needs to be included in the Roll's model. The model may also not give sufficient attention to the possibility that topographically distinct regions of the perforant pathway may be carrying somewhat different kinds of information to the hippocampus.

More generally, a greater amount of attention may be needed to be given to the question of how distributed is the representation of information in the hippocampus, what kind of information is represented, for how long, and for what purpose. If the hippocampus does contain an autoassociative net, then it presumably stores complex information at least for a certain period of time. Single unit recording work suggests that interesting conjunctions of features are represented in individual neurons as well as networks of neurons in humans and other animals. If such representations persist for a moderate period of time, it is hard to believe that their only function is to guide storage in the association cortex for only a brief period of time following learning. Rolls seems to imply that the hippocampus detects useful conjunctions of widely distributed cortical activations and only modulates cortical storage under those conditions in which the conjunctions are of interest. The modulation may be non-specific as point-to-point specificity is probably not preserved in the hippocampus, but learning might only be facilitated in those cortical association areas that have just been active.

As a model of a theory of amnesia, Rolls' account may need to explain how damage to the hippocampus can leave priming of novel as well as familiar information unaffected, and perhaps also explain why such damage disrupts free recall of targets and direct memory for various aspects of context more than recognition of targets. It is also not clear that disruption of the functions performed by Rolls' model will produce any degree of retrograde amnesia. This may not be a deficiency, however, until it is shown convincingly that selective hippocampal lesions cause a retrograde amnesia that extends back some considerable time. Nevertheless, more attention should be paid to seeing whether disruption of the model's functions can produce the pattern of impairment typically seen in amnesics. A comprehensive model of amnesia may also have to consider the forniceal projections of the hippocampus to the midline diencephalic structures, damaged in some amnesics, and also the polysensory association cortex projections to these diencephalic structures.

Much of the information that we currently possess about the pattern of cognitive and memory performance shown by amnesic patients and about lesions that cause this pattern of performance is still uncertain although some parts of it are obviously more certain than others. Even so, theorists wishing to model amnesia in a realistic fashion cannot afford to ignore the constraints suggested by this information. It may be that if they cannot produce a biologically plausible model of a claimed feature of amnesia, then this feature will require more careful investigation as it may result from a hitherto unidentified kind of artefact. For example, if no biologically plausible model of amnesia can satisfy the claim that amnesics are more impaired at free recall of targets and at direct memory for context than they are at recognizing targets, then some doubt is cast on this claim. More realistically models of different theories may vary in the number of implausible assumptions that they need to make, and this may be used in choosing between them. Similarly, if a model of a structure's processing and the disruption of that processing cannot produce the probable symptoms of amnesia, then damage to that structure is unlikely to contribute to amnesia. In other words, it is to be hoped that not only will network models of amnesia be guided by our current neuropsychological and neuroanatomical knowledge of the condition, they will also help guide the direction of research aimed at improving such knowledge.

For the time being the following points are worth noting. First, amnesia very probably involves damage to two or more processing/storage systems of neurons, which will be interconnected. Temporarily extensive retrograde amnesia may require damage to association cortical regions that project to and receive projections from the structures, lesions to which cause severe anterograde amnesia. It remains to be determined whether temporarily extensive retrograde amnesia is caused by some kind of retrieval deficit, by a storage failure or both. If episodic and factual memories are stored long-term in association cortex, one very important issue to resolve is how many of the cortical relay stages show the kind of synaptic changes that underlie storage. It is of some interest that Routtenberg and Nelson (see Mishkin and Appenzeller (1987)) have argued that the phosphorylation of the brain protein, F1, by the enzyme kinase C, underlies the synaptic changes resulting from repeated electrical stimulation of certain neurons, and that this phosphorylation mechanism operates most extensively in the final stages of the monkey visual system. This suggests that it is mainly at the final relay stages of sensory processing where memories about facts and episodes are laid down. In the language of Rolls' model, these would be the regions where the hippocampus guides cortical storage rather than at the earlier cortical stages of sensory processing. Lesions of the subcortical structures in the medial temporal lobes, midline diencephalon and cholinergic basal forebrain disrupt another system or systems. There are two pairs of chief candidates. The first, derived from Mishkin's hypothesis, postulates that there is a hippocampal system and an amygdalar system. Given their anatomy, inputs and physiology, these two systems must perform distinct functions, which together produce good direct memory of facts and episodes, and, in isolation, produce moderately good memory. One possibility, consistent with the context-memory deficit hypothesis, is that the hippocampal system is most important for spatial memory (and perhaps other currently undefined kinds of context-memory) whereas the amygdalar system is most important for memory of temporal order, cross-medal memory, and associations between events and reinforcement. The alternative candidate, derived from Zola-Morgan's work, postulates that there is a hippocampal-polysensory association cortex loop and a less well defined loop between polysensory association cortex and structures in the midline diencephalon. These two systems may be concerned with different kinds of consolidation although of what information is a matter of speculation. Finally, although the cholinergic basal forebrain is highly interconnected with all the structures, just mentioned, it may act to some extent independently in facilitating the consolidation of information in the association cortex regions to which it also projects.

Second, at present, biologically realistic models of amnesia can only be based on the functions of the hippocampus as too little is known about the other candidate structures. It is not known, for example, whether long-term plastic changes occur in the midline diencephalon or in the basal forebrain, and the details of association cortex projections to the midline diencephalon is far from understood, as is the neural architecture of the midline deincephalon.

Third, network models should be used for refining and discriminating between the main theories of the functional deficit that underlies amnesia so as to produce new and more precise predictions. More psychological work also needs to be done in order to confirm whether or not amnesics show preserved indirect memory for novel information, under exactly what conditions they show direct memory deficits that are worse for some kinds of information than they are for others, and whether they do show genuinely accelerated forgetting at some point after learning.

Finally, more attention needs to be given to two aspects of network models. The first has already been mentioned and concerns the way information is represented in a network, something that is generally blurred over in current models, which are good at demonstrating how inputs can be transformed, but less explicit about what is represented by the inputs and transformed outputs. This is obviously critical in explaining amnesia where rival theories talk not only about information storage, but also about the nature of the information that is being manipulated and stored. As a related issue, it is believed that amnesics encode or represent information normally at learning so whatever information is represented by the candidate structures has also been represented elsewhere in the brain. This raises in acute form what the candidate structures are doing. Is the information being re-represented in a different way? If so, in what way, and how does this help long-term direct memory to operate normally? Second it is easier to specify the necessary conditions for recognition and recall than it is to specify the sufficient conditions. There is no generally accepted psychological theory of recognition and recall, but it is almost certain that recognition of an event involves more than merely the reactivation of the same distributed set of neurons that were activated when that event was initially experienced. In healthy people, the systems damaged in amnesics, must contribute to the feeling of familiarity that is associated with learnt facts and episodes, but without a psychological theory it is hard to know whether a network model can produce this feeling. In future therefore, neural network models of amnesia, will have to be liaised with developments in psychological theories of episode and fact recognition and recall in healthy people.

References

Daum I, Channon S and Canavan AGM (1989) Classical conditioning in patients with severe memory problems. Journal of Neurology, Neurosurgery and Psychiatry 52:47-51.

Dudai Y (1989) The Neurobiology of Memory:Concepts. Findings and Trends. Oxford University Press, Oxford.

Heit G, Smith ME and Halgren E (1988) Neuronal encoding of individual words and faces by the human hippocampus. Nature 333:773-775.

Hirst W, Johnson MK, Kim JK, Phelps EA, Risse G and Volpe BT (1986) Recognition and recall in amnesics. Journal of Experimental Psychology:Learning, Memory and Cognition 12:445-451.

Hirst W, Johnson MK, Phelps EA and Volpe BT (1988) More on recognition and recall with amnesics. Journal of Experimental Psychology:Learning, Memory and Cognition 14:758-762.

Jacoby LL and Witherspoon D (1982) Remembering without awareness. Canadian Journal of Psychology 36:300-324.

Lye RH, O'Boyle DJ, Ramsden RT and Schady W (1988) Effects of a unilateral cerebellar lesion on the acquisition of eye-blink conditioning in man. Journal of Physiology 403:58P.

McClelland JL and Rumelhart DE (1986) Amnesia and distributed memory. In:McClelland JL, Rumelhart DE and the PDP Research Group (eds) Parallel Distributed Processing, volume 2:Psychological and Biological Models. MIT Press, Cambridge, Mass.

Mayes AR (1988) Human Organic Memory Disorders. Cambridge University Press, New York.

Mayes AR, Meudell PR, Mann D and Pickering A (1988) Location of lesions in Korsakoff's syndrome:neuropsychological and neuropathalogical data on two patients. Cortex 24:1-22.

Mishkin M and Appenzeller T (1987) The anatomy of memory. Scientific American 256:62-71.

Mishkin M, Malamut B and Bachevalier J (1984) Memories and habits:two neural systems. In:Lynch G, McGaugh JL and Weinberger NM (eds) Neurobiology of Learning and Memory. Guildford Press, New York.

Morris RGM (1989a) Does synaptic plasticity play a role in information storage in the vertebrate brain. In:Morris RGM (ed) Parallel Distributed Processing:Implications for Psychology and Neurobiology. Oxford University Press, Oxford.

Morris RGM (1989b) Introduction:computational neuroscience:modelling the brain. In:Morris RGM (ed) Parallel Distributed Processing:Implications for Psychology and Neurobiology. Oxford University Press, Oxford.

Press GA, Amaral DG and Squire LR (1989) Hippocampal abnormalities in amnesic patients revealed by high-resolution magnetic resonance imaging. Nature 341:54-57.

Rolls ET (1989) Parallel distributed processing in the brain:implications of the functional architecture of neuronal networks in the hippocampus. In:Morris RGM (ed) Parallel Distributed Processing:Implications for Psychology and Neurobiology. Oxford University Press, Oxford.

Schacter DL (1990) Toward a cognitive neuropsychology of awareness:implicit knowledge and anosognosia. Journal of Clinical and Experimental Neuropsychology 12:155-178.

Shimamura AP (1989) Disorders of memory:the cognitive science perspective. In:Boller F and Grafman J (eds) Handbook of Neuropsychology, volume 3. Elsevier, Amsterdam.

Shoqeirat MA (1989) Contextual memory deficits and rate of forgetting in amnesics with different aetiologies. Unpublished Ph.D. thesis, Manchester University.

Singer W (1990) Mechanisms of use-dependent synaptic plasticity in visual cortex. Paper given at the Open Network Conference on Neural Mechanisms of Learning and Memory. London, 3-6 April.

Squire LR, Haist F and Shimamura AP (1989) The neurology of memory:quantitative assessment of retrograde amnesia in two groups of amnesic patients. Journal of Neuroscience 9:828-839.

Squire LR, Shimamura AP and Amaral DG (1989) Memory and the hippocampus. In:Byrne J and Berry W (eds) Neural Models of Plasticity. Academic Press, New York.

Zola-Morgan S, Squire LR and Amaral DG (1986) Human amnesia and the medial temporal region:enduring memory impairment following a bilateral lesion limited to field CA1 of the hippocampus. Journal of Neuroscience 6:2950-2967.

Zola-Morgan S, Squire LR and Amaral DG (1989) Lesions of the amygdala that spare adjacent cortical regions do not impair memory or exacerbate the impairment following lesions of the hippocampal formation. Journal of Neuroscience 9:1922-1936.

Zola-Morgan S, Squire LR, Amaral DG and Suzuki WA (1989) Lesions of perirhinal and parahippocampal cortex that spared the amygdala and hippocampal formation produce severe memory impairment. Journal of Neuroscience 9:4355-4370.

ACTIVITY PATTERNS IN CORTICAL MINICOLUMNS

Steen S. Christensen, Rodney M.J. Cotterill and Claus Nielsen

Department of Biophysics
The Technical University of Denmark
Building 307, DK-2800 Lyngby, Denmark

ABSTRACT

The activation of cortical minicolumns has been investigated in a model in which the neurons lying in a given cortical layer are regarded as a collective unit. The behaviour of such a neuronal group is found to depend on the interplay between the excitatory and inhibitory cellular sub-populations. Likewise, the interactions between two assemblies, lying in different cortical layers in a given minicolumn, depend upon the nature of the connections between them. There is evidence of a control mechanism that stems from the balancing influences of excitation and inhibition. Because the interlayer connections are not symmetric, different layers are found to exhibit different types of behaviour, in accordance with physiological observations.

1. INTRODUCTION

The aim of the project described in this paper is a study of the dynamics of neuronal activations in a model of the cerebral cortex which takes into account the known anatomical detail. The underlying philosophy is that because information about that detail is now so extensive, it is no longer advisable to attempt to model cortical funtion on the basis of a single type of cell that interacts with its fellow cells in a manner that is mathematically expedient but biologically untenable. The shortcomings of such simplistic models have been discussed by Crick and Asanuma (Crick and Asanuma, 1986; Crick 1988; Crick 1989) , and the present investigation attempts to avoid the pitfalls which those authors have enumerated.

Our work has attached special significance to several anatomical structures which have come to light in recent years, and it has attempted to discover what significance these would have for the dynamical behaviour of cortical activations. The structures in question are the minicolumn arrangement discovered by Mountcastle (1979) and

Szentágothai (1979), and the interconnections between the various cortical layers in such a minicolumn, these having been reported by Gilbert and Wiesel (1983, 1985).

The advantage of taking such anatomical detail into account is that it indicates natural groupings of neurons. There are about 300 neurons in a minicolumn, and this indicates that there would be approximately 50 of these cells in a given cortical layer, in such a unit. That number would be made up of two sub-populations, one excitatory and the other inhibitory, and a central aspect of our work was simulation of the dynamical properties of such a cellular assembly. This being accomplished, we then examined the interactions between two such assemblies, and that study provided a natural stepping stone to an investigation of the dynamics of an entire minicolumn.

This strategy, progressing from the part to the whole, suggested a natural structure for the present paper, so the sections describe, in turn, the known anatomical details of a typical minicolumn, the study of an individual cellular assembly, the dynamics observed in two coupled assemblies, and finally the dynamical behaviour of an entire minicolumn under various stimuli.

2. CORTICAL STRUCTURE

Although evidence for the existence of cortical minicolumns could not be said to be definitive, as yet, there is nevertheless good evidence for the minicolumn as a functional unit (Braitenberg 1977, 1978). If one considers the lateral connections between cells in a given cortical layer, it is observed that these are excitatory over a short range, but inhibitory over longer distances, and this suggests a natural division which happens to coincide with the observed diameter of a minicolumn, namely about 30 μm (Kohonen, 1989). Moreover, this diameter indicates that there would be very roughly a million such minicolumns in the primary visual area, and it is interesting to note that this is about the same number as that of the axons of which each optic radiation is composed (Kuffler, Nicholls and Martin 1984), these numbers being relevant to the human brain. The suggestion is thus that each axon in an optic radiation provides an input to a single minicolumn in the primary visual area.

It is now well established that this input enters the cortex at layer IV, and the question obviously arises as to how the other cortical layers are interconnected. Such information has primarily been supplied by the work of Gilbert and Wiesel (1983, 1985), and their main findings can be summarized as follows (see Fig. 1).

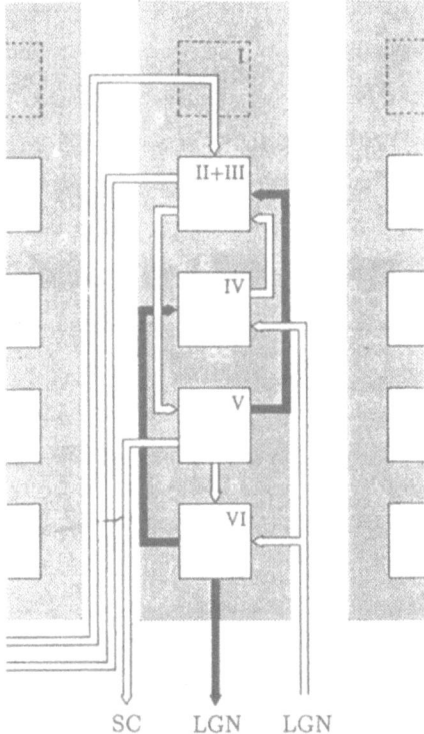

SC   LGN   LGN

Fig. 1. Idealized view of the interconnections between the cellular assemblies in a given cortical minicolumn (indicated in grey). Excitatory connections are shown in white and (net) inhibitory connections in black. The white squares indicate cellular assemblies, comprising 50 to 60 neurons in a given layer in a given minicolumn. The lack of such a square at layer I reflects the paucity of cell bodies in that layer. SC and LGN indicate the superior colliculus and lateral geniculate nucleus, respectively.

Firstly, regarding the input, they find that this makes contact not only with layer IV, in fact, but also with layer VI. And the first suggestion of a finely-balanced control comes from the fact that the latter layer sends inhibitory connections up to layer IV. Layer IV itself sends excitatory connections up to layer II + III, and these send excitation down to layer V. This layer sends net inhibition up to layer II + III, in that the excitatory axons of the pyramidal neurons in layer V activate inhibitory interneurons in layer II + III. So again we see evidence of a balance between excitation and inhibition in a cortical sub-circuit. Layer V also sends excitation to layer VI, and the latter sends connections back to the lateral geniculate nucleus (LGN).

There appears to be little doubt that the latter connections, from layer VI back to the LGN, are excitatory, but because the reticular formation is also involved, and because it is known that this exerts an influence on the LGN that is at least locally inhibitory (Crick 1984), we believe that it is appropriate to look upon the overall connection between layer VI and the LGN as being one of inhibition. This, then, sets up the third and final excitation-inhibition sub-circuit.

The lateral interactions between a minicolumn and its neighbours (in the same cortical area) are, as mentioned earlier, primarily inhibitory. These, then, are the anatomical features that are being built into the model in our ongoing studies, and the goal was to see how they influence the dynamical interactions between cellular assemblies both within a given minicolumn, and also between minicolumns in different cortical areas.

3. CELLULAR ASSEMBLIES

As mentioned earlier, there would be approximately 50 to 60 cells in a given cortical layer within a single minicolumn, and an important aspect of our work was the investigation of the behaviour of such an assembly, allowing for the fact that some of these neurons would be excitatory whereas others would be inhibitory. These two sub-assemblies would naturally interact with one another, so a full description of the dynamics of the assembly would require several different factors to be taken into account. For a start, excitatory cells would excite one another, so the activation of just a few of the members of this sub-set would soon spread excitation to the other members, and the level of activity would increase rapidly as the excitation spread throughout the group, rather in the manner of a bush fire. Simultaneously, however, activation is given by the excitatory cells to members of the inhibitory sub-set. There is good anatomical underpinning for this idea, because this appears to be the major role of the inhibitory interneurons, which are a widespread feature of cortical anatomy. And these inhibitory neurons obviously have a dampening effect of the excitatory cells. In the present study, however, we did not include the possibility that inhibitory neurons could inhibit each other, because this does not appear to happen in the real cortex. This absence notwithstanding, there are nevertheless many different types of interaction to be taken into account, for there are also the signals that enter from outside the cellular assembly; these are assumed to feed into both the excitatory and the inhibitory sub-populations.

In studying the response of such a cellular assembly, our goal was to be able to subsequently treat it as a unit, which responded to a given time-dependent input with a readily calculable time-dependent output, and to do this, it was necessary to solve a pair of simultaneous differential equations. One of these described the rate of change of the number of excitatory cells that were active, while the other described the analogous dependence on time of the activation in the inhibitory sub-population. These two rate equations were as follows:

$$dN_e = s_2 N_e (M_e - N_e) dt + \alpha(M_e - N_e) dt - s_1 N_i N_e dt - \lambda N_e dt \qquad (1)$$

$$dN_i = s_3 N_e (M_i - N_i) dt + \beta(M_i - N_i) dt - \lambda N_i dt \qquad (2)$$

where M_e and M_i are the total number of excitatory and inhibitory cells, respectively, in an assembly; N_e and N_i are the number of cells in these same sub-assemblies that are currently active; s_1 and s_3 are the synaptic coupling coefficients between the two sub-assemblies, while s_2 refers to the self-activation within the excitatory group; λ is the decay coefficient (assumed to be the same for both sub-assemblies); and α and β are the coupling coefficients for activation from the outside, for the excitatory and inhibitory sub-populations respectively.

The time dependence of N_e and N_i are thus given by

$$N_e(t) = N_e(t_o) + \int_{t_o}^{t} [s_2 N_e (M_e - N_e) + \alpha(M_e - N_e) - s_1 N_i N_e - \lambda N_e] dt \qquad (3)$$

$$N_i(t) = N_i(t_o) + \int_{t_o}^{t} [s_3 N_e (M_i - N_i) + \beta(M_i - N_i) - \lambda N_i] dt \qquad (4)$$

We solved these equations by using a fourth order Runge-Kutta method, and we employed discrete time steps that were equivalent to about a twentieth of a nerve action potential. We investigated the time course of the activity levels in the two sub-populations, for a variety of values of the various parameters. In all cases we examined the effect of first injecting a standard level of external stimulation, this being followed by removal of that stimulation for a period lasting twice the initial injection period. Following this, we then increased the stimulation level by a factor of ten, and continued to apply this for the same duration as previously. Immediately following this, we decreased the stimulation to the former lower level, and held it there for twice as long as the two earlier stimulations, whereafter all external stimulation was removed. It was our intention, in this way, to observe whether the response of the overall cellular assembly was linearly related to the input. We observed that such a linear dependence is seen only over a limited range of the input stimulus, and that beyond that range, on either side, the system behaves

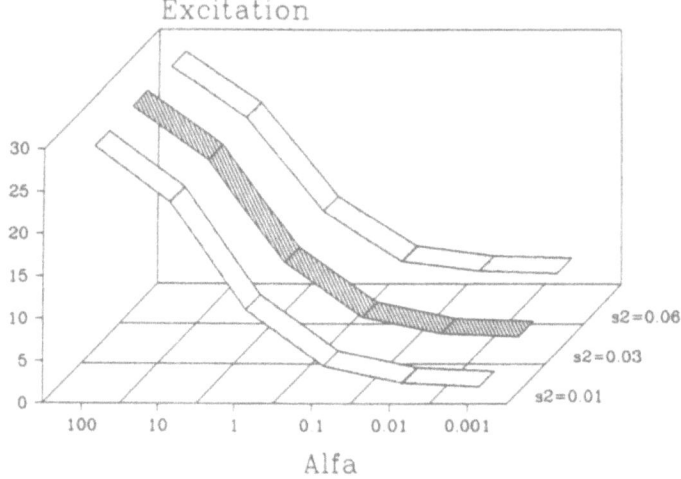

Fig. 2. The overall results of the study of an individual cellular assembly indicate that the response (to an input here called Alpha) saturates for sufficiently large input, irrespective of the size of the self-activation coefficient s_2.

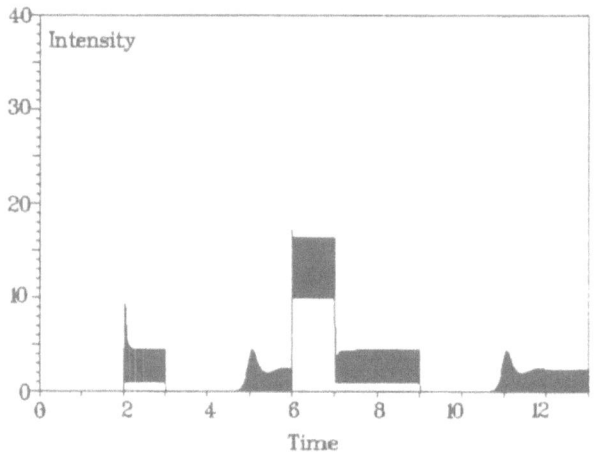

Fig. 3. The level of activity (black areas) for a given level of injected stimulation (white blocks) for a single cellular assembly in which the relevant parameters were $s_1 = 0.30, s_2 = 0.03, s_3 = 0.01, \lambda = 0.2$.

in a quite non-linear fashion. In particular, as the injected stimulus increases, a saturation behaviour is observed, further increase in the stimulus leading to no observed increase in the response (see Fig. 2).

Turning to the results for one specific set of the parameters ($s_1 = 0.30, s_2 = 0.03, s_3 = 0.01, \lambda = 0.2$) we see (Fig. 3) that the tenfold increase in injected stimu-

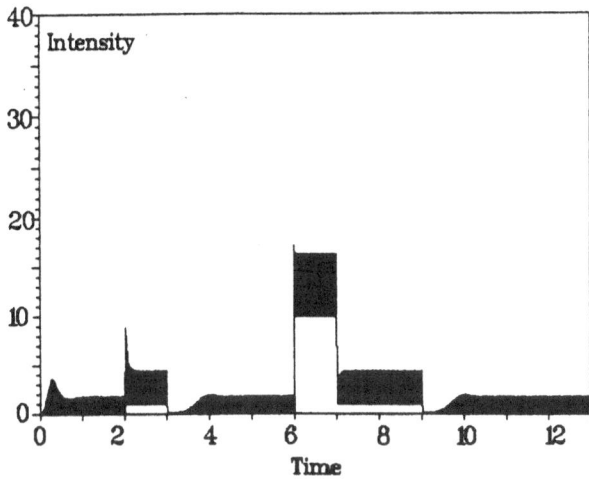

Fig. 4. The same as Fig. 4, but with a 2% level of noise.

lation does not lead to a tenfold increase in resultant activity. On the contrary, the latter factor lies closer to four. In this diagram, the white blocks indicate the injected stimulation, and the black areas show the response. Particularly noteworthy is the fact that in all cases the onset of stimulation leads to a transient overshoot, this indicating that it takes some time for the inhibition to reach its maximum effect. The difference between Fig. 3 and Fig. 4 lies only in the fact that the latter run included a 2% noise level which, in the computer simulations, involved the use of a random number generator. One sees that the general effect of the noise is to decrease the swings in the activity level seen when, after a decay that almost reaches the zero level, the self- excitation causes the activity to flair up again. This flairing up is observed to start at timesteps 5 and 11 in Fig. 3, and it is noticeable from Fig. 4 that the noise not only dampens down the oscillations in the latter but also causes it to set in at an earlier time.

4. THE CORTICAL MINICOLUMN

In the study of a single cortical minicolumn, further parameters had to be taken into account, because the coupling between the different layers would be influenced by the number of available interlayer synapses, and also the propensities of the various types of neuron. We were particularly concerned about the number of GABA neurons in the different layers, and in this respect we were guided by the numbers published by Henry, Schwark, Jones and Yan (1987) (see Fig. 5).

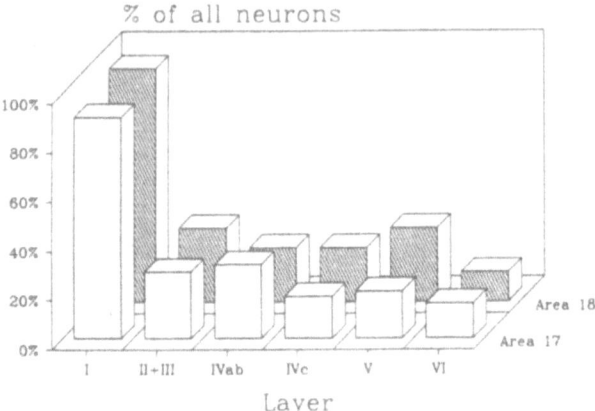

Distribution of GABA-immunoreaktive neurons in two visual areas

Fig. 5. The distribution of GABA neurons amongst the different cortical layers is not uniform, as indicated by these proportions taken from the work of Henry, Schwark, Jones and Yan (1987). The numbers for area 17 were used in the present calculations.

In the real situation, the input from the LGN actually comprises two components, namely the X part, which is spatially well resolved but temporarily rather sluggish, while the Y component shows just the opposite characteristics, namely relatively good temporal resolution, but fairly widespread spatially. We attempted to include these factors in our simulations, and this can be seen by comparing Figs. 6 and 7, the former showing the excitation level at layer IVab, which receives the Y input, and the latter showing the analogous situation in layer IVc, which receives the X excitation. In these two figures, one has differentiated between the activity levels for the excitatory and inhibitory sub-populations, and although the injected stimulation levels were the same in both cases, it is particularly noteworthy that the excitatory activation in layer IVab shows very little temporal variation in the response, except when the stimulus is injected, just after timestep 1, and when it is removed, at timestep 9.

It was particularly interesting to notice the marked difference between the responses of the cellular assemblies lying in II + III, on the one hand, and layer V, on the other. These are seen in Figs. 8 and 9, respectively. For a start, one notices that it is the Y stimulation which has the apparently dominating effect, as can be seen by comparing Fig. 8 with Fig. 7. But the most noteworthy fact arises from

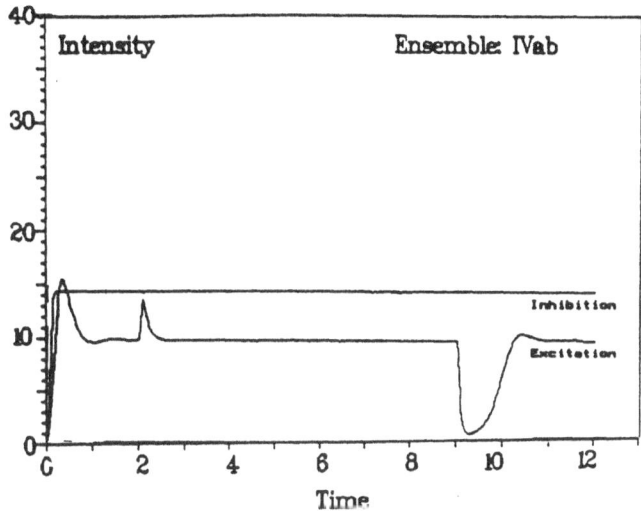

Fig. 6. The responses of the inhibitory and excitatory sub-populations of an assembly of neurons at cortical layer IVab, which receives the Y stimulation from the LGN. One sees that there is very little temporal variation in the amplitude of the response of the excitatory sub-population, except just after the stimulus is switched on, and again just after it is switched off.

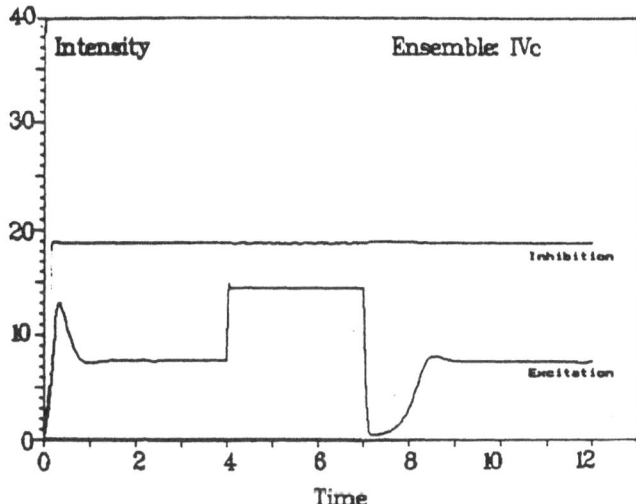

Fig. 7. The responses of the excitatory and inhibitory sub-populations for the assembly of neurons at layer IVc, which receives the X stimulation from the LGN. One sees a more marked difference in the excitatory response activity than is the case for layer IVab.

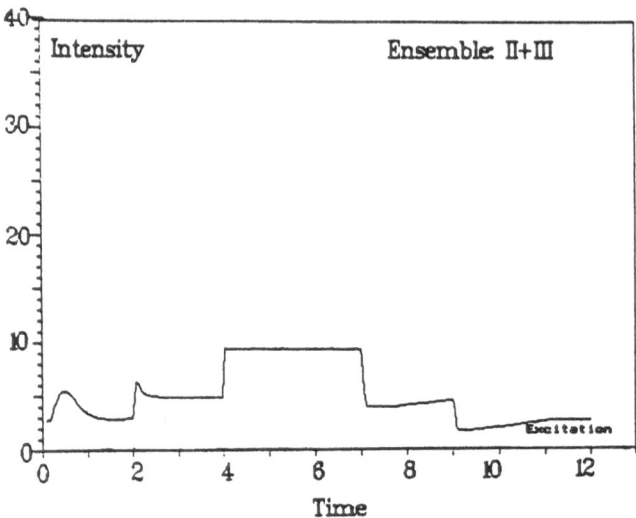

Fig. 8. The responses in the activity levels of the excitatory and inhibitory sub-populations for the neural assembly at layer II + III in a given cortical minicolumn.

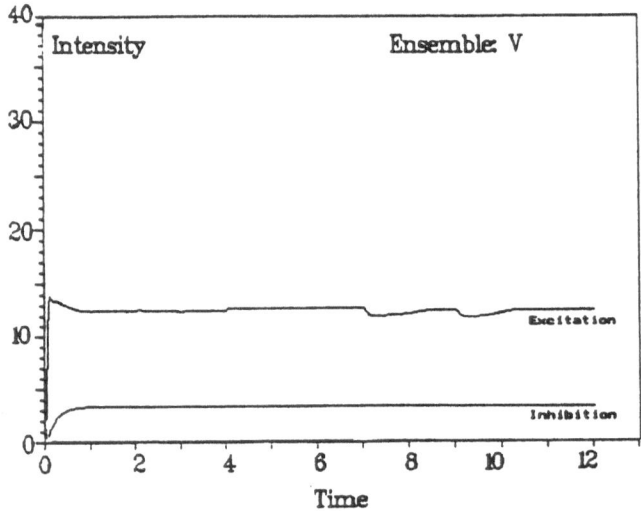

Fig. 9. The responses in the excitatory and inhibitory sub-populations in the cellular assembly at layer V in a given cortical minicolumn. It should be noted that the temporal variation in the amplitudes is much lower than that observed in layer II + III.

a comparison of Figs. 8 and 9, because it is clear from the latter that almost no variation is observed in the activity level of the excitatory sub-population in layer V. In other words, the marked contrast between the responses in these two different cortical layers shows that whereas the assembly at layer II + III is able to discriminate between different input levels, the same is not true of the assembly on layer V. We believe that this marked difference in responses is a reflection of the non-symmetrical connections present within a given minicolumn. The point is that whereas layer II + III receives both excitation and inhibition, layer V receives only excitation. We believe that this difference provides the basis for the more faithful response of layer II + III to what it is receiving from layer IV. It is interesting to note that this is in general agreement with the physiological observations of Pollen and his co-workers (Pollen, Gaska and Jacobsen, 1989). They have observed that it is actually more difficult to detect activity in layer II + III, for a given stimulation from the LGN, than it is to pick up activity in layer V. One could say that layer II + III carries what could be called high-grade information, whereas the response in layer V is of a more low-grade character.

5. DISCUSSION AND CONCLUSIONS

The quite pronounced difference between the responses of layer II + III and layer V is the chief result of the present study, and it is intriguing that such a difference should be seen between the very two layers which are responsible for sending signals to other cortical areas (Maunsell and van Essen, 1983). We see that the layer that is responsible for sending signals in the forward direction is capable of a high level of discrimination. The layer responsible for sending signals in the reverse direction, on the other hand, seems not to be able to discriminate particularly well, and one could speculate as to how these differences could be of service to the overall functioning of the cerebral cortex. Perhaps a hint comes from the additional fact that the layer V of the primary visual cortex sends connections to the superior colliculus (SC in Fig. 1). This part of the brain is responsible for control of gaze, and it could be that only relatively coarse information is required for this function; perhaps it is sufficient for the superior colliculus merely to rapidly point the eyes in roughly the correct direction to pick up things of current interest to the system. Just why the same low demand might be made of the reverse projections is, however, not yet clear.

These studies, although obviously still at a rather primitive stage, do hold promise for the revelation of new facts concerning the interactions between different cortical areas. Still missing in our work, until now, is a detailed investigation of what happens when the visual stimulus moves, and it could be that this will be reflected in temporal and spatial responses between the various minicolumns in a given area, effects which, in the present limited study, had no chance of being observed.

REFERENCES

Braitenberg, V. "Cell Assemblies in the Cerebral Cortex" in: *Lecture Notes in Biomathematics* (R. Heim and G. Palm, eds.), Springer, Berlin, 1977, pp. 171-188.

Braitenberg, V. *Cortical Architectonics: General and Areal* (M.A.B. Brazier and H. Petsche, eds.), Raven Press, New York, 1978.

Crick, F., and Asanuma, C. "Certain aspects of the anatomy and physiology of the cerebral cortex" in: *Parallel Distributed Processing*, Vol. 2, (J.L. McClelland and D.E. Rumelhart, eds.), Bradford MIT Press, Cambridge, Mass. 1986.

Crick, F. "The recent excitement about neural networks". Nature **337**, 129-133 (1989).

Crick, F. "The function of the thalomic reticular complex: The searchlight hypothesis". Proc. Nat. Acad. Sci. USA **81**, 4586-4590 (1984).

Crick, F. *What Mad Pursuit*, Basic Books, New York, 1988, p. 161.

Gilbert, C.D. and Wiesel, T.N. "Intrinsic Connectivity and Receptive Field Properties in Visual Cortex". Vision Research **25**, 365-374 (Pergamon, New York, 1985).

Henry, S.H.C., Schwark, H.D., E.G. Jones and Yan, J. "Numbers and proportions of GABA-Immunoreactive Neurons in Different Areas of Monkey Cerebral Cortex". Journal of Neuroscience **7**, 1503-1519 (1987).

Hopfield, J.J. "Neural Networks and Physical Systems with Emergent Collective Computational Abilities". Proc. Nat. Acad. Sci. USA **79**, 2554-2558 (1982).

Kohonen, T. *Self-Organization and Associative Memory*, Springer, Berlin, 1989.

Kuffler, S.W., Nicholls, J.G. and Martin, A.R. "From Neuron to Brain", Sinauer Associates, Sunderland, Mass., 1984, p. 21.

Maunsell, J.H.R. and van Essen, D.C. "The Connections of the Middle Temporal Visual Area and their Relation to a Cortical Hierarchy in the Macaque Monkey". Journal of Neuroscience **3**, 2563-2586 (1983).

Mountcastle, V.B. "An Organizing Principle for Cerebral Function: The Unit Module and the Distributed System" in: *Neuroscience 4th Study Programme* (F.O. Schmitt, ed.), MIT Press, Cambridge, Mass. 1979.

Pollen, D.A., Gaska, J.P. and Jacobsen, L.D. "Physiological Constraints on Models of Visual Cortical Function" in: *Models of Brain Function* (R.M.J. Cotterill, ed.), Cambridge University Press, Cambridge, 1989, pp. 115-136.

Sterling, P. "Microcircuitry and Functional Architecture of the Cat Retina". Trends in Neuroscience **9**, 186-192 (1986).

Szentágothai, J. "Local Neuron Circuits of the Neocortex" in: *Neuroscience 4th Study Programme* (F.O. Schmitt, ed.), MIT Press, Cambridge, Mass. 1979.

Wiesel, T.N. and Gilbert, C.D. "Morphological Basis of Visual Cortical Function". Quarterly Journal of Experimental Physiology **68**, 525-543 (1983).

DYNAMICS AND MEMORY IN RANDOM AND STRUCTURED NEURAL NETWORKS

Karl E. Kürten

HLRZ c/o KFA Jülich, D-5170 Jülich, FRG
and
Institut für Theoretische Physik, Universität zu Köln,
D-5000 Köln   , FRG

Abstract.   These notes provide a selection of results on
modelling collective neural phenomena from completely random
networks to networks with optimized architectures.   The model
based on binary threshold elements operating in discrete time
displays   emergent   fascinating   dynamical   behaviour;   in
particular we demonstrate that it undergoes dynamical phase
transitions and that it provides an impressive potential for
content addressable memory.

1 Introduction

Cellular   automata and artificial neural   networks   have
long been attracting the attention of scientists across   an
immense field of disciplines,   such as neurobiology, computer
science,   artificial   intelligence and   theoretical   physics.
These simple mathematical objects not only serve as models of
living nervous systems,   but can also be viewed as archetypes
of new computing architectures and intelligent machines.   For
the   theoretical physicist they represent a   novel   nonlinear
dynamical system characterized by disorder and frustration.

One drawback of some of the currently popular neural
network models is high or even full connectivity of the
neuron-like elements [1-3] rarely found in nature. Otherwise,
highly connected networks of respectable size, suitable for
such cognitive tasks as pattern recognition and   image
processing,   raise immense wiring problems in   hardware
realization   and   make   real-time   software   simulations
computationally unfeasible. In fact, realistic biological
networks are rather sparsely interconnected, and systems with
low connectivity have often been solved exactly in the
thermodynamic limit [4-6]. Accordingly we concentrate on
exploring   dynamical   properties   of   sparsely   connected
networks.

274

2 Cellular automata model

The network consists of N Boolean state variables σ_i, $i=1,\ldots,N$ whose dynamics evolve in discrete time steps. Each cell of the assembly is supposed to receive at most K input lines ($1 \leq K \leq N$). The state of unit σ_i at time $t+1$ depends only on the value of its input variables at the previous time step according to the updating rule

$$\sigma_i(t+1) = f_i(\sigma_{j_1(i)}(t),\ldots,\sigma_{j_K(i)}(t)) \qquad i = 1,\ldots,N . \qquad (1)$$

The function f_i represents one of the $2^{(2^{**}K)}$ possible Boolean rules which act like a K-input binary logical gate. According to the corresponding 2^K-element truth table, each transition function can be represented by a 2^K-digit binary number or the corresponding decimal number between 0 and $2^{(2^{**}K)}-1$.

Biologically motivated cellular automata mimicking the activity of the immune and the nervous system define their rules by a set of thresholds and synaptic weights describing the strength of excitatory and inhibitory multi-cell interactions. However, both formulations are equivalent since it can be easily shown by a polynomial orthogonal transformation that any Boolean function f_i of K inputs can be written as

$$f_i = \text{sign}\{c_{i0} + \sum_{j_1} c_{ij_1}\sigma_{j_1}(t)+..+ \sum_{j_1<\cdots<j_K} c_{ij_1\cdots j_K}\sigma_{j_1}(t)..\sigma_{j_K}(t))\}(2)$$

The sums are taken over all cells with which cell i connects and self-excitations are excluded. The quantity c_{i0} represents a threshold. The coupling coefficients $c_{ij_1\cdots j_{K'}}$ usually not symmetric with respect to interchange of cell i, define the weight of a K-order cell interaction, while the bracket term represents the total synaptic input to cell i.

Allowing arbitrary coupling coefficients each of the $2^{2^{**}K}$ rules can be assigned a subspace of the 2^K-dimensional hypercube $|c_{ij_1\cdots j_K}| \leq 1$. However, it can be shown that a minimal space of couplings $c_{ij_1\cdots j_K} \in \{0,+1,-1\}^{2^{**}K}$ already generates all possible Boolean functions of order K [7].

Restricted to low connectivity Kauffman [8] applied the model with multi-cell interactions and *randomly* chosen Boolean functions to simulate gene regulation, whereas Caianiello [2] applied the fully connected model restricted to two-cell interactions with

$$f_i = \text{sign}\{c_{i0} + \sum_{j_1} c_{ij_1}\sigma_{j_1}(t)\} \qquad (3)$$

to mimick the dynamics of formal neurons, consequently called the linear threshold model. Since (2) disregards subscript symmetries of the couplings, the number of available degrees of freedom is 2^K in a K-order network compared to only $K+1$ in the restricted linear version (3).

Due to the discreteness of Boolean functions there exist
only a finite number of states. Hence, the motion driven by
(1) will inevitably relax to an attractor, either a limit
cycle or a fixed point. Cycling phenomena, often interpreted
as the reponse of the network to stimuli expressed as initial
conditions, are of genetic and neurobiological interest. In
Kauffman's evolutionary model for cell differentiation the
total number of cyclic modes scales with the highly limited
number of different cell types in living organisms, whereas
in neural network models attractors can be useful as a
repository of content-addressable memories.

3 The infinite-range model

In the thermodynamic limit analytical predictions can be
derived for the dynamics of (1) provided that
i)   the connectivity of the network is chosen at *random*
ii)   the network is sparsely connected ($K \propto \log(N)$) and
iii) the synaptic weights or the Boolean transition
functions are chosen according to a given distribution ϱ.
Under these constraints the time evolution of the normalized
Hamming distance between two initial configurations

$$H(t) \quad = \quad \frac{1}{2N} \sum_{\nu=1}^{N} |\sigma_{\nu}^{(1)}(t) - \sigma_{\nu}^{(2)}(t)| \tag{4}$$

can be derived exactly and takes the form of a polynomial
spline function of order K:

$$H(t+1) \quad = \quad \Phi[H(t)] = \sum_{\nu=1}^{K} (-1)^{\nu+1} \binom{K}{\nu} a_{\nu} H^{\nu}(t) \tag{5}$$

For the Kauffman model comprising all possible Boolean
transition functions, the coefficients a_{ν} take the values
$2p(p-1)$, p being the probability that the output values of
the randomly chosen functions f_i are unity. This is in
contrast to the linear threshold model, where the
coefficients usually differ depending on the distribution of
the synaptic weights and the thresholds.
    Obviously, $H \equiv 0$ is a natural fixed point of eq.(5). The
dynamical long-term behaviour of the system then depends only
on whether this fixed point is stable or unstable. The issue
can be decided by the slope of $\Phi(H)$ evaluated at the fixed
point. The critical line representing the border line of
instability thus only depends on the first order coefficient
of expansion (5) and is given by

$$\frac{d\Phi}{dH} \bigg|_{H=0} \quad = \quad K a_1 = 1 \tag{6}$$

A value of $Ka_1 < 1$ marks an ordered phase, where two slightly
different identical initial conditions usually evolve to
highly correlated attractors or even to the same attractor.
A value $Ka_1 > 1$ implies that the system is in a chaotic phase
characterized by an extreme sensitivity to the initial
condition reminiscent of the occurence of chaos in continuous

time models [9]. Chaos is obviously favoured by a larger
number of inputs K. Expanding eq.(5) around the critical
point $a_1 = 1/K$ reveals that a small initial distance between
two state points will diverge (decay) exponentially in the
chaotic (ordered) phase. However, the term *chaotic* phase is
strictly applicable only in the limit N -> ∞. On the critical
line the asymptotic time behaviour is special: H(t) either
remains constant or follows an inverse-t law [10].

A very general result is that for K ≤ 2 H≡0 is the only
attractive fixed point such that the system remains always in
the ordered phase independent of the network parameters [10],
whereas for K > 2 the manipulation of one or another network
parameter can induce a dynamical phase transition from order
to chaos or vice versa.

A quantity of obvious interest is the average length <P>
of accessible cycles, in an ensemble of nets of a given type.
Computer simulations show that the manner in which <P>
increases with N is distinctly different in the two phases.
Within the chaotic phase <P> grows exponentially with N,
whereas <P> has a power-law dependence on N in the ordered
phase [5,8]. Along the phase boundary, the increase appears
to be linear [5].

4 The model in finite dimension.

The mean field or infinite-range model can be easily
modified to a finite dimensional one by injecting some two-
dimensional spatial structure [11,12]. One route to
generalize the model is to arrange the cells on the sites of
regular lattices. One important issue is how the dynamical
behaviour of the network changes when the interactions are of
near-neigbour character. Note that for models based on
geometrically correlated couplings such as nearest-neighbour
or distant dependent interactions [13] to date no analytical
solutions have been found.

Computer simulations have been performed for systems
where the cells reside on regular two-dimensional lattices
and experience nearest-neighbour interactions: i) honeycomb
lattice, with three nearest neighbours (K=3); ii) square
lattice, with four orthogonal neighbours (Von Neumann
neighbourhood, K=4); and iii) same as ii), but each cell
allowed to interact with itself (Moore neighbourhood, K=5).
In contrast to the situation with long-range interactions,
chaotic activity does not seem to occur in the K=3 case (i)
which has also been found for the Kauffman model [12]. The
mean cycle length increases linearly with N for K=3, whereas
the increase is exponential for K=4 and K=5. However, the
variation of the mean cycle length in lattice models follows
a much weaker exponential law than found in their infinite-
range counterparts, reflecting the expected shift in the
critical parameters. Moreover, the time evolutions of the
Hamming distance (4) behave qualitatively quite differently
in the two phases [11].

The chief finding of these studies is that any kind of geometrical structure has a powerful effect in suppressing chaotic activity, suggesting that short-range lattice models are less susceptible to disorder than their infinite-range counterparts.

Finally we remark that networks with exclusively long-range or exclusively short-range interactions are not realistic expressions of the biological situation. Such networks appear useful only for highly specialized technical applications. However, hybrid network topologies containing both nearest-neighbour *and* suitable long-ranged interactions [14], emerging from an optimization process can lead to quasi-optimal performance of networks designed for useful cognitive tasks including pattern recognition and image processing. Such architectures are reminiscent of general ideas, in particular Braitenberg's, about the inter-connectivity of cortical pyramidal cells making short-range connections with basal dendrites and long-range connections with apical dendrites [15].

5 Self-organization through synaptic plasticity

The first decisive step towards a 'dynamical' neural network model with activity-dependent synaptic couplings was Hebb's classical postulate that the efficacy of an excitatory synapse increases when the two neurons it links fire simultaneously [16]. In fact, conditioning experiments suggest strongly that temporal correlations between pre- and post-synaptic firings strongly enhance the *excitatory* synaptic strength and that the *excitatory* synaptic efficiency decreases considerably, if the pre-synaptic cell is silent and the post-synaptic cell is active.

Following these lines we studied several theoretically possible training rules designed to demonstrate their effectiveness in gradually leading to networks showing more ordered behaviour [18]. One possible general ansatz for the time evolution of the modification of the coupling coefficients is

$$|c_{ij}(t+1)| = |c_{ij}(t)|(1 + \delta \, f(\sigma_i(t), \sigma_j(t)) \qquad , \quad (7)$$

where the learning constant δ determines the rate of modification and the function f represents a specific training rule. Such a rule is local both in space and time: local in space because the change depends only on firing states of the neurons i and j; local in time because it depends only on the present time but not on the states of these neurons in the past. For the 'genuine' Hebb rule the function f then takes the form

$$f(\sigma_i(t), \sigma_j(t)) = [\sigma_i(t)+1][\sigma_j(t)+1][\text{sign}(c_{ij}(t))+1] \qquad (8)$$

We have carried out a number of interesting simulations in which besides the 'genuine' Hebb rule several sets of rules have been imposed on the dynamics of our network model.

Initially, each specimen net was assembled with quasi-random connectivity which placed it in the chaotic phase. For almost any choice of a local rule it was found that there exists a number of training steps at which a phase transition from chaotic to ordered behaviour occurs. Both the average period of cyclic modes and the average number of cycles per net show a rapid decline with the number of training steps. The occurence of a phase transition is indicated by the dependence of the mean cycle length on the number of cells. As for random networks, an exponential dependence was found, when only a small number of training steps had been completed, whereas a power law dependence is seen after a large number of steps.

In summary, the available results show that in analogy to lattice models activity-dependent plasticity algorithms, inducing correlated structures into the network architecture, tend to suppress or even eliminate chaotic modes entirely [18].

6 Memory and learning

In connectionist systems information is stored throughout the network distributed all over across the values of the synaptic couplings. A single synapse carries information about a variety of different experiences.

In order to store p arbitrary configurations $S^{(\mu)}$ $\mu=1,\ldots,p$ as fixed points of eq.(2) the coupling constants have to be chosen such that the condition

$$S_i^{(\mu)} h_i (S_1^{(\mu)},\ldots,S_N^{(\mu)}) = \kappa_{i\mu} > \kappa \qquad (9)$$

holds for each cell i and each pattern μ. Moreover, the positive global polarization parameter κ has to be chosen as large as possible in order to ensure large basins of attraction of the individual patterns.

As has been demonstrated in ref. [19] the retrieval performance as well as the storage capacity of the model can be largely improved if the connectivity is *not* chosen at random but adapted to the specific information the network is asked to capture.

We are now faced with a combinatorial optimization problem, where each cell i has $\binom{N}{K}$ different ways to choose its incoming connections in order to maximize the minimal polarization parameter $\kappa_{i\mu}$ defined in eq.(9).

Since an exhaustive neighbour search is not possible for networks of respectable size one can first adopt a simple trial and error scheme [19] : Whenever a random neighbour choice fails to fulfill a minimal embedding condition (9) after a short learning session, we choose other connections at random in order to increase the magnitude of the global polarization parameter κ.

According to the biological law that low-efficacy synapses degenerate the strategy can be improved by substituting only those synaptic weights whose magnitudes are close to zero.

They hardly contribute to the stability, rather they induce synaptic noise. Substantial improvement has finally been achieved by weighting the connections with the magnitudes of their synaptic efficiencies such that the probability of being exchanged increases with decreasing magnitude of the synaptic weight [19].

Note that there are two levels of optimization:

i) Variation of the connectivity by a Monte Carlo procedure

ii) Variation of the synaptic weights for fixed connectivity with the aid of an arbitrary, not necessarily optimal learning procedure

The main result of our studies is that networks even with an appreciable degree of dilution , but optimized connectivity, show a quantitatively similar retrieval performance as their fully connected counterparts [14]. Moreover, due to the fact that sparsely connected networks exhibit appreciably fewer spurious attractors the fraction of perfectly recalled patterns is substantially larger than in fully connected networks.

Furthermore, work in progress suggests strongly that it is far more important to aim at optimal architectures than to concentrate on optimal, time consuming learning procedures for the modification of the coupling coefficients. Hence, Hebbian one-step learning via

$$c_{i\,j_1} = \sum_{\mu=1}^{p} s_i^{(\mu)} s_{j_1}^{(\mu)} \tag{10}$$

can easily be adopted which simplifies step ii) appreciably, since the synaptic weights are given explicitly.

We remark that according to exact results in the thermodynamic limit for networks with *random* connectivity even imperfect storage of p randomly chosen patterns is only possible up to the critical $\alpha_c = 2/\pi$ [6] with $p = \alpha K$. However, our results even for α above one demonstrate clearly that a pattern-specific connectivity allows the network not only to store the information perfectly but also leads to a respectable size of the basins of attraction [22].

Finally, the performance of the network model can be improved by allowing higher order interactions of multiplicative character (2). Restricting the three-cell interactions to the subspace containing the optimized connectivity which evolved within two-cell interactions, the additional coefficients can consistently be determined from the second order Hebbian rule

$$c_{i\,j_1\,j_2} = \sum_{\mu=1}^{p} s_i^{(\mu)} s_{j_1}^{(\mu)} s_{j_2}^{(\mu)} \tag{11}$$

The improvement is dramatic, particularly in view of the minor technical effort in order to include the second order contributions. In summary, a pattern-specific connectivity successfully overcomes overloading instabilities arising in network models with *randomly* chosen connectivity. Self-consistent inclusion of second order correlations increases the stability of the engraved information substantially [22].

7 Conclusion

The issue of stability is of central importance in this short and biased overview, since instability can lead to chaotic or even catastrophic behaviour. The results indicate most clearly that random networks of automata generally remain stable up to some critical network parameter values and become suddenly unstable as these values are exceeded. Moreover, reducing randomness by practically any kind of structure such as nearest-neighbour or distance-dependent interactions, self-organization or forcing structures as well as optimal training has a powerful effect in suppressing chaotic activity.

Strongly motivated by the view that self-organization of the architecture, as it occurs in biological networks, involves optimization processes we demonstrate that optimally *structured* networks outperform their completely connected counterparts substantially.

8 Acknowlegements

The author thanks J.W. Clark, L.van Hemmen, U. Keller, G. Kohring, R. Rohwer, M.L. Ristig , W. von Seelen and D. Stauffer for numerous helpful and stimulating discussions.

9 References

[1] J.W. Clark , J.Rafelski and J.V. Winston 1985, Physics Reports, 123 (4), 215-273
[2] E. Caianiello, 1961, J.Theor. Biol.1, 204-235
[3] J.J. Hopfield, 1982, Proc.Natl.Acad.Sci.79,2554-2558
[4] B. Derrida and Y. Pomeau, 1986, Europhys.Lett.1,45-49
[5] K.E. Kürten, 1988, Phys.Lett. A129,3,157-160
[6] B. Derrida, E. Gardner and A. Zippelius,1987, Europhys. Lett. 4, 167-173.
[7] K.E. Kürten, to be published
[8] S.A. Kauffmann, 1984, Physica 10D,145-156
[9] K.E. Kürten and J.W. Clark, 1986,Phys.Lett.A114,413-418
[10] K.E. Kürten, 1988, J.Phys.A21, L615-619
[11] K.E. Kürten,1989 , J.Phys. France 51,2313-2323
[12] D. Stauffer, 1987, Phil.Mag.B, 56,901-16
[13] K.E. Kürten, 1988, Neural Networks from Models to Applications, eds. L.Personnaz and G. Dreyfus, I.D.S.E.T. Paris p.353-359
[14] K.E. Kürten,1990, Parallel Processing in Neural Systems and Computers, Eds. R.Eckmiller,G.Hartmann and G.Hauske (North Holland) p.191-194
[15] V. Braitenberg,1978, Lect. Notes Biomath. (Springer Verlag Berlin), 21, p.171
[16] D.O. Hebb,1949, The Organization of Behavior,Wiley, N.Y.
[17] J.P. Rauschecker and W. Singer,1981, J.Physiol.(London), 310,215-239

[18] K.E. Kürten, 1988, Chaos and Complexity, World Press, pp. 224-229, Singapur eds. R.Livi, S.Ruffo, S.Ciliberti and M.Buiatti

[19] K.E. Kürten,1990, J.Phys. France 51,1585-1594

[20] L. Personnaz, I. Guyon and D. Dreyfus,1987, Europhys. Lett.,4(8),863-867.

[21] G.A. Kohring,1990, J.Phys.France 51, 145-155.

[22] K.E. Kürten, Complexity and Evolution, Les Houches 1990

ADDITIONAL PAPER

(not given
at conference)

COUPLED EXCITABLE CELLS

C.L.T.Mannion

Department of Electrical Engineering, Univ. of Surrey,
Guildford, Surrey, U.K.

J.G.Taylor

Department of Mathematics, King's College,
Strand, London, WC2R2LS, U.K.

Abstract. Coupled excitable cells are analysed, using two types of models (S^1's and Fitzhugh-Nagumo) both analytically and by simulation, to determine regions of their parameter spaces which lead to synchronised oscillations. These may give an underlying model of the coupled oscillations observed in visual cortex.

1 INTRODUCTION

There has been a great deal of interest elicited by the discovery [1], subsequent confirmation [2], [3] and further extension [4] of synchronised coupled oscillatory neurons in the cat visual cortex. Almost zero phase shift occurs in the observed cross-correlation functions of pairs of neurons with similar feature sensitivity, even across a distance of up to several millimetres.

The main aspects of this phenomenon which have been investigated have been orientation sensitivity and binocularity, although motion and direction sensitivity have also been investigated more recently [4]. Since this temporal synchronisation may help to solve the binding problem [5] it is of importance to understand how the synchronisation may be generated. This paper is to be regarded as a contribution to the solution to that question.

Various models have been proposed to answer the above query about the source of the observed oscillations. The simplest uses the developing theory of coupled limit cycle oscillators, based on their each being described by a phase variable θ_i, say, with θ_i being defined modulo the period T of the cycle [6]. This allows for a great simplification in the study of neuronal activity, and very interesting results ensue. However, unless the neurons are spontaneously active (for which there is rather little evidence in visual cortex) the description of the onset of oscillation by external stimuli would be invalid. This is because the period is not defined before oscillation is evoked. This difficulty becomes clearer if a more complete description of the oscillators is given.

Let us consider, as an example, a set of supercritical Hopf bifurcations with variables r_i, θ_i, for which

$$dr_i/dt = r_i(I_i - s_i - r_i^2)$$

$$(1)$$

$$d\theta_i/dt = r_i$$

For external inputs I_i less than the thresholds s_i there is only the stable fixed point $r_i = 0$, $\theta_i =$ constant. When $I_i > s_i$, this point becomes unstable, leading to the stable limit cycle $r_i = (I_i - s_i)^{1/2} = r_{i0}$, $\theta_i = r_{i0}t$. This latter system can be described as motion on S^1's provided the relaxation time, proportional to $r_{i0}^{-1/2}$ is small in comparison to the time variation of I_i. However at threshold, when $I_i = s_i$, $r_{i0} = 0$, the S^1 description cannot be used since T is infinite (and then becomes complex for smaller values of the inputs I_i). Because the time dependence of the synchronisation is non-trivial, it might be difficult to model this without being able to approximate the stimulus-evoked bifurcation in the first place.

An alternative approach [7] has been to use time-averaged firing rate equations for coupled pairs of feedback-inhibition neurons, the bifurcations being stimulus evoked, although helped by time-delays which decrease stability. Again, valuable results ensue in this model, but due to the time averaging, detailed timing aspects are not be available.

This latter approach seems to be a halfway-house between the extreme simplicity of the coupled S^1's and a more complex model using excitable cells. In this paper we will investigate various aspects of coupled oscillatory neurons when modelled as S^1's, at one extreme, or as excitable cells at the other. In this latter arena we will be particularily concerned with the spike generation process. To be analysed effectively this should be modelled by means of the Hodgkin-Huxley (HH) system of equations . To achieve a little simplicity we use the Fitzhugh-Nagumo model (FHN) of the nerve impulse [8], based on the Bonhoeffer van-der Pol oscillator (BVP). This latter is a reduction of the full HH system from a four variable system to one of two variables. As noted by Fitzhugh [8] " The BVP model is not intended to be an accurate quantitative model of the axon,

in the sense of reproducing the experimental curves; it is meant rather to
exhibit as clearly as possible those basic dynamic interrelationships between the
variables of state which are responsible for the properties of threshold,
refractoriness, and finite and infinite trains of impulses"

Before we begin our analysis of these models let us review briefly the data
from the living system as presented in [4]. We may extract from this reference
various features which must ultimately be explained by any model claiming to be
satisfactory. Such an explanation may only be available when suitable inhibitory
and excitatory cell interactions with suitable time delays and complicated enough
neurons are included. In order to be able to assess that we must have the general
features of the data before us at the start of any such modelling.

The data of [4] present various regularities. The first is the dependence
of the oscillatory frequency and amplitude for oscillatory activity of a cell (as
seen in the autocorrelogram) on the velocity of the input stimulus (a bar being
driven across the receptive field of a cell at its optimal orientation). The data
of table 6 of paper 2 of [4] are plotted in figure 1.

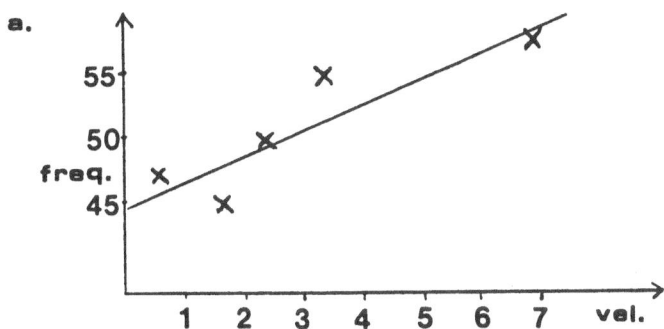

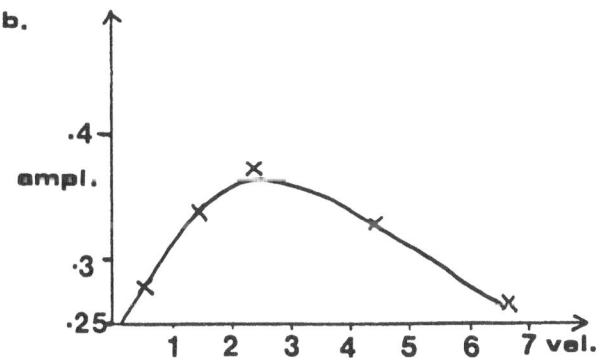

Figure 1.
(a) Variation of the frequency of the oscillation of the cell, in inverse
seconds, as a function of the stimulus amplitude.
(b) Variation of the oscillation amplitude as a function of the input in degrees
per second. Both (a) and (b) are taken from table 6 of the second paper of ref.
[4].

There is in general a slight but steady increase of frequency with stimulus
velocity, whilst a maximum of the oscillatory amplitude occurs at a value (2-3
degrees per second) which is much less than the value (of order 12 degrees per
second) at which there is a maximum firing rate response of the cell to the
signal (and at which the oscillatory amplitude is negligible).

Another feature is the variation of frequency and amplitude of oscillations
to the length of the stimulus bar; this is shown in figure 2(a) and (b) for the
two cases respectively.

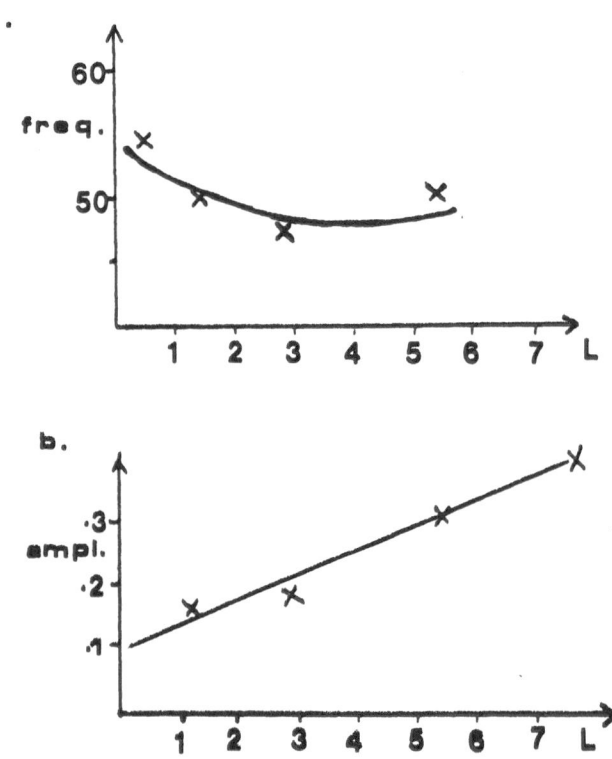

Figure 2.
(a) Variation of the frequency of the oscillation of a cell with the length L of the stimulus bar.
(b) Variation of the amplitude of oscillation with L. Both (a) and (b) are taken from table 7 of the second paper of ref. [4].

From fig.2(a) the frequency is roughly constant, whilst from fig.2(b) the amplitude is gradually increasing. Finally the dependence of frequency and amplitude on the orientation θ of the stimulus bar are shown in figure 3.

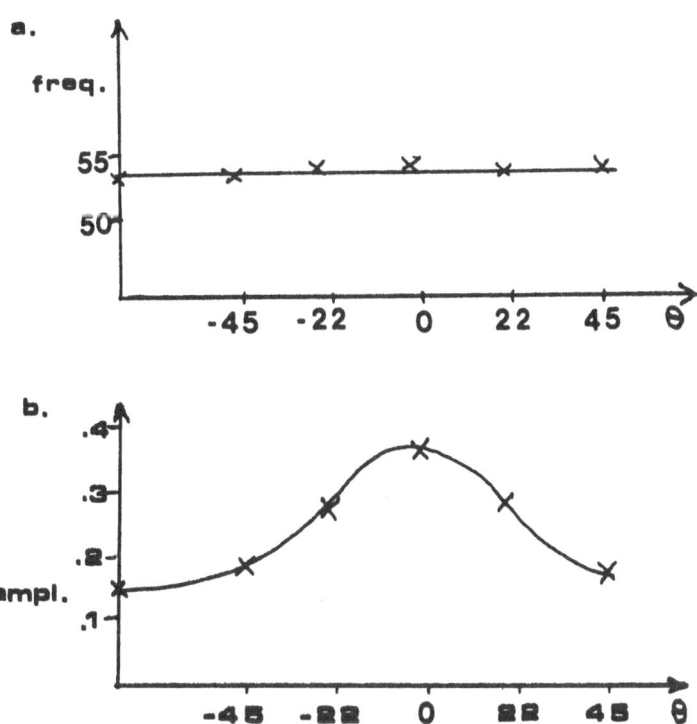

Figure 3.
(a) Variation of the frequency of oscillation of a cell with orientation of the stimulus bar.
(b) Variation of the amplitude of oscillation of a cell with the stimulus bar orientation.

It is clear from fig.3 that there is no dependence of the frequency on θ, whilst the amplitude has a very clear peak at the optimal orientation,with a gradual but definite fall-off on either side.

We begin in the next section with the reduction of a class of non-linear neuron models, including the FHN and leaky integrator cases, to a system of coupled S^1's. Synchronisation in this latter is analysed in the next section. In the following a similar analysis is performed for coupled BVP oscillators, first for a pair and then for any number of such oscillators. These results are summarised in the final section.

2. COUPLED S^1 MODELS

These models are clearly the simplest to analyse since they involve only a single variable for each of the neurons, this being the phase in the firing cycle at which the neuron is presently situated. This does not allow analysis of the setting up or decay of the oscillations, as noted in the introduction. However since the stimulus input is present for roughly a second or so on each oscillating neuron, unsynchronised oscillations which may occur initially are driven to synchronisation. Such a scenario may be recognised in the data of [3], especially as shown in figure 9 of that reference.

Let us initially consider conditions under which S^1 models can arise. We will only consider the case in which the dynamics is described by two variables, denoted by x_i, y_i (for i=1 to N, where N is the number of oscillators). This model includes the FHN model, but excludes the more complete HH and compartmental HH models. Reduction of such more general cases to coupled S^1's requires further analysis.

It is assumed that the external input I_i is strong enough to cause each cell to fire. The equations for each cell without coupling are taken to be

$$dx_i/dt= F(x_i,y_i) + I_i \qquad\qquad (1a)$$

$$dy_i/dt= G(x_i,y_i) \qquad\qquad (1b)$$

so each of the equations (1) will describe an oscillation in the activity variable x_i, with a related change in the recovery variable y_i, due to the size of the external input I_i. The form of the function F may be N-shaped in its dependence on x, whilst G will be linear (or quadratic, for bursting cells [9]);

if F is linear and G is zero then the cell i is a leaky integrator neuron without active membrane.

Since we are working with neurons of zero size then the variable x_i is to be regarded as the potential at the axon hillock. The coupling between the cells may therefore be assumed to involve only the activity variables x_i. The simplest form of the interaction is thus a linear sum of terms in the x_j's. In the FHN model this could be either proportional to x_j itself or some other threshold value of x_j, corresponding to a normalised action pulse. The leaky integrator model could have a function describing the non-linear manner in which the firing rate depends on the activity, as is usual in many neural net models. Thus (1) becomes

$$dx_i/dt = F(x_i,y_i) + \epsilon \Sigma_j a_{ij} f_j(x_j(t-t_{ij}) + I_i(t) \qquad (2a)$$

$$dy_i/dt = G(x_i,y_i) \qquad (2b)$$

It is to be noted that in (2a) time delays are included to take account of the time taken by the signal from the j'th neuron to arrive at the i'th due to the finite velocity of the nerve impulse. The functions f_i may be linear, sigmoidal or step functions, as noted above. A parameter ϵ has been included in the coupling term, so emphasing the weak coupling nature of the following discussion.

There is a general method of reducing the system (2) to coupled equations for the phases of the separate oscillators [10] in the case ϵ is small; see also [11]. This method uses a transformation to angle variables θ_i and variables A_i corresponding to the distance from the oscillation in the x-y plain, as

$$x_i = X(\theta_i) + \epsilon A_i Y'(\theta_i), \quad y_i = Y(\theta_i) - \epsilon A_i X'(\theta_i) \qquad (3)$$

Following the singular perturbation theory manipulations of [10] and [11] there results the equations

$$dA_i/dt = \Phi(\theta_i)A_i + \Psi(\theta_i)\Sigma_j a_{ij}F(\theta_i(t-t_{ij})) + 0(\epsilon) \qquad (4a)$$

$$d\theta i/dt = w_i + \epsilon A_i \Omega(\theta_i) + \epsilon \Sigma_i a_{ij} T(\theta_i)F(\theta_j(t-t_{ij})) \qquad (4b)$$

where $F(x) = f(X(x))$, $\Phi \Psi \Omega T$ are defined in terms of X,Y and their derivatives and w_i are the frequencies of the uncoupled neurons. The details of the method of two-time perturbation theory of [10], [11], may be used to deduce that

$$\theta_i = w_i t + \psi_i(\tau) \tag{5}$$

where $\tau = \epsilon t$ and the phases $\psi_i(\tau)$ satisfy the set of coupled equations

$$d\psi_i/d\tau = \Sigma_j \ a_{ij} \ H(\psi_j - \psi_i + (w_j - w_i)t - t_{ij}) \tag{6}$$

with the function H being an odd periodic one with H(0)=0. Also H'(0)=1, following the analysis of [11] for $f_j = x_j$. Thus the system (2) has been reduced to a set of coupled oscillators on S^1's, although with time delays t_{ij}. Moreover the connection weights entering in (6) are exactly those of (2). The form of H is also obtainable directly from the above construction, but it is not clear how useful it would be since it involves the poorly known functions X,Y, which satisfy

$$dX/d\theta = F(X,Y) + I \ , \ dY/d\theta = G(X,Y) \tag{7}$$

where I is the external input.
It seems helpful to return to work directly with the variables $\theta_i = w_i t + \psi_i(t)$ in this case, with the resulting dynamics being

$$d\theta_i/dt = w_i + \Sigma_j a_{ij} H(\theta_j - \theta_i + (w_j - w_i)t - t_{ij}) \tag{8}$$

We will now use this form (8) to investigate possible synchronisation. We will assume that the inputs I_i change the frequencies w_i of the uncoupled oscillators slowly, so that the assumptions used in the derivation of (8) are valid.

The labelling hypothesis requires synthesis of the phases θ_i across a suitable set of neurons when certain inputs w_i occur. A possible approach to this has been recently analysed [12] using the requirement that all of the phases are used in the labelling of an input. This is in contradiction to the experimental data reported in [1]-[5] and described in the first section. In any case such a method of labelling would be expected to reduce the capacity of the system for labelling. In order to analyse this question we need to understand how different subsets of the phases θ_i can be synchronised according to different values of the w_i's. For that we proceed as follows.

Let θ_{ij} denote the differences of the phases $(\theta_i - \theta_j)$, so that (8) for θ becomes

$$d\theta_{ij}/dt = w_{ij} + \epsilon\Sigma_k[a_{ik}H(\theta_{ki}-t_{ik}) - a_{jk}H(\theta_{kj}-t_{jk})] \qquad (9)$$

where $w_{ij}=w_i-w_j$. The linearised version of (9) is

$$d\theta_{ij} = \Omega_{ij} - \epsilon\Sigma_k(a_{ik}\theta_{ik} - a_{jk}\theta_{jk}) \qquad (10a)$$

with

$$\Omega_{ij} = w_{ij} + T_{ij} \qquad (10b)$$

$$T_{ij} = \epsilon\Sigma_k(a_{jk}t_{jk} - a_{ik}t_{ik}) \qquad (10c)$$

and $A=H'(0)$. On the other hand the version of (9) linearised about $\theta_{ij}=0$ is

$$d\theta_{ij}/dt = w_{ij} - \epsilon\Sigma_k(A_{ik}\theta_{ik} - A_{jk}\theta_{jk}) \qquad (11)$$

with $A_{ik}=H'(-t_{ik})$. We assume that $H'(0)$ or the $H'(-t_{ij})$ are all positive, following the remark made earlier that $H'(0)=1$ for linear coupling.

There are various possibilities that might arise in the analysis of (10), but we will consider couplings for which $T_{ij}=0$ (which seems reasonable on symmetry grounds) so that (10a) reduces to (11), although with a_{ij} replacing A_{ij}. Modulo this replacement our discussion of the two equations can therefore be reduced to that solely of (11).

The inputs w_i may be divided into subsets in which there is rough equality. Such would be the case for iso-orientation cells in area 17 or 18, considered in [1] to [5], for a period of about one second. These subsets have w_{ij}'s all zero, whilst the w_{ij}'s are not expected to be so in general for values of i and j in different subsets. Restricting our analysis to a single subset, synchrony will occur if the solution $\theta_{ij}=0$ of (11) for any pair i,j in the subset is stable. From (11) this is true if the real parts of all of the eigenvalues of the matrix M, with elements

$$M_{ij,kl} = \epsilon(A_{il}\delta_{ik} - A_{jl}\delta_{jk}) \qquad (12)$$

are all positive. This is a condition expressible on the principle minors of M; thus for a two element system this requires $A_{12}>0$, for a three element system a set of conditions including $(A_{12}+A_{21})>0$, $(A_{13}+A_{31})>0$, etc.

If the above conditions are satisfied in each of the subsets with common value for the input w_i then phase synchronisation will occur between all cells in the subset. Such synchronisation is not expected to arise between the cells of different subsets. In particular if all of the eigenvalues of the total matrix (12) have positive real parts then the θ_{ij}'s for i,j in the same subset will converge exponentially fast to zero whilst for i,j in different subsets such will not be the case. Thus we expect synchronisation of the phases in subsets with the same inputs, but lack of such synchrony between different subsets.

This scenario may be affected by perturbations from one subset to another. If such perturbations could be avoided then the capacity of the system would be large, equal to the number of all subsets of the oscillators; it would thus be exponential in N, growing like 2^N.

It is more realistic to assume that synchronisation may occur over subsets labelled by spatial positions of several subsets conjointly, for example in the case of orientation detectors with sensitivity not more than 60 degrees or so apart. Synchrony between such subsets might then be possible if the matrix elements of M are small between units with a greater difference of sensitivity, so preventing perturbation of the synchronisation otherwise occurring.

Thus our basic model for the coupled S^1's is a set of subsets $\{S_n\}$ of cells, where n may take the values 1 to 10, corresponding to the 10 or so distinct orientations to which such cells are sensitive. The cells in each subset S_n are coupled to each other so that the sub-matrix of M in (12) has only eigenvalues with positive real parts. There is weaker coupling of cells in S_n to cells of subsets S_{n+1} and S_{n-1}, so that the larger sub-matrix of M for S_n and its related S_{n+1} and S_{n-1} still only have positive real parts for the eigenvalues. Stability will ensue if matrix elements joining subsets S_n and S_m with [n-m]>1 are small enough. Such seems to be consistent with the neuro-anatomical data for layers 2 and 3 in area 17 [13]. Thus our model seems to have some experimental basis. We have neglected inhibitory couplings here, but may consider these as involved in setting up the orientation selectivity in the first place.

It is also important to consider learning rules which will lead to the greatest capacity. There are various possibilities for this, which we will consider elsewhere.

The most appropriate architecture to consider in the above model is that in which the cells in the oscillator layer are labelled by their receptive field and orientation sensitivity. These cells are fed directly by the inputs for that orientation, both at their own receptive field position and from nearby receptive field positions. These latter connections are of lesser strength to prevent receptive field enlargement. There are also excitatory feedbacks both to iso-orientation columns in nearby hypercolumns and to nearby oscillatory layer cells, all with small connection weights. These latter connections should produce synchronisation of oscillations of nearby cells, with orientation sensitivity which is not too different (say to within 60 degrees). The direct connections should achieve sensitisation and synchronisation of cells in different iso-orientation columns. These connections may be considered as arising from layer 4 in the cortex, with the oscillatory layers being 2 and 3. The corresponding architecture is shown in figure 4. This is supported by anatomical evidence [13]. The role of inhibition is less clear here, although it may function as an automatic gain control, or so as to generate the orientation selectivity in the cortex in the first place.

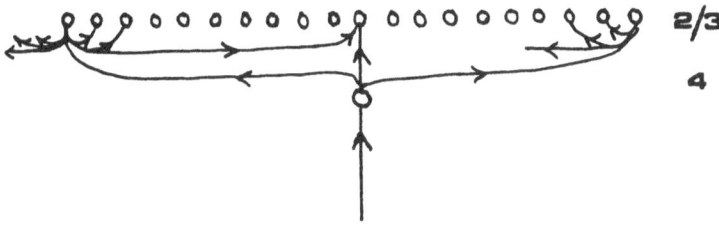

Figure 4.
Architecture used in the simulation of a set of 20 coupled S^1 oscillators in figs.5 and 6. The details of the connections is discussed in the text.

It is also possible that if inhibitory cells receive input from about half a hypercolumn distant they may prevent too extensive activation of oscillations throughout a hypercolumn, and only allow iso-orientaion oscillations. There need not therefore be a variation of connectivity as suggested above between the oscillator cells.

Twenty coupled S^1 oscillators were coupled with the architecture of fig.4 The result for the phases of the fifth and tenth is shown in figure 5 (the phase of the ninth oscillator, for example, is identical to that of the tenth, as expected by the excitation it receives).

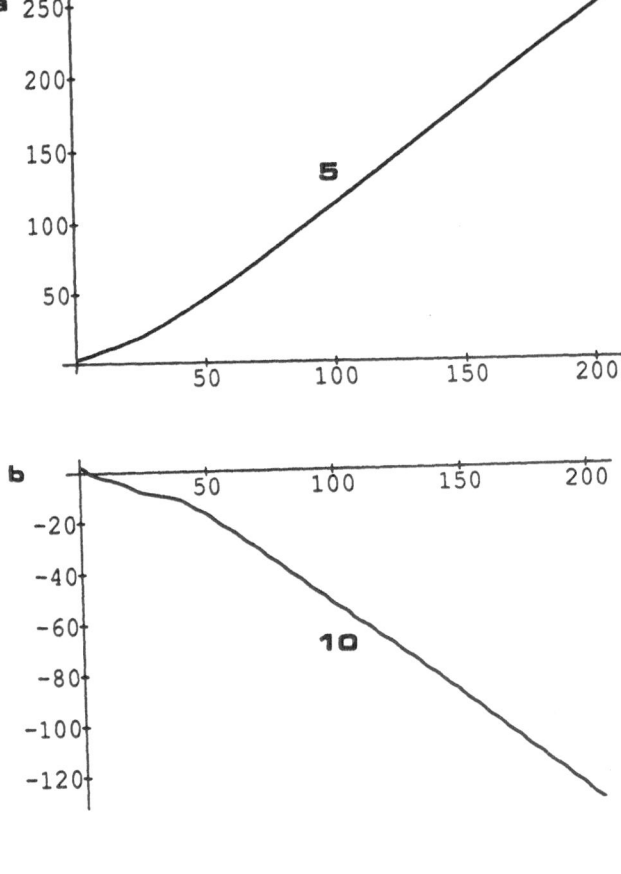

Figure 5.
The phase shifts for the oscillators 5 and 10 in the array of coupled oscillators of figure 4. The short range coupling is .002 and the long range coupling is .0025.

As can be seen from figure 5, there is no synchronisation between the cells 5 and 10, as expected form the above analysis.
Learning is added to the dynamical activity of the cells in figure 6. The learning rule is chosen as the simplest case:

$$\Delta(\theta_i-\theta_j)=(\text{constant})\sin(\theta_i-\theta_j) \qquad (12a)$$

where the right hand side must be periodic in the phase difference $(\theta_i - \theta_j)$, and is expected to vanish when the phases are equal. The simulation was performed for four coupled oscillators, with them being coupled all to all. The inputs were taken to be equal on the first and third cells, that value being different from the input for the second and fourth cells. As can be seen the phases of each of the two pairs of cells converge to the same values. These values were different between the two pairs.

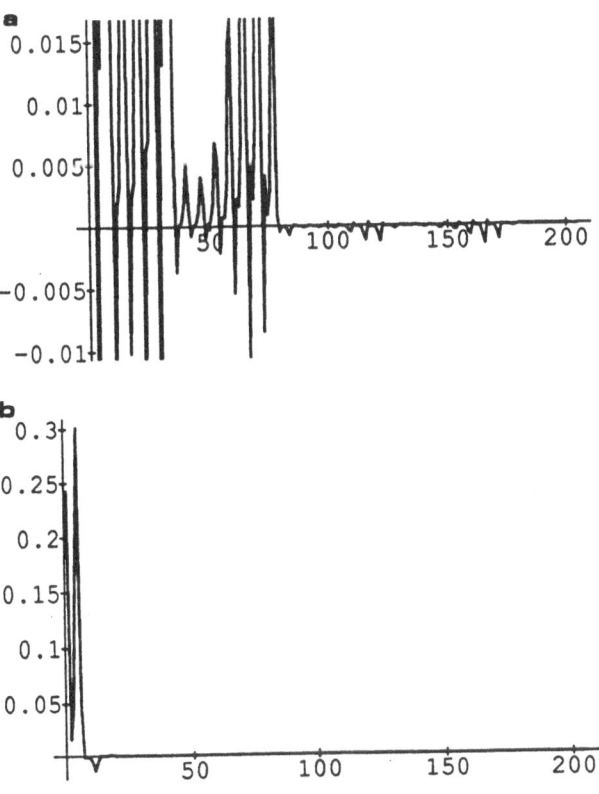

Figure 6.
Learning between four coupled oscillators by the rule (12a). The inputs on the first and second cells is constant, and twice that on the third and fourth cells. The phase differences of the first and second cells tends to zero as the learning proceeds, as seen in figure (a), as does that between the third and fourth cells, given in (b).

In order to be able to take a better account of the temporal activity of single neurons we now turn to a system of coupled BVP oscillators. The i'th of these has membrane potential x_i and recovery variable y_i. The coupling between the different oscillators is taken to feed only to the membrane potentials, as in the BVP model, so the i'th BVP oscillator satisfies the dynamical equations

$$dx_i/dt = c[y_i + x_i - (1/3)x_i^3 + I_i(t) + \Sigma_j a_{ij} x_j (t - t_{ij})] \qquad (13a)$$

$$dy_i/dt = -(1/c)[x_i - a + by_i] \qquad (13b)$$

In (13a) the a_{ij} are the usual connection weights and the t_{ij} are the time delays, as before. The system (13) can be generalised to have different parameters a,b,c for the various neurons instead of the common value assumed. This extension may in particular be used to model the various classes of neurons in the visual cortex; we will not pursue that further here. We will also not consider the extension of the model to take account of the compartments other than the axon hillock. Moreover it is possible to extend the model to a more general class of non-linearities than the cubic, along the lines of those discussed in [9].

We should also note here that coupled BVP oscillators have been analysed in [14] in some detail. However that discussion is based solely on coupling through the recovery variable (13b) so as not to perturb the limit cycles of the individual cells. Such a perturbation is at the centre of our interest here. It is also the case that it is also biologically correct, since activity from other cells will couple directly to the membrane potential x_i. Thus the results of [14] do not have relevance for our analysis.

Let us first consider the process of bifurcation of a single BVP oscillator to a limit cycle from a stable equilibrium point by external current. The analysis of [8] in this case is especially simple when the parameters are chosen to satisfy

$$1 - (2b/3) < a < 1, \quad 0 < b < 1, \quad b < c^2 \qquad (14)$$

In the range (14) the limit cycle arises due to the fact that when the intersection of the x and y null-clines of (13) is between the turning points of the cubic x-null-cline then the equilibrium point is unstable, and a stable limit cycle oscillation results. For I=0, however, the equilibrium point is outside this region, and is therefore stable. As discussed carefully in [8], a suitably negative stimulus shifts the x null-cline so as to lead to oscillation whilst the stimulus is on.

The main question to be asked is therefore what is the extension, if any, of the parameter range (14) to the parameters in (13) in order that a similar phenomenon of evoked oscillations occurs. A subsidiary question is as to the possible synchronisation of the resulting oscillations by different time-varying inputs $I_i(t)$. Let us first consider the case N=2, with no self-interaction terms, and simplify by taking $a_{12}=a_{21}=d$.

Stability analysis of (13) is based on the condition that the eigenvalues λ of the Jacobian of the vector field given by the right hand side have negative real parts. This Jacobian may be evaluated in terms of those for the separate BVP oscillators with d=0. If these latter are denoted J_1, J_2 then the eigenvalue condition for the Jacobian of (13) becomes

$$\det(J_1-\lambda 1).\det(J_2-\lambda 1)-c^2d^2(\lambda+(b/c))^2 =0 \qquad (15)$$

The values of $\det(J_i-\lambda 1)$ are given by $(\lambda-l_1)(\lambda-l_2)$, where l_1, l_2 are given solely in terms of the equilibrium point x_0 for the uncoupled BVP oscillators with d=0, and no external inputs. Using the expression [8]

$$l_1+l_2=-(b/c)+(1-x_0^2)c, \quad l_1l_2=1-(1-x_0^2)b \qquad (16)$$

then (15) reduces to

$$\lambda^2-\lambda(l_1+l_2\pm cd)+l_1l_2\mp bd=0 \qquad (17)$$

Stability is therefore obtained at the eqilibrium point if

$$x_0^2>1-(b/c^2)\pm d, \quad x_0^2>1-(1/b)\pm d \qquad (18)$$

where both sign choices ++,-- in (18) must be considered. Thus the stabilty is guaranteed if

$$d<(1/b)-1 \qquad (19a)$$

$$x_0<-\gamma \quad \text{or} \quad x_0>\gamma \qquad (19b)$$

where $\gamma=(1-(b/c^2)-d)^{1/2}$. The second condition only makes sense provided

$$d<1-(b/c^2) \qquad\qquad (20)$$

For d=0 the conditions (19a) and (20) reduce to the last two conditions in (14); the first two conditions arise from the requirement that the null-clines intersect in a point to the right of the minimum of the x null-cline, and the y null-cline intersects the x-axis to the left of this minimum. This condition generalises, when d is non-zero, to

$$(1+d)^{1/2}[1-(2b/3)+(bd^2/3)-(bd/3)] < a < (1+d)^{1/2} \qquad\qquad (21)$$

Conditions (19a),(20) and (21) are satisfied, for example, by the values of a=0.7, b=0.8, c=3, 0<d<0.25, which agree with those used in simulations in [8], other than for d.The above conditions are also sufficient to show that there is only one equilibrium point of (13a) when N=2; more generally this is valid if

$$d+(1/b) > 1 \qquad\qquad (22)$$

Instability, then, is expected to ensue whenever the external input causes one or other of the fixed points of the oscillators to lie inside the interval $(-\gamma,+\gamma)$. This will occur due to suitably large external input, possibly aided by the input from other BVP oscillators. However we do not expect the latter to bring about oscillations of the first BVP node unaided, with the small value of d being considered.

Thus the picture we arrive at is that of input exciting one BVP oscialltor into its stable limit cycle whilst the second neuron is at its stable equilibrium point, which varies in phase with the oscillations of the first. Such a scenario is amenable to further analysis: the condition (19b) was obtained, when input is present, by assuming identical inputs to derive (18). However we expect the stability analysis to be valid provided the inputs are not too different. Moreover there are destabilising effects to be expected from the time delays in (14a), as discussed, for example, in [7] and [15].

Direct simulation of (14) for N=2 is shown in figure 7.

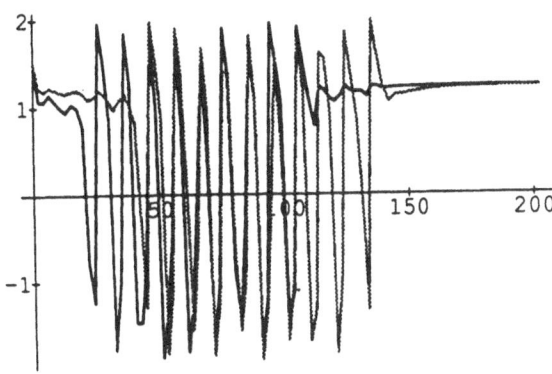

Figure 7.
Simulation of a pair of coupled FHN neurons with values c=0.3, d=0.1. Cell 1 is
in black, cell 2 in grey. A Gaussian shaped input, with width of 30 units of
time, is drawn across the two cells, with a time delay of 30 in the excitation of
the second compared to the first. Note the manner in which the spikes from cell 1
give a small input te cell 2 so as to synchronise the second cell when it comes
on.

We see in figure 7 that the receptive field of oscillator 2 is not
enlarged by its coupling to oscillator 1, but yet the synchronisation of
oscillations is brought about by the coupling. This result gives a possible
mechanism for synchronisation of the oscillators; it occurs by small couplings
which do not enlarge the receptive fields of the receiving cells, but cause
oscillations in them set up later by inputs to be ultimately synchronised.

We add here that if the value d is taken to be antisymmetric between the
two cells then the firing of the cells are exactly out of phase. This was
simulated in the presence of a Gaussian input to excite one of the cells or both
them. We should also note that all the simulations for the FHN neurons were
performed using an adaptive step size in a fourth order Runge-Kutta program.

The zero phase shift noted above can only be expected to be valid provided
the cells are not too distant if coupling between cells is by nerve impulses
along axons. Certainly above a few millimetres the time lag from impulse
propagation becomes an appreciable portion of the total period. The time delayed
case can be analysed following the methods of [15]. It is also to be noted that
the conduction over more than a few millimetres of sub-threshold effects will be
expected to be reduced by membrane properties, as discussed, for example, in
[16]. This is a further reason for expecting only a limited range of
synchronisation. However it is of interst to note that there is a great

difference between the coupling term in (14a) and that arising from nerve impulse propagation. Thus there is no appreciable time delay at all in direct current spread, although the rise time to maximum is determined by the membrane time constant. This may be a mechanism for explaining how there is zero phase shift in the oscillations across some millimetres. On the other hand if the spread were by nerve impulses then a phase shift of 5 msec or so should have been observed in references [2] to [5].

The above analysis may be extended to the case of arbitrary N if it is assumed that the couplings a_{ij} (i different from j) are small, and $a_{ii}=0$. If all the couplings have the same value d, then (22) is still sufficient to prove the existence of a single fixed point in the absence of input, and (19a),(20),(21) generalise by replacing d in (19a),(20) by $d[1/2N(N-1)]^{1/2}$, whilst (21) becomes

$$(1+d)^{1/2}[1-(2b/3)+d(5/3-N)+d^2/3]< a < (1+d)^{1/2} \qquad (23)$$

Thus provided these conditions are satisfied the same synchronisation mechanisms for N=2 will occur. A simulation of the case N=4 is shown in figure 8. Only the synchronisation between the first and third neurons occurs, as is shown there.

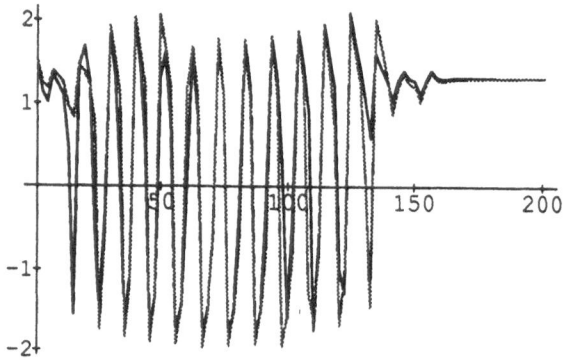

Figure 8.
Simulation of N=4 FHN neurons ; the cells are fully interconnected with the value of d=0.05 The inputs are four Gaussian pulses separated in time. The overlap of the activities of the second and third neurons is shown.

We also show in figure 9 the recovery variables for the four neurons for the case of figure 8. The shapes of these variables clearly show the presence of the moving Gaussians.

302

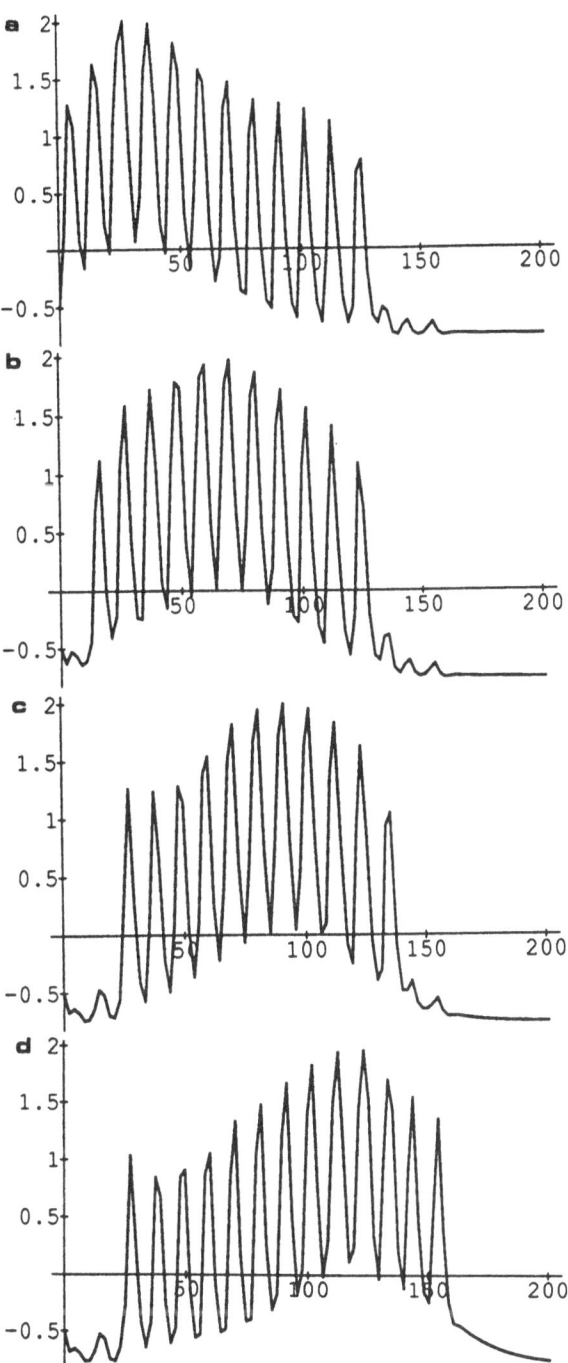

Figure 9.
Recovery variables for the four FHN neurons of figure 8. The curves (a) to (d)
correspond to the neurons 1 to 4. The details of the inputs are given in the
text.

It is possible to extend the above stability analysis to general but small interactive couplings a_{ij} in (13).

4 DISCUSSION

We started this paper with a set of graphs summarising the results of the coupled oscillator experiments on cats of Singer and co-workers. Let us now turn to discussing what insight our analysis of the S^1 and FHN models can throw on these results. The S^1 model is the simplest, so let us consider it first.

The basis of that model is the set of equations (20) which arise from the class of non-linear models (14), under the assumption that oscillations are present. The S^1 models wil not be able to describe any dependence of the amplitude of the oscillation on the external features of the input, but only the manner in which the frequency depends on the latter.

The curve of figure 1(a) indicates that the phase θ increases roughly with the input w. This agrees with the equations (8) on neglect of the couplings.

References

[1] C.M.Gray and W.Singer,Soc.Neuroscience Abstr.404.3,(1987)

[2] C.M.Gray et al, Nature 338,334,(1989)

[3] R.Eckhorn et al,Biol. Cybern. 60.121(1988)

[4] A.K.Engel et al,Eur.J.Neurosci. 2,588,607(1990)

[5] W.Singer, Concepts in Neuroscience 1,1(1989)

[6] D.Kammen, P.Holmes and C.Koch, pp273 etseq in Models of Brain Function, ed R.J.Cotterill, Camb Univ Press(1989); P.Baldi, J.Buhmann and J.Meir,pp908 et seq in Proc INNC'90, Paris, Kluwer Academic (1990)

[7] T.B.Schillen and P.Konig, pp139 et seq in Parallel Processing in Neural Systems and Computers, ed R.Eckmiller, G.Hartmann and G.Hauske, Elsevier (1990)

[8] R.Fitzhugh, Biophys.J. 1,445(1961)

[9] R.Rose and J.Hindmarsh, Proc.Roy.Soc.Lond.B 225,161(1985)

[10] J.C.Neu,Siam J.Appl.Math. 36,509(1979)

[11] J.D.Murray, Mathematical Biology, Springer,(1980)

[12] L.F.Abbott,J.Phys. A Math.Gen. 23,3835(1990)

[13] K.A.Martin, Quart.J.Exp.Physiol.73,637(1988)

[14] Asymptotic Methods for Relaxation Oscillators

[15] Marcus and Westervelt

[16] S.W.Kuffler, J.G.Nicholls and A.R.Martin,Chap.7, From Neuron to Brain,Sinauer Assoc. Publ.,Mass,2nd ed(1984)